COMMITTEE ASSIGNMENT POLITICS IN THE U.S. HOUSE OF REPRESENTATIVES

Congressional Studies Series
Ronald M. Peters, Jr., General Editor

COMMITTEE ASSIGNMENT POLITICS IN THE U.S. HOUSE OF REPRESENTATIVES

SCOTT A. FRISCH

AND

SEAN Q KELLY

UNIVERSITY OF OKLAHOMA PRESS : NORMAN

Also by Scott A. Frisch

The Politics of Pork: A Study of Congressional Appropriation Earmarks (New York City, 1998)

Library of Congress Cataloging-in-Publication Data

Frisch, Scott A., 1964–
    Committee assignment politics in the U.S. House of Representatives / Scott A. Frisch, Sean Q Kelly.
        p.   cm.—(Congressional studies series ; v. 5)
    Includes bibliographical references and index.
    ISBN 0–8061–3720–7 (alk. paper)
        1. United States. Congress. House—Committees. I. Kelly, Sean Q. II. Title. III. Series.

JK1429.F75 2005

                                                      2005050656

Committee Assignment Politics in the U.S. House of Representatives is Volume 5 in the Congressional Studies Series.

The paper in this book meets the guidelines for permanence and durability of the Committee on Production Guidelines for Book Longevity of the Council on Library Resources. ∞

1 2 3 4 5 6 7 8 9 10

For Elizabeth and Colin
and
For Sheen and Shriya: I hope you remember the times
when I was home more often than the times I was gone.

CONTENTS

Figures and Tables   ix

Acknowledgments   xiii

Chapter 1:   Committee Assignment Politics   3

Chapter 2:   Assignment Process and Process Change   33

Chapter 3:   Committee Request Motivations   68

Chapter 4:   Committee Requests and Constituency
             Characteristics   96

Chapter 5:   House Members and the Assignment Process   138

Chapter 6:   Leadership and Committee Assignments   175

Chapter 7:   Inside the Black Box   224

Chapter 8:   Who Gets What and Why   255

Chapter 9:   Gender, Race, and Request Success   289

Chapter 10: Committee Assignment Politics Reconsidered   326

Appendix 1: Measuring Voting Power   339

Appendix 2: Content Analysis of Committee Request Letters   345

Notes   351
References   381
Name Index   395
General Index   401

FIGURES AND TABLES

FIGURES

1.1.	Committee assignment politics framework	16
2.1.	Voting power in the Republican Committee on Committees, by region, 86th Congress	40
2.2.	Seats in the Republican Conference, by region, selected Congresses	45
2.3.	Voting power in the Republican Committee on Committees, by seats, 97th Congress	48
2.4.	Voting power in the Republican Committee on Committees, by region, 97th Congress	49
2.5.	Voting power in the Republican Committee on Committees, by seats, 101st Congress	52
2.6.	Voting power in the Republican Committee on Committees, regional and leadership representation, 101st Congress	53
2.7.	Voting power in the Republican Committee on Committee, by seats, 105th Congress	54
2.8.	Voting power in the Republican Committee on Committee, regional and leadership representation, 105th Congress	56
2.9.	Voting power in Democratic Steering and Policy Committee zone elections	62

2.10.   Voting power in the Democratic Steering and Policy
        Committee   63
2.11.   Democratic seats in the House   64
4.1.   Average number of committee requests, first-term members   99
4.2.   Average number of committee requests, incumbents   100
4.3.   Proportion of successful committee requests, all members   132
4.4.   Proportion of successful committee requests,
        first-term members   133
4.5.   Proportion of successful committee requests, incumbents   134
7.1.   Republican Executive Committee cleavage structure   230
7.2.   Winning coalition size, Republican Executive Committee   241

TABLES

2.1.   Republican Committee on Committees representative
        structure   37
2.2.   Republican Committee on Committees voting power indices   42
2.3.   Democratic Committee on Committees representative
        structure   59
3.1.   Motivation types and committee preferences
        (two previous studies)   74
3.2.   Motivation types and committee preferences (Deering and
        Smith results)   76
3.3.   Motivations expressed in committee request letters
        (by motivation type)   77
3.4.   Motivations expressed in committee request letters
        (by committee and motivation type)   79
3.5.   Committees reclassified by motivation type   90
4.1.   Number of committees requested   98
4.2.   Committee assignment preferences   102
4.3.   Party and electoral status differences in
        committee preferences   105
4.4.   Committee requests and constituency characteristics   110
4.5.   Committee requests and interest group scores   118
4.6.   Committee requests and department-specific awards   122

4.7.   Committee requests and department-specific awards   124
4.8.   Committee request success   128
4.9.   Request success differences by leadership regime   135
4.10. Influence committee requests   136
5.1.   Committee request justifications   145
5.2.   Committee type and request justification   147
5.3.   Committee requests and previous occupations   149
6.1.   Michel support for committee assignment winners   188
6.2.   Democratic Party loyalty and committee assignments
       (by institutional era)   220
6.3.   Democratic Party loyalty and committee assignments
       (by leadership era)   221
6.4.   Republican Party loyalty and committee assignments
       (by leadership era)   222
7.1.   Republican Executive Committee annual rosters   233
7.2.   Republican Executive Committee vote distribution   236
7.3.   Cleavage indicators used in faction correlation analysis   239
7.4.   Republican Executive Committee factional structure
       (97th–101st Congresses)   242
7.5.   Republican Executive Committee factional structure
       (98th Congress)   244
7.6.   Republican Executive Committee factional structure
       (99th Congress)   246
7.7.   Republican Executive Committee factional structure
       (100th Congress)   248
7.8.   Republican Executive Committee factional structure (100th
       Congress, Appropriations Committee assignments)   250
7.9.   Republican Executive Committee factional structure
       (101st Congress)   250
8.1.   Electoral marginality and first-term request success   263
8.2.   Electoral marginality and incumbent request success   264
8.3.   Electoral opposition and Democrats' request success   267
8.4.   Predecessor's committee status and first-term
       request success   269
8.5.   Former congressional staff's first-term request success   273

8.6.   Family ties and first-term request success   276
8.7.   Hypothesized relationship of model variables to
       request success   278
8.8.   First-term Democrats' request success (multivariate)   280
8.9.   First-term Republicans' request success (multivariate)   282
8.10. Incumbent Democrats' request success (multivariate)   284
8.11. Incumbent Republicans' request success (multivariate)   286
8.12. Summary of multivariate request success findings   287
9.1.   Gender differences in committee preferences   295
9.2.   Female members' request success   296
9.3.   Gender and request success probabilities   298
9.4.   Differences in committee preferences of African American
       and white Democrats   316
9.5.   Request success of African American and white Democrats   318
9.6.   Request success probabilities for African American and
       white Democrats   320
9.7.   Request success of African American and white
       Democrats (by historical period)   322
10.1. Committee assignment politics findings summary   330
A1.1. Hypothetical voting schemes   342
A2.1. Content analysis coding scheme   348

Acknowledgments

This book began with a phone call from Scott A. Frisch to Sean Q Kelly in March 2000. We had met and become friends while we were both teaching at East Carolina University in Greenville, North Carolina, and kept in touch as we each moved on to happier university environments. Frisch reported that during a trip to the Robert H. Michel Papers at the Dirksen Congressional Center, he had discovered the committee request letters of Republican members of the House and other interesting materials. These data would enable us to test theories premised solely on the behaviors of House Democrats and examination of data for House Democrats, remedying what we agreed was a major gap in the data on House committees. A second obvious gap in the literature also occurred to us: Extant committee request data existed for only a handful of Congresses. We quickly resolved that our research design would be both comparative *and* longitudinal.

The task that we assigned ourselves was not an easy one; it required us to track down appropriate collections and visit the archived papers of former members of Congress throughout the country. In fact, scholars more able than us had rejected the idea, noting that "collecting request data for 50 years (26 congresses) would [be] prohibitively difficult" (Adler and Lapinski 1997, 906). We instantly discovered, however, that we shared an obsession for collecting the most complete dataset possible, despite the difficulties. For four years, we collected archival data from the papers of more than twenty members of Congress and interviewed dozens of members of Congress and congressional staff, mostly in Washington, D.C.; altogether, we traveled more than forty thousand combined air miles. We also discovered that we each possessed compulsions that, while different, complemented those of the other. A dynamic mixture of obsession and compulsion has fueled our collaboration over the last several years, and this book *is* collaboration in the truest sense; we have labored together, if not always shoulder to shoulder (thank goodness for e-mail, telephones, faxes, and the Internet), throughout the entire process.

While working on our data collection, we crossed paths with many helpful archivists across the country who went above and beyond the call of duty and were critical to our research, including (but not limited to) Frank Mackaman (Robert H. Michel Papers, Dirksen Congressional Center); Nina Dietz, Robert Matuozzi, and Laila Miletic-Vejzovic (Thomas S. Foley Congressional Papers, Washington State University); Todd Kosmerick (Carl Albert Center, University of Oklahoma); Judy Robinson (Wilbur Mills Papers, Hendrix College); Nancy Martin (Frank Horton Papers, University of Rochester); Evelyn Taylor (Robert J. Lagomarsino Collection, California State University Channel Islands); and Jason dePreaux (the Center for American History, University of Texas at Austin). Jason Lantzer performed admirably by collecting archival documents from the unprocessed Charles Abraham Halleck Papers (Indiana University).

We presented ten conference papers, most of which figured into this finished project. We were fortunate to receive insightful comments from a number of discussants and helpful participants, including Bob Boatright, Gary Cox, Keith Hamm, Sukie Hammond, Mark Wrighton (on several occasions), and Garry Young. Jonathan Strand provided important insights into the mysteries of weighted voting, and Dave Reilly also offered insightful comments at several points in the evolution of this research. Nancy McGlen, Karen O'Connor, and Jean Reith Schroedel provided extensive comments on our work with women's committee assignments. Generous with their comments, advice, and encouragement were Larry Dodd, E. Scott Adler, Pete Baxter, Larry Evans, Rick Hall, Keith Krehbiel, Lance

LeLoup, Cathy Rudder, Dave Rohde, Barry Rundquist, and Ken Shepsle. We were particularly fortunate to have Ron Peters as our editor; he helped us improve our work to the best of our limited abilities, as did the other reviewer of the manuscript. Melanie Mallon, our outstanding copyeditor, helped to clarify our thinking and writing. Any bad decisions or errors of fact or interpretation that we might have made should not be blamed on any of these people; they did their best to warn us when we were headed for trouble.

The Dirksen Congressional Center and the Caterpillar Foundation provided substantial financial support for this research. Additional funding was provided by the Gerald R. Ford Presidential Library, the Carl Albert Center at the University of Oklahoma, the Thomas S. Foley Institute at Washington State University, California State University Bakersfield and Channel Islands, the Institute for Humane Studies, and the Niagara University Research Council and the College of Arts and Sciences. Thanks are also due to the members and former members of Congress and congressional staff who took their valuable time to talk with us about committee assignments.

Lance LeLoup and Ed Weber of the Thomas S. Foley Institute and Department of Political Science at Washington State University were gracious hosts during two visits to Pullman, Washington. Joe Jenkins and Joe and Carol Hoenegis opened their homes during our trips to Washington State and Illinois, respectively. The Department of Political Science at the University of Alabama, and especially Steve Borrelli, were very welcoming during a visit to the Tom Bevill Papers. Carmen Warschaw, Brett Palmer, and Larry Rothrock helped arrange interviews that otherwise would not have been possible. We offer special thanks to the members of Congress who granted us permission to access their papers when the archives were closed to research (William E. Frenzel, Frank Horton, Robert Livingston, and James Wright).

Last, and most important, our spouses (Elizabeth Rothrock and Sheen Rajmaira) and kids (Colin Frisch and Shriya Kelly) displayed an unusual tolerance for our travel habits and our childlike excitement at each new archival discovery. Sheen demonstrated unusual courage in reading every word that we wrote on the subject and provided helpful comments along the way. Grants did not cover all our research expenses.

Our thanks are due to the Frisch Foundation and the Kelly Charitable Trust and their directors (Rothrock and Rajmaira) for their blind faith in us and our project and their generous financial support; we also offer the same thanks, though with less enthusiasm, to several credit card companies.

Committee Assignment Politics in the U.S. House of Representatives

CHAPTER ONE

COMMITTEE ASSIGNMENT POLITICS

The notion that you are doing it exclusively for pork barrel interests
rather than what interests you isn't true. First of all, most of the
people in Congress don't have marginal seats, and the notion that
they are obsessed with things that can ensure their reelection just isn't
that relevant for a lot of people. . . . There are a lot of reasons why they
would want certain committees, but I think that surviving the next
election is, for most members, not necessarily the decisive reason.

REPRESENTATIVE HOWARD BERMAN (D-CA)

Henry Waxman (D-CA) was elected to Congress along with seventy-four other first-term Democrats in the Watergate election of 1974.[1] Waxman immediately sought membership on the Interstate and Foreign Commerce Committee, a powerful committee with a broad jurisdiction. He did not pursue membership on the Commerce Committee (as it is frequently known) to protect the dominant commercial interests in his wealthy, urban district. His motivation for pursuing this assignment was his deep interest in health policy. Waxman described his interest in a letter to Speaker Carl Albert, requesting assignment to the Commerce Committee:

While a member of the California State Legislature, I have concentrated my legislative activities in the fields of health and consumer affairs. I was Chairman of the Assembly Committee on Health and the Select Committee on Medical Malpractice, as well as a member of the Assembly Committee on Health Manpower and the California State Health Advisory Council. I would hope to continue my involvement in the health field as a Member of the House. I feel that my expertise in this area would permit me to make a real contribution to the committee's deliberations.[2]

Waxman's interest in health policy was forged by personal experience and a strong sense of social justice. When Waxman's grandmother had become ill, his family had difficulty supporting the cost of her medical care. According to Waxman, "Everyone was so apprehensive whether we could pay for her medical bills and she ended up going to a nursing home, because we couldn't care for her any longer. . . . It made me very sensitive to the difficulties of a lot of elderly people" (Waxman quoted in Getlin 1990).

Waxman was assigned to the Commerce Committee as a first-term member, gaining membership on the Health and the Environment Subcommittee.[3] In 1979, Waxman's fifth year in Congress, the California Democrat challenged the seniority system by running for the vacant subcommittee chair against a more senior candidate, Richardson Preyer (D-NC). Although Preyer was supported by the Democratic leadership and was endorsed by the *Washington Post,* Waxman defeated him when the Democratic members of the Commerce Committee voted 15–12 to reject Preyer. Waxman's challenge to the seniority system, and to a respected member (Preyer), was opposed most strenuously by Richard Bolling (D-MO) and majority leader James Wright (D-TX), even though Waxman had much higher party-unity scores than Preyer. Bolling strongly objected to campaign contributions from Waxman's political action committee (PAC) to ten other members of the Commerce Committee, nine of whom voted against Preyer.

Waxman used two issues in his campaign to defeat Preyer. He maintained that since Preyer and his family were important stockholders in Richardson-Merrill, one of the nation's largest pharmaceutical manufacturers, Preyer had a serious conflict of interest on the subcommittee that regulates the drug industry. In addition, Preyer, who represented a district in North Carolina, had publicly disputed claims that cigarettes posed a health hazard. Waxman, an ardent opponent of the tobacco industry, claimed that he would be better able to represent the view of the majority of the Democratic Caucus in this area of health policy.

Waxman used his position as chair of the Health and Environment Subcommittee to become one of the most influential members of the House. According to Waxman, some of his most important achievements in the area of health policy include

> [the] Ryan White CARE Act, the Nutrition Labeling and Education Act, the Breast and Cervical Cancer Mortality Prevention Act, the Safe Medical Devices Act, the Patent Term Restoration and Drug Competition Act, and the Orphan Drug Act. Rep. Waxman has also passed legislation that improves the quality of nursing homes and home health services and that sets policy for childhood immunization programs, vaccine compensation, tobacco education programs, communicable disease research, community and migrant health centers, maternal and child health care, family planning centers, health maintenance organizations, and drug regulation and reform. Throughout the 1980s, Rep. Waxman championed national health care reform and improvements in the Medicare and Medicaid programs. He successfully led the fight for improved prenatal and infant care for low-income families, for protection against impoverishment for the spouses of persons in nursing homes, and for more services in the community for people needing long-term care. He has also been a long-time advocate for comprehensive prescription drug coverage in Medicare.[4]

By almost any standard, Waxman's career has been one of extraordinary accomplishment. Waxman has scored legislative victories at the expense of tobacco companies, the American Medical Association, pharmaceutical manufacturers, auto manufacturers, oil companies, Christian conservatives, and food manufacturers. Henry Waxman has dependably fought for policies that are consistent with his liberal world view, policies that have been opposed by some of the most powerful interest groups in the United States.

Waxman's case is contrary to much of the accepted wisdom in political science about the behavior of congressional members and the composition of congressional committees. In his classic treatment of the committee assignment process, Kenneth A. Shepsle describes the essence of distributive theory:

> The committee assignment process . . . conspires with other factors—the career orientation of congressmen, weak party and House leadership, the seniority system, and reliance on committees as the principal gatekeepers for the House—to keep subgovernments in business. The accommodation of interests at the stage in which members seek committee assignments is the necessary first step in the creation of enduring relationship among legislators, lobbyists, and agency personnel in particular policy areas. A reelection oriented legislator, on a committee in which he may preserve or promote projects or interests in his district, is in a position to collaborate with interest groups and agency bureaucrats. In exchange for lobbying/bill drafting services, research, and campaign contributions from interest groups and the expediting services for district projects and interests by agency personnel, the strategically located legislator provides "good public policy" for the former and authorizations and appropriations for the latter. (1978, 247)

How does the Waxman example pose a challenge for the distributive perspective developed by Shepsle? Waxman selected a committee for public policy reasons, not electoral considerations related to assisting the predominant interest in his district—in fact, it would be very difficult to identify a predominant interest in Waxman's wealthy Los Angeles district. Waxman was elected from a congressional district that was known from the moment it was drawn as "the Waxman district," and he has never been seriously challenged in either a primary or a general election. In Congress, he openly opposed a fellow Democrat from North Carolina who had more seniority and who was backed by the tobacco lobby (two elements of the quintessential iron triangle); he was elected subcommittee chair by members of the Commerce Committee over the tobacco industry's choice. Throughout his career, he has aligned himself with interest groups representing the public interest—consumer groups, environmentalists, advocates of universal health care—against narrow economic interests, and he has been successful.

Republican William Thomas, another Californian who has been influen-tial in health policy for many years, represents another type of member. If the Henry Waxman case highlights the importance of policy concerns to a member of Congress, Bill Thomas's case highlights the importance of power in the motivations of members. Thomas was elected in 1978, and as might be expected of the representative from Bakersfield, California—a heavily agricultural region—and consistent with constituency-centered formulations of the committee request process, he requested an assignment to the Agriculture Committee, presumably so that he could service the agricultural interests in his district. During his electoral campaign, he sought the endorsement of minority leader John J. Rhodes (R-AZ), who replied in a letter, "Personally, I'll do all I can to see that your request is fulfilled."[5] Thomas, however, took the unusual step of contacting the ranking minority member of the committee, William Wampler, seeking his endorsement for placement on the Cotton Subcommittee. Wampler's reply was more direct than the leader's: "Once selected for membership on the Full Committee, I can assure your appointment to the Subcom-mittee on Cotton—a crop of unique importance to California's Eighteenth Congressional District."[6]

Thomas was initially placed on Agriculture, and Wampler, true to his word, delivered a seat on the Cotton Subcommittee. Thomas announced his assignment to his constituents on the front page of his first newsletter: "Much of a Congressman's legislative work is done on various commit-tees, where proposals are heard, amended, approved or rejected. . . . I am happy to report that I'll be helping to form Congressional policy on agri-culture as a member of the House Committee on Agriculture."[7] Thomas also received assignment to the Standards of Official Conduct Committee (also known as the Ethics Committee, hereafter referred to as Ethics), which he told his constituents was "a great honor." Although this com-mittee assignment is not typically sought after, it is frequently viewed within the Republican Conference as a stepping stone to an exclusive committee. According to Republican leader Robert H. Michel (R-IL), membership on the Ethics Committee was often seen as penance that one had to serve to be appointed to an important committee.[8]

Although Thomas received his first-choice committee assignment at the beginning of his first term, he *immediately* sought a transfer off the

Agriculture Committee, even before his first reelection effort. On May 14, 1980, the Republican Conference filled a vacancy on the powerful Rules Committee. First-term member Thomas was one of six members nominated for the position, which was awarded to fourth-term member Gene Taylor (R-MO). Thomas again requested a transfer to the Rules Committee when the Republican Committee on Committees (RCC) met at the beginning of the 97th Congress (January 4, 1981), and again he was unsuccessful—the only vacancy on the committee was awarded to outgoing minority leader John Rhodes. In February 1982, Thomas turned his attention away from a Rules Committee seat and requested consideration for any future vacancy on the Ways and Means Committee.[9] Thomas repeated this request at the beginning of the 98th Congress, and this time he was successful, defeating Hank Brown (R-CO) on the second ballot for the second and final vacancy on Ways and Means. In his spring 1983 newsletter, Thomas addresses the importance of Ways and Means to his constituents:

> In January, I was appointed as a member of the House Ways and Means Committee, a new assignment which will closely involve me in legislation important to the 20th District. . . . Many people have asked how my leaving the Agriculture Committee will affect California agriculture's interests in Congress. I am confident that Sen. Pete Wilson (Calif.) will protect our farm concerns in House-Senate conferences on agriculture legislation. In addition, I will promote fair treatment for our state's farm exports when the Ways and Means Committee considers trade and tariff legislation. If anything, our area's farm concerns will be better represented by my new assignment.
>
> Regarding taxation, the old joke goes that the Ways and Means Committee's job is to find "ways" to separate taxpayers from their "means." It is true that a liberal majority of the House has called for repeal of the third year of the 1981 tax cut. . . . However, I will oppose a move to undo this tax relief, because without it, families, individuals and businesses will be unable to stimulate the recovery of our economy.[10]

Bill Thomas became an influential leader on tax and entitlement policy on Ways and Means and now serves as the chair of that committee. In a unanimous vote, the Republican Steering Committee appointed him chair at the start of the 107th Congress, even though another member who sought the chair, Phil Crane (R-IL), had ten more years of seniority. A PAC established by Thomas gave generously to his Republican colleagues before his assignment.

Like Waxman, Thomas is from a safe district; he has never received less than 60 percent of the vote. Like Waxman, his committee assignment experience (especially after his initial assignment to the Agriculture Committee) is best understood by looking at motivations other than reelection. A former political scientist, Thomas understood where institutional power resided and, from his earliest days in Congress, he pursued a committee assignment that would provide him with institutional influence. When a seat on Rules did not seem possible, Thomas instead set his sights on the larger Ways and Means Committee, and today he is considered one of the most powerful members of Congress.

Drawing conclusions about the applicability of any theoretical model based on two cases is hazardous business. We do not contend that the experiences of Henry Waxman and Bill Thomas are typical or, taken alone, invalidate the constituency-centered perspective on the committee assignment process, or the relationship among committee assignments, reelection, and public policy. However, both of these cases illustrate that the committee request and assignment process is more complex than existing models suggest. In congressional studies, analysts commonly argue that members of Congress are primarily motivated by their desire to be reelected and thus seek assignment to committees that allow them to service directly the interests of their constituencies. If reelection had been Bill Thomas's primary concern, he would have been wise to remain on the Agriculture Committee rather than seek assignment first to the Rules Committee and then to the Ways and Means Committee. Thomas could directly influence agricultural policy in ways that were more readily explicable and easily understandable to his constituents from the Agriculture Committee than from Ways and Means (or Rules). Bill Thomas's pursuit of membership on the Rules Committee before he had finished his first term suggests that he was primarily motivated by something other than concerns about reelection (we suggest he was seeking power within the institution); no other House committee is more difficult to explain to one's constituents than the Rules Committee.

We are not suggesting that Waxman and Thomas are unconcerned about reelection. Reelection is the sine qua non for policy influence and power; furthermore, members of Congress have a fiduciary responsibility to protect and advance the interests of their constituents. In their committee work, however, and through other institutional activities, members of Congress can resolve "conflicts" between their need to be reelected and their policy and power motivations by discovering creative ways to use the jurisdiction of their committees to serve the interests of their constituencies and then claim credit for benefiting the district. For instance, Bill Thomas trumpets his ability to help constituents in his heavily agricultural district while serving on a committee with a jurisdiction that expands well beyond agricultural issues:

> In my capacity as Chairman of the Committee on Ways and Means, I am working vigorously to ensure that global markets are open for free and fair trade. . . . I authored legislation (H.R. 3009, the Trade Act of 2002) to enhance the President's ability to negotiate trade agreements that will open markets and expand trade. Since this legislation was signed into law in August 2002, free trade agreements with Chile and Singapore have been implemented pursuant to the law's authority. The United States is in the process of negotiating other free trade agreements with more than 50 countries. This legislation [has provided] benefits for developing countries through the extension and expansion of several trade preference programs, such as the African Growth and Opportunities Act, the Caribbean Basin Trade Partnership Act, and the Andean Trade Preference Act. *These preference programs are especially important to the 22nd Congressional District because they make U.S. inputs, such as California cotton, more attractive to our trading partners.* (emphasis added)[11]

In his statement, Representative Thomas emphasizes the local benefits created by committee legislation, though the benefits of such legislation are far more general; that is, the policy contains benefits for Americans in all 435 congressional districts and are not narrowly focused on his Twenty-second District as one might expect from a member who is solely interested in bolstering his chances of being reelected. Thomas's committee work allows him to satisfy his electoral need to appear responsive to his constituents' interests while primarily pursuing his broad public policy and influence goals. Simply because Thomas makes apparent a constituency connection does not mean that he was motivated to pursue the committee assignment for reelection purposes. In this respect, as Richard F. Fenno has argued, members of Congress have multiple motivations (reelection, good policy, and influence in the House) that shape their behavior, and "the opportunity to achieve [these] goals varies widely among committees. House members, therefore, match their individual patterns of aspiration to the diverse patterns of opportunity presented by the House committees" (1973, 1).[12]

THE CENTRALITY OF COMMITTEES

The House sits, not for serious discussion, but to sanction the conclusions of its Committees as rapidly as possible. It legislates in its committee rooms; not by the determinations of majorities, but by the resolutions of specially-commissioned minorities; so that it is not far from the truth to say that Congress in session is Congress on public exhibition, whilst Congress in its committee-rooms is Congress at work.

WOODROW WILSON, *CONGRESSIONAL GOVERNMENT*

On the surface, Congress appears to be a majoritarian institution. A majority of members in the House and in the Senate must vote policy proposals into law. In practice, Congress is largely a "minoritarian" institution. House committees exercise influence over legislation throughout the policy process. All legislation introduced into the House is referred to the committee or committees that have jurisdiction over the subject matter of the bill. Public policy is crafted in committees comprising small groups of members—and even then, by a smaller minority within the committee itself (Hall 1996)—and committee proposals are rarely spontaneously changed by a majority on the House floor. Committees not only shape public policy, they also act as gatekeepers, with the power to limit the range of policies considered by the whole House. The rules of the House are such that legislation of any significant weight must first be considered in committee before receiving consideration on the floor. Who is sitting in the committee room when public policy is made is perhaps more important than the votes taken on the floor to pass the legislation. Because of the powerful influence committees exert on the contours of public policy, political analysts have taken an intense interest in the composition of congressional committees.[13]

The important role of committees in the legislative process has made them a source of suspicion for political analysts since the inception of the republic. The founders were especially suspicious of political parties and committees, which they believed might develop into power centers in their own right. These factions would seek to promote their group interest over the public interest at every opportunity.[14] Standing committees in a legislature might conspire to dupe the chamber into acceding to what James Madison referred to as a "wicked project," something that served the narrow interests of individual committee legislators— such as their interest in reelection through service to factions in their district—at the expense of the common good.

Woodrow Wilson's classic *Congressional Government* contains a strong indictment of the committee system. According to Wilson, the committee system of the late nineteenth century lacked "unity or method" resulting in the "unsystematic, confused, and desultory action of the House" lacking "any common purpose in the measures which its committees from time to time recommend" (1885/1981, 59). Domination of the committee system by senior members discouraged the initiatives of less senior members, and committees were the first and last stop for innovative policy ideas that did not please committee chairs, who serve as the executioners: "The fate of bills committed is generally not uncertain. As a rule, a bill committed is a bill doomed. When it goes from the clerk's desk to a committee-room it crosses a parliamentary bridge of sighs to dim dungeons of silence whence it will never return. The means and time of its death are unknown, but its friends never see it again" (63). Reformers in the 1950s, 1960s, and 1970s used a similar critique of the committee system to bolster their case for significant changes in the House committee system (Zelizer 2004).

In *The Giant Jigsaw Puzzle*, Shepsle (1978) provided a formal and empirical foundation for the subfield of congressional studies and for the suspicions expressed by traditional scholars. Building on the construct of self-interest rooted in the reelection motivation, he explained that members of Congress would self-select for committees in which their constituents had an interest.[15] Party leaders seeking to minimize conflict largely accommodated such requests. Committees, he argued, thus would comprise members who represented similar constituencies with similar political interests, and who represented in Washington, D.C., interest groups that were clients of the committee; committees thus would seek to deliver policies and benefits to their clients and constituents while distributing the costs of such policies across all constituencies. E. Scott Adler suggests that comprehensive reform of the committee system has failed largely because of the benefits that the current system provides to committee members (2002). In short, from the perspective of Shepsle and distributive theory, committees were, in fact, the factions that the founders feared they would become; committees did short-circuit the pursuit of the common good as Jefferson, Madison, Wilson, and others predicted.

Given the centrality of committees to the legislative process, much research effort has focused on the composition of congressional committees. In recent years, a lively scholarly debate has reemerged over the committee assignment process in the U.S. House of Representatives. This debate primarily revolves around whether committee assignments, which are made by the Republican and Democratic committees on committees, reflect the individual interests of members of Congress, the institutional interests of Congress, the interests of the congressional parties, or some combination of these (Shepsle 1978; Krehbiel 1991; Cox and McCubbins 1993b; Maltzman 1997; Hall and Grofman 1990).[16] Committee assignments are the fulcrum of the differences among these models. Each model makes implicit or explicit assumptions about individual and collective behaviors that ultimately shape committee composition. Despite the centrality of committee assignments to our understanding of the policy dynamics of Congress, the empirical research on committee assignments has been hamstrung by data limitations, not the least of which is the absence of data that would provide political scientists the ability to test the generalizability of existing theories to House Republicans. In addition, the extant datasets have been limited to a handful of Congresses.

Committee assignment politics is complex; congressional studies' understanding of the politics of committee assignments is lacking. This book is an exploration of a significant new data source on committee assignments; we have collected the committee assignment requests of Democratic and Republican House members throughout most of the post–World War II period, from the papers of former congressional members. We use an explanatory framework to guide our exploration and to illustrate the richness of committee assignment politics and how assignment politics may influence the policy dynamics of House committees. We are not advancing our framework as a new theory of congressional organization. Our framework is not meant to replace existing theories; however, we contend that our framework and findings can illuminate areas of theoretical strength and weakness in existing theories and provide guidance for how theory-building in this area might proceed.

Throughout this work we emphasize interparty comparisons. The vast majority of the literature on congressional committees focuses exclusively on the behavior of Democrats. This was often justified by the lack of data, and the fact that the Democrats had established near-permanent majority status in the House; understanding the Republican Party appeared to be irrelevant to understanding the House. However, conclusions regarding Democrats were often assumed to be equally applicable to House Republicans. Thus, testing these models to determine whether they are generalizable across parties is a worthy enterprise. We also emphasize change over time. Both the House of Representatives and the congressional parties have undergone substantial changes over the postwar period; we seek to assess what these changes have meant for committee assignment politics.

COMMITTEE ASSIGNMENT POLITICS

In the extended republic of the United States, and among the great variety of interests, parties, and sects which it embraces, a coalition of a majority of the whole society could seldom take place on any other principles than those of justice and the general good.

JAMES MADISON, *FEDERALIST* #51

The committee assignment politics (CAP) framework is a foundation for understanding the politics of committee assignments and its potential impact on the dynamics of House policy making (see figure 1.1). The most fundamental assumption of the CAP framework is that *politics matters*. Individual political actors have multiple interests that they seek to advance in competition with other similarly interested individuals. Competition occurs within the context of political institutions that structure political competition in ways that shape and limit the success of individual actors. With respect to the committee assignments and committee politics, we argue that the committee assignment process is itself an arena of such intense competition and political struggle—between individual members seeking to advance their multiple interests and within the party committees on committees, where party leaders and members of the committee are seeking to advance their own interests— that the result of the process will be committees that are relatively heterogeneous and representative of the floor, as informational theory suggests. The CAP framework implies that relatively heterogeneous committees will result because of political competition rather than the rational process on which informational theory is predicated (Krehbiel 1991); rather than relying on questionable assumptions, such as the exogenously induced preferences of members and the majoritarian postulate to produce heterogeneous committees, we argue that multiple individual motivations in the context of political competition will produce the same result that informational theory predicts.

Our CAP framework is partly informed by previous scholarship and existing committee theories, but CAP is also grounded in our interviews of congressional members and in the written testimony of House members contained in thousands of committee request letters and other process-related documents. We argue that members of Congress are motivated by multiple goals; they are interested in being reelected but also in pursuing their conception of good public policy and developing influence within the institution (Fenno 1973). Members' goal-seeking behavior is constrained by district and personal considerations. The committee assignment process unites individual members in a competition to advance their interests in the context of a complex interplay of their individual goals, their collective choices, and the politics of the assignment

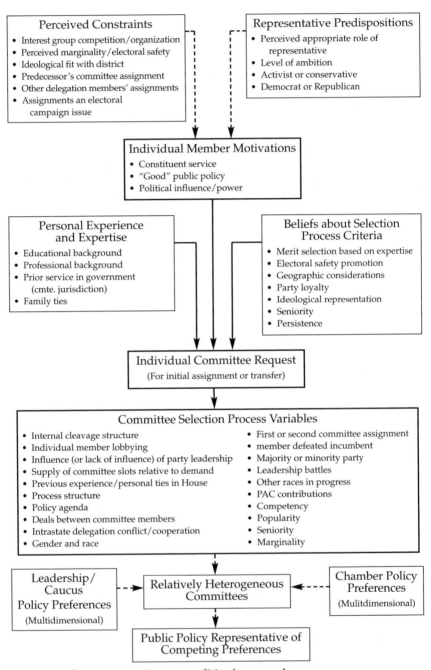

Perceived Constraints

- Interest group competition/organization
- Perceived marginality/electoral safety
- Ideological fit with district
- Predecessor's committee assignment
- Other delegation members' assignments
- Assignments an electoral campaign issue

Representative Predispositions

- Perceived appropriate role of representative
- Level of ambition
- Activist or conservative
- Democrat or Republican

Individual Member Motivations

- Constituent service
- "Good" public policy
- Political influence/power

Personal Experience and Expertise

- Educational background
- Professional background
- Prior service in government (cmte. jurisdiction)
- Family ties

Beliefs about Selection Process Criteria

- Merit selection based on expertise
- Electoral safety promotion
- Geographic considerations
- Party loyalty
- Ideological representation
- Seniority
- Persistence

Individual Committee Request

(For initial assignment or transfer)

Committee Selection Process Variables

- Internal cleavage structure
- Individual member lobbying
- Influence (or lack of influence) of party leadership
- Supply of committee slots relative to demand
- Previous experience/personal ties in House
- Process structure
- Policy agenda
- Deals between committee members
- Intrastate delegation conflict/cooperation
- Gender and race

- First or second committee assignment
- member defeated incumbent
- Majority or minority party
- Leadership battles
- Other races in progress
- PAC contributions
- Competency
- Popularity
- Seniority
- Marginality

Leadership/ Caucus Policy Preferences

(Multidimensional)

Relatively Heterogeneous Committees

Chamber Policy Preferences

(Mulitdimensional)

Public Policy Representative of Competing Preferences

Figure 1.1. Committee assignment politics framework.

process—which is a competitive arena itself—that has important implications for committee composition and hence the policy output of Congress. At the core of the framework (in the heavily framed boxes in figure 1.1) are the concepts that are central to our understanding of committee assignment politics. We do not directly or quantitatively consider in this work the concepts linked to the core by dashed lines; we do consider directly those linked to the core by solid lines. As the framework suggests, we view committee assignments as potentially influenced by various factors, which are not equally weighted all the time, nor present in all cases. We offer the CAP framework as a heuristic tool aimed at illustrating a complex political process and guiding the analysis of a vast amount of new data.

Member Motivations

Members of Congress have multiple motivations, including a desire to serve their constituents, to advance what they believe to be good public policy, and to achieve institutional influence and political power (Fenno 1973; see also Deering and Smith 1997). Members differ from one another according to the mix of motivations, some motivated primarily by one of these concerns, others by a complex mixture of the three. Shaping their motivations are perceived constraints and their personal predispositions. In large part, perceived constraints emanate from district considerations.[17] Members with well-organized single interests in their districts may feel more constrained to serve constituent interests than members whose districts are characterized by higher levels of competition between interest groups, which provides some autonomy from constituency pressures on the members. Electorally safe members may feel free to pursue policy and power interests without tremendous concern about serious electoral challenges, while marginal members may feel the need to focus on constituent concerns. Ideological fit with the district is also important. Members whose ideology is consistent with their constituents may not feel as constrained in pursuing their interests, whereas a liberal representing a primarily conservative district (or vice versa) may feel a need to pay more attention to constituency concerns. On occasion, committee assignments may become an issue in an election. For instance, an incumbent may claim that the challenger could not gain a slot on an important committee, and the challenger, in response, will seek a commitment from the party leadership to place her or him on the committee. Winning puts the challenger in the position of pursuing or accepting such an assignment. Members may also be constrained by the committee assignments of a predecessor or by the assignments held by other members of the state delegation. A member taking the seat of a popular former member who actively publicized the benefits of membership on a particular committee may feel obligated to request a seat on that committee. Although a member may desire a seat on a given committee, the presence of another member from the same state may discourage such a request.

Motivations are also shaped by the individual member's predispositions. Many members of Congress believe their primary role is to reflect the interests of their constituents faithfully and to endeavor to promote the interests of their district in Congress. Members who come to office with this predisposition are likely to be motivated primarily by constituent concerns. Other members believe that the role of the representative is also to promote the general welfare of the state or nation. These members will likely be motivated by public policy concerns but may believe that these interests can best be served by pursuing their own political ambitions. In addition, members' predispositions as activists or conservatives—the degree to which they believe policy change, in particular, is necessary or appropriate—will shape their motivations. Activists are more likely to be motivated by policy concerns, and conservatives, by constituency concerns. Finally, Democratic and Republican members of Congress will differ in important ways. For congressional members, partisan affiliation is more than a casual association; it reflects fundamental differences in policy and will therefore shape member behaviors.

Our understanding of members' motivations deviates substantially from theories of congressional organization founded on the reelection motivation. These theories typically build on David R. Mayhew's theoretical construct of the congressional member as a "single-minded seeker of reelection" (1974, 5). The distributive model of congressional organization asserts that members of Congress seek membership in committees that will best serve their interest in reelection. Our focus on multiple motivations also differs from the orienting approach of informational theory. According to Krehbiel (1991, 77), members' preferences are induced exogenously by the "values, wants, and needs" of the electorate, in other words, an electoral imperative (Rohde 1995).

Our grounding in the multiple-motivations tradition leads us to understand members as motivated by a more complex combination of impulses that includes reelection concerns but also encompasses the desire of many members to exercise policy and institutional influence. We consider the interplay of motivations and committee assignment requests in chapters 3 and 4 and demonstrate that motivations beyond reelection are important to most representatives. Evidence from multiple data sources confirms that constituency concerns, although considered by members, do not determine committee preferences for most representatives. Most congressional members expect more than reelection from their committee assignments; they expect professional fulfillment, which means assignments need to be responsive to their other professional goals.

Committee Requests

In the CAP framework, committee requests are influenced by members' motivations, but also by members' personal backgrounds and beliefs about the factors that are most important in the assignment process, and how these factors advantage them in the assignment process. Many members, especially first-term members, may consider their experiences to be important in the request decision (as Henry Waxman did). Based on education, work experience, or experience in dealing with the issues that fall within a committee's jurisdiction as a state legislator or in some other official capacity, members may request a particular committee. Often incumbents will seek to capitalize on their congressional experience when requesting a committee. Newly elected members frequently emphasize experience working on a congressional staff, and those first-term members who are family members of other current or former members typically emphasize this family relationship.

Requesters will also tailor their choices based on what they believe the committee on committees considers most important in a candidate. For instance, many members believe that party loyalty is an important consideration in the assignment process, especially for highly sought-after committees. Those members who have records as party loyalists may be emboldened when seeking a preferred committee assignment, given their record. By contrast, members who have less impressive credentials may avoid such a request altogether, believing they have no chance of receiving such an assignment. A similar argument can be made about the importance of member ideology in influencing member requests. Other members who believe that assignments are decided on merit or expertise may request assignments that they are unlikely to receive because of their background and personal experience. As we demonstrate in chapter 5, members of Congress routinely shape their campaigns and arguments for committee assignments according to the type of committee they are pursuing, and Democrats and Republicans differ significantly in how they perceive the role of experience in the assignment process.

Beliefs about how the assignment process treats other member and district characteristics also influence member requests. Some members perceive a bias in the process toward assisting members who have won election by a slim margin, while others see a bias toward placing members from safe districts on more important committees. Seniority and persistence often factor into the decision to request a committee assignment. Members who have accumulated seniority may feel more entitled to a place on a desired committee, especially when they have previously requested assignment to that committee and have been turned down. Finally, geographic considerations matter; members perceive bias in the assignment process favoring members from specific states or regions or bias favoring members based on the size of the state.

Committee Selection Process

The committee assignment process itself—the decision-making process within the party committees on committees—is more complex than the political science literature suggests, and in fact, it is far more complex than requesting members of Congress believe. The political science literature typically portrays the assignment process as governed by constrained self-selection: Party committees on committees routinely accommodate members' committee requests within the constraints of the supply of available committee slots. According to this view, the assignment process is routine and dispassionate, guided by the principle of conflict avoidance.

The CAP framework suggests that the process is influenced by a swirl of competing political forces, some of which are structural in nature, others of which bear the hallmarks of pure politics. First, the structure of the assignment process itself is dynamic. As we illustrate in chapter 2, the assignment process has changed significantly in both parties over the postwar period, which has pitted factions within the party against one another over the structure of the assignment process. In the Republican Party, this conflict often pitted large states against small states; in the Democratic Party, liberals against conservatives. Second, committee assignments are subject to the broad internal cleavage structure of the party, which may become apparent in the appearance of coalitions within the assignment process. In chapter 7 we demonstrate that votes within the RCC over the course of several Congresses were marked by fairly stable coalitions of members. Internal cleavages or unity within state delegations can influence the ability of a state delegation's representative within the committee on committees to advance the interests of delegation members who are seeking assignments (see chapter 2). Third, committee assignments are subject to simple considerations of the supply of committee seats, which is partly a function of the minority or majority status of the party, and the decisions of other members to surrender committee assignments or to leave the chamber. The assignment process is not, however, simply a reflection of supply-and-demand considerations. It is subject to an array of political factors that can influence the accommodation of members' requests. As we demonstrate in chapter 5, members seeking assignments often subject members of the committee on committees to intense campaigning, which can influence the assignment process. Members of the party committees on committees consider the personal characteristics of individual requesters and are often influenced by the personal popularity of a member, the perceived competence (or incompetence) of a committee requester, previous experience, and personal ties (see chapter 8). Gender and race considerations may also influence decisions of the committee on committees (see chapter 9).

A number of other factors combine to make the process an overtly political one. Party leaders vary considerably in the desire to influence the assignment of members to committees and their skill at making their wishes come true (see chapter 6). The policy agenda may influence the assignment process. If a major reauthorization is scheduled to occur, a highway bill for example, there may be an effort to place vulnerable members in positions where they can take credit for the benefits of the legislation. Deals between members of the committee on committees often influence the outcome of voting on assignments. In voting, members of both parties' committees on committees take into account whether a request is for a first or second committee assignment for the member, how the requesting member voted in past leadership elections, the requesting members' record of raising money for the party, other committee assignment races that are forthcoming, the marginality of the requester, and whether the requesting member defeated an incumbent member of the other party. Finally, majority status provides that party with greater numbers of choice committee positions to distribute as well as the ability to increase the number of seats available, whereas minority status increases the competition within the assignment process because there are fewer choice assignments to go around.

The committee request and assignment process within the CAP framework is far less routine than theoretical literature suggests. According to distributive theory, members' interests—largely influenced by constituency characteristics—are routinely matched with existing committee vacancies during the assignment process. This routinized self-selection suggests that the committee assignment process is aimed at minimizing conflict within the assignment process by emphasizing nonpolitical factors and by accommodating members' requests within the constraints of the supply of committee seats. This view has developed despite empirical studies that generally indicate only about 50 percent of members are assigned to their preferred committee (see chapter 4).

Informational theory views the assignment process as dictated by the interests of the chamber, though the empirical literature is devoid of empirical consideration of the assignment process per se. The chief innovation of informational theory is the contention that congressional committees are organized to serve the collective interests of the parent body rather than the narrow interests of individual members, as distributive theory suggests. Informational theory is built on two assumptions: (1) Committee composition is subject to majoritarian principles—if a committee comprised members who were unrepresentative of the floor median, a majority on the floor would reject that committee's slates; and (2) the consequences of proposed public policies are uncertain. Legislative organizations must amass information about policy options and provide their members with information about the potential costs and benefits of legislative proposals. Congressional committees exist to collect and communicate this information to members of the parent body. Given the legislature's interest in the work of its committees, the majority on the floor seeks committees that are representative of the majority. The floor majority in the chamber serves as a check on the behavior of committees by punishing high-demand behavior (Krehbiel 1991).

The majoritarian postulate is the subject of intense debate (Hall 1996). Like most elements of congressional politics, the assignment process within each party is controlled by a small number of members, a minority of both their party and the floor. This presents two important reasons to be skeptical of the claim that committee assignments are subject to the majoritarian principle. First, committee slates developed within the committee on committees and presented to the party caucuses have never been seriously challenged in a caucus. Second, the acceptance on the floor of committee slates proposed by the party caucuses is routine, and there is no evidence that the House floor, in the modern era, has ever considered this step as anything other than pro forma.

Party-cartel theory suggests that multiple motivations drive members' committee request behavior (Cox and McCubbins 1993). Members who are motivated by constituency concerns will gravitate toward committees with narrow policy jurisdictions and targeted externalities that serve the interests of dominant constituencies in the district, such as the Agriculture, District of Columbia, Interior, and Merchant Marine and Fisheries committees. Members who are motivated by policy concerns will gravitate toward committees with more expansive jurisdictions and either mixed externalities (Armed Services, Education and Labor, Banking and Finance, Foreign Affairs, and Judiciary committees) or uniform externalities (committees on Energy and Commerce; Government Operations; House

Administration; Post Office and Civil Service; Public Works and Transportation; Science, Space, and Technology; and Veterans' Affairs). Finally, members who are seeking influence will gravitate toward the "control" committees (Appropriations, Budget, Rules, and Ways and Means).[18] Over the last category of committees, party leadership will try to exercise particular control, the theory suggests, by placing party loyalists on the committees to provide the leadership with influence over the committees that dictate the broad policy agenda of Congress. In the case of the first two sets of committees, party-cartel theory implies that self-selection will dominate the assignment process; in the case of the control committees, party loyalty will determine which candidates are successful. The strength of party-cartel theory is its reliance on multiple motivations and the resulting typology of committee request behavior. However, the assignment process it not as frictionless as party-cartel theory suggests with respect to most committees, and, as we argue above, the CAP framework implies that leadership control will be highly contingent over all committee assignments, including assignments to the control committees, because of the mixed motivations of leaders and the competition within the committees on committees.

Committee Composition and Public Policy

Our CAP framework suggests that committees will be relatively heterogeneous in representation of interests within a committee, and that public policy output will reflect competition between conflicting policy preferences within the committees and the chamber. Although empirical analysis of the assignment composition–pork barrel nexus is beyond the scope of this study, our framework has implications for existing theories' expectations in this regard. The CAP framework expects that competition between individuals who are motivated by different interests combined with competition in the committee assignment process will result in committees that, for the most part, represent various policy interests and will, therefore, be fairly representative of the interests of the chamber as a whole. Note that we argue that they will be *relatively* heterogeneous. In a comparatively small number of districts dominated by large-scale single interests, many members will feel obligated to request committees that are narrowly focused on their constituency's interests. The number of large-scale single interests than *can* dominate a district is limited primarily to agriculture and the military; the former requires a great deal of space and supporting industries, and the latter requires space and tends to employ large numbers of people. The Agriculture and Armed Services committees offer targeted jurisdictions that enable members to appear responsive to constituents' interests; predictably, these committees are often pointed to as examples of the power of distributive theory. A small number of committees will represent homogeneous interests. Most districts are not dominated by single interests; they are composed of multiple and competing interests. Members representing these districts will feel free to pursue assignment to committees that have jurisdiction over issues of personal or policy importance to them, and their reasons for pursuing assignment to any particular committee will be different.

In this respect, our framework suggests a different policy dynamic than is predicted by distributive theory, which posits that constituency-based requests routinely accommodated in the assignment process will result in committees that are homogeneous with respect to policy preferences. Routine self-selection may occur within this subset of committees. In the absence of high levels of competition for seats on these committees, the committees on committees will accommodate member requests. These committees are Agriculture, Armed Services, and Interior. In these cases, our framework suggests that committees will comprise preference outliers.

Our expectation that committees will be relatively heterogeneous is similarly predicted by informational theory—though informational theory predicts uniformly heterogeneous committees—which posits heterogeneous committees as a result of the majoritarian principle and the interests of the chamber in informational committees: "Objects of legislative choice in both the procedural and policy domains must be chosen by a majority of the legislature" (Krehbiel 1991, 16). From this perspective, committees will be heterogeneous in deference to the interests of the majority in the chamber; the majority has the ability to reject committees that are not representative.

Similar to informational theory, our framework suggests that most committees will be heterogeneous and that the public policy that comes out of these committees will generally serve the interests of the chamber rather than the narrow interests of the members of the committee. The challenge we raise for informational models is our explanation for *why* most committees will be heterogeneous. *We contend that most committees will be relatively heterogeneous because of committee assignment politics.* Members who have different interests and beliefs pursue the same committees; the committee assignment process itself incorporates heterogeneous interests and therefore selects from requesting members based on shifting interests and alliances. Some committees may well be composed of preference outliers; however, committees are kept in check by party leaders and ultimately by the floor. In short, Arthur Maass was essentially correct when he argued that "the result of [the] committee assignment process is that some committees are fairly representative of the House as a whole and some are quite unrepresentative" (1983, 102).

Ultimately political analysts focus on the committee request and assignment process and the question of committee composition to gain understanding of the nature of congressional policy making, to determine whether Congress makes policy to satisfy the interests of minorities in the chamber or the interests of the nation as a whole. From the perspective of the CAP framework, there are significant reasons to believe that congressional policy, in general, will be responsive to the multiple interests of the nation. We expect that most committees represent heterogeneous policy preferences, necessitating significant bargaining within committees and partisan contingents to serve the interests of the majority within the committee. Policies are rarely unidimensional; they often contain elements within them that will stimulate cleavages within the committee: spenders versus budget hawks, centralizers versus devolutionists, urban versus rural interests, Republicans versus Democrats, and so forth. Building a coalition within a committee, even one composed of preference outliers, will prove difficult.

During committee consideration, committee members need to consider their ability to create a winning coalition on the floor. In the absence of many homogeneous committees, the committee-based logrolling behavior predicted by distributive theory is impossible. For instance, members of the Agriculture Committee, seeking to provide benefits targeted to their constituencies, might be able to engage in a logroll with members of the

Armed Services and Interior Committees, but that would not provide them with the majority they would need to pass the legislation on the floor. In a quest to build a majority on the floor, the Agriculture Committee would need to limit the scope of benefits in order to build support; legislation seeking to provide an inordinate set of benefits to a narrow constituency would be a loser. Furthermore, authorizing committees, like Agriculture, do not control the congressional purse strings. The Appropriations Committee jealously guards its power to spend federal dollars and is not willing to defer this power to the authorizing committees who seek funds. In short, the politics of the legislative process will cause this handful of committees, in many cases, to curb their desire to service the narrow interests within their jurisdiction.

The party leadership also has the means to influence the legislation approved by congressional committees. Party leaders control the scheduling of legislation for consideration on the floor; they also have substantial influence over the Rules Committee, which controls the conditions under which the legislation will be considered on the floor. Committee leaders and members who are politically astute pay attention to the signals they receive from the leadership about the scope of committee legislation; party leaders can rein in committee legislation if the committee fails to anticipate and respond to leadership signals before legislation leaves the committee room.

• • •

Our CAP framework bears some similarities to elements of existing theories but also suggests expectations that are not suggested by these theories. First, members of Congress are largely motivated by a desire to influence public policy and develop influence within the institution; most members are not obsessed with reelection. For that reason, there will be a modest linkage between constituency interests and committee requests and assignments. Second, the two political parties are different. Despite the fact that Democratic and Republican House members are motivated by very similar concerns, their ability to achieve their individual goals, such as preferred committee assignments, is shaped by their political party structure, their party leadership, and the culture of their party. For instance, in our consideration of committee request success, we demonstrate that the party committees on committees weigh the personal characteristics of requesters differently, based in part on the interests of the party. The interests of the party are shaped, again in part, by the party's majority or minority status. Political parties matter, political context matters, and theorists should consider the differential effects of parties and context within the institution. Third, given these findings, it is somewhat unsurprising to find that most committees are not composed of preference outliers, as Krehbiel and others have also found (for instance, Krehbiel 1991; Groseclose 1994). On the other hand, as we suggest above, the motivational and institutional factors that result in heterogeneous committees require additional consideration; some committees, by our estimation, will be outlier committees, and political parties do significantly shape the complexion of committees based on collective partisan interests. Finally, our framework suggests that evidence for pork barrel spending of the type expected by distributive theory will not be widespread, a finding that is supported as often as not in the empirical literature (for instance, Frisch 1998; Stein and Bickers 1995).

RESEARCH DESIGN

Over forty years ago, Nicholas Masters (1961) published the first major empirical study of House committee assignments. A great deal has been learned in the intervening years; however, one of the major agenda items outlined by Masters, and largely ignored by subsequent scholars, concerns the differences between the two parties in their committee assignment behavior. There has been little comparative research largely because of the dearth of data on House Republicans. Scholars have identified the inaccessibility of committee request data for Republicans as a major reason for the failure to engage in a truly comparative exercise (for example, Eulau 1985). Congressional scholars have generally assumed that Republican members behaved in a manner similar to Democrats. Shepsle virtually ignores Republicans: "While the approach employed in this study is quite general, the empirical focus is on Democratic committee assignments, 1958–1974. . . . Although the descriptive materials of this study are primarily related to the committee process of the majority party, I believe that the theoretical forces are of a much more general nature. I do hope that scholars undertake separate studies of the committee assignment process for the Republicans" (1978, 7).

We contend that the examination of party differences in members' committee requests will have important consequences for the study of committees and congressional organization. Further, a consciously comparative approach to the study of the two parties will provide additional evidence useful in the ongoing debates over the organization and influence of committees in Congress. Thus, this study is comparative in nature. We do not take for granted that members of both parties will behave in the same ways. Throughout this work, we take a comparative approach to determine whether members of the two congressional parties behave in appreciably different ways and what the consequences are for committee composition, and to consider these differences in light of theories built primarily on the behavior of a single party's members. We believe that changes in Congress over time have shaped the committee assignment processes in important ways. Thus, our research design is also diachronic.

Committee Assignment Request Data

Much of the analysis that follows is based on examination of the committee requests of individual members of Congress. Our data include both the briefing books used by the party committees on committees during the actual assignment process and the preference letters submitted to the committees on committees from individual members, explaining, in many cases, why they are seeking membership on a particular committee. For Democrats, we have committee request data from the 80th Congress through the 103rd Congress (with the exception of the 85th Congress); for Republicans, our data are from the 86th through the 102nd Congress. All totaled we have committee request data for 2,480 members of Congress over this period for both Democrats (1,366) and Republicans (1,114). Committee preference data are almost exclusively from the committees on committees' briefing books. The request letters alone provide a particularly rich dataset, which provides tremendous insight into the calculations of requesters; we use these letters also for some of the qualitative elements of our analysis (chapters 3 and 5; see also appendix 2).

Most studies of committee behavior over the last several decades have relied on examination of the actual committee assignments of members of Congress. The assumption of these studies, based on the self-selection assumption of distributive theory, was that members of Congress largely served on committees on which they *wanted* to serve. As we will demonstrate, this is a questionable assumption. Members of Congress often do not receive their preferred committee assignment; therefore, assuming that the observed committee assignment is an indication of intent is a seriously flawed approach. With committee request data in hand, we are able to examine both the foundations of these theories and their implications in more depth, and with more accuracy, than previous studies have done. In addition to the quantitative and qualitative data collected from the archives, we have also conducted extensive interviews with members and former members of Congress and congressional staff. Our work reflects various methodologies, both quantitative and qualitative, and is based on primary source materials and on extensive interview data.

Despite the enormous effort involved in collecting these data, and the vast amount of new information that they represent, we are not able to present data for more recent Congresses. We do not have data for the Republicans during their time in the majority beginning in the 104th Congress. This limitation is the result of how we collect our data. Because we collect these data from congressional archives, we must wait until a member who was active in the assignment process retires (or dies). The member's papers are transferred to an archival repository, the collection is processed at the archive, and the collection is opened to researchers (and it is often the case that members place restrictions on access to the papers for several years). This can create a significant lag. The major implication of this study is that some of the party differences we highlight are not merely differences between Democrats and Republicans but instead are differences between a majority and a minority party. That said, our interviews with members and staff who are currently active in the assignment process suggest that, beyond process changes, many of the patterns that we identify here persist in recent Congresses.

ORGANIZATION OF THE BOOK

This study is organized within the CAP framework. We begin with a comparative description and analysis of the committee assignment structure over the last half-century, emphasizing the Republican assignment process, which political scientists have largely ignored. Our purpose in closely detailing the assignment process is twofold. First, we demonstrate that the structure of the assignment process has varied over the last half century. Second, we redress a significant problem in the congressional literature: the dearth of information on the committee assignment process among Republicans. Discussions of the GOP process have mechanically cited Masters' *APSR* article from the 1960s. This presents a static view of the GOP that was outdated almost as soon as it was published and became even more so with each passing year (though it is still routinely cited as the authoritative source on the subject). It is also the case that most of the descriptive work on the Democratic Steering Committee is nearly three decades old and requires updating (Dodd 2004).

In chapters 3 and 4, we examine the motivations of members seeking committee assignments. We focus in particular on our assertion that members are driven by multiple motivations that go well beyond electoral and constituency considerations. Using content analysis in chapter 3, we examine request letters and find that most members seek committee membership as a means to shape public policy or to exercise influence in the House. In chapter 4, we examine the relationship between objective constituency characteristics and committee assignments. Our analysis demonstrates that, except for a small subset of committees, there is no definite constituency-request linkage. Chapter 5 focuses on an analysis of members' beliefs about the committee assignment process and the strategies they employ to achieve preferred committee assignments.

In chapters 6 through 9, our attention shifts to the politics of committee assignments inside the assignment process. In chapter 6, we examine the role of the party leadership in the assignment process, finding that party leaders do exercise influence, but that influence varies between parties and across party leaders. Chapter 7 uses a unique dataset, the individual votes of members in the RCC, to analyze factions inside the RCC. Chapters 8 and 9 analyze request success. Far from indicating a routinized self-selection process, our analysis shows that success is a function of both the personal characteristics of the requester (including elements suggested by the informational and party-cartel theories) and the supply and demand of committee slots. Further, these factors differ across parties, and across party leaders, suggesting, ultimately, that committee assignment is a function of politics and time.

We conclude by summarizing our findings within the context of both the CAP framework and existing theories about congressional committees. We suggest areas of weakness and strength in these theories, and make suggestions for improving these theories; we also suggest several directions for further research using these and other data that will provide additional insight into the policy dynamics of Congress.

CHAPTER TWO

Assignment Process and Process Change

Everyone believes the system tilts against him or her. Everyone wants it to tilt toward him or her. It may be impossible to construct a tiltless system.

BILL FRENZEL (R-MN)

One of the research agenda items discussed by Masters (1961) concerned the differences between the parties in their committee assignment processes: "The study of committee assignments should . . . throw light on . . . the differences between the parties in performing this organizational task" (345). Despite the direction provided by Masters' classic article, interparty comparison has languished, in large part because of the dearth of research into the Republican process. Our research design is premised on the assumption that Masters was correct, that comparative examination of the politics of committee assignments can have important consequences for the study of Congress and can shed substantial light on the ongoing debate over the organization and purpose of congressional committees.

Previous treatments of the committee assignment process have viewed the structure of the assignment process as a static black box; unchanging over time and largely irrelevant to committee assignments, the party committees on committees are neutral arbiters that impartially mediate between competing members and their interests. Our CAP framework suggests there are good reasons for taking a close look at the structure of the committees on committees themselves. The structure of the committee assignment mechanism itself is likely to be a matter of competition within the party to gain advantage in the assignment process; for this reason, we expect the structure of the process to be more dynamic and subject to change and intraparty conflict than previously thought. Interparty comparison of the committees on committees' structure will provide insight into differences between individual partisans in terms of their success in achieving their goals through the assignment process. Finally, change in the assignment processes employed by the two parties illustrates that the description of the assignment process provided by Masters is in need of substantial revision, especially to the degree that political scientists still reflexively refer to Masters as the authoritative source on the subject.

We explore in greater detail than has been done in five decades the structure and evolution of the Republicans' committee assignment process, and we engage in a conscious comparison with the Democratic assignment process. Our major focus is the representative and voting structure of the RCC from the 86th to the 105th Congress, and the structure of voting power within the committee.[1] Throughout this period members of the Republican Conference as well as party leaders frequently sought to reform the committee assignment process, with the perhaps conflicting goals of making the process more broadly representative of the Republican membership and to provide the party leadership with greater control over the process. It is our contention that each successive reform had important consequences for the ability of individual members to pursue their individual goals, and for the party leadership to pursue the collective goals of the Republican Conference.

POWER INDEXES

Because the Republicans' committee assignment process relied on weighted voting for seventy years, it is useful to examine the effect of the different schemata on the power of various actors. We use two measures of voter power: the Banzhaf Power Index (BPI) and the Johnston Power Index (JPI). Each power index seeks to quantify the relative importance of each voter in making a committee assignment decision. Power scores range between 0 and 1, and the sum of the power of all voters is equal to 1. The closer an individual actor's score is to 1, therefore, the more important the actor is in making decisions. (See appendix 1 for detailed information on BPI and JPI.)

REPUBLICANS' COMMITTEE ASSIGNMENT PROCESS

At 12:30 A.M. on Friday, February 28, 1919, Republican members of the House of Representatives agreed to a committee assignment process based on weighted voting that would remain in place (with alterations discussed below) for the next seventy years.[2] The process was proposed by James R. Mann (R-IL), who had just been defeated in his attempt to be elevated from minority leader to Speaker after the Republicans reclaimed the House majority. Mann's proposal was an alternative to a seventeen-member committee on committees' slate that had been put forward by supporters of the newly elected Speaker of the House, Frederick Gillett (R-MA). The Mann substitute created a full committee on committees (the RCC) comprising one Republican member chosen by the members from each state delegation that had elected at least one Republican to the House. It was soon apparent (as reported in the *New York Times* later that same morning) that the new committee assignment system, which gave each RCC member voting power equal to the total Republican House membership from his state, concentrated power in RCC representatives from a few large states with big Republican delegations.

According to contemporaneous accounts and historical research, the new process allowed Mann and his allies to control committee assignments, committee chair assignments, and appointments to the important Steering Committee, which at the time set party policy. Paul DeWitt Hasbrouck (1927) points out that since Mann supporters were the majority in the larger states, they could effectively control committee voting. There were more Gillett supporters on the full RCC (20 state representatives to 12 for Mann); however, with weighted voting, the votes lined up to 124 for Mann and 92 for Gillett.

Historian Herbert F. Margulies captures nicely the creation of the Republicans' committee assignment process:

> Mann perpetrated a coup against his tormentors. Gillett's manager, Samuel Winslow of Massachusetts, offered a resolution for the election of a seventeen-member Committee on Committees, consisting of some Mann allies but chiefly Gillett people. Mann was ready with a substitute. Each of the thirty-six Republican state delegations should elect a member of the Committee on Committees, presumably the head of the delegation. Each of these members would cast a number of votes equal to his state's Republican representation in the House. On the surface the proposal seemed to the Gillett coalition to be inoffensive, since the motion would provide additional places on the committee, and quick calculation indicated that Gillett men would be in the majority. Thus the caucus gave noisy approval to Mann's motion without a record vote. Only later did the Gillett men realize that mainly because of the seventy-five votes that would be cast by the members from New York, Pennsylvania and Illinois, Thomas Dunn, J. Hampton Moore, and Mann, the Mann forces would easily control. (1996, 194)

When and how an RCC subcommittee emerged to do the actual work of assigning Republicans to committee is uncertain (Brown 1922). At some point early in RCC history, a small group comprising members from the large states became the main decision-making body. What is certain is that by the 83rd Congress (1953), a subcommittee of the RCC, selected by the Republican leader, was responsible for assigning members to standing committees. Between the 83rd and 86th Congress, that subcommittee comprised only members from the states with the largest Republican delegations: California, Illinois, Michigan, New Jersey, New York, Pennsylvania, and Ohio, with the minority leader (or majority leader, if the Republicans were in control of the chamber) serving as nonvoting chair.

The RCC in the 86th Congress

Prior to the 86th Congress, Republicans from small states were not represented on the subcommittee that made the committee assignment decisions. This apparently led to considerable resentment and certainly

TABLE 2.1
Republican Committee on Committees representative structure
(selected Congresses)

Executive Committee representative structure, 86th Congress

	States represented	Number of members represented	Votes in RCC
California	California	14	14
Illinois	Illinois	11	11
Michigan	Michigan	11	11
New Jersey	New Jersey	9	9
New York	New York	24	24
Ohio	Ohio	14	14
Pennsylvania	Pennsylvania	14	14
Idaho	Ariz. (1), Colo. (1), Fla. (1), Idaho (1),		
North Carolina	Ind. (3), Iowa (4), Kans. (3), Ky. (1), Maine (1), Mass. (6), Minn. (5), Mo. (1), Neb. (2), N.H. (2), N.C. (1), N.Dak. (1), Okla. (1), Ore. (1), S.Dak. (1), Tenn. (2), Tex. (1), Utah (1), Va. (2), Wash. (6), W.Va. (1), Wisc. (5), Wyo. (1)	56	2
Total		153	99

Executive Committee representative structure, 97th Congress

	States represented	Number of members represented	Votes in RCC
California	California	21	21
New York	New York	17	17
Illinois	Illinois	14	14
Ohio	Ohio	13	13
Pennsylvania	Pennsylvania	13	13
Virginia	Virginia	9	9
Michigan	Michigan	7	7
New Jersey	New Jersey	7	7
Five-member states	Ind., Minn., Tex.	15	15
Four-member states	Fla., Kans., Mo., N.C., S.C., Wisc.	24	24
Three-member states	Ala., Iowa, Ky., Neb., Tenn.	15	15
Two-member states	Ariz., Ark., Colo., Conn., Idaho, La., Maine, Mass., N.Mex., Utah, Wash., W.Va.	24	24

TABLE 2.1 (*continued*)
Republican Committee on Committees representative structure
(selected Congresses)

Executive Committee representative structure, 97th Congress (*continued*)

	States represented	Number of members represented	Votes in RCC
One-member states	Alaska, Del., Ga, Md., Miss., Mont., N.H., Okla., Ore., R.I., S.Dak., Vt., Wyo.	13	13
Total		192	192

RCC representative structure, 101st Congress

	States represented	Number of members represented	Votes in RCC
Republican leader	n/a	n/a	12
Republican whip	n/a	n/a	6
California	California	18	18
Florida	Florida	9	9
Illinois	Illinois	8	8
Michigan	Michigan	7	7
New Jersey	New Jersey	6	6
New York	New York	13	13
Ohio	Ohio	10	10
Pennsylvania	Pennsylvania	11	11
Texas	Texas	8	8
Virginia	Virginia	5	5
Four-member states	Ariz., Iowa, La., Mo., N.C., Wisc.	24	24
Three-member states	Conn., Colo., Kans., Ky., Minn., Ind., Tenn., Wash.	24	24
Two-member states	Ala., Neb., Md., N.H., N.Mex., Okla., Ore., R.I., S.C., Utah	20	20
One-member states	Alaska, Ark., Ga., Hawaii, Idaho, Maine, Mass., Miss., Mont., Nev., Vt., Wyo., Guam	13	13
Second-term members	n/a	n/a	1
First-term members	n/a	n/a	1
Total		176	196

TABLE 2.1 (*continued*)
Republican Committee on Committees representative structure
(selected Congresses)

Steering Committee representative structure, 105th Congress

	States represented	Number of members represented	Votes in RCC
Speaker	n/a	n/a	5
Republican leader	n/a	n/a	2
Whip	n/a	n/a	1
Conference chair	n/a	n/a	1
NRCC chair	n/a	n/a	1
Appropriations chair	n/a	n/a	1
Budget chair	n/a	n/a	1
Rules chair	n/a	n/a	1
Ways and Means chair	n/a	n/a	1
E. North Central	Ind. (6), Mich. (6), Ill. (10)	22	1
Atlantic Coast	N.Y. (13), N.J. (7)	20	1
Mid-Atlantic	Ohio (11), Pa. (10), Md. (4)	25	1
Great Plains	Iowa (4), Kans. (4), Wisc. (4), Mo. (4)	16	1
Cotton South	Ala. (5), Fla. (15), Ga. (8)	28	1
Tidewater South	N.C. (6), S.C. (4), Va. (5), Ky. (5), Tenn. (5)	25	1
W. South Central	La. (5), Okla. (6), Tex. (13)	24	1
West	Ariz. (5), Colo. (4), Wash. (6)	15	1
California	California	23	1
Small states	Alaska (1), Del. (1), Mont. (1), Ore. (1), S.Dak. (1), Wyo. (1), Ark. (2), Conn. (2), Idaho (2), Minn. (2), Nev. (2), N.H. (2), N.Mex. (2), Miss. (3), Neb. (2), Utah (3)	28	1
Second-term members	n/a		1
First-term members	n/a		1
Total		226	26

played a role in Charles Halleck's (R-IN) overthrow of minority leader Joseph W. Martin, Jr. (R-MA) in 1959.[3] When Halleck became Republican leader in the 86th Congress, he expanded the subcommittee to include some small-state representation. Halleck appointed to the subcommittee two additional members to represent the smaller states on a regional basis.

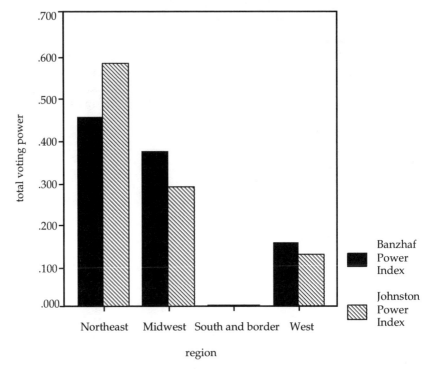

Figure 2.1. The structure of voting power in the Republican Committee on Committees, by Region, 86th Congress.

Unlike the large-state representatives, each of these regional members was given only a single vote in committee assignment voting.

Masters (1961) describes the structure of the 86th Congress, though he does not mention that this was the first year that Republicans used regional representatives on the subcommittee.[4] Examining the RCC structure of representation in the 86th Congress, one immediately notices that the large states (California, Illinois, Michigan, New Jersey, New York, Ohio, and Pennsylvania) still seemed to wield enormous power within the committee. Although their members constituted only 63 percent of the Republican Conference, representatives of these states controlled 98 percent of the votes in the RCC. Masters' conclusions are not surprising: "This [structure] concentrates the power over committee assignments in the hands of the senior members from the large state delegations" (1961, 348).

Figure 2.1 illustrates the RCC voting power structure in the 86th Congress.[5] The appointments made by the Republican leader kept the committee assignment process firmly in the grip of the states of the Midwest and Northeast, in addition to California accounting for the apparent voting power of the West in the committee. Indeed, only two of the votes (out of ninety-nine) in the RCC were granted to states outside this power nexus (one each to Idaho and North Carolina), and those two votes were intended to represent the interests of more than one-third of the Republican Conference, mainly southern and western states.

In the 86th Congress, New York, with the largest number of votes in the RCC, was a dominant actor within the committee (see table 2.2). New York's BPI and JPI of .24 and .43, respectively, reveal that New York had 1.8 to 3.6 times the power in the RCC of the next most powerful states (California, Ohio, or Pennsylvania). As the two indices indicate, it would be difficult to form a winning coalition in the RCC without New York.

The small states represented by congressional members from Idaho and North Carolina were vastly overmatched in the committee (BPI = .02, JPI = .01), with one tenth to one fortieth of the power of New York. In short, it was theoretically unlikely that the small states would have an appreciable impact on the outcomes of the committee assignment process for the members they sought to represent. The extent to which they did gain representation on committees was in spite of the institutional structure that the RCC used.

In light of this analysis, it is understandable that Masters found widespread discontent among Republicans from small states with the committee assignment process. These members complained that the process deprived them of seats on important committees. Furthermore, Masters relates that small-state Republicans complained "that the Republican procedure allows no mechanism whereby the small state delegations can combine their voting power in the Committee-on-Committees" (1961, 350). Clapp captures what was likely a common Republican member response to the assignment process:

> On the Republican side of the aisle the business of filling vacancies simply boils down to a decision to be made by about four

TABLE 2.2
Republican Committee on Committees voting power indices
(selected Congresses)

Measure/Congress	Mean	Minimum (least powerful actors)	Maximum (most powerful actor)	Range	N
BPI 86th	.0287	.0004 (one-member states)	.2390 (New York)	.2386	34
JPI 86th	.0289	.0001 (one member states)	.4290 (New York)	.4289	34
BPI 97th	.0207	.0050 (one-member states)	.1100 (California)	.1050	47
JPI 97th	.0199	.0040 (one-member states)	.1360 (California)	.1320	47
BPI 101st	.0207	.0050 (one-member states)	.0920 (California)	.0870	49
JPI 101st	.0208	.0020 (one-member states)	.1010 (California)	.0990	49
BPI 105th	.0194	.0000 (states in groups dominated by a single state)	.2670 (Speaker)	.2670	50
JPI 105th	.0189	.0000 (states in groups dominated by a single state)	.6990 (Speaker)	.6990	50

Note: BPI = Banzhaf Power Index; JPI = Johnston Power Index.

people. If you don't set well with any one of them, you can't get on. They come from big states and they have the votes to select whomever they want. They parcel out assignments and exercise veto power according to what they think is best for the Republican Party. They think alike and they are very senior, and they are not representative of what most people would like the Republican

Party to be. To them, the sine qua non is to "be regular" according to their views of regularity, and regularity is rewarded. (1964, 188)

Republican members who complained about the Republicans' committee assignment process apparently had empirical grounds for such complaints, and our findings confirm Masters' conclusions about the process.

When forty-four new Republican members were elected to the 87th Congress, Halleck further expanded the subcommittee to include a member to represent the first-term members. An additional member was added to the subcommittee for the 88th Congress, ensuring that second-term and first-term Republicans would be represented. Like the regional representatives, the first- and second-term class representatives were provided with only one vote apiece.

When Gerald R. Ford (R-MI) became minority leader at the start of the 89th Congress, he altered the composition of the RCC subcommittee, or the Executive Committee, as it became known officially, by changing the regional basis of small-state representation to a method based on the number of Republicans a state had in the House. His system included one representative for all one-member states, two for all two-member states, and three for all three-member states. The voting power, however, remained disproportionately in favor of the large states, because the representative of all one-member states cast only one vote, the two-member-state representative had two votes, and the member chosen to vote for the three-state grouping was allowed only three total votes. In addition, the Republican leader on the Executive Committee, not the members of the individual states, selected these representatives.[6]

In spite of these changes, some sentiment remained within the conference that the RCC did not adequately represent the smaller states. At the opening of the 92nd Congress (January 26, 1971), Alabama representative Bill Dickinson introduced a resolution for consideration of the full conference that would have dramatically altered the voting mechanism for committee assignments. The plan called for a single fifteen-member committee made up of five members of the leadership, eight members selected on a regional basis (adopting the same regional configuration as in the Republican Policy Committee), and two members representing the first- and second-term classes. The plan was soundly defeated, 82–27.[7]

In a letter to minority leader Gerald Ford, dated January 23, 1973, Vermont representative Richard W. Mallary openly expressed the hostility small-state members felt toward the process:

> I have deferred writing to you to comment on the distribution of committee assignments for a while so that I could give them fair consideration and not respond in undue haste. Even after a week, I must report that I am disappointed that neither of my requests were honored and I was not informed in time to modify my choices.
>
> As I told you in our discussion, I am a pragmatic politician and as such, I have analyzed the committee assignments and reached two conclusions: (1) it is a mistake to come from a small state—especially if it is in New England; (2) there is no evidence that any benefits accrue from quiet attention to business and reasonably close cooperation with leadership.[8]

Evidently, the changes made to try to make the Executive Committee more representative were not sufficient to eliminate member discontent. Representatives from the small states continued to resent the process throughout the Ford years, and this resentment continued to build during the period when John Rhodes was Republican leader.

In subsequent Congresses, the numbers of Republican members from the Northeast and Midwest began to decrease as Democrats replaced liberal Republicans in the Northeast, and Republican strength in the South and West grew (see figure 2.2). This created significant pressure within the Republican Conference to reform the RCC representative and voting structure to reflect changing regional interests within the conference.

Bowing to pressure from small-state Republicans in particular, the House Republicans adopted a voting scheme intended to provide representation in the RCC for all states with Republican members in the House—the Stangeland proposal. Near the end of the Rhodes era, representative Arlan Stangeland (R-MN) initiated a proposal, which was cosigned by eight other small-state Republicans, to increase representation of small-state members on the Executive Committee:

> [W]e believe that the structure of the Executive Committee of the Committee on Committees is unfair in that it discriminates against

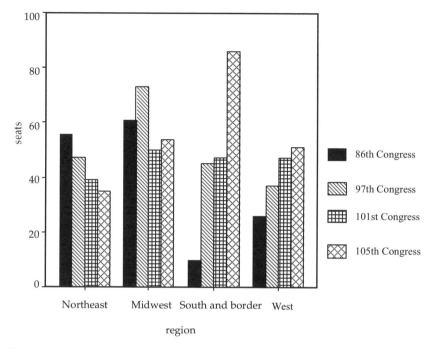

Figure 2.2. Seats in the Republican Conference, by region, selected Congresses.

smaller states. Eight states with a combined total of 83 Republican members are given 83 votes. The balance of the states representing 72 Republican Members receive 10 votes with the remaining 2 votes allocated one each to the 95th class and the 96th class.

We believe there is no reason why the Executive Committee should not and could not reflect 1 man 1 vote. It is totally unfair for 1 member to represent his full delegation of 17 Members with 17 votes, while another Member represents 15 states with a total of 15 Members with 1 vote. With the importance of the committee assignments, we believe that a Republican in a 1 Member state is just as important as every other Member of our Conference and his representation on the Executive Committee of the Committee on Committees should reflect that fact.

Therefore, we are proposing changes in the Rules to state in effect that each Member of the Conference will have equal representation on the Executive Committee of the Committee on Committees. It must be in the Rules of the Conference that the multi-state groups be allowed to caucus and select their representative on the Executive Committee of the Committee on Committees just as individual states do.[9]

The Stangeland proposal was adopted and used to determine Executive Committee voting power in the 97th Congress.

The RCC in the 97th Congress

Under the new plan, states that elected seven or more Republicans to the House elected one representative to the Executive Committee (see table 2.2) to represent that state. The remaining states were grouped by number of Republicans elected to the House (those states that elected five members, those that elected four members, and so forth). The members of each multistate grouping elected a representative to a seat on the Executive Committee. Each Executive Committee member exercised the number of votes equal to the total number of members in the group of states being represented. If the number of votes in a small-state grouping exceeded the number of votes exercised by the state with the largest number of Republican representatives, that grouping was then represented by two members, each exercising half the votes of the members represented. Members of the RCC could serve indefinitely. Finally, the restructured Executive Committee included the Republican leader and Republican whip, ex officio, *without* vote.

One of the interesting features of this arrangement is that it groups states that are very different. For instance, representatives in the two-member states represented constituents from the four corners of the country: Washington State, Arizona, Louisiana, and Maine, among others. Examination of the other RCC Executive Committee groupings reveals similarly interesting patterns. It is difficult to conceive of the complex task that a group's representative would face in trying to represent the shared interests of states that are so different from one another. Furthermore, it is difficult to imagine how a representative of one of these state groupings would settle conflicts that might emerge within that group over committee assignments.[10] By contrast, those states with seven or more Republican members had their own representative and thus may have been able to exercise their common interest more readily. The single state representative, giving his or her candidate an edge in committee voting, could mediate any competition that might exist between members from the same state for a committee assignment.

The RCC voting structure in the 97th Congress (see figure 2.3) was vastly different from that in the 86th Congress. States with between one and six members now registered significant voting power within the RCC, voting power that equaled or exceeded that of the larger states. Further, the largest state in terms of voting power, California (BPI = .11; JPI = .14), no longer maintained a near monopoly on power in the committee assignment process. The descriptive statistics in table 2.2 confirm a significant change in voting power. In the 86th Congress, the power discrepancy between the most powerful and least powerful states was between .24 and .43; in the 97th Congress, this discrepancy was cut in half to between .11 and .13.

Figure 2.4 indicates that, in one respect, changes in the voting weights in the RCC were consistent with shifting regional patterns of representation within the Republican Conference. As representation in the Republican Conference evidenced gains in the South and West, voting power within the committee reflected, to some extent, this shift in political power.

At the same time that regional voting power seemed to be equalizing, however, this seeming surge in power was diffused throughout the process. Excluding Virginia, which had a separate vote of its own, the twenty-seven southern votes in the RCC (due to the region because there were twenty-seven southern members) were distributed among five distinct state groupings and constituted the majority necessary to select a representative in only one of those, the four-member state group. Likewise, the fourteen votes due to the western states were distributed between two distinct groups (two-member and one-member states) and did not constitute a majority of votes in either grouping. Thus, while voting power in the RCC was somewhat equalized, that power was sufficiently divided in a manner that would theoretically allow the larger states to dominate voting in the RCC.

Predictably, small-state Republicans continued to complain about their relative lack of power within the RCC. Substantial gains in Republican representation in the House following the 1978 and 1980 elections

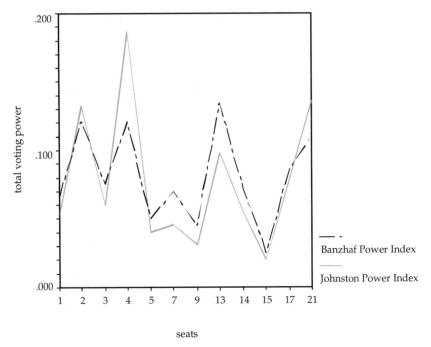

Figure 2.3. The structure of voting power in the Republican Committee on Committees, by number of seats, 97th Congress. Seats are actual numbers of seats held by state delegations with Republican representation in the 97th Congress. Numbers shown on the x-axis reflect actual Republican delegation sizes.

did not result in proportional gains in the ratios of representation on the most important committees. Anger with the committee ratios determined for the 97th Congress so enraged House Republicans that fourteen members of the conference sued the Democratic leadership in federal district court, charging that the ratios "diluted the power and influence of Republican members and thus the political rights of voters in Republican districts as well."[11] Although the courts refused to intercede, the legal challenge demonstrates the level of dissatisfaction with committee assignments that existed within the Republican membership.

In addition, the system initiated in the 97th Congress following the adoption of the Stangeland amendment allowed for the possibility that the small states could, if they were to act collectively, manage to form a

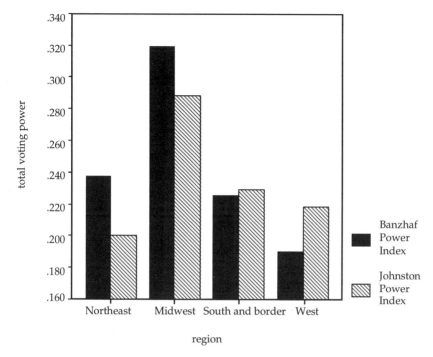

Figure 2.4. The structure of voting power in the Republican Committee on Committees, by region, 97th Congress.

coalition that could defeat the large states. As we show in chapter 7, this in fact occurred in the 100th Congress; by combining their forces with Texas—a large state with many of the western and southern tendencies common in the smaller states—the smaller states were able to defeat a number of large-state candidates in Executive Committee voting.[12] This alliance, which caused many in the Republican Conference to view the committee assignment system as in need of repair, led to reforms that were enacted before committees were organized for the 101st Congress.

The RCC in the 101st Congress

Widespread dissatisfaction with the committee assignment process continued to be a problem. After the small-state victories at the start of the 100th Congress, dissatisfaction with the process spread to include not only the small-state members, but many large-state members as well. In the 100th Congress, Republican Leader Michel appointed a Task Force on Conference Rules and Procedures, with a Subcommittee on Committee Assignments specifically charged with the responsibility of reforming the assignment process.

Proposing a system that would provide representation from more focused regional groupings, Republican whip Trent Lott (MS) highlighted the problems inherent in the existing system: "The advantage of this system would be that the members within small subregions would be compatible. The current multi-state group system—which might include one representative from Washington and another from Maine in a group—would not happen. This would help alleviate members from both ends of the political spectrum with conflicting interests ending up in the same group. There would not be the big state/little state problem."[13]

Lott and others also urged an expanded role for the Republican leadership in the committee assignment process. One member expressed support for returning the sole power of making committee assignments to the Republican leader.[14] However, most Republicans assumed a position similar to that of Lott, who argued, "The Leader [should] have more input without having to look out for his/her own state's interests. In addition, the Leader could have, perhaps, as many as six votes out of 15 directly responsible to him, but would still have a buffer in not having absolute control."[15]

Subcommittee chair Robert J. Lagomarsino (R-CA) transmitted the results of the subcommittee's work to Leader Michel in September 1987. The subcommittee recommended significant reforms in the committee assignment process, including making the leader a voting member of the Executive Committee, electing regional representatives based on compact state groupings, and providing representation for first-term members and women. Regional representatives would be elected by a caucus of their members and be entitled to a number of votes in the RCC equal to the number of members in their caucus. The leader would control a number of votes equal to the number of votes due to the smallest regional grouping; first-term and women's representatives would be elected by their caucuses but would be afforded a single vote in the RCC.

In the wake of the Lagomarsino Report, only minor reforms were enacted in the Republicans' committee assignment process. Most important, the Republican leader was given twelve votes, and the Republican whip, six votes in the RCC. In addition, the Executive Committee became the sole committee on committees; the larger committee on committees, with representation from every state with a Republican member and that simply served to ratify Executive Committee decisions, was eliminated. Finally, the Republican leader was given the power to appoint all Republican members to the Rules Committee, subject to conference approval.

Analysis of the reformed voting structure in the RCC indicates that the intentions of the reformers were not achieved. Although the Republican leader gained twelve votes, his voting power was fairly low (BPI = .06, JPI = .03) compared with the larger states, such as California (BPI = .11, JPI = .14).[16] The collective voting power of the leader and whip was significant (BPI = .09, JPI = .06), but it was not the amount of power that could control the committee assignment process and command party unity on its own.

Furthermore, a qualitative split in the Republican leadership did not guarantee that the leader and whip would vote together when committee assignments were at stake. Republican leader Robert Michel was widely considered more moderate and accommodating within the Republican Conference and toward Democrats. In the RCC Michel sought to soothe regional and ideological divisions and promote the interests of individual members, as he explained in an interview, referring to the more conservative southern members of the RCC: "Some of those guys [in the RCC] just had a bias against the Northeast. . . . You know, they'd say, 'Oh, he's too damn liberal,' and I'd always have to keep telling these guys that, listen guys, the numbers, the total numbers are important, and they've got to do it for their district, you know."[17] Indeed, Michel felt his goal was to keep peace in the family: "Well, of course, as leader and chairman of the committee, my whole objective was to make everybody happy, pleased with the committee assignment, pleased with the process, at least, that they got a fair shake, that there was no lingering animosities if the debate got heated inside."[18]

The Republican whip Newt Gingrich (GA), on the other hand, was more ideologically driven, sought to increase party unity by rewarding

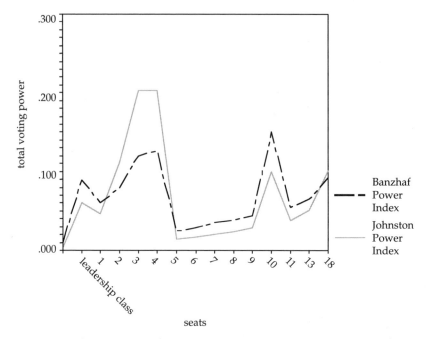

Figure 2.5. The structure of voting power in the Republican Committee on Committees, by number of seats, 101st Congress. Class = first- and second-term class representatives. Leadership = Republican leader and whip. Seats are actual numbers of seats held by state delegations with Republican representation in the 101st Congress. Numbers shown on the x-axis reflect actual Republican delegation sizes.

and punishing Republican members, and took a more confrontational approach to the Democratic majority.[19] Thus, personal, ideological, political, even regional concerns might prevent these two actors from working together in the committee assignment process.

Regional balance in the RCC reveals that the distribution of voting power closely mirrors the increasing influence of the southern and western wings of the Republican Conference, although the Midwest remained the single most powerful region in the RCC. This is somewhat misleading, however, since the state groupings continued to diffuse the power of all except the large states across several groups; the small states continued to wield little influence in the process due to this arrangement.

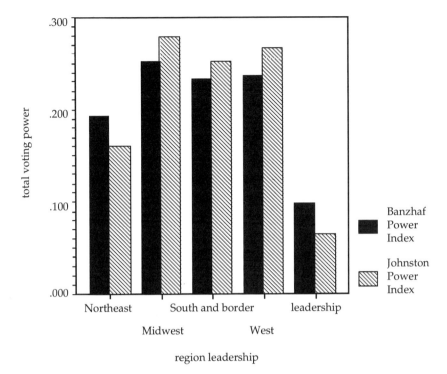

Figure 2.6. The structure of voting power in the Republican Committee on Committees, regional and leadership representation, 101st Congress. Leadership = Republican leader and whip. Class representatives omitted.

The RCC in the 105th Congress

In the wake of the Republican Revolution in the 104th Congress the RCC was yet again restructured to provide more formal power to the Republican leadership in the committee assignment process and was renamed the Steering Committee. Consistent with the recommendations of the Lagomarsino Report, state groupings were given geographic coherence by bringing together states with similar regional interests. The members of the regional groupings would elect representatives of these groupings. Second, the House Republicans significantly limited their use of weighted voting.

Finally, and ultimately most important, the Republican Party leadership was given significant power in the Steering Committee. The Speaker was

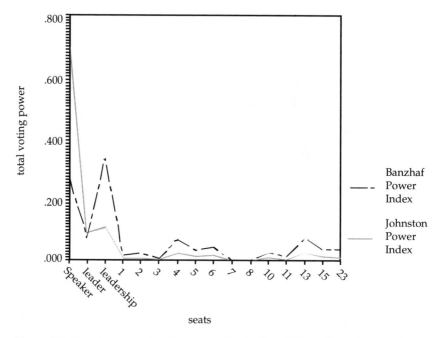

Figure 2.7. The structure of voting power in the Republican Committee on Committees, by number of seats, 105th Congress. Other leadership includes whip and the chairs of the Republican Conference, National Republican Congressional Committee, Appropriations, Budget, Rules, and Ways and Means. Seats are actual numbers of seats held by state delegations with Republican representation in the 105th Congress. Numbers shown on the x-axis reflect actual Republican delegation sizes. Class representatives omitted.

granted five votes, and the majority leader, two votes; all other members were granted a single vote. Further, the ranks of the leadership were expanded to include the whip, conference chair, NRCC chair, and the chairs of the "control committees" in the House (Appropriations, Budget, Rules, and Ways and Means). Combined, the leadership now controls fourteen of the twenty-five votes in the RCC; if they vote together, the leadership can dominate the committee assignment process. Figure 2.7 illustrates the dramatic result of these reforms: The Speaker has become the single most dominant actor in the committee assignment process (BPI = .27, JPI = .70); all things being equal, it is difficult for a successful coalition to exclude the Speaker.

It is interesting to note that the voting power of the Speaker in the 105th Congress exceeds the voting power of New York in the 86th Congress (see table 2.2). The descriptive statistics in table 2.2 confirm a significant change in voting power. In the 86th Congress, the power discrepancy between the most powerful and least powerful states was between .24 and .43; in the 97th Congress, this discrepancy was cut in half to between .11 and .13.

Almost without regard to the number of seats a state controls, it has very little individual power within the Steering Committee. Having said that, we should note that voting power varies significantly between states, and some states under this structure have no voting power. For instance, New York, in the Atlantic Coast group, has in its membership the power to decide the election of their representative to the Steering Committee. New Jersey has zero voting power within this group. In a sense, New York can behave as a dictator within this voting group. Likewise, Florida and Texas can control the selection of their representative, robbing other group members of any voting power.

In this system, all regions lose power as the leadership gains power (see figure 2.8). At the same time, the southern and border states emerge as the most powerful region in the committee, followed by the West, Midwest, and Northeast. In this respect, the story of the RCC comes full circle. During the 86th Congress, the primary regional cleavage was between the Northeast and Midwest versus the South and West; under this new voting structure—to the degree that we can talk about regional power—the South and West have more relative power than the Northeast and Midwest. This is consistent with shifting electoral patterns in the country: Over the last two decades, the Republican Party's influence in the Northeast and Midwest has waned while its fortunes in the South and West have strengthened substantially.

THE DEMOCRATIC COMMITTEE ASSIGNMENT PROCESS

The historical development of the contemporary Democratic committee assignment process is well documented in the political science literature.[20] However, the voting structure of the reformed Democratic committee assignment process—not to mention a comparison of the assignment

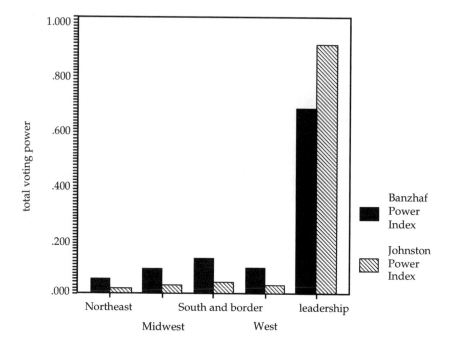

Figure 2.8. The structure of voting power in the Republican Committee on Committees, regional and leadership representation, 105th Congress. Leadership includes Speaker, leader, whip, and the chairs of the Republican Conference, National Republican Congressional Committee, Appropriations, Budget, Rules, and Ways and Means. Class representatives omitted.

process between the two parties—has never been undertaken. Comparison with the Republicans' committee assignment process requires understanding of the major institutional arrangements that the Democrats have used to make committee assignments and, to the degree possible, comparison of the underlying voting structure used by the Democrats to that of the Republicans. One major difference between the parties' committee assignment processes makes extensive comparison difficult: Democrats have never used weighted voting to distribute power in the process.

The Ways and Means Committee

Democratic committee assignments were made by the Democratic members of the Ways and Means Committee, acting as the committee on committees, between the 62nd Congress (1911–1912) and the 94th Congress (1975–1976). Members of the Ways and Means Committee were elected by a vote of the Democratic Caucus to be both the Democratic committee on committees and the committee responsible for tax, entitlement, and trade policy. Each member of the committee assumed responsibility for a relatively coherent geographic zone comprising roughly equal numbers of Democratic members. Voting within Ways and Means followed a simple one-person–one-vote majority rule, thus each voter was functionally equal. In reality, however, there were likely to be significant power discrepancies within the committee:

> Each member does not carry equal weight on the committee. The status and rank of each Democratic member of Ways and Means are carried over to the Committee-on-Committees. The ranking Democrat serves as chairman and the status of the other ranking members is unquestionably enhanced by the fact that they also serve as Ways and Means subcommittee chairmen when the Democrats are in the majority. These are the senior members in an institution that respects seniority. (Masters 1961, 348)

The Democratic Steering and Policy Committee

Under the control of its powerful chair, Wilbur D. Mills (D-AR) from 1957 to 1975, the secretive Ways and Means committee assignment process became a source of suspicion for rank-and-file Democrats. The caucus reforms that preceded the 94th Congress stipulated that the Democratic Steering and Policy Committee (DSPC) assume the responsibility for committee assignments. Consistent with the general spirit of other congressional reforms of the time, members sought to democratize the committee assignment process by creating a representative system that would reflect the interests of the Democratic Caucus.[21] Many junior members of the Democratic Caucus—several of whom sought access to seats on more influential committees—likely believed that creating a more representative process would enhance their chances of obtaining sought-after committee assignments.

Also consistent with other caucus reforms, Democrats gave an expanded role to the party leadership in constituting the DSPC. The DSPC as originally constituted was composed of three sets of members.[22] The first set comprised the Democratic leadership: the Speaker—who served as the DSPC chair—the Democratic leader, the Democratic whip, and the caucus chair. Second, eight members were appointed to the committee by the Speaker. Third, the members of the Democratic Caucus, through zone elections, chose twelve regional members (see table 2.3).

Before convening the DSPC to make committee assignments for the next Congress, the twelve regional members were chosen by members of their regional caucus. Regional zones were determined based on two criteria. First, states were included in a zone to emphasize geographic compactness, that is, grouping together states with common interests. Second, the number of states in a zone was determined so that the number of Democratic members within each zone was roughly equal. Caucus rules limited zone representatives to two consecutive terms on the DSPC.

Because zone representatives in the DSPC were elected in zone elections, it is possible to measure voting power by the number of seats and by regional and leadership power, comparable to the analysis presented for the RCC. Consider figure 2.9, which reflects the size of Democratic Caucus delegations and their resulting voting power in the DSPC. For the most part, the regional groupings seem to ensure a linear increase in voting power based on how many seats a state sends to the House. Several caveats are necessary here. First, consider the scale on the y-axis; the overall BPI and JPI values are very small, peaking at about .05, and indicating that the additional voting power of adding members is negligible. Second, a number of states have zero voting power because of the nature of the zone groupings. For instance, in Region III, Michigan controls enough votes (twelve of twenty) to determine the outcome of regional zone elections; thus regional partners have no voting power (see table 2.3). This is also true in Regions X and XII.

Figure 2.10 illustrates the distribution of voting power within the DSPC by region, including the voting power of the leadership. Although the

TABLE 2.3
Democratic Committee on Committees representative structure
(selected Congresses)

Ways and Means Committee representative structure, 86th Congress

	States represented	Number of members represented	Votes in Ways and Means
Arkansas	Ark. (6), Del. (1), Kans. (3), Okla. (5)	15	1
Rhode Island	R.I. (2), Conn. (6), Maine (2), Mass. (8), Vt. (1)	19	1
California	Calif. (16), Alaska (1), Ariz. (1), Nev. (1), Utah (1)	20	1
Illinois	Ill. (14), Wisc. (5)	19	1
Louisiana	La. (8), Ala. (9), Miss. (6)	23	1
New York	N.Y. (19)	19	1
Virginia	Va. (8), S.C. (6)	14	1
Missouri	Mo. (10), Iowa (4), Minn. (4)	18	1
Florida	Fla. (7), Ga. (10)	17	1
Texas	Tex. (21), N.Mex. (2)	23	1
Tennessee	Tenn. (7), N.C. (11)	18	1
Michigan	Mich. (7), Ind. (8), Ohio (9)	24	1
Montana	Mont. (2), Colo. (3), Idaho (1), Neb. (2), N.Dak. (1), Ore. (3), S.Dak. (1), Wash. (1)	14	1
Pennsylvania	Pa. (16), N.J. (5)	21	1
Kentucky	Ky. (7), Md. (7), W.Va. (5)	19	1
Total		283	15

Democratic Steering and Policy Committee structure, 97th Congress

	States represented	Number of members represented	Votes in DSPC
Speaker	n/a	n/a	1
Democratic leader	n/a	n/a	1
Whip	n/a	n/a	1
Caucus chair	n/a	n/a	1
Speaker-appointed members (8)	n/a	n/a	8
Region I	Calif. (22)	22	1
Region II	Ariz. (2), Colo. (3), Hawaii (2), Mont. (1), Nev. (1), Ore. (3), Wash. (5)	17	1
Region III	Mich. (12), Minn. (3), Wisc. (5)	20	1
Region IV	Ill. (10), Ind. (6), Ky. (4),	20	1

TABLE 2.3 (*continued*)
Democratic Committee on Committees representative structure
(selected Congresses)

Ways and Means Committee representative structure, 86th Congress (continued)

	States represented	Number of members represented	Votes in Ways and Means
Region V	Ark. (2), Iowa (3), Kans. (1), Mo. (6), N.Dak. (1), Okla. (5), S.Dak. (1)	19	1
Region VI	Tex. (19)	19	1
Region VII	Ala. (4), Fla. (11), La. (6), Miss. (3)	24	1
Region VIII	Ga. (9), N.C. (7), S.C. (2), Tenn. (5)	23	1
Region IX	Md. (7), N.J. (8), Va. (1), W.Va. (2)	18	1
Region X	Ohio (11), Pa. (13)	23	1
Region XI	N.Y. (22)	22	1
Region XII	Conn. (4), Mass. (10), N.H. (1), R.I. (1)	16	1
Total		243	24

Democratic Steering Committee structure, 107th Congress

	States represented	Number of members represented	Votes in DSC
DSC chair	n/a	n/a	1
DSC co-chair	n/a	n/a	1
DSC vice-chair	n/a	n/a	1
Vice-chair, deputy whip	n/a	n/a	1
Whip	n/a	n/a	1
Caucus chair	n/a	n/a	1
Caucus vice-chair	n/a	n/a	1
Assistant to the leader	n/a	n/a	1
DCCC chair	n/a	n/a	1
Deputy whips (3)	n/a	n/a	3
Leader-appointed members (16)	n/a	n/a	16
Region I	Southern Calif. (17), Nev. (1) Utah (1), N.Mex. (1), Colo. (1)	21	1
Region II	Northern Calif. (15), Hawaii (2), American Samoa (1), Guam (1)	19	1
Region III	Mich. (9), Minn. (5), Wisc. (5)	19	1
Region IV	Ill. (10), Ind. (4), Ky. (1)	15	1

TABLE 2.3 (*continued*)
Democratic Committee on Committees representative structure
(selected Congresses)

Democratic Steering Committee structure, 107th Congress (*continued*)

	States represented	Number of members represented	Votes in Ways and Means
Region V	Ark. (3), Iowa (1), Mo. (4), Kans. (1), N.Dak. (1), Ore. (4), Wash. (6), Okla. (1)	21	1
Region VI	Tex. (17)	17	1
Region VII	La. (2), Miss. (3), Tenn. (4), Ala. (2)	11	1
Region VIII	Ga. (3), N.C. (5), S.C. (2), Fla. (8)	18	1
Region IX	Md. (4), N.J. (7), W.Va. (2), Va. (3)	16	1
Region X	Ohio (8), Pa. (10)	18	1
Region XI	N.Y. (19)	19	1
Region XII	Conn. (3), D.C. (1), Mass. (10), P.R. (1), R.I. (2), V.I. (1)	18	1
Appropriations ranking member	n/a	n/a	1
Budget ranking member	n/a	n/a	1
Energy and Commerce ranking member	n/a	n/a	1
Rules ranking member	n/a	n/a	1
Ways and Means ranking member	n/a	n/a	1
Organization Study and Review chair	n/a	n/a	1
Total		212	46

regions have formal equality with the leadership (one person–one vote), power is distributed among the regions that slightly favor the South and Northeast over the Midwest and West. When compared to the regional distribution of seats in the Democratic Caucus (see figure 2.11), the distribution of voting power largely mirrors the distribution of seats, though the Midwest seems to be at something of a disadvantage.

Compared with the Republican leadership, the Democrats give very little voting power directly to the Speaker or minority leader when they are in the minority (BPI = .04 and JPI = .04 compared to BPI = .27 and JPI

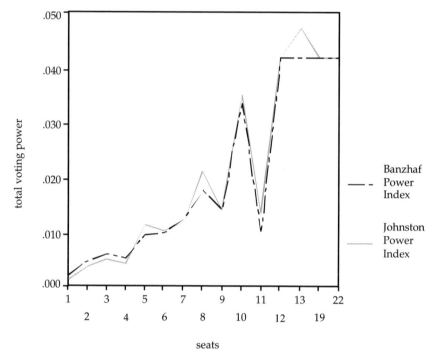

Figure 2.9. Voting power in Democratic Steering and Policy Committee zone elections, by number of seats, 97th Congress. Seats are actual numbers of seats held by state delegations with Republican representation in the 97th Congress. Numbers shown on the x-axis reflect actual Republican delegation sizes. Leadership omitted. Because Republicans used weighted voting, leadership matters independently. Democratic committee-on-committees rules specifying one vote per member made regional membership important.

= .70 for Republican Speakers since the 104th Congress). As a result, the Democratic Speaker is not a formally dominant actor in the assignment process. However, the Speaker is given eight appointed positions on the DSPC, and when combined with the other formal leaders included on the committee (leader, whip, and caucus chair), the leadership vote makes up 50 percent of the votes in the committee assignment process.

Since many of these actors, in one way or another, are in place because of their dedication to supporting the partisan legislative agenda and goals, it is likely that they will often vote together. When combined, the leadership retains a tremendous amount of power over the assignment

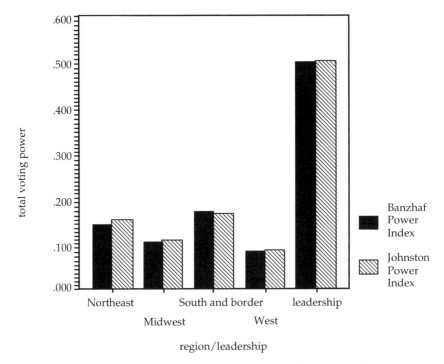

Figure 2.10. The structure of voting power in the Democratic Steering and Policy Committee, regional and leadership representation, 97th Congress. Leadership includes Speaker, leader, whip, caucus chair, and eight Speaker-appointed members.

process. If considered as a monolithic voting bloc—that is, as a single voter with twelve votes against twelve voters with one vote each—the leadership attains the power of a dictator within the assignment process (BPI = 1.0, JPI = 1.0).[23] Even if we consider only the top four leaders as a unified voting bloc, significant power still resides in the leadership (BPI = .20, JPI = .68), about comparable to the Republican Speaker since the 105th Congress.

The Democratic Steering Committee

Two important changes in the structure of the DSPC have occurred since the separation of function from the Ways and Means Committee. First, there has been a steady increase in the size of the body. When it

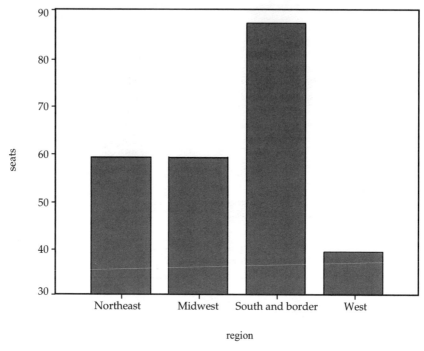

Figure 2.11. Democratic seats in the House, by region, 97th Congress.

was originally tasked with the assignment responsibility, there were twenty-four members. Sinclair details the growth of the DSPC:

> Late in 1980 the secretary of the caucus and the chairs of the four most important committees (Appropriations, Budget, Rules and Ways and Means) joined the committee as ex officio members. The chair of the DCCC [Democratic Congressional Campaign Committee] and the chief deputy whip were added, first as nonvoting members, later as full members. When the chief deputy whip position was split into three positions in 1991 and then a fourth chief deputy whip was added in 1992, all were made ex officio members of the Steering and Policy Committee. In the 102nd Congress, the Speaker was temporarily granted a ninth appointment because Vic Fazio, as caucus vice chair and chair of the DCCC, held two of the

positions with ex officio membership. To allow for appointment of
two freshmen from the large 103rd Congress class, the rule was rewritten
to give the Speaker the power to appoint as many as ten members. In
the 103rd Congress (1993–1994), the committee had thirty-five
members: thirteen ex officio (because Fazio still held two slots) twelve
regionally elected, and ten appointed by the Speaker. (1995, 89)

The second major alteration occurred when the Democrats lost the
House majority in 1994. Minority leader Richard Gephardt (D-MO) initiated a change that broke the DSPC into two parts—a Steering Committee to assign members to standing committees and to select ranking
members (or chairs if the Democrats were in the majority) and a Policy
Committee to help formulate and publicize party policy (Salant 1994).[24]
The creation of separate committees had the benefit of including more
Democrats in responsible, party leadership positions. In the wake of the
tremendous losses in the number and quality of committee assignments
suffered by Democratic members, Gephardt sought to create additional
positions of importance for many of his members.

The newly constituted Democratic Steering Committee (DSC) for the
104th Congress was expanded to thirty-nine members. The DSC has
continued to expand; by the 107th Congress, its size had grown to forty-
six. Of the forty-six, thirteen were members of the elected leadership
(including a member who was elected to be co-chair of the DSC and two
who were elected to be vice chairs); twelve were elected by regions to
support candidates from those regions; five ex officio members served
as ranking members of the five most important committees; and sixteen
members were appointed by the Democratic leader (Schneider 2002; See
table 2.3). In actual operation, the DSC now acts upon a slate of candidates put together by the minority leader (and based on discussions
with leadership appointees representing the various groups represented
in the Democratic Caucus).[25] One senior Democratic member who had
served on the DSPC under Speakers Thomas P. (Tip) O'Neill, Jr, and Jim
Wright, referred to the DSC under the leadership of Richard Gephardt
as a "rubber stamp" of candidates proposed by the leadership.[26] More
recently, Nancy Pelosi (D-CA) has moved to reunite the policy and

committee assignment functions in a newly constituted Steering and Policy Committee.

• • •

Both parties have frequently altered the size, structure, and composition of their committees responsible for making committee assignments. Committees on committees need to be able to accommodate the multiple goals of members as well as the multiple and sometimes conflicting goals of party leaders. Marginal changes in the composition of the committee assignment panels were common to adjust to incremental changes in party composition and member goals. In addition to these marginal changes, each party has had to alter the process dramatically in response to nonincremental changes that followed significant elections. Suspicion of the Ways and Means process and demands for reform conspired with the rapid decline of Ways and Means chair Wilbur Mills to lead the Democrats to take the assignment task away from the Ways and Means Committee and to create a separate Steering and Policy Committee that was both more representative and more subject to leadership control. The 1980 Reagan election represented the arrival of the new Republican conservatives from the South and West, who received greater representation through the Stangeland proposal in committee assignments, which ensured that representation on the RCC was no longer dominated by the large northeastern and midwestern states.

Finally, the Republican victory in 1994 after forty years in the congressional minority led to large-scale changes on both sides of the aisle. The Republicans rewarded their new Speaker with considerable power on the committee on committees and effectively ended a system of weighted voting that favored larger states. The Democrats adapted to their newfound minority status by splitting the policy and committee assignment roles and by increasing the size of the committee assignment panel to the point where it is now nearly double the size of the original DSPC.

It is not coincidental that the change in partisan control of the House after the 1994 election resulted in a Republican process that is meant to enhance the power of leadership in securing its policy agenda; in many ways, the Republican process was modeled after the process Democrats used when in the majority. The Democratic process has been altered to look more like the Republican process when the Republicans were in the minority. A large group (the committee on committees) is responsible for ratifying the choices made by a smaller group of leaders. This process values the perception of equity and representation over party unity and achieving policy goals. As the minority party, the Democrats must now be concerned with keeping all the various factions satisfied rather than enforcing unity to promote a positive policy agenda.

Masters' frequently cited depiction (1961) of the committee assignment processes in the House is a static one, as are the descriptions that are found elsewhere (for instance, Shepsle 1978). In reality, both parties have altered their committee assignment processes in response to changing political circumstances that are prompted by changes inside and outside the institution. That the fundamental structure of the assignment process is, itself, a source of conflict is an important part of the assignment puzzle that has not been fully addressed in the literature or incorporated into existing theories of congressional organization. In the next chapter, we begin the process of empirically examining the motivations behind the decisions of individual members to request committee assignments.

CHAPTER THREE

COMMITTEE REQUEST MOTIVATIONS

My request for Appropriations is derived from my twofold desire to (1) utilize what I believe are my legislative skills on negotiating, compromising, and coalition building to advance a prudent, fiscally responsible approach to our federal budget process, and (2) to serve the greatest number of my constituents as possible.

HAROLD ROGERS (R-KY)

The CAP framework rests on the premise that members of Congress are motivated by several impulses to pursue particular committee assignments. We suggest that members of Congress have multiple goals: They seek to address constituency concerns to ensure reelection; they seek to promote good public policy; and they seek institutional influence. As we argue in chapter 1, members pursue these goals within the context of perceived constraints and the members' personal predispositions. In this chapter, we focus on members' expressed motivations for pursuing committee assignments through a systematic analysis of the letters they write to the party leadership in search of a committee assignment. As a means of measuring motivation, we capitalize on the committee request letters submitted by individual members to the party committees on committees. (See appendix 2 for a discussion of our coding scheme and the advantages and potential hazards of this approach.)

Our CAP framework is based on a multiple-motivations approach, which suggests that members of Congress will cite multiple motivations for pursuing committee assignments. Sometimes these motivations will be consistent with one another; sometimes they will be contradictory. The degree of consistency will be driven, as the CAP framework suggests, by perceived constraints and representatives' predispositions (neither of which we can directly measure). Members from districts marked by a high level of interest homogeneity—as in many districts with large agricultural or military interests—may allow their reelection interests to tip the balance among competing motivations. Members who come from districts that are more heterogeneous may satisfy conflicting motivations in favor of policy or influence concerns. As our framework suggests, however, the balance among motivations will also be influenced by members' personal predispositions: beliefs about the appropriate role of a representative and of government and their personal levels of ambition. The complexity of motivations leads us to believe that concerns about reelection will not dominate members' motivations for pursuing committee assignments except when members feel especially constrained; the lack of an obsession with reelection should be especially true of incumbents who have been successfully reelected. In this and the next chapter, we examine to what degree committee request data supports this expectation and provide a broader evaluation of analysts' assumptions that members of Congress are motivated by multiple goals.

MOTIVATIONS AND GOALS

The multiple goals approach is, of course, not unique to us. It is informed by a long tradition within congressional studies research that is most prominent in the work of Fenno (1973), Kingdon (1973), Dodd (1977), and Deering and Smith (1997), and has figured significantly in the work of others. It does, however, contrast with the narrow focus on the reelection motivation of several existing theories of congressional organization. Distributive theory, for instance, holds that members of Congress seek assignment to particular committees because the committee will provide the members with an opportunity to service their constituency by delivering particularized benefits to their district, benefits that will promote the member's reelection. In examining members' motivations, distributive theory leads one to expect that reelection will dominate members' discussions of their reasons for seeking assignment to a committee. Informational theory likewise emphasizes committee preferences that are exogenously induced (Rohde 1995; also see chapter 1).

Over the last four decades, congressional studies have increasingly focused on the individual goals and motivations of members of Congress as a means for understanding congressional organization. Despite the focus on individual behavior, the distinction between motivations and goals is unclear, with the two terms often used interchangeably (Eulau 1984). Goals are strategic; they refer to the end to which political actors aspire. A member of Congress might have as a goal ascending to a party leadership position or committee chair, or influencing the defense policy of the nation. Motivations are predispositions that shape the means by which members seek to achieve their goals.

David Mayhew emphasized the reelection goal over all other goals in his study of congressional organization. He posits an abstract member of Congress who is a "single minded seeker of reelection" (1974, 5), arguing that any other goals that a member of Congress might have are dependent upon achieving reelection. Mayhew contends that congressional organization revolves around this goal to such a degree that "if a group of planners sat down and tried to design a pair of American national assemblies with the goal of serving members' electoral interests year in and year out, they would be hard pressed to improve on what exists" (1974, 81–82). Mayhew argues that the committee structure of Congress is aimed at creating committees that can promote the reelection goal by providing opportunities to deliver particularized benefits, pork barrel projects, to their districts and providing a platform for taking positions by promoting policies of interest to their narrow constituencies.

Mayhew's formulation is the behavioral foundation of distributive theory and has been subject to intense criticism on at least two grounds. Critics have argued that reelection cannot be accurately referred to as a "goal" of members of Congress. Contrary to the conceptualization of goals outlined above, Mayhew's reelection goal cannot be considered an ultimate end to which a member aspires. Considered in this light, Mayhew's formulation becomes tautological: Members of Congress run for election in order to run for reelection. Heinz Eulau puts it another way:

> Of course, reelection is not just a necessary condition, it is *the* necessary condition for anything else, including achieving influence [in] the Legislature, or making policy there, or representing, in one way or another, clientele or constituency interests. To elevate reelection into a "goal" constitutes a truism, as if one were to say that eating or sleeping are "goals." Because legislators recite reelection as a "goal" over and over again, whether their reelection is really in jeopardy or not, even sophisticated political scientists seem to believe that reelection can serve as an independent variable in a model of committee assignments. (1984, 609; emphasis added)

Considered this way, it is perhaps more accurate to refer to reelection as a *motivation* rather than a goal; it is a necessary means for achieving the goals of congressional members.

Critics of Mayhew have also focused on the implications of the reelection motivation for the structure of Congress. If members of Congress were solely interested in reelection, it would not be in their interest to devote significant amounts of their scarce resources—their time, their staff—to anything but the promotion of their own reelection. Why would a member of Congress seek membership on any committee other than those committees that are able to address the particular interests of their constituents (Hall 1996)? Dodd makes this point eloquently:

> Were members solely preoccupied with reelection, we would expect them to spend little time in Washington and devote their personal efforts to constituents speeches and district casework . . . *Members of Congress would give little attention to committee work, and then only to committees that clearly served reelection interests.* The primary activity of Congress people in Congress, rather, would be extended, televised floor debates and symbolic roll call votes, all for show. (1979, 271–72; emphasis added)

We would expect members to pursue assignment to committees like Agriculture, which services the interests of well-defined constituencies, and avoid membership on committees such as Budget, Ways and Means, or Rules, which serve the collective interests of the nation or the congressional institution.

In his classic study *Congressmen in Committees*, Richard Fenno (1973) characterizes members of Congress as being motivated by multiple goals: Reelection, making good public policy, and developing influence within the House. According to Fenno, members of Congress "probably hold all three goals. . . . But each congressman has his own mix of priorities and intensities—a mix which may, of course, change over time" (1). Congressional committees, he contends, vary in their utility to serve each of these goals, and he argues that members with dominant goals will gravitate toward committees that best allow them to address their goals. A long-time member of Congress supported this view: "I think different members have different motivations. Some members have a particular policy interest and want to go on [a committee] because of that policy interest; some members right from the beginning look at the select committees like Appropriations, Ways and Means, and Commerce, as they want to be on one of the committees that have power."[1]

In examining how members' goals influenced their choice of committees, Fenno interviewed members of Congress and asked them, "Why did you want to get on the _____ committee in the first place?" Fenno found a relationship between members' goals and their tendency to gravitate toward specific committees. For instance, the Interior and Post Office committees provide opportunities to service the interests of narrow reelection constituencies; the Education and Labor and Foreign Affairs committees enable members to pursue an interest in making public policy; the Appropriations and Ways and Means committees enable members to pursue institutional influence (Fenno 1973, 2–14).

Eulau (1984) criticizes Fenno for not fully appreciating that the "goals" that he was measuring in his research were highly sensitive to the committee slots available to members, and that members might adjust their goals according to the available committee slots. In other words, Fenno's goals are, in fact, motivations. Fenno's typology of multiple goals, renamed multiple motivations by subsequent researchers, is preferred by many congressional scholars who believe that it is a more realistic characterization of members of Congress and holds more promise for understanding the individual behavior of members and the subsequent dynamics of committee politics. Accordingly, a number of scholars have sought to test Fenno's typology using interview methodology (Bullock 1972, 1973, 1976; Smith and Deering 1984; Deering and Smith 1997).

Charles S. Bullock III (1976) points out that Fenno's question assumes that the member *wanted* to serve on a particular committee, which is not necessarily the case; members often wind up on committees that they did not request. In Bullock's interviews with members, he instead asked, "What committees did you want to serve on? Why?" Subsequent analysts adopted this interview protocol as superior to Fenno's (Smith and Deering 1984; Deering and Smith 1997). Table 3.1 lists the findings of the two definitive studies on individual motivations and committee requests, Bullock (1976) and Deering and Smith (1997). For the most part, these two studies reach similar conclusions about the motivations leading members to request certain committees. Two committees that did not exist when Bullock conducted his research, Budget and Small Business, are added to Deering and Smith's list as influence and constituency committees, respectively; Government Operations and Rules move from undesired to policy and influence committees, respectively.[2] These findings have become the basis of the most widely accepted typology of congressional committees (Deering and Smith 1997).

The most significant element of these studies is that the authors acknowledge that members are subject to multiple motivations. Contrary to what one might expect based on Mayhew's assumption that members are motivated primarily by reelection, these studies suggest that members' committee requests are often motivated by the desire to make policy and their quest for influence in addition to their concerns about reelection or constituency concerns. In fact, Bullock, examining first-term members who as a group might be considered more electorally vulnerable on average, finds that "although reelection was highly ranked, it was not the most common motivation expressed by freshman in explaining their committee preferences" (1976, 205).

What these studies do not explicitly allow for is the possibility that individual requests for committees may be the result of mixed motivations, and that, in turn, committees can be classified by the mixture of motivations that led members to seek membership on the committee. Consider table 3.2. Although many of the committees in Deering and

TABLE 3.1
Motivation types and committee preferences (two previous studies)

Motivation type	Committee requested	
	Bullock (1976)	*Deering and Smith (1997)*
Constituency/reelection	Agriculture	Agriculture
	Armed Services	Armed Services
	Interior	Interior
	Merchant Marine	Merchant Marine
	Public Works	Public Works
	Veterans' Affairs	Science
		Small Business
		Veterans' Affairs
Policy	Banking	Banking
	Education and Labor	Education and Labor
	Energy and Commerce	Energy and Commerce
	Foreign Affairs	Foreign Affairs
	Judiciary	Government Operations
		Judiciary
Influence/prestige	Appropriations	Appropriations
	Ways and Means	Budget
		Rules
		Ways and Means
Undesired	District of Columbia	District of Columbia
	Government Operations	House Administration
	House Administration	Post Office
	Internal Security	Ethics
	Post Office	
	Rules	
	Science	

Smith's study indicate that members who requested the committee were compelled by similar motivations, in the case of several of these committees, two or more motivations seemed to be in relative balance, suggesting that some committees might be better described as mixed-motivation committees. The most often-cited motivation for requesting Appropriations was the committee's prestige, but almost equal numbers of members cited constituency and policy motivations, and when the two are combined, the constituency and policy mentions outnumber the mentions of prestige. Similarly, almost equal numbers regarding Budget mention policy and prestige. These studies also implicitly assume that motivations do not vary across political parties; in neither of these studies do the authors compare members of the two parties to determine whether they are similarly motivated to request certain committees.

Whether motivations are mixed or discrete, one thing is clear in our interviews with staff who are close to the committee assignment process: Members are motivated to seek committee assignments for many reasons, some electoral, but many personal. When asked what he believed motivated members to seek assignment to a particular committee, a Republican staff member replied, "Past interests and past professions. . . . things like that play a big factor in members' getting appointed and members' motivations for getting on committees. I'm sure that some of them are influenced by political considerations—what will give them the best chance of getting reelected."[3] A senior Democratic staff member remarked on member motivations, highlighting a change in attitude since the Democrats became the minority party:

> Some people need it for their district; some need it because they are marginal members and those things. For a lot of members, it's fulfillment; a lot of them want to be challenged; a lot of them just want to achieve, and so it becomes partially that. In the minority, especially, it's become a real thing to have something to do. For a lot of members on a lot of committees, especially since we don't use the committees as much as we used to, the committees are controlled by the majority; they have got a lot of time on their hands, and so they want to be in a place where more is happening. . . . It's a personal achievement type of thing.[4]

MEMBER MOTIVATIONS

Mayhew's characterization of members of Congress as single-minded seekers of reelection leads us to expect that members seeking committee assignments will be primarily motivated by reelection concerns. Table 3.3 examines the distribution of member motivations using our data. Consider the motivations expressed by all members in our sample. Less than

TABLE 3.2
Motivation types and committee preferences (Deering and Smith results)

Motivation type	Committee requested	Motivation mentioned[a]		
		Constituency	Policy	Prestige
Constituency	Agriculture	23	8	0
	Armed Services	20	10	0
	Interior	14	3	0
	Merchant Marine	12	0	0
	Public Works	10	3	0
	Science	17	8	0
	Small Business	16	4	0
	Veterans' Affairs	10	1	0
Policy	Banking	18	27	1
	Education and Labor	5	8	0
	Energy and Commerce	15	16	0
	Foreign Affairs	2	16	0
	Judiciary	1	6	0
	Government Operations	1	11	0
Prestige	Appropriations	12	10	15
	Budget	0	6	7
	Rules	0	1	4
	Ways and Means	2	14	11
Undesired	District of Columbia	1	1	1
	House Administration	0	0	0
	Post Office	3	0	0
	Ethics	0	1	0

Source: Calculated by the authors from Deering and Smith (1997, 87), table 3-6.
[a]Number of mentions in interviews during the 97th, 100th, and 101st Congresses.

half (41.2 percent) of the 289 members in our sample cited constituency concerns as the motivation for seeking membership on a committee; nearly as many (just under 5 percent less) cited a desire to make policy; and less than a quarter of the members sought committee membership to wield influence in the chamber. We might expect that members would express different motivations depending on their electoral status; members might be more concerned about servicing their constituents early in their careers and seek to shape policy and accrue influence after

TABLE 3.3
Motivations expressed in committee request letters (by motivation type)

| | All Members | | | Democrats | | | Republicans | | |
	All	*First-term*	*Incumbent*	*All*	*First-term*	*Incumbent*	*All*	*First-term*	*Incumbent*
Motivation									
Constituency	161	115	46	75	60	15	86	55	31
	41.2%	59.3%	23.4%	37.7%	57.7%	15.8%	44.8%	61.1%	30.4%
Policy	142	62	80	82	41	41	60	21	39
	36.3%	32.0%	40.6%	41.2%	39.4%	43.2%	31.3%	23.3%	38.2%
Influence	88	17	71	42	3	39	46	14	32
	22.5%	8.8%	36.0%	21.1%	2.9%	41.1%	24.0%	15.6%	31.4%
Total	391	194	197	199	104	95	192	90	102

Note: N = 289, multiple responses are possible; 92nd, 93rd, 97th, 98th, 100th, and 101st Congresses. Percentages are column percentages.

solidifying their electoral fortunes (Dodd 1977). Our results suggest support for this expectation. Well over half (59.3 percent) of all first-term members cite constituency as critical, while less than a quarter (23.4 percent) of incumbents were motivated by constituency concerns. Larger proportions of incumbents, compared with first-term members, cite policy (40.6 percent versus 32.0 percent) and influence (36 percent versus 8.8 percent) as motivating factors in seeking a preferred committee.

Interparty results provide extensive support for our expectation that partisans will differ. Members of both parties were motivated by constituency concerns, but significant proportions of members are also motivated by policy and influence. In addition, as we suggest, there are interesting contrasts between the two parties. First-term Democrats are more likely to express a policy motivation for seeking their initial committee assignment (39.4 percent) compared with first-term Republicans (23.3 percent); first-term Republicans are more likely to mention interest in exercising influence through their committee assignment (15.6 percent) than are first-term Democrats (2.9 percent). Incumbent Republicans are closely split among the three motivations, whereas the vast majority of incumbent Democrats express an interest in either shaping policy or wielding influence through their committee assignment (43.2 percent and 41.1 percent, respectively).

These results are significant for several reasons. First, they provide evidence that the behavior of House members reflects a complex combination of motivations. Second, they provide supporting evidence for the findings of others (Bullock 1971, 1973, 1976; Deering and Smith 1997), that constituency concerns are not necessarily foremost in the minds of members seeking committee assignments. Finally, they suggest some evidence for the proposition that there are differences between members of the two political parties, a proposition that, to date, has largely been ignored in the literature.

Committee Types and Motivations

Table 3.4 presents the results of our analysis using the Deering and Smith approach, thus allowing for comparison with table 3.2. Unlike Deering and Smith, however, we provide results for Democratic and Republican requesters separately in addition to aggregated results. Comparing the aggregate results of our analysis with their findings suggests a significant amount of overlap between the two analyses. Six of the eight committees classified as constituency committees by Deering and Smith also evidence a dominant constituency motivation in our aggregate results. Our results suggest that the two other committees—Science and Small Business—emerge in our analysis as committees that members seek primarily for policy reasons. Admittedly, however, our conclusion is based on a small number of cases, so the difference between the findings should be approached cautiously.

Of the six committees classified as policy oriented, our data and analysis suggest overlap with Deering and Smith in three cases, Banking, Foreign Affairs, and Judiciary, but for the three other committees, our results suggest possibly different conclusions. Requests for Education and Labor suggest that constituency motivations are dominant among those members requesting the committee (75 percent), and those members requesting Government Operations are equally split between policy and

Table 3.4

Motivations expressed in committee request letters
(by committee and motivation type)

Committee	All Members			Democrats			Republicans		
	Constituency	Policy	Influence	Constituency	Policy	Influence	Constituency	Policy	Influence
Agriculture	21	1	—	10	1	—	11	—	—
	95.5%	4.5%		90.9%	9.1%	15.8%	100%		
Appropriations	8	11	18	6	6	7	2	5	11
	21.6%	29.7%	48.6%	31.6%	31.5%	36.8%	11.1%	27.8%	61.1%
Armed Services	30	13	—	11	7	—	19	6	—
	69.8%	30.2%		61.1%	38.9%		76.0%	24.0%	
Banking	9	14	—	7	12	—	2	2	—
	39.1%	60.9%		36.8%	63.2%		50.0%	50.0%	
Budget	—	14	18	—	13	16	—	1	2
		43.8%	56.3%		44.8%	55.2%		33.3%	66.7%
Education and Labor	3	1	—	3	1	—	—	—	—
	75.0%	25.0%		75.0%	25.0%				
Energy and Commerce	39	29	7	15	17	4	24	12	3
	52.0%	38.7%	9.3%	41.7%	47.2%	11.1%	61.5%	30.8%	7.7%
Foreign Affairs	4	15	3	2	4	1	2	11	2
	18.2%	68.2%	13.6%	28.6%	57.1%	14.3%	13.3%	73.3%	13.3%
Government Operations	—	1	1	—	—	—	—	1	1
		50.0%	50.0%					50.0%	50.0%
House Administration	1	3	1	1	3	1	—	—	—
	20.0%	60.0%	20.0%	20.0%	60.0%	20.0%			
Judiciary	—	2	—	—	1	—	—	1	—
		100%			100%			100%	
Merchant Marine	3	1	—	1	1	—	2	—	—
	75.0%	25.0%		50.0%	50.0%		100%		
Interior	15	7	—	7	6	—	8	1	—
	68.2%	31.8%		53.8%	46.2%		88.9%	11.1%	
Post Office	1	—	—	1	—	—	—	—	—
	100%			100%					
Public Works	9	3	1	5	1	1	4	2	—
	69.2%	23.1%	7.7%	71.4%	14.3%	14.3%	66.7%	33.3%	

Table 3.4 (*continued*)
Motivations expressed in committee request letters
(by committee and motivation type)

	All Members			Democrats			Republicans		
	Constituency	*Policy*	*Influence*	*Constituency*	*Policy*	*Influence*	*Constituency*	*Policy*	*Influence*
Rules	1	2	11	—	—	—	1	2	11
	7.1%	14.3%	78.6%				7.1%	14.3%	78.6%
Science	1	2	—	—	1	—	1	1	—
	33.3%	66.7%			100%		50.0%	50.0%	
Small Business	1	1	—	—	—	—	1	1	—
	50.0%	50.0%					50.0%	50.0%	
Veterans' Affairs	1	—	—	—	—	—	1	—	—
	100%						100%		
Ways and Means	7	13	16	—	2	5	7	11	11
	19.4%	36.1%	44.4%		28.6%	71.4%	24.1%	37.9%	37.9%

Note: N = 289. Data for 92nd, 93rd, 97th, 98th, 100th, and 101st Congresses. Percentages are row percentages within each subgroup (i.e., all members, Democrats, and Republicans).

influence motivations; again, the total number of requests for these committees is small, so some caution is warranted. The most significant difference that we identify among the policy committees is in motivations for pursuing membership on Energy and Commerce. Slightly more than half the members who requested Energy (52 percent) cited constituency motivations, with the bulk of the other requesters citing policy concerns (38.7 percent).

Our results for the committees classified as prestige (or influence) committees (Appropriations, Budget, Rules, and Ways and Means) suggest different conclusions from those of Deering and Smith. First, although our results suggest support for the conclusion that members seek membership on Budget and on Rules primarily for purposes of influence (56.3 percent and 78.6 percent, respectively), our results also imply that motivations for pursuing Appropriations and Ways and Means are mixed. A plurality of members cite influence as a motivation for pursuing membership on Appropriations (48.6 percent), but large numbers of members cite policy (29.7 percent) and constituency (21.6 percent) as well. In the case of Ways and Means, policy and influence motivations compete, with a plurality of members indicating that influence is the prime motivation for seeking the committee (44.4 percent), while a similarly large proportion of members indicate that policy is a motivating concern (36.1 percent).

Constituency Committees

Committees that are most often associated with the constituency motivation differ somewhat according to political party. Both Democrats and Republicans mention constituency concerns as their motivation for pursuing an assignment to the Agriculture Committee. Members of both parties who request membership on Agriculture usually refer to the rural complexion of their district as the single most important factor for pursuing membership. Richard Durbin's (D-IL) expression of interest in the Agriculture Committee is typical of members who requested the committee: "[A]griculture plays a key role in our local economy. Farm related business and agribusiness concerns, such as ADM and Staley, are located within the district. I found during the course of the campaign frequent questions concerning farm policy. The constituents who I will serve are most concerned about agricultural issues as they affect the nation and our local economic well-being."[5]

First-term Republican Webb Franklin (MS) was likewise motivated by constituency interests to request membership on Agriculture:

Mississippi 2 is a district with a primarily agricultural economy. Cottonwood, soybeans, rice, catfish and wheat are the major cash crops of the area. The constituents, many of whom are farmers, have historically been represented on the Agriculture Committee by their Congressman. . . . Its jurisdiction and influence are vital to the interests of this congressional district. . . . As the needs of the district require representation on the agriculture committee, I ask for a speedy confirmation of my appointment.[6]

Members from districts with heavy agricultural involvement may feel the need to serve on the Agriculture Committee, even if the work of the committee does not interest them. A letter from H. Allen Smith (R-CA), member of the Executive Committee, to Minority Leader Ford illustrates this situation: "Bob Mathias is on Agriculture. He has to be because of his district. However, it isn't a very interesting committee to him personally and he would like to also be on some other committee. In view of the fact that he is an Olympic champion, loves people and has done a lot of traveling, he would like to be on Foreign Affairs."[7]

This result is hardly surprising. In congressional studies, the Agriculture Committee is the most common example of a constituency-oriented committee. The committee and its policy products are often pointed to as emblematic of the distributive theory of congressional organization. It is not always the case, however, that members from heavily agricultural areas demand seats on the Agriculture Committee. One such member publicly stated a preference for Agriculture while indicating he had no interest whatsoever in serving on the committee.

Constituency concerns play similar roles among Democrats and Republicans who seek membership on Armed Services, on Interior, and on Public Works, though there is some variation. Democrats requesting Armed Services mention policy as a motivation slightly more often than do Republicans (38.9 percent versus 24 percent, respectively); Democrats requesting Natural Resources similarly mention policy as a motivation more often than do Republicans (46.2 percent versus 11.1 percent, respectively); and Republicans requesting Public Works mention policy more often than do Democrats (33 percent versus 14.3 percent, respectively).

Two committees requested by only Democrats in our sample are Education and Labor, and Post Office, and both were requested primarily for constituency reasons. Education and Labor has generally been considered a committee that is requested for policy reasons. Our results suggest that it is a committee with important constituency concerns for Democrats, who, consistent with John R. Petrocik's (1996) conception of issue ownership, count educators and union members, both of whom are significantly affected by the policies considered in Education and Labor, as important elements of their electoral coalition. Similarly, Post Office had the potential to serve an important Democratic constituency: government employees. Indeed, some Republicans trying to transfer off the committee complained about the degree to which it was used to curry favor with these constituencies. Richard W. Mallary (R-VT) told Minority Leader Ford, "Let me again, for the record, indicate that I have no compelling interest in the Post Office and Civil Service Committee, which I find serves largely as a vehicle for Democratic office seekers to buy Federal and postal employees' votes with Federal funds."[8] It is therefore not surprising that when the Republicans gained the House majority in 1995, they quickly moved to abolish the committee.

Republicans request two other committees for constituency reasons in contrast to Democrats: Energy and Commerce and Merchant Marine. Deering and Smith classify Energy and Commerce as a policy committee, yet almost two-thirds of Republicans (61.5 percent) in our sample cited constituency concerns as their motivation for requesting the committee. First-term Maine Republican William Cohen's letter to the RCC is typical of many Republicans' desire to sit on the Interstate and Foreign Commerce Committee, as it was called at the time, for constituency reasons: "[M]y first choice is the Interstate and Foreign Commerce Committee. The broader range of its jurisdiction affects many areas of concern to my constituents in Maine, including such questions as health care, and its delivery system; the environment and its effects on the vast natural resources of Maine; the transmission of power; and the improvement of both intra and interstate transportation."[9]

Policy Committees

Several differences between partisans also emerge when we examine motivations for pursuing what are typically considered the policy committees. One has already been noted: Democrats are motivated to seek assignment to Education and Labor over constituency concerns. Democrats' reasons for requesting Energy and Commerce are almost evenly split between constituency- and policy-related concerns (41.7 percent and 47.2 percent, respectively). This narrow split is nicely illustrated by two first-term Democrats who requested Energy and Commerce in the 97th Congress. Gus Savage (D-IL) expressed his desire to sit on the committee entirely in terms of the interests of his constituency: "In Illinois, [a] leading export and major industrial state, [my district] is one of the foremost industrial districts. It houses more of my state's steel and automobile industries then any other Illinois district. Also, it contains the only access to St. Lawrence Seaway Ports in Illinois, including the only foreign and free trade zone in the Midwest."[10]

Ron Wyden (D-OR), by contrast, couched his motivation in terms of his policy interests:

> [D]uring my campaign for Congress, I said that . . . domestic issues—specifically energy, health care, and transportation—would be my top priority. These issues, as you know, are all within the jurisdiction of [the] energy and commerce committee . . . during my seven years as director of a major senior citizens' organization, my energies have been directed almost exclusively at the kind of issues that come before the energy and commerce committee.[11]

In addition to these two committees, one other anomaly is worth noting. Though the majority of Democrats who pursue assignment to the Foreign Affairs Committee (57.1 percent) cite policy as their motivation, they are more likely than Republicans are to mention constituency as a motivation (28.5 percent versus 13.3 percent, respectively). James Bilbray (D-NV) noted in his request to the DSPC, "I have a deep interest in national security matters stemming from Nevada's unique contribution to our nation's security. Southern Nevada is the home of the Nellis Air Force Base as well as the Nevada Test Site."[12]

Eliot Engel (D-NY) cited the demographics of his district and the ways that membership on the committee would allow him to be responsive to constituent concerns: "The 19th congressional district is comprised of a broad spectrum of ethnic and racial communities. For example, issues affecting Israel, Northern Ireland and South Africa take on a very personal role in the lives of many constituents. The Foreign Affairs Committee will allow me to address their concerns."[13]

Clement Zablocki (D-WI) expressed his constituency motivation for pursuing an assignment to Foreign Affairs: "The fourth Congressional District of Wisconsin is populated largely by Germans and Poles and for that reason I am extremely anxious to serve on this committee. . . . I do feel that I could best serve the people of my district as a member of the Committee on Foreign Affairs."[14]

Examination of the results among Republicans suggests support for the assertion that requests to serve on Foreign Affairs are strongly motivated by policy concerns. An overwhelming 73.3 percent of Republicans mention policy as a motivation for seeking an assignment to the committee. Christopher Smith (R-NJ) requested membership on the committee based on his personal interests and then enumerated a list of policy concerns that he would consider during his service on the committee:

> Ever since my college experience as an exchange student . . . I have had [a] deep and vital interest in international matters. I [am] particularly concerned about the following . . . Free emigration and human rights for Soviet Jews . . . an accounting of the 2500 MIAs in South East Asia . . . the ever-present problem of world hunger . . . the proper role of A.I.D . . . [t]he questionable practice of selling high-technology products[,] . . . which possess military capabilities, to political adversaries like the Soviet Union [and] China. . . . I could go on but, suffice it to say, I believe I will be able to make a genuine contribution to the Congress by my participation on this important committee.[15]

Examination of the committees considered attractive by members due to their policy concerns reveals three departures from the conventional wisdom. First, as was noted above, Republicans requesting Energy and Commerce are more likely to mention constituency concerns as a motivation for requesting the committee. Second, both policy and influence are cited as motivations for pursuing Government Operations, though the small number of cases makes this finding suspect. Finally, requests for Banking evidenced both constituency and policy motivations for pursuing the committee.

Requesting assignment to Banking, first-term member Patrick Swindall (R-GA) revealed his interest in addressing the financial interests located in his suburban Atlanta district, which he described as "a center for banking in the Southeast," going on to say, "[A] large number of my constituents are directly involved in the banking industry. Many more of my constituents and supporters are involved in business and industry and, consequently, have a very substantial stake in the banking industry . . . and the importance to my constituency of the banking finance and urban affairs committee would certainly enhance my reelection effort."[16]

On the other hand, Jack Buechner (R-MO) indicated his interest in the policy jurisdiction of the Banking Committee as his reason for seeking an assignment to the committee: "I have deep background in mortgage financing and apartment construction both in urban and rural (FMHA) areas. So I believe I will be able to significantly contribute to the committee as well as hold our party's position on what will probably be a new housing bill to be introduced by the Democrats."[17]

Influence Committees

Our results for requests to Budget indicate that requesters are motivated by influence, though Democrats had a greater tendency to note their policy interests when requesting Budget than did Republicans (44.8 percent versus 33.3 percent, respectively). In his letter requesting an assignment to Budget, Leon Panetta (D-CA)—who would later go on to chair the Budget Committee and head the Office of Management and Budget in the Clinton Administration—discussed at length his interest in shaping policy in the committee:

> As you may know, I am deeply interested in the budget process. During the 95th Congress, I introduced legislation to put Congress on a two-year budget cycle, a change which I believe would give us more time for careful study and oversight in the budgeting and appropriations process. . . . [W]hether or not Congress goes to a two-year budget, they believe strongly that we must examine all programs for advanced budgeting potential, so that we can maximize time for consideration of the budget needs of more important or complicated programs. In addition, I believe we must find ways to force the executive branch to identify areas of potential waste in programs, so that Congress can make careful choices in its budgeting process and avoid the meat-axe approach that we saw used in the last Congress.[18]

The Rules Committee represents a special case. Both parties consider the Rules Committee to be an arm of leadership and have placed assignment of Rules Committee members in the hands of their leader. The Democrats were first to adopt this practice (beginning in the 94th Congress), and the Republicans made a similar change in the 101st Congress. Therefore, we have fewer letters requesting Rules Committee assignment, and none for the Democrats in the years we have chosen to analyze.

Chip Pashayan (R-CA) put his motivation for requesting assignment to Rules in plain language: "My priority would be to advance the leadership's position, both in the Rules Committee and on the floor."[19] Future Speaker Dennis Hastert (R-IL) made his intentions known in slightly more eloquent form:

> Bob, as you know, I have given a great deal of thought to this decision, and feel that service on the Rules Committee will provide me with the opportunity to become more involved in the day[-]to[-]day decision-making process affecting the direction of Congress. . . . [I] would like to be into position to do more. A position on the Rules Committee, I believe, would allow me to fulfill that desire. . . . I know what it means to compromise without losing your undershorts, and I feel that the Rules Committee provides an excellent opportunity to utilize this ability. And Bob, I also know how to listen and appreciate that in this position the leadership must be heard. The minority can take a beating in Rules, and often has, but I'd like the opportunity to tackle this challenge, and maybe work a little coalition building in the process.[20]

Differences between the parties emerge as we turn to an examination of two other influence committees: Appropriations and Ways and Means. Among Democrats, motivations to seek assignment to Appropriations are distributed among constituency, policy, and influence concerns. In light of this nearly equal distribution, it is difficult to say that Democrats are motivated to pursue this committee for any dominant reason. In looking at how members expressed their interest in Appropriations, one is just as likely to find any of these three motivations.[21] Requesting a seat on the committee, Daniel Akaka (D-HI) felt motivated by constituency concerns: "Hawaii's economy depends heavily on defense spending because of its vital position in the Pacific."[22] Katie Hall (D-IN), in writing to the DSPC, showed an interest in shaping policy through membership on Appropriations: "As a former member of the Indiana Senate, I am keenly aware of the role of the Appropriations Committee in setting funding priorities within the budgetary process. In these days of competing alternatives, I would welcome the opportunity to share my perspective as an educator, former state legislator and representative of an area hard-hit by the realities of shrinking federal dollars, out migration and wide scale unemployment."[23]

Nancy Pelosi (D-CA), on the other hand, expressed having an interest in shaping the broad spending priorities of the nation through her membership on the Appropriations Committee: "My goal in Congress is to serve on the Appropriations Committee because I believe that the 13 Appropriations bills, more than any other legislation, are a declaration of our national values. It is the place where the needs reflective of the great diversity of our country must be accommodated."[24]

A majority of Republicans requesting Appropriations cited the influence of the committee as a motivation for seeking an assignment. Lawrence Coughlin (R-PA) noted the centrality of the committee in the legislative process and its import to achieving Republican objectives: "My interest in the work of that committee is personal, and I have no major public works or other situations in my district that are particularly affected. I come from a Republican district that should permit me to sustain committee positions on fiscal matters. . . . Going into my third term, I believe I understand the responsibilities [that] accompany the assignment to the Appropriations Committee."[25] James Abdnor (R-SD) likewise acknowledged the centrality of the committee to advancing party priorities: "I believe that I could serve on the Appropriations Committee, and thereby help promote the interests of republicanism."[26]

Democrats' motivations for seeking assignment to Ways and Means fell squarely into the influence column. Republicans, on the other hand, were equally split between policy and influence. Doug Bereuter (R-NE) expressed his reasons for seeking an assignment to Ways and Means: "I am quite interested in all areas of the committee's jurisdiction. . . . My special interests would lie in the areas of reciprocal trade agreements and in the health areas where I have been active during the past term and in my four years as a state senator."[27] D. French Slaughter (R-VA) was even more specific about how he wanted to use a position on Ways and Means: "With our Medicare system financially strapped and the need for financing long-term care growing, I would like to utilize my experience in this issue area on the Ways and Means Committee in order to help shape Federal health policy in a constructive and cost-efficient manner that will emphasize quality care provided through the private sector."[28]

MIXED MOTIVATIONS

In contrast to the findings of Bullock (1976) and Deering and Smith (1997), our findings suggest a more complex reality. Democrats and Republicans differ in their motivations to pursue committees. Previous studies have assumed that Democrats and Republicans were similarly motivated to pursue similar committee assignments. Our results suggest that this is not the case. We believe the reality is more complex also because the committee requests of congressional members are often responses to mixed motivations.

We classified committees allowing for multiple motivations expressed by each member. If a member expressed two motivations that all fell into the same category, the motivations were coded as "pure" constituency, policy, or influence; if a member expressed two different motivations, they were coded as "mixed." This approach results in a five-category typology: pure constituency, policy, or influence; mixed motivations; constituency and policy; and policy and influence.[29]

The results of this approach are presented in table 3.5. Among Democrats, the modal response of members suggests that ten of sixteen committees fall into the pure motivation categories; among Republicans, twelve of sixteen fall into the pure motivation categories. Six of sixteen committees fall into mixed-motivation categories for Democrats, five of seventeen for Republicans. This presentation is meant to be illustrative of the degree to which motivations are mixed, and to suggest that there may be dynamics within committees that transcend the categories that have become enshrined in the literature.

This finding has implications for our understanding of the policy dynamics of congressional committees. Many congressional analysts assume, consistent with the tenets of the distributive model, that members sharing

TABLE 3.5
Committees reclassified by motivation type

Motivation type	Committee requested	
	Democrats	*Republicans*
Constituency	Agriculture	Agriculture
	Armed Services	Armed Services
	Education and Labor	Energy and Commerce
	Interior	Interior
	Post Office	Merchant Marine
	Public Works	Public Works
		Veterans' Affairs
Mixed constituency/ policy	Energy and Commerce	Banking
	Foreign Affairs	Science
	House Administration	Small Business
	Merchant Marine	Foreign Affairs
	Judiciary	
Policy	Banking	Foreign Affairs
	Judiciary	Judiciary
	Science	
Mixed policy/influence	Appropriations	Government Operations
	Budget	Ways and Means
Influence	Ways and Means	Appropriations
		Budget
		Rules

Note: Reclassification of committees into five motivation types based on analysis of committee request letters from 92nd, 93rd, 97th, 98th, 100th, and 101st Congresses. Undesired committees omitted.

common motivations will seek membership on congressional committees such that committee members will share policy preferences that transcend political party. Our findings suggest that motivations vary between parties, within partisans seeking the same committee, and ultimately within partisan contingents on committees that have important political and policy consequences.

Consider Democratic requests for the Armed Services Committee. This committee is often held up, after Agriculture, as a prime example of a constituency-oriented committee. Members, it is argued, seek membership on this committee if their district contains significant defense interests; using their position on the committee, similarly motivated members display a pro-defense bias that leads to high levels of defense spending (perhaps higher than optimal), often on programs that benefit their districts as much as the national interest. Our results suggest support for the idea that Democrats and Republicans requesting the committee are both motivated by constituency concerns. At the same time, a larger proportion of Democrats seeking membership on the committee mention policy concerns (38.9 percent) than do Republicans (24.0 percent).

The request letters for Armed Services indicate the different motivations between members of the two parties seeking assignment to the committee. In most of the letters to the RCC, members seeking membership on Armed Services appeared to be motivated by constituency concerns. A characteristic letter to the RCC came from newly elected member Duncan Hunter (R-CA), who indicated he was motivated by constituency interests: "This district contains the largest U.S. Navy base, the West Coast Marine training center, both sites under consideration for the new Navy hospital and most of the defense industries of the San Diego area."[30]

Beginning in the 1970s, a few Democratic members began to seek membership on the Armed Services Committee for policy reasons rather than constituency concerns. In fact, these Democrats sought to influence the military establishment regarding race and gender and to restrain defense spending in favor of spending on social programs. This shift is evident in the request letters of members like first-term member Ronald Dellums (D-CA)—an African American member concerned about the racial inequities in military conscription during the Vietnam War—who indicated a strong policy interest in committee membership that reached beyond his narrow geographic constituency:

> One of my major concerns is the role of minority servicemen. . . .
> I am just as concerned with the broader area of GI rights and the
> overall role of the military in our society. Visits to a number of military installations in our country served to heighten my desire to
> become a member of this important committee. Opportunities to

talk with command personnel, enlisted and civilian men and women provided [me] with an insight I believe can be translated into meaningful input on the Armed Services Committee.[31]

In 1973 Dellums and Patricia Schroeder (D-CO)—an anti–Vietnam War activist and an early feminist leader—were assigned to the heavily pro-defense Armed Services Committee. When they were first assigned, the chair of the committee, F. Edward Hebert (D-LA), resentful of the presence of these two new members who were clearly outside the pro-defense culture of the committee, commented, "That girl and that black are each worth about half. I'll give them one chair" (Schroeder 1998, 41).[32]

From the committee, Dellums, Schroeder, Les Aspin (D-WI), and a few other Democrats fought to change military policies regarding the treatment of minorities and allowing women into combat, and sought to downsize the military and shift money away from military programs toward domestic programs. Over the long run, a number of these policy initiatives were successful, but these policy-oriented Democrats were often frustrated that most of the members of the committee, especially the Democrats, were heavily pro-defense. In a letter to Speaker Tip O'Neill, Schroeder expressed her frustration:

> The Democratic majority of the House of Representatives must take the lead imposing fiscal integrity on the military budget. . . . [O]ur ability to restrain defense spending is impaired by the fact that the committee of jurisdiction, the committee on armed services, is unrepresentative of the national Democratic Party. . . . On defense issues, the unrepresentativeness of the Democrats on the committee is . . . extreme. . . . On four major defense votes over the last two years which would have reduced defense expenditures and on which a majority of Democrats in the House voted for a reduction, only six [committee] Democrats voted with the House Democratic majority all four times and twelve committee Democrats voted against the Democratic House majority every single time.[33]

Representative Schroeder then focused on upcoming assignments to the Armed Services Committee as a means for changing the culture of the committee. She advocated assigning members to the committee who were more representative of the House Democratic Party:

[T]here are six Democratic vacancies on the committee, due to retirements and the new party ratio. The appointment of national Democrats to these vacancies would reduce the pro-Pentagon bias of the committee somewhat. Six new members together with the six current members who have some concern for fiscal control over the Defense Department would mean that there would be twelve cost conscious Democrats and 15 big defense spenders. So, if all six new members were national Democrats, the committee would still not be reflective of the national party; yet, it would be much more representative than it is now.[34]

As it turns out, Armed Services had seven vacancies in the 98th Congress because of one transfer off the committee. Nine members requested assignment to the committee. Of those nine, seven expressed a clear motivation for seeking the committee. Four sought the committee purely for constituency-related reasons, two because of policy concerns, and one member evidenced mixed constituency and policy motivations for seeking a committee seat. The two members who did not express a clear motivation both had reasons to be pro-defense. Of the seven who were assigned to the committee, only two were motivated by the policy concerns of committee members who were "national Democrats" like Dellums and Schroeder.

The Armed Services Committee was not significantly changed by the assignments made by the DSPC in the 98th Congress. However, the conflict between national Democrats and Armed Services Democrats persisted, and Schroeder and Dellums were able to make significant strides in changing military policy through their service on the committee. Dellums ascended to the chair of the committee in the 103rd Congress and served as the ranking minority member until his retirement. He successfully implemented procurement reforms in the Pentagon once a Democrat was in the White House. Schroeder was able to use her position on the committee to address issues of gender bias in the military and, with the coming of the Clinton Administration and her old ally Les Aspin heading the Defense Department, was successful in achieving limited involvement of women in combat positions.

Proponents of distributive theory will point to this case as support for their expectation that constituency concerns will dominate in committees.

Committee assignments are, on the legislative side, at the root of the "cozy little triangle" problem. A system that permits "interesteds" to gravitate to decision areas in which their interests are promoted provides the fertile environment in which clientelism flourishes. Short of total disruption of current committee assignment practices (in which case clientelism would probably emerge in some other guise), cozy little triangles are likely to dominate the policy process. The interest-advocacy-accommodation syndrome provides the legislative underpinnings for these relationships. (Shepsle 1978, 248)

Although constituency can play an important role in motivating members' pursuit of committee assignments, conflicting motivations may have important consequences for the dynamics of committees, and gross generalizations can ignore important aspects of committee politics.

• • •

Our analysis of member motivations provides support for the multiple-motivations perspective employed in our framework and the work of other analysts who rely on this assumption as a foundation for their models. Our empirical exploration provides support for our contention—and the contention of others—that members are motivated by more than electoral concerns to pursue particular committee assignments. Evidence from the request letters indicates that members are motivated by policy concerns and the desire to accrue political power as much or more than they are concerned about reelection or the need for their committee assignment to reflect some major interest in their district. Variations in members' motivations are influenced by perceived constraints and predispositions unique to the member and his or her political circumstances, as we describe in chapter 1.

The similarity between our aggregate findings and those of Deering and Smith suggest that using member request letters as a data source is a valid research strategy that has been overlooked, or more accurately, simply dismissed. This approach holds promise for helping us to understand more fully how member motivations shape the quest for a committee assignment, and ultimately to better understand committee performance. While providing a richness of understanding, divining individual motivations based on a content analysis of members' request letters may seem to some a somewhat soft methodology. In the chapter that follows, we examine the relationship between objective measures of constituency characteristics and committee requests.

CHAPTER FOUR

COMMITTEE REQUESTS AND
CONSTITUENCY CHARACTERISTICS

The heterogeneous Interstate and Foreign Commerce Committee is
peculiarly geared to the requirements of my heterogeneous district.
REPRESENTATIVE TORBERT H. MACDONALD (D-MA)

Our CAP framework suggests that constituency concerns are
simply one element of a complex request calculus that incorporates both district and individual concerns into the committee
request. The findings in the previous chapter support this contention,
illustrating that constituency motivations, while important, are only one
component of members' motivations for pursuing a particular committee. Even when representatives are motivated by constituency concerns,
the motivation is complex.[1] Congressional members who are constrained
by the presence of a large, well-organized single interest in their district
will likely pursue membership on a committee that can be narrowly
responsive to that constituency interest. However, these conditions will
exist in a relative handful of districts, leaving most members free to pursue
committee assignments that are aligned with their personal interests.
Thus, we expect to find only a modest relationship between objective
measures of constituency interest and committee requests.

Our framework also leads us to focus on the limited ability of the party committees on committees to accommodate committee requests in a highly competitive environment. The committees on committees are usually able to accommodate members who are constrained by constituency considerations and who request assignment to constituency-oriented committees like Agriculture and Interior. The intense competition among members for assignment to other types of committees, however, severely limits the committee on committees' ability to accommodate all requests. Unlike many previous studies, which find high levels of accommodation of members' requests, our data show that a large percentage of members are *not* assigned to their preferred committee. Routine accommodation of members' requests is a widely accepted feature of the process and it plays a central role in distributive theory, which conceives of self-selection as a mechanism for producing homogeneous committees, committees composed of preference outliers (Weingast and Marshall 1988). Our findings suggest that this assumption may have less support in empirical reality than previously thought.

GENERAL PATTERNS OF COMMITTEE REQUESTS

Table 4.1 provides descriptive information on the number of requests submitted by members, broken down by electoral status (first-term member versus incumbent) and political party. First-term Democrats in the House submitted concentrated request lists to the DSPC. Just under half of these members (46.9 percent) requested only one or two committees, and almost three-quarters (73.2 percent) of first-term Democrats requested fewer than three committees. A majority of first-term Republicans, by contrast, requested four or more committees.

Looked at over time (see figure 4.1), the number of first-term Republican requests generally exceeds Democratic requests over the period between the 86th and 102nd Congresses. The average number of committee requests from new Democrats ranges between one and a half and three, while the number of Republican requests averages between three and four, increasing to over a half-dozen in the 100th and 101st congresses before returning to lower levels.

TABLE 4.1
Number of committees requested

Number of committees requested	All members		First-term members		Incumbents	
	Democrats	*Republicans*	*Democrats*	*Republicans*	*Democrats*	*Republicans*
1	755	479	176	41	579	438
	55.3%	43.0%	24.8%	9.1%	88.4%	66.2%
2	196	151	157	50	39	101
	14.3%	13.6%	22.1%	11.1%	6.0%	15.3%
3	207	196	187	126	20	70
	15.2%	17.6%	26.3%	27.9%	3.1%	10.6%
4 or more	208	288	191	235	17	53
	15.2%	25.9%	26.9%	52.0%	2.6%	8.0%
N	1366	1114	711	452	655	662
	Phi = .150		Phi = .298		Phi = .277	
	(.000)		(.000)		(.000)	

Note: Number in parenthesis is p, the Monte Carlo significance of Phi based on 10,000 simulations. Random number seed = 2000000. Data on member requests are drawn from committee-on-committees briefing books and committee request letters. Data for Democrats include all Congresses from the 80th through the 103rd, with the exception of the 85th. Data for Republicans range from the 85th Congress through the 102nd.

In contrast to first-term Democrats, the requests of incumbent Democrats represent a more stable pattern. The vast majority of incumbent Democrats who sought to modify their committee assignments requested only a single committee (88.4 percent). A large percentage of Republican incumbents also restrained their transfer requests to a single committee, but compared with incumbent Democrats, surprisingly large numbers of Republicans request two or more committees, suggesting substantial dissatisfaction with initial committee assignments. As figure 4.2 indicates, this gap between incumbents of the two parties seems to have emerged during the 94th Congress.

One explanation for these observed differences may involve the greater levels of uncertainty in the minority party leadership. The number

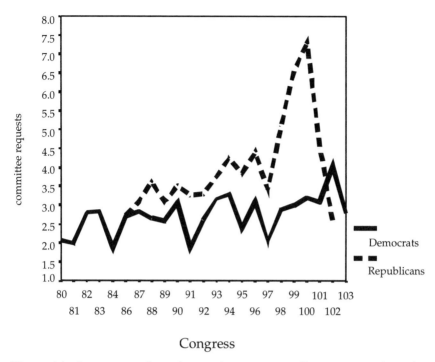

Figure 4.1. Average number of committee requests, first-term members, by party and Congress. Data on member requests are drawn from committee-on-committees briefing books and committee request letters. Data for Democrats include all Congresses from the 80th through the 103rd, with the exception of the 85th. Data for Republicans range from the 85th Congress through the 102nd.

of available committee slots largely results from two factors: the number of party members who are not returning to the committee, and the committee ratios that are set by the majority party. Although the RCC knows the number of nonreturning members long before the committee assignment process begins, committee ratios are variable and subject to modification by the majority. Given the uncertainty that surrounds the number of available committee seats, new members might increase the number of committees requested in order to increase their chances of receiving an acceptable assignment. Additionally, the Republican leadership may encourage new members to provide them with flexibility by providing a more complete accounting of the committees that are acceptable.

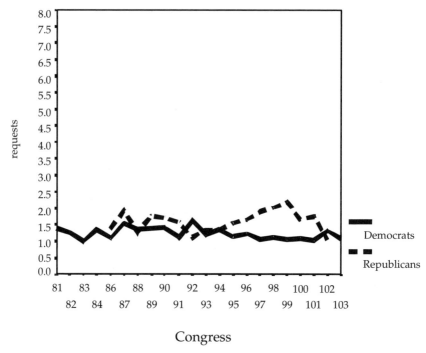

Congress

Figure 4.2. Average number of committee requests, incumbents, by party and Congress. Data on member requests are drawn from committee-on-committees briefing books and committee request letters. Data for Democrats include all Congresses from the 80th through the 103rd, with the exception of the 85th. Data for Republicans range from the 85th Congress through the 102nd.

As a result of the limited number of committee slots available to the minority, and the conditional nature of additional committee seats being made available by the majority, the Republican leadership may have had to place its members in a higher percentage of unwanted committee assignments. Comments in his letter requesting a seat on the Appropriations Committee suggest that Mickey Edwards of Oklahoma was one Republican who felt his assignment was not optimal: "I am currently in an intolerable assignment. My district is totally urban. I am on the Interior Committee."[2] Harold Hollenbeck (R-NJ) was even more adamant about his committee assignments and his ability to represent his district:

I desire a change in my committee assignments. At present I serve on Science and Technology and Standards of Official Conduct. This is hardly a "choice" or even "decent" selection of assignments both logically and parochially . . . although much worthwhile legislation emerges from the [Science] Committee, it has little direct impact on my District and it is difficult for my constituents to relate to most of the technical concepts involved . . . Ethics hardly enables one to aid his constituency.[3]

THE DISTRIBUTION OF COMMITTEE PREFERENCES

Table 4.2 illustrates the distribution of first requested committees by electoral status and party. Several interesting patterns are apparent. First, incumbent demand for the influence (or control) committees is much higher than that for first-term members. As a proportion, incumbents are more likely to request Appropriations, Budget, Rules, and Ways and Means than are their less senior colleagues. This finding is consistent with Shepsle's original finding among Democrats (1978). Requests for influence committees are rarely granted to newly elected members; they are typically made aware of this by their more senior colleagues; and the strategies of first-term members are shaped by the likelihood that they will receive a desired committee.

First-term members focus their requests on several committees that incumbents do not request. Among the committees generally considered to be constituency committees, first-term members are more likely than incumbents to request Agriculture and Public Works. Banking, Education and Labor, and Energy and Commerce committees, usually considered to be policy oriented, tend to be more popular among first-term members than among incumbents. First-term members are more than five times more likely to request the Banking Committee than are incumbents, almost five times more likely to request Education and Labor, and almost two times more likely to request Energy.

The distribution of preferences also suggests interesting interparty differences among incumbents and first-term members, as demonstrated in table 4.3. Requests for the influence committees are roughly the same across incumbents of both parties. One obvious difference is the Rules

TABLE 4.2
Committee assignment preferences

Committee type	Committee	All			Incumbent			First-term		
		All members	Democrats	Republicans	Both parties	Democrats	Republicans	Both parties	Democrats	Republicans
Service	District of Columbia	17 0.7%	14 1.0%	3 0.3%	16 1.2%	13 2.0%	3 0.5%	1 0.1%	1 0.1%	—
	House Administration	21 0.8%	12 1.0%	9 0.8%	20 1.5%	11 1.7%	9 1.4%	1 0.1%	1 0.1%	—
	Post Office	15 0.6%	12 0.9%	3 0.3%	8 0.6%	6 0.9%	2 0.3%	7 0.6%	6 0.8%	1 0.2%
	Ethics	3 0.1%	—	3 0.3%	3 0.2%	—	3 0.5%	—	—	—
Constituency	Agriculture	170 6.9%	93 6.8%	77 6.9%	32 2.4%	14 2.1%	18 2.7%	138 11.9%	79 11.1%	59 13.1%
	Armed Services	199 8.0%	101 7.4%	98 8.8%	88 6.7%	32 4.9%	56 8.5%	111 9.5%	69 9.7%	42 9.3%
	Interior	112 4.5%	64 4.7%	48 4.3%	63 4.8%	33 5.0%	30 4.5%	49 4.2%	31 4.4%	18 4.0%
	Merchant Marine	34 1.4%	22 1.6%	12 1.1%	24 1.8%	17 2.6%	7 1.1%	10 0.9%	5 0.7%	5 1.1%
	Public Works	102 4.1%	74 5.4%	28 2.5%	23 1.7%	12 1.8%	11 1.7%	79 6.8%	62 8.7%	17 3.8%
	Science	59 2.4%	27 2.0%	32 2.9%	31 2.4%	13 2.0%	18 2.7%	28 2.4%	14 2.0%	14 3.1%

Small Business	11 — 0.4%	1 — 0.1%	10 — 0.9%	10 — 0.8%	—	10 — 1.5%	1 — 0.1%	1 — 0.1%	—
Veterans' Affairs	10 — 0.4%	6 — 0.4%	4 — 0.4%	8 — 0.6%	5 — 0.8%	3 — 0.5%	2 — 0.2%	1 — 0.1%	1 — 0.2%
Policy									
Banking	112 — 4.5%	75 — 5.5%	37 — 3.3%	18 — 1.4%	4 — 0.6%	14 — 2.1%	94 — 8.1%	71 — 10.0%	23 — 5.1%
Education and Labor	65 — 2.6%	52 — 3.8%	13 — 1.2%	11 — 0.8%	8 — 1.2%	3 — 0.5%	54 — 4.6%	44 — 6.2%	10 — 2.2%
Energy and Commerce	319 — 12.9%	189 — 13.8%	130 — 11.7%	110 — 8.4%	64 — 9.8%	46 — 6.9%	209 — 18.0%	125 — 17.6%	84 — 18.6%
Foreign Affairs	188 — 7.6%	75 — 5.5%	113 — 10.1%	113 — 8.6%	32 — 4.9%	81 — 12.2%	75 — 6.4%	43 — 6.0%	32 — 7.1%
Government Operations	43 — 1.7%	28 — 2.0%	15 — 1.3%	37 — 2.8%	24 — 3.7%	13 — 2.0%	6 — 0.5%	4 — 0.6%	2 — 0.4%
Judiciary	73 — 2.6%	37 — 2.7%	36 — 3.2%	17 — 1.3%	9 — 1.4%	8 — 1.2%	56 — 4.8%	28 — 3.9%	28 — 6.2%
Influence									
Appropriations	412 — 16.6%	212 — 15.5%	200 — 18.0%	269 — 20.4%	137 — 20.9%	132 — 19.9%	143 — 12.3%	75 — 10.5%	68 — 15.0%
Budget	170 — 6.9%	124 — 9.1%	46 — 4.1%	160 — 12.1%	119 — 18.2%	41 — 6.2%	10 — 0.9%	5 — 0.7%	5 — 1.1%
Rules	72 — 2.9%	25 — 1.8%	47 — 4.2%	65 — 4.9%	21 — 3.2%	44 — 6.6%	7 — 0.6%	4 — 0.6%	3 — 0.7%
Ways and Means	273 — 11.0%	123 — 9.0%	150 — 13.5%	191 — 14.5%	81 — 12.4%	110 — 16.6%	82 — 7.1%	42 — 5.9%	40 — 8.8%
Total	2480	1366	1114	1317	655	662	1163	711	452

Note: N = 2,480. Six requests for House Un-American Activities are excluded. Percentages are column percentages. Data on member requests are drawn from committee-on-committes briefing books and committee request letters. Data for Democrats include all Congresses from the 80th through the 103rd, with the exception of the 85th. Data fro Republicans range from the 85th Congress through the 102nd.

[a]Categories are based on the committee typology developed by Deering and Smith (1997).

Committee. This difference reflects the fact that for most of this period, the Speaker filled Democratic slots on this committee, while in the Republican Party, the RCC was invested with Rules assignment power, leading members to request this committee assignment on occasion. Another difference is that incumbent Democrats request membership on the Budget Committee more often than Republicans do by nearly three to one. The Budget Committee plays an important agenda-setting role in congressional fiscal policy and is heavily dominated by the majority party, the Democrats during the period that our data cover. Republicans may not have found service on the committee attractive, preferring instead to serve on the Ways and Means Committee, which plays a more important role in tax policy, a core political and policy concern of the Republican Party. In fact, incumbent Republicans are slightly more likely than incumbent Democrats to request Ways and Means.

Incumbent Democrats are more likely than incumbent Republicans to request an assignment to Education and Labor and to Energy and Commerce (1.2 percent versus 0.5 percent, and 9.8 percent versus 6.9 percent, respectively). Given the jurisdiction of Education and Labor, Democratic members of the committee would have an opportunity to serve two important constituencies in their electoral coalition. Membership on Energy and Commerce might be more attractive to Democrats because of its jurisdiction over many health-care and environmental issues that that are important to many Democratic voters and that regularly recur on the congressional policy agenda, providing many opportunities to engage in substantive policy making.

Incumbent Republicans, on the other hand, were more likely than incumbent Democrats to request Armed Services and Foreign Affairs (8.5 percent versus 4.9 percent, and 12.2 percent versus 4.9 percent, respectively). These differences may be related to the policy foci of the two parties. Over the post–World War II period, the Republican Party has claimed ownership of military and foreign policy issues (Petrocik 1996). For this reason, Republicans might have been more interested in serving on these two committees than many Democrats would. Indeed, many Democrats without significant military interests in their district might find membership on the Armed Services Committee to be frustrating and avoid it (see chapter 3).

TABLE 4.3
Party and electoral status differences in committee preferences
(Monte Carlo probabilities)

| | Committee preference differences | | | |
	Democrats	p	Republicans	p
All members	Banking	.000	Foreign Affairs	.000
	Budget	.000	Judiciary	.088
	District of Columbia	.023	Rules	.000
	Education and Labor	.000	Small Business	.005
	Post Office	.072	Ways and Means	.005
Incumbents	Budget	.000	Agriculture	.060
	District of Columbia	.011	Armed Services	.004
	Energy and Commerce	.073	Banking	.002
	Government Operations	.069	Foreign Affairs	.000
	Merchant Marine	.042	Rules	.002
			Small Business	.002
			Ways and Means	.041
First-term members	Banking	.003	Appropriations	.039
	Education and Labor	.002	Judiciary	.091
	Public Works	.001		
	Ways and Means	.058		

Note: Committees listed are those more likely to be requested by members of each party. Committees are listed when $p < .10$; p is the Monte Carlo significance of Phi based on 10,000 simulations, random number seed 2000000. Data on member requests are drawn from committee-on-committees briefing books and committee request letters. Data for Democrats include all Congresses from the 80th through the 103rd, with the exception of the 85th. Data for Republicans range from the 85th Congress through the 102nd.

Incumbent preferences for the remaining committees tend to parallel one another closely. One interesting departure is in requests for Post Office. Though the number of requests is small, Democrats request the committee more than Republicans by three to one.

Among first-term members, we observe different request patterns between members of the two parties. Democratic newcomers are about two to four times more likely than are first-term Republicans to request Banking, Education and Labor, and Public Works.

Republican newcomers, on the other hand, were more likely than Democrats to request two influence committees: Appropriations and

Ways and Means. Requests for these two committees make up almost one-quarter (23.8 percent) of all first-term Republican requests. Fifteen percent of first-term Republicans versus 10.5 percent of first-term Democrats request Appropriations, and 8.8 percent of first-term Republicans request Ways and Means compared with 5.9 percent of first-term Democrats. Considering Shepsle's (1978) finding among first-term Democrats, the fact that many first-term Republicans request Appropriations and Ways and Means is surprising. Shepsle's theoretical model suggests that first-term members will focus their requests on committees where the likelihood of success in receiving the committee assignment is relatively high. However, these committees are highly sought after and the likelihood of success is quite low, much lower, in fact, in the minority party, given the small number of slots granted to the minority party.

This interparty difference is likely a function of differences in early socialization practices in the two parties. Perhaps because of their status as an almost permanent majority in the House during the period of study, the Democratic Party developed an extensive process for mediating member demands within the committee assignment process to reduce conflict within the process. Democrats tend to engage new members in extensive counseling prior to the committee request process, advising new members that they are unlikely to receive important committee assignments in their first term and encouraging them to consult with their zone representative, who will probably repeat this message. Republicans, on the other hand, did not engage in systematic counseling before soliciting assignments; thus, many Republicans might lodge such a request if only to get on record as having requested the committee. An interview with one Republican leadership aide involved in the assignment process confirmed this view: "It doesn't hurt for them to express that they want to be there. Especially down the road, when they can say 'I've requested this three times.'"[4]

First-term Democrats focused their efforts more on gaining slots on Banking, Education and Labor, and Public Works compared with first-term Republican efforts to gain these slots. Requests for these committees may hold the promise for new Democrats of becoming involved in core Democratic policy issues. Newly elected Republicans were more likely than new Democrats to request Judiciary. Assignment to Judiciary or to

Foreign Affairs provides the potential of being active in shaping core Republican policies.

THE SELF-SELECTION HYPOTHESIS

Distributive theory is premised on self-selection; that is, individual members will seek committee assignments that are consistent with some dominant interest within their district. In the classic example of the Agriculture Committee, members who request Agriculture will come from districts that have higher concentrations of agricultural interests than districts represented by members who do not request assignment to the committee. Thus, the self-selection hypothesis suggests that the district characteristics of members requesting a given committee will differ significantly from those members who do not request that committee. Based on our understanding of member motivations, developed above, we expect the relationship between constituency characteristics and committee requests will be evident in a handful of committees but mostly nonexistent across all committees.

Monte Carlo Approach to Self-Selection

In the analysis that follows, we combine our committee request data (see appendix 1) with the district-level data collected by Scott Adler (Adler and Lapinski 1997). We use nonparametric, difference-of-median methodology to analyze the data. Our purpose is to determine whether demand for committee assignments comes disproportionately from members whose constituencies demand a high level of benefits consistent with the committee's jurisdiction. Timothy Groseclose (1994), Christopher Z. Mooney and Robert D. Duval (1993), and others highlight the problems associated with the use of traditional asymptotic methodologies, such as difference-of-means tests, with data such as these. Of primary concern here is that results from asymptotic tests can be affected when data are heavily skewed across groups (see Mooney and Duval 1993; Mooney 1997), as they are in this case. Typically, analysts employ an 80-20 test for determining whether to use asymptotic methodologies; that is, if less than 20 percent of one's cases fall into one category, asymptotic tests are unreliable. This is certainly the case with our data. For instance, 170

(6.9 percent) congressional members requested assignment to the Agriculture Committee out of a total of 2,480 requests; such an imbalance could result in incorrect inferences.

Following Groseclose (1994) and others (Adler and Lapinski 1997; Maltzman 1997; Peterson and Wrighton 1998), we employ a Monte Carlo approach. Monte Carlo methodology uses repeated random sampling of the observed data to determine whether the test group—in this case, those requesting a committee assignment—represents districts that are consistently, significantly different from the districts of all nonrequesting members of the House. In considering the results of these tests, interpretation relies on the value of p, the probability that the observed values for the test group (requesters) are drawn from a population other than the universe of all members. We adopt a standard significance level of .05 for accepting the hypothesis that committee requests come from a population of high-demand legislators that are distinct from the overall population of members.

Results of the Monte Carlo Analysis of Self-Selection

Table 4.4 presents the results of an extensive analysis of the self-selection hypothesis for incumbents and first-term members of both parties.[5] The expectations of distributive theory are supported only by the findings for the Agriculture, Armed Services, Foreign Affairs, and Interior committees. All measures of district interest for the Agriculture Committee suggest that the median value for the requesters' districts is significantly different from the median value of the nonrequesters' districts. This finding holds for both incumbent and first-term requesters of both parties. This finding is consistent with our analysis in the previous chapter, which suggested that members of Congress seeking assignment to the Agriculture Committee overwhelmingly mention constituency as their motivation. These combined results support the characterization of Agriculture, in particular, as the poster child of distributive theory.

Our results also indicate that those who request membership on Armed Services have districts that are distinct from those of members who do not request an assignment to the committee; without exception, those members who request Armed Services have a greater military presence in their district, no matter how that presence is measured (percentage of workforce or number of installations). Members requesting Interior tend to come from districts that are more sparsely populated than the districts of members who do not request the committee. Members requesting Interior also tend to have more land in their district that is held in public trust. These findings hold for all but incumbent Democrats, and only when the measure of district demand is measured by population density. Our findings in this analysis are also consistent with our findings about members' motivations for seeking these particular committees. In both cases, committees members' motivations leaned toward constituency concerns.

Requests for Foreign Affairs suggest self-selection behavior from incumbents of both parties and first-term Democrats with high concentrations of foreign-born constituents; first-term Republican members' districts do not evidence the same pattern, suggesting that demand for this committee is constant across all first-term Republicans. This finding is not entirely consistent with our examination of members' motivations. Democrats evidenced mixed motivations for seeking assignment to Foreign Affairs; in fact, we classified it as a mixed constituency/policy committee. These findings are somewhat more surprising for Republicans, who seemed primarily motivated by policy concerns. However, a number of Republicans expressed mixed motivations for pursuing assignment to the committee. Political scientist Mark Siljander (R-MI), in his letter to the RCC, evidenced both constituency and policy motivations for requesting Foreign Affairs: "I have a special interest in being assigned to the committee, which has been heightened by my recent visit to Israel and Lebanon and my discussions with Bachir Gemayel, the late president-elect of Lebanon. I also think this would be an effective assignment as my state of Michigan is especially sensitive to any foreign trade with Japan."[6]

Ed Zschau (R-CA) likewise expressed a combination of constituency- and policy-oriented motivations:

> The heart of my district is the Silicon Valley, known worldwide
> for its leadership in high technology (particularly electronics),

TABLE 4.4
Committee requests and constituency characteristics

Committee type[a]	Committee • Indicator	Incumbent			First-term		
		All	Democrats	Republicans	All	Democrats	Republicans
	Post Office						
	• % Federal workers	.404	.063	n/a	n/a	n/a	n/a
Constituency	**Agriculture**						
	• % Rural population	+.000	+.011	+.000	+.000	+.000	+.000
	• % Ag. workforce	+.000	+.000	+.000	+.000	+.000	+.000
	Armed Services						
	• % Mil. workforce	+.000	+.000	+.004	+.000	+.000	+.000
	• # Mil. installations	+.000	+.000	+.047	+.000	+.000	+.000
	• # Major mil. install.	+.000	+.000	+.029	+.000	+.000	+.000
	Interior						
	• % Population density	+.034	.427	+.030	+.000	+.000	+.000
	• Federal Land	+.011	+.026	+.021	+.000	+.000	+.000
	Merchant Marine						
	• Coastal district	+.000	+.006	.111	+.037	1.0	+.006
	• Marine academy	+.035	.223	.081	1.0	1.0	1.0
	• 25 most active ports	.106	.248	.769	.765	.093	1.0
	Public Works						
	• % Transportation	.848	.686	.960	.243	.135	.494
	• % Construction	.249	.159	.863	.483	.431	.739
	• Flood Potential	.052	.559	+.032	.343	.868	.222
	• % Unemployed	.677	.428	.981	+.012	.180	.196
	Science						
	• % Mil. workforce	+.040	.226	.138	.657	.967	.549
	Small Business						
	• % Urban	.643	n/a	.975	n/a	n/a	n/a
	• Population density	.959	n/a	.605	n/a	n/a	n/a
	Veterans' Affairs						
	• % Veterans	.795	.100	.057	n/a	n/a	n/a
	• # Beds VA Hospital	.582	.460	.641	n/a	n/a	n/a
Policy	**Banking**						
	• % African American	.397	.395	.775	.+006	.095	.466
	• % Urban	.345	n/a	.559	+.000	+.001	+.015
	• % Unemployed	.198	.899	.071	.295	.789	.682
	• 50 largest cities	.792	1.0	1.0	+.040	.322	.117
	• Banking assets	.488	.333	.641	.999	.960	.888
	• % Employed in finance	.900	.666	.602	.266	.289	.739

Table 4.4 (*continued*)
Committee requests and constituency characteristics

Committee type[a]	Committee • Indicator	Incumbent			First-term		
		All	Democrats	Republicans	All	Democrats	Republicans
Policy	**Education and Labor**						
	• % Blue collar	**+.019**	.136	.051	.072	.174	.231
	• % Unionized	**+.035**	.256	**+.018**	**+.001**	**+.004**	.068
	• % Public schools	+.006	.132	+.019	**+.035**	.121	.329
	• Median income	.274	.319	n/a	.876	.704	.620
	• Population density	.122	.264	.546	**+.001**	**+.007**	.231
	Energy and Commerce						
	• % Retail/wholesale	.056	.403	**+.041**	**+.049**	.082	.305
	• % Transportation	.245	.488	.511	.919	.528	.612
	Foreign Affairs						
	• % Foreign born	**+.001**	**+.001**	**+.009**	**+.008**	**+.005**	.541
	Government Operations						
	• District close to D.C.	1.0	1.0	1.0	.177	1.0	.067
	• % Federal workers	.987	.442	.508	.146	.172	n/a
	Judiciary						
	• % African American	.689	.570	.791	.396	.511	.292
	• % Urban	.717	.669	.977	.202	.174	.547
	• 50 largest cities	.767	1.0	.690	.414	.101	.810

Note: Significant levels (*p*) for Monte Carlo difference-of-median tests. Number of simulations = 10,000, Random number seed = 2000000. Committes with no district-specific indicators of interest omitted. Indicator data provided by E. Scott Adler, from his analysis of U.S. census data.

Null Hypothesis: Committee assignment preferences are unrelated to district characteristics.

bold   Monte Carlo *p* < .05 (one-tailed).

none   Results fail to support high-demand hypothesis at either standard.

n/a   No or too few cases to draw a conclusion.

+   Districts of members significantly overrepresentative of characteristic (as predicted by distributive theory).

–   Districts of members significantly underrepresentative of characteristic (contrary to prediction of distributive theory).

Sign omitted if critical *p* is not significant.

[a]Categories based on the committee typology developed by Deering and Smith (1997).

venture capital, and entrepreneurship. . . . A primary objective of my first term in Congress is to help formulate a Republican initiative in high technology, particularly as it relates to national industrialization policy and economic growth. . . . I'm seeking a committee assignment complementary to the needs of high technology and my district.[7]

Results for several other committees suggest weaker support for the self-selection component of distributive theory. Almost half the indicators for Education and Labor show some support for the idea that members with strong constituency interests might pursue assignment to this committee. First-term Democrats and incumbent Republicans who request the committee tend to have a greater union presence in their constituency than do those who do not request the committee. Republican incumbents request the committee also if a large proportion of students in their districts are in public schools. Republican members elected from districts with high levels of unionization may feel especially pressured to seek assignment to Education and Labor because they represent districts that would ordinarily be considered Democratic districts. Jack Kemp (R-NY), who represented the city of Buffalo—the site of two major public universities—and who was something of a labor leader, expressed several reasons for seeking an assignment to the committee: "The large number of colleges and universities in the 39th District, my concern with the financial crisis our schools are facing, the problem of campus unrest, in addition to my experience as co-founder and president of the AFL Players Association lead me to believe that an assignment on this committee would be an excellent opportunity to serve the 39th District."[8]

Education and Labor is considered an example of a policy committee by Deering and Smith (1997), yet these findings suggest that it has some of the characteristics of a constituency committee. Our finding is not especially surprising considering our analysis of motivations, which suggests that Democrats, in particular, evidence constituency-oriented reasons for seeking assignment to the committee; our sample did not include any Republican requests, but our casual impression of the requests is that requests for Education and Labor from Republicans are motivated, at least partly, by constituency concerns.

Results for Merchant Marine hint that members who request these committees are unrepresentative of all requesting members. Incumbent Democratic and first-term Republican requesters for Merchant Marine are no more likely to be from coastal districts than are other members. This finding is somewhat surprising given the tendency of the literature to point to Merchant Marine as the typical constituency-oriented committee, but considering our findings in chapter 3—which suggest that Democrats, in particular, expressed mixed motivations for pursuing an assignment to the committee—it is perhaps less surprising.

Results for Energy and Commerce suggest support for the hypothesis among incumbent Republicans who tend to represent districts with higher percentages of constituents involved in retail or wholesale trade than districts represented by other requesters. Here again, our results in the preceding chapter are instructive: Democrats expressed mixed constituency-policy motivations for seeking the committee, whereas Republicans sought the committee for constituency reasons.

Most of the p-values for members seeking membership on Banking do not suggest that committee requesters are unrepresentative of all requesters (five of thirty-six, 13.9 percent, are significant). However, first-term requesters of both parties seem to come from more highly urbanized districts, likely because the committee had jurisdiction over programs related to the Department of Housing and Urban Development (HUD), many of which benefit urban areas. Charles Schumer (D-NY) expressed his interest in the committee by citing precisely this concern: "The banking committee is my strong first choice. Not only does the banking committee handle the New York City loan guarantees, but it also has jurisdiction over UDAG, CDBG [Urban Development Action Grant and Community Development Block Grant] and housing grants, which are a prime concern to my district."[9] All of the other results for Banking suggest that there is not uniform demand for this committee within either party. It seems generally plausible to consider this a policy-oriented committee.

Results for the remaining six committees (Government Operations, Judiciary, Post Office, Public Works, Science, Small Business, and Veterans' Affairs) do not appear to support the self-selection expectations of distributive theory. Few of the district measures indicate that requesters' districts are significantly different from those members who are not requesting the committee. This is perhaps especially surprising given that several of these committees—Public Works, Science, Small Business, and Veterans' Affairs—are widely considered to be constituency committees.

One way to evaluate the overall performance of the distributive theory is to consider the degree to which the p-values confirm or disconfirm the expectations of the theory. First, consider the p-values for all incumbents. Of the thirty-nine p-values presented for all incumbents, fourteen achieve significance at the .05 level (35.9 percent). Results for Democratic and Republican incumbents indicate much the same conclusion. Among Democratic incumbents, p-values reach the .05 level in eight of thirty-seven tests (21.6 percent). The overall results for incumbent Republicans are better: p-values reach the .05 level in twelve of thirty-seven tests (32.4 percent).

Next, consider the results among first-term requesters. Among all first-term members, tests achieve significance at the .05 level in seventeen of thirty-seven tests (45.9 percent). For first-term Democrats, the self-selection hypothesis is supported eleven out of thirty-four times at the .05 level (32.4 percent). Among first-term Republicans, support for the self-selection hypothesis is only slightly lower: nine out of thirty-three (27.3 percent) achieve statistical significance at the .05 level.

Our results suggest support for the assertion of our CAP framework, which suggests that district characteristics will influence committee requests under narrow conditions: When district interests are narrow and the policy jurisdiction of the committee neatly maps onto those interests, members will be drawn to those committees. In the majority of cases, one or both of these conditions do not hold, and we would expect to find only mild support for the district-request linkage. Four of the fifteen committees considered here (26.7 percent) are requested by members who come from districts with distinct policy interests that are addressed by the committee: Agriculture, Armed Services, Foreign Affairs, and Interior. Constituency interests may be linked to request behavior in three additional committees: Education and Labor, Energy and Commerce, and Merchant Marine. Thus, assuming the most liberal interpretation of our results (the interpretation that would be most charitable to distributive theory and the self-selection hypothesis), request behavior related to seven of these fifteen committees (46.7 percent) evidence constituency-related self-selection behavior on the part of requesting members.

These results represent modest support for the central assertion of distributive theory: Members gravitate to committees that reflect some dominant constituency interest. However, they also suggest that factors beyond narrow constituency concerns motivate member behavior, a finding that supports our analysis in chapter 3. It is worth pointing out that evidence supporting the constituency-based self-selecting behavior of member requests finds more support among the constituency committees than among the policy committees (Deering and Smith 1997). Of the 100 indicators used in the analysis of the constituency committees, 49 (49 percent) support the self-selection hypothesis, and 33 of 118 (28.0 percent) used in the analysis of policy committees support the self-selection hypothesis. To the degree that self-selection behavior is apparent in this analysis, it is more apparent among the constituency committees than it is among the policy committees.

In chapter 3 we conclude that committees can be classified as pure and as mixed-motivation committees. Considering these results in that context, we find a similarly strong relationship. Among those committees that we classify as attracting members based primarily on constituency concerns, thirty of sixty-eight (44.1 percent) of the indicators support the self-selection hypothesis; among mixed-motivation committees, four of twenty-one (19.0 percent) indicators are significant; and among policy committees, two of twenty-seven (7.4 percent) indicators are significant. The results within the parties evidence the same pattern: 43.3 percent (constituency), 25 percent (mixed), and 5.3 percent (policy) for Democrats, and 51.5 percent, 7.1 percent, and 12 percent for Republicans. These results are consistent with our findings in chapter 3.

INTEREST GROUP SCORES AND COMMITTEE REQUESTS

Krehbiel (1991) criticizes the use of geographic measures to determine member "interests." He contends that district-level measures obscure the fine distinction between district constituency and reelection constituency.

Members of Congress may, through their committee assignments, seek to appeal to a narrower reelection constituency that is attentive to the member's actions in Congress through his or her committee assignment. Actual voting behavior, as revealed in interest group scores that indicate a member's narrow, policy-specific interests, may provide a direct link between constituency interests and committee assignments.

Krehbiel examines the relationship between interest group scores and membership on several committees. The evidence, he suggests, provides little support for the distributive argument that members will seek assignment to committees that reflect their electoral interests. Krehbiel's approach has at least three shortcomings.[10] First, distributive theory holds that *interests* are causally prior to committee requests and assignments. By examining the relationship between interest group scores—which, at least in the case of first-term members, are calculated *after* the member has served on the committee—and committee assignments, Krehbiel threatens to reverse the causal direction of the argument. Furthermore, a sociological argument might be advanced that membership on the committee influences voting behavior: One is not a high demander until *after* joining the committee, where the member is socialized into the high-demanding behavior of the committee. Evidence linking interest group scores with committee membership might be evidence for a sociological rather than the rational choice argument. Second, examining committee membership ignores the possible influence of the committee assignment process. Members make requests for membership on committees but their assignment to committees is contingent on the assignment process. It is possible that the assignment process could either increase or decrease the number of members who are preference outliers on the committee. In short, failure to find a relationship reflects something about the assignment process rather than the behavior of requesting members. Third, Krehbiel examines only a small subset of committees and subcommittees, leaving the reader to wonder about the results for other committees.

We use our request data to reexamine Krehbiel's findings. By examining requests, we are able to purge many of the possible effects of the sociological problem, and completely purge the committee assignment problem. Additionally, we are able to examine all committees and compare the behavior of Democratic and Republican members. However, we can not solve the causal problem. The interest group scores are calculated after first-term members have requested and been assigned to committees. This is not the case for incumbent members, who have a voting history prior to their requests for changes in committee assignments. Thus, we need to be cognizant of differences between first-term and incumbent members that may reflect the influence of committee membership on interest group scores. Distributive theory suggests that the policy preferences of members requesting a given committee will differ significantly from those members who do not request that committee. As in the case of district characteristics, we expect a mild relationship between this measure of policy preferences and committee requests.

Table 4.5 presents the results of our analysis. Consistent with our analysis of district-level measures, these results suggest support for distributive theory for the Agriculture and Education and Labor committees, especially among first-term members. First-term members requesting the Agriculture Committee tend to support agriculture-related interest groups than do those who do not request the committee. This is especially true among first-term Republicans who request the committee. Republican support of these groups persists among incumbents but is not evidenced among Democrats. Likewise, first-term members requesting Education and Labor tend to be more responsive to education and labor interests relative to first-term members who do not request the committee. This tendency is less obvious among incumbents seeking assignment to the committee. Results for Armed Services also indicate some support for the expectations of distributive theory. First-term Republicans tend to be more supportive than nonrequesters of defense interests, and incumbent Democrats tend to be more supportive relative to all incumbent non-requesters. Finally, there is scattered evidence of possible self-selection behavior relative to Interior and possibly Banking.

These interest-related findings show less evidence of self-selection behavior among members than when district-level measures are used. Strong support for the proposition that the Agriculture Committee is the object of desire for members with agricultural interests in their districts

Table 4.5
Committee requests and interest group scores

Committee requested	First-term members				Incumbent members			
	Policy preferences measure[a]	All	Democrats	Republicans	Policy preferences measure[a]	All	Democrats	Republicans
Agriculture	AFBF	.003	.232	.032	AFBF	.103	.584	.045
	NFO	.043	.117	.008	NFO	.022	.235	.000
	NFU	.191	.348	.424	NFU	.245	.172	.006
Appropriations	CCUS	.384	.601	.042	CCUS	.362	.630	.721
	NTU	.590	.796	.495	NTU	.775	.992	.708
Armed Services	ASC	.158	.727	.010	ASC	.002	.015	.466
Banking	CCUS	.576	.623	.331	CCUS	.239	n/a	.469
	NFIB	.012	.523	1.0	NFIB	.910	n/a	.902
Budget	CCUS	.161	.483	.239	CCUS	.011	.296	.231
	NFIB	.927	.684	1.0	NFIB	.000	.145	1.0
	NTU	.236	.762	.038	NTU	.227	.821	.401
Education and Labor	AFT	.038	.357	n/a	AFT	n/a	n/a	n/a
	COPE	.411	.538	.233	COPE	.335	.308	n/a
	NEA	.001	.544	n/a	NEA	.297	.261	.038
	UAW	.000	.104	n/a	UAW	.002	.066	.032
Energy and Commerce	CCUS	.321	.992	.634	CCUS	.230	.145	.093
	LCV	.196	.361	.897	LCV	.549	.887	.071
Foreign Affairs	ASC	.411	.995	.606	ASC	.378	.336	.008

Government Operations	AFSCME	.057	n/a	.340	AFSCME	.702	.379	.747
Interior	CCUS	.138	.296	.435	CCUS	.094	.353	n/a
	LCV	**.049**	.427	**.037**	LCV	.693	.211	.192
Judiciary	LWV	.829	.751	.975	LWV	.699	.415	.783
Public Works	CCUS	.606	.977	n/a	CCUS	.460	.611	n/a
	LCV	.901	.324	.550	LCV	.736	.562	.162
Small Business	CCUS	n/a	n/a	.190	CCUS	n/a	n/a	.571
	NFIB	n/a	n/a	.290	NFIB	n/a	n/a	1.0
Ways and Means	CCUS	.031	.203	.515	CCUS	.832	.511	.380
	NFIB	.407	.753	1.0	NFIB	.815	.911	.584
	NTU	.771	.745	.566	NYU	.082	.132	.680

Note: Significance levels (p) for Monte Carlo difference-of-median tests. Number of simulations = 10,000. Random number seed = 2000000. Committes with no district-specific interest group score omitted.

Null Hypothesis: Committee assignment preferences are unrelated to policy preferences.

Bold	Monte Carlo $p < .05$ (two-tailed).
underline	Monte Carlo $p < .10$ (two-tailed).
none	Results fail to support high-demand hypothesis at either standard.
n/a	No or too few cases to draw a conclusion.

[a]Policy preferences measure acronyms: AFBF (American Farm Bureau Federation); AFSCME (American Federation of State, County, and Municipal Employees); AFT (American Federation of Teachers); ASC (American Security Council); CCUS (Chamber of Commerce of the United States); COPE (Committee on Political Education of the AFL-CIO); LCV (League of Conservation Voters); LWV (League of Women Voters); NEA (National Education Association); NFIB (National Federation of Independent Business); NFO (National Farmers' Organization); NFU (National Farmers' Union); NTU (National Taxpayers Union); UAW (United Auto Workers).

abounds, but evidence for other committees is less than overwhelming. Overall, the strongest indications of self-selecting behavior are evident in Armed Services and in Interior along with Agriculture; Education and Labor continues to be a question mark.

Our combined evidence to this point suggests that members' request behavior is consistent with a multiple-motivations approach; constituency characteristics do not seem to be particularly important determinants of request behavior. Our results indicate only mild support for both distributive and informational theories to the degree that these theories tend to focus on constituency-centered motivations. Though far from universal, self-selection seems to characterize the request behavior of members seeking membership on committees that offer the greatest opportunity to be responsive to focused constituencies within a district. It appears, however, that members' interests are heterogeneous—perhaps because it is difficult to identify a single dominant interest within their district—as informational theory suggests; mixed interests lead members to seek assignment to various committees they believe will advance their interest in reelection.

DISTRICT PROGRAMMATIC INTERESTS
AND COMMITTEE REQUESTS

Bruce A. Ray (1980, 1982a) has suggested that members of Congress (in particular, newly elected members) gravitate toward committees where there is already a significant federal presence in their district to keep those funds flowing to the district. By looking at past spending patterns in districts, it should be possible to predict the committees that members of Congress will request. The Ray thesis implies that members of the House will request membership on committees that have jurisdiction over programs that have delivered significant benefits to their districts in the past. In this case, Ray suggests that past federal-spending patterns in congressional districts—that is, how much money has been spent in the district in the past on federal programs—is the appropriate measure of constituency interest rather than the demographic and policy-oriented measures employed above. In this section, we seek to determine the linkage between spending patterns and committee request behavior.

Spending Data

District-specific spending data were compiled by Kenneth Bickers and Robert Stein from the Federal Assistance Awards Data System (FAADS).[11] These data represent spending from federal direct-assistance programs to congressional districts. Excluded expenditures include transfer payments and contingent liability programs, such as federal insurance programs. In its disaggregated form, the data contain records of individual transactions between departmental programs and district-level expenditures. Each record in the dataset contains information on the district receiving the award, the department and program responsible for the outlay, the number of awards, new awards, and total outlays through the department and program. For our purposes, we aggregate these data by the federal department responsible for the awards and expenditures to each district and by Congress for the 98th through the 103rd Congresses. In turn, we combine our committee request data with the Bickers and Stein data on district awards and expenditures.

A Test of the Ray Thesis

The Ray thesis holds that members of Congress will gravitate to committees that have jurisdiction over programs that are important to their constituencies. To test this hypothesis, we seek to determine whether individual requests for committee assignments come from members whose districts have disproportionately benefited from programs within the jurisdiction of the requested committee in the preceding Congress. We operationalize the independent variable in two ways: first, the *number* of department-specific awards to the district in the Congress preceding the member's committee request; and second, the logged *value* of all district-specific awards to the district in the Congress preceding the member's committee request. Values are logged because of the large interdistrict variances in the data. We employ the same difference-of-median methodology that we have used throughout the chapter's analysis.

Table 4.6 displays the results of the Monte Carlo simulation based on the number of new awards. Consider first the findings for the analysis of all members. Five of the nine committees evidence support for the Ray hypothesis: Agriculture, Public Works, Science, Energy and Commerce.

Table 4.6

Correlations between committee requests and number of department-specific awards

Committee type[a]		Number of awards$_{t-1}$		
	Committee • Department	All members	Democrats	Republicans
Constituency	**Agriculture** • *Agriculture*	**+.02**	.27	**+.01**
	Armed Services • *Defense*	.12	.49	<u>+.08</u>
	Interior • *Interior*	.27	.14	.28
	Public Works • *Transportation*	**+.01**	<u>+.06</u>	**+.02**
	Science • *NASA*	**+.01**	.50	**+.001**
	Small Business • *SBA*	.37	.16	.40
Policy	**Banking** • *HUD*	.23	<u>+.09</u>	.39
	Education and Labor • *Education*	.39	.25	<u>+.09</u>
	• *Labor*	.31	.45	.13
	Energy and Commerce • *Commerce*	**+.02**	**+.02**	.46
	• *Energy*	.18	.18	.45
	• *NRC*	**+.01**	**+.04**	.23

Note: Significance levels (*p*) for Monte Carlo difference-of-median tests. Number of simulations = 10,000. Random number seed = 2000000. Data on department-specific awards from Kenneth Bickers and Robert Stein. (See http://www.polsci.indiana.edu/faad/ for details.) Committees with no district-specific awards in the year prior to the assignment request by department are omitted.

Null Hypothesis: Committee assignment preferences are unrelated to past awards to the district.

bold   Monte Carlo *p* < .05 (one-tailed)

<u>underline</u>   Monte Carlo *p* < .10 (one-tailed)

none   Results fail to support distributive model hypothesis at either standard.

n/a   No or too few cases to draw a conclusion.

+   Districts of members significantly overrepresentative of characteristic (as presented by distributive theory).

–   Districts of members significantly underrepresentative of characteristic (contrary to prediction of distributive theory).

Sign omitted if critical *p* is not significant.

[a]Categories based on the committee typology developed by Deering and Smith (1997).

The remaining committees indicate little or no support for the hypothesis that members will request committees that have jurisdiction over programs of import for their constituencies.

Comparative analysis of request behavior by party suggests interesting interparty differences. Requests for Public Works suggests that Democratic requesters' districts are receiving significantly more programmatic benefits than nonrequesting Democrats, though the support is relatively weak. Stronger support for the Ray thesis comes from Energy and Commerce, where Democratic requesters' districts seem to be benefiting significantly more from programs administered by several departments within Energy and Commerce's jurisdiction.

Among Republicans, on the other hand, the results suggest strong support for the Ray thesis for three committees: Agriculture, Public Works, and Science. Republicans requesting these committees represent districts that have received a larger number of programmatic awards from departments within the committees' jurisdiction than nonrequesting members. Here it is interesting to note that the analysis for Republican members does reflect the classic distinction between constituency and policy committees: all three of the committees that support the analysis are classic constituency-oriented committees.

Table 4.7 presents the same analysis using logged department-specific outlays. The overall results are even less flattering for the Ray thesis and the expectations of the distributive model. Only those members who requested Agriculture and Energy and Commerce hailed from districts that benefited from higher median levels of outlays than those who did not request the committee.

However, the interparty comparisons reveal interesting results. Democrats requesting Banking were more likely than nonrequesting Democrats to come from districts that received higher median levels of HUD funding. More interesting yet, similar to the results in table 4.5, Republicans requesting Armed Services, Public Works, Science, Education and Labor, and Banking had higher median district expenditures from relevant departments than nonrequesting Republicans.

• • •

By examining the relationship between district characteristics and committee requests using objective measures of constituency interest,

TABLE 4.7

Correlations between committee requests and number of department-specific awards

Committee type[a]		Committee • Department	Logged outlays$_{t-1}$		
			All members	Democrats	Republicans
Constituency		**Agriculture** • *Agriculture*	**+.000**	**+.003**	**+.03**
		Armed Services • *Defense*	.18	.24	**+.04**
		Interior • *Interior*	.22	.42	.24
		Public Works • *Transportation*	.11	.21	<u>+.09</u>
		Science • *NASA*	.11	.27	**+.05**
		Small Business • *SBA*	.41	.13	.23
Policy		**Banking** • *HUD*	.12	<u>+.08</u>	**+.05**
		Education and Labor • *Education*	.44	.24	**+.03**
		• *Labor*	.22	.20	.35
		Energy and Commerce • *Commerce*	**+.02**	**+.01**	.24
		• *Energy*	.25	.35	.44
		• *NRC*	.39	.29	.15

Note: Significance levels (*p*) for Monte Carlo difference-of-median tests. Number of simulations = 10,000. Random number seed = 2000000. Data on department-specific awards from Kenneth Bickers and Robert Stein. (See http://www.polsci.indiana.edu/faad/ for details.) Committees with no district-specific outlays in the year prior to the assignment request by department are omitted.

Null Hypothesis: Committee assignment preferences are unrelated to past awards to the district.

bold	Monte Carlo *p* < .05 (one-tailed)
<u>underline</u>	Monte Carlo *p* < .10 (one-tailed)
none	Results fail to support distributive model hypothesis at either standard.
n/a	No or too few cases to draw a conclusion.
+	Districts of members significantly overrepresentative of characteristic (as presented by distributive theory).
–	Districts of members significantly underrepresentative of characteristic (contrary to prediction of distributive theory).

Sign omitted if critical *p* is not significant.

[a]Categories based on the committee typology developed by Deering and Smith (1997).

the relationship between policy interests and committee requests, and the programmatic interests of the district and committee requests, we find support for our contention that members are driven by mixed motivations to pursue committee assignments, but only mild support for constituency-driven explanations of request behavior.

Our results clearly suggest that requests for the Agriculture Committee are heavily influenced by constituency considerations (regardless of the measure employed); Agriculture's status as the stereotypical constituency committee remains unchallenged by our findings. District interests are also influential in motivating members to pursue an assignment to Armed Services. Programmatic concerns seem to be more prevalent among Republican requesters than among Democratic requesters. Requests for another committee that is often considered a typical constituency committee, Interior, seem primarily motivated by district interests rather than programmatic concerns.

Three other committees provide mixed evidence. Requests for Public Works—often considered a constituency committee—did not generally come from members motivated by relevant district characteristics; often requests came from members whose districts have been the target of past Department of Transportation awards, regardless of party. Requests for Banking—considered a policy committee—generally did not come from members representing homogeneous district interests, but requests did tend to come from members representing districts that had benefited from HUD spending in the past. Similarly, requests for Energy and Commerce were not related to district interests, but Democratic requesters tended to come from districts that had benefited from past spending by the Department of Commerce.

Results for the remaining committees are mixed. Although this analysis shows moderate support for the assertion that committee requests are driven by constituency concerns, our results suggest that a general theory based on this assumption, as attractive as the assumption might be, is built upon a foundation that has less-than-overwhelming support. This conclusion is buttressed by our discussion of member motivations in chapter 3, which suggests that requests often do not reflect narrow constituency concerns.

ASSIGNMENT SUCCESS

Distributive theory is particularly reliant on the assumption that the committee assignment process largely accommodates the committee requests of members; not only do members gravitate toward similar types of committees, but they are assigned to those committees by compliant party leaders. It is frequently taken for granted that members receive the committees that they request.[12] In table 4.8, we examine members' first committee requests and their success at achieving an assignment to their preferred committee.

Table 4.8 shows mixed support for the assumption that member requests are routinely accommodated. More often than not, members *do not* receive their preferred committee assignment. First-term members tend to have a better chance of getting a slot on a preferred committee overall (48.3 percent versus 39.4 percent for incumbents). This pattern is consistent across parties. First-term Democrats are more likely to receive a requested committee than are incumbent Democrats (54.1 percent versus 48.9 percent, respectively), and first-term Republicans are more likely to receive a preferred committee assignment than are incumbent Republicans (39.2 percent versus 31.1 percent, respectively).

Interparty comparison indicates that Democrats were more likely to receive a preferred assignment than are Republicans. First-term Democrats are more likely to receive their preferred committee assignment relative to first-term Republicans (54.1 percent and 39.2 percent). Likewise, incumbent Democrats are far more successful than their Republican counterparts are at receiving their preferred committee assignment (48.9 percent to 31.1 percent).

Interparty differences are relatively easy to explain. As the majority party throughout this period, Democrats had more flexibility in responding to the demands of their members through manipulation of committee ratios and the overall size of the committees. What is less obvious, and more vexing, is the discrepancy between our findings and those of previous studies. David W. Rohde and Kenneth A. Shepsle (1973) used Democratic committee request data from 1959, 1961, 1963, and 1967 to conclude that 46 percent of first-term Democrats and 39 percent of Democratic incumbents received their first-choice committee.

Using a longer dataset (1961–1973), Shepsle (1978) increased the figure to 58 percent for newly elected members. Irwin N. Gertzog (1976) found that 70 percent of newly elected members of the 89th, 90th, and 91st Congresses received their first-choice committee. Steven S. Smith and Bruce A. Ray (1983) found that 62.9 percent of Democratic first-term members were successful in the 95th through 97th Congresses. Using the longest time series yet (86th through 97th Congresses, with the 91st omitted), Cox and McCubbins (1993b) found that roughly 60 percent of Democratic first-term members received their first-choice assignment at some point during their first Congress, and about 55 percent of transfer requests were accommodated. Taken together, these studies find that about 60 percent of first-term Democrats, and 47 percent of incumbent Democrats, are granted preferred assignments. These estimates are somewhat higher than ours are, and the former is substantially higher; these numbers are also much different from our findings among Republican members.

Our results differ from the results of previous studies for four reasons. First, Gertzog (1976) relies on interview data of members *after* committee assignments have been made to determine member preferences. Members of Congress (and their staff) may be unwilling to admit that they were assigned to a committee that was not their first choice, and may seek to rationalize their committee assignment relative to their constituents' concerns.[13] This tendency inflates the success rate reported by Gertzog.

A second study (Smith and Ray 1983) relies on committee-on-committees ballot totals to determine member committee requests and as such excludes members who are not nominated by the committee on committees for their preferred assignment. Third, with the exception of Gertzog, all the studies that report success ratios of first-term and incumbent members exclude the minority party (Republicans in all cases) from request data collected, artificially inflating the success rate of committee aspirants. Finally, previous conclusions have been based on data limited to eleven Congresses at most.

The perception of self-selection has been further exaggerated by several studies that express success in terms of a member receiving *any* requested committee (Shepsle 1978; Weingast and Marshall 1988), which overestimates support for the self-selection hypothesis.[14] This approach

TABLE 4.8

Committee request success

Committees[a]

		All members				Democrats				Republicans			
		First-term		Incumbent		First-term		Incumbent		First-term		Incumbent	
	Committee requested	Request denied	Request granted	Request denied	Request granted	Request denied	Request granted	Request denied	Request granted	Request denied	Request granted	Request denied	Request granted
Service	District of Columbia	—	1 100%	7 43.8%	9 56.3%	—	1 100%	5 38.5%	8 61.5%	—	—	2 66.7%	1 33.3%
	House Administration	1 100%	—	11 55.0%	9 45.0%	1 100%	—	6 54.5%	5 45.5%	—	—	5 55.6%	4 44.4%
	Post Office	—	7 100%	6 75.0%	2 25.0%	—	6 100%	4 66.7%	2 33.3%	—	—	2 100%	—
	Ethics	—	—	1 33.3%	2 66.7%	—	—	—	—	—	—	1 33.3%	2 66.7%
	Service committee totals	1 11.1%	8 88.9%	25 53.2%	22 46.8%	1 12.5%	7 87.5%	15 50.0%	15 50.0%	—	—	10 58.8%	7 41.2%
Constituency	Agriculture	35 25.4%	103 74.6%	13 40.6%	19 59.4%	20 25.3%	59 74.7%	4 28.6%	10 71.4%	15 25.4%	44 74.6%	9 50.0%	9 50.0%
	Armed Services	50 45.0%	61 55.0%	48 54.5%	40 45.5%	27 39.1%	42 60.9%	8 25.0%	24 75.0%	23 54.8%	19 45.2%	40 71.4%	16 28.6%
	Interior	10 20.4%	39 79.6%	37 58.7%	26 41.3%	9 29.0%	22 71.0%	14 42.4%	19 57.6%	1 5.6%	17 94.4%	23 76.7%	7 23.3%
	Merchant Marine	1 10.0%	9 90.0%	12 50.0%	12 50.0%	1 20.0%	4 80.0%	9 52.9%	8 47.1%	—	5 100%	3 42.9%	4 57.1%
	Public Works	22 27.8%	57 72.2%	11 47.8%	12 52.2%	17 27.4%	45 72.6%	5 41.7%	7 58.3%	5 29.4%	12 70.6%	6 54.5%	5 45.5%
	Science ,	10 35.7%	18 64.3%	13 41.9%	18 58.1%	3 21.4%	11 78.6%	3 23.1%	10 76.9%	7 50.0%	7 50.0%	10 55.6%	8 44.4%
	Small Business	1 100%	—	6 60.0%	4 40.0%	1 100%	—	—	—	—	—	6 60.0%	4 40.0%
	Veterans' Affairs	—	2 100%	3 37.5%	5 62.5%	1 100%	—	2 40.0%	3 60.0%	—	1 100%	1 33.3%	2 66.7%
	Constituency committee totals	129 30.8%	289 69.5%	143 51.3%	136 48.7%	79 30.2%	183 69.8%	45 35.7%	81 64.3%	51 32.7%	105 67.3%	98 64.1%	55 35.9%

Committee												
Policy												
Banking	30 / 31.9%	64 / 68.1%	11 / 61.1%	7 / 38.9%	22 / 31.0%	49 / 69.0%	—	4 / 100%	8 / 34.8%	15 / 65.2%	11 / 78.6%	3 / 21.4%
Education and Labor	16 / 29.6%	38 / 70.4%	6 / 54.5%	5 / 45.5%	12 / 27.3%	32 / 72.7%	3 / 37.5%	5 / 62.5%	4 / 40.0%	6 / 60.0%	3 / 100%	—
Energy and Commerce	143 / 68.4%	66 / 31.6%	79 / 71.8%	31 / 28.2%	79 / 63.2%	46 / 36.8%	49 / 76.6%	15 / 23.4%	64 / 76.2%	20 / 23.8%	30 / 65.2%	16 / 34.8%
Foreign Affairs	49 / 65.3%	26 / 34.7%	63 / 55.8%	50 / 44.2%	22 / 51.2%	21 / 48.8%	11 / 34.4%	21 / 65.6%	27 / 84.4%	5 / 15.6%	52 / 64.2%	29 / 35.8%
Government Operations	2 / 33.3%	4 / 66.7%	25 / 67.6%	12 / 32.4%	2 / 50.0%	2 / 50.0%	15 / 62.5%	9 / 37.5%	—	2 / 100%	10 / 76.9%	3 / 23.1%
Judiciary	24 / 42.9%	32 / 57.1%	7 / 41.2%	10 / 58.8%	13 / 46.4%	15 / 53.6%	3 / 33.3%	6 / 66.7%	11 / 39.3%	17 / 60.7%	4 / 50.0%	4 / 50.0%
Policy committee totals	264 / 53.4%	230 / 46.6%	191 / 62.4%	115 / 37.6%	150 / 47.6%	165 / 52.4%	81 / 57.4%	60 / 42.6%	114 / 63.7%	65 / 36.3%	110 / 66.6%	55 / 33.3%
Influence												
Appropriations	119 / 83.2%	24 / 16.8%	162 / 60.2%	107 / 39.8%	55 / 73.3%	20 / 26.7%	73 / 53.3%	64 / 46.7%	64 / 94.1%	4 / 5.9%	89 / 67.4%	43 / 32.6%
Budget	7 / 70.0%	3 / 30.0%	103 / 64.4%	57 / 35.6%	4 / 80.0%	1 / 20.0%	71 / 59.7%	48 / 40.3%	3 / 60.0%	2 / 40.0%	32 / 78.0%	9 / 22.0%
Rules	6 / 85.7%	1 / 14.3%	50 / 76.9%	15 / 23.1%	3 / 75.0%	1 / 25.0%	11 / 52.4%	10 / 47.6%	3 / 100%	—	39 / 88.6%	5 / 11.4%
Ways and Means	75 / 91.5%	7 / 8.5%	124 / 64.9%	67 / 35.1%	35 / 83.3%	7 / 16.7%	39 / 48.1%	42 / 51.9%	40 / 100%	—	85 / 77.3%	25 / 22.7%
Influence committee totals	207 / 85.5%	35 / 14.5%	439 / 64.1%	246 / 35.9%	97 / 76.9%	29 / 23.1%	194 / 54.2%	164 / 45.8%	110 / 94.8%	6 / 5.2%	245 / 75.2%	82 / 24.8%
Column totals	601 / 51.7%	562 / 48.3%	798 / 60.6%	519 / 39.4%	327 / 45.9%	384 / 54.1%	335 / 51.1%	320 / 48.9%	275 / 61.0%	176 / 39.0%	463 / 69.9%	199 / 31.1%

Note: Percentages are row percentages within categories.
[a] Categories based on the committee typology developed by Deering and Smith (1997).

increases the likelihood of a member being "successful": The more committees a member asks for, the more likely that member will be assigned
to one of those requested. This is especially true if the member submits
a lengthy list of committees; a member who listed all committees in
order of preference would have a 100 percent chance of receiving a
"preferred" committee.[15]

Table 4.8 also presents substantial variation across committees in the
accommodation of requests. First-term members who request an appointment to a constituency committee tend to have the greatest amount of
success compared with policy and influence committee requests (69
percent success for constituency committees compared with 46.6 percent
and 11.9 percent for policy and influence committees). This same pattern
holds within parties, with requests for constituency committees being
granted more often than requests for policy or influence committees.
The pattern generally holds for incumbents and across parties. In short,
the party committees are more likely to accommodate members' requests
for the constituency committees compared with the other committees in
Congress. These, in turn, are the same committees that are most likely to
draw requests from members with focused interests within their districts.

Consideration of interparty differences regarding specific committees
also suggests interesting patterns. Among Democrats, especially first-
term members, the party leadership does a reasonable job of responding
to requests for constituency committee requests. The same is generally
true for the Republican leadership, with the exception of Armed Services.
As a popular committee eliciting a great deal of demand from both first-
term and incumbent members, the leadership was not successful at
meeting demands for this committee; Energy and Commerce and Foreign
Affairs, among the policy committees, presented problems for the leadership in both parties, as is indicated by the high rate of denials for these
committees. Assignment to these committees represented a special challenge for Republicans in particular, with 70.0 percent being denied a
seat on Foreign Affairs (a very popular request in the Republican ranks),
and 72.3 percent being denied a seat on Energy and Commerce. In short,
while the committee assignment process seeks to accommodate members'
preferences, it is by no means perfect. In fact, our analysis suggests that
denial is as likely as success, contrary to the findings of others.

VARIATION IN OVERALL REQUEST SUCCESS

The analysis presented above assumes that request success does not vary over time. Our data allow us to determine whether the responsiveness of the assignment process to member demands has changed in significant ways over time. Figure 4.3 illustrates the proportion of first committee requests that were satisfied by Congress. Immediately apparent in the graph is the fact that Democrats over this period had greater success achieving a preferred committee relative to their Republican counterparts. Also apparent is some year-to-year variation in request success, no doubt attributable to a combination of individual requests and intraparty turnover due to retirements and electoral defeats. Most striking, however, is a secular decline in the overall success rates, in both parties, over the period. An ocular test—that is, just eyeballing it—suggests that the decline begins around the 93rd or 94th Congress and is more precipitous among Republicans than among Democrats.

To better understand this puzzle, we separate the two partisan series by electoral status. It is possible that the decline evident in figure 4.3 is the result of the declining fortunes of either first-term members or incumbents in receiving an assignment. Figure 4.4 is an illustration of this pattern among first-term members of the two parties; figure 4.5 illustrates the pattern among incumbents. Careful consideration of these two series suggests two things. First, the pattern persists regardless of electoral status, and Republicans are less likely to be successful than their Democratic colleagues. Second, the decline of success appears to be more acute among incumbents than among first-term members.

Several alternative explanations present themselves. It might be that the Democratic leadership was becoming less likely to increase the size of committees to accommodate members' demands for committee assignments. This explanation fails to comport with the data, which indicate that there has been a constant and linear increase in the number of committee slots over the entire period.

A second possibility suggests some central role for the individual party leaders over the period. Table 4.9 indicates the success rates of members during the regime of each leader. The results suggest that there is substantial variation from regime to regime in both parties.

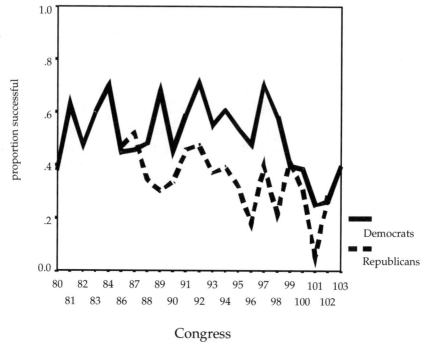

Congress

Figure 4.3. Proportion of successful committee requests, all members, by party and Congress. Data on member requests are drawn from committee-on-committees briefing books and committee request letters. Data for Democrats include all Congresses from the 80th through the 103rd, with the exception of the 85th. Data for Republicans range from the 85th Congress through the 102nd.

More important, the results suggest that a significant shift took place around the 94th Congress. Prior to the 94th Congress, 57 percent of Democrats were successful in receiving their preferred committee assignment. Beginning with the 94th Congress, the success rate dropped a full 10 percent. Success was higher than the mean when O'Neill was Speaker, though still below the previous period; significantly lower under Wright; and only marginally improved under Thomas S. Foley (D-WA). A similar pattern is apparent among Republicans. Prior to the 93rd Congress, 41 percent of Republicans were successful in receiving their first committee request; after the 93rd Congress, only 30 percent on average received their preferred request.[16] Rates of success under Rhodes and Michel were about equally poor.

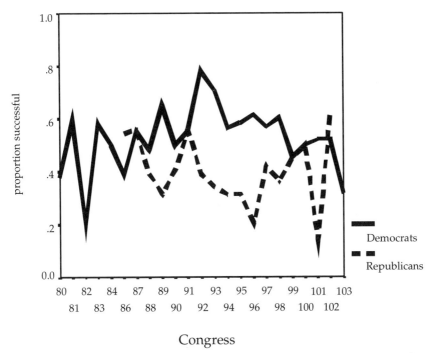

Congress

Figure 4.4. Proportion of successful committee requests, first-term members, by party and Congress. Data on member requests are drawn from committee-on-committees briefing books and committee request letters. Data for Democrats include all Congresses from the 80th through the 103rd, with the exception of the 85th. Data for Republicans range from the 85th Congress through the 102nd.

A systemic shift apparently occurred over this period. We suggest that a confluence of two factors produced this shift. First, the reforms in the Democratic Party in the late 1960s and early 1970s appeared to many as a rejection of the seniority system, creating an atmosphere of greater democratization of the institution, in this case, in the committee assignment process. Democrats committed to placing at least one first-term member on several of the influence committees, increasing hope that first-term members would have broader access to committees that were well outside of their grasp to that point. This would lead to an increased number of requests from first-term Democrats for more valuable committee assignments. Incumbents, on the other hand, had reason to believe that they would be able to advance more rapidly than had

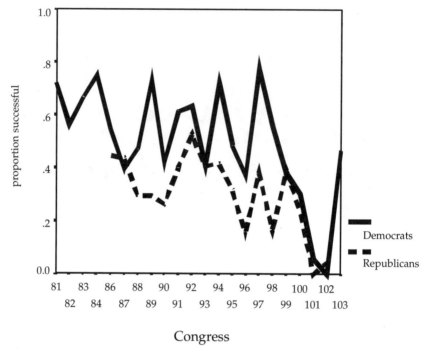

Congress

Figure 4.5. Proportion of successful committee requests, incumbents, by party and Congress. Data on member requests are drawn from committee-on-committees briefing books and committee request letters. Data for Democrats include all Congresses from the 80th through the 103rd, with the exception of the 85th. Data for Republicans range from the 85th Congress through the 102nd.

happened in the past. Although there was no concomitant reform movement within the Republican Party, the general atmosphere of democratization infected junior members of the GOP as well, leading to heightened expectations about committee assignments.

Equally important during this period were the ballooning federal deficits. Beginning with the "guns and butter" policies of Lyndon Johnson in the 1960s, through the stagflation of the 1970s, and climaxing with the tax cuts and increasing military spending of the 1980s and early 1990s, federal budget deficits were becoming increasingly important in congressional politics. With revenue in short supply, service on the authorizing committees held less value for members, and the value of seats on the money committees (Ways and Means and Appropriations,

TABLE 4.9
Request success differences by leadership regime

Democrats

Committee on Committees	Chair	Congresses	Mean success (%)	N	
Ways and Means	Robert L. Doughton	80–82	55	139	Mean 80th–93rd
Ways and Means	Jere Cooper[a]	83–85	67	55	
Ways and Means	Wilbur Mills	86–93	56	427	57%
Steering and Policy	Carl Albert	94	61	94	Mean 94th–103rd
Steering and Policy	Tip O'Neill	95–99	54	365	
Steering and Policy	Jim Wright	100–101	32	113	47%
Steering and Policy	Tom Foley	101–103	36	173	

Republicans

Committee on Committees	Chair	Congresses	Mean success (%)	N	
Executive Committee	Charles Halleck	86–91	44	143	Mean 86th–92nd
Executive Committee	Gerald R. Ford	89–92	39	240	41%
Executive Committee	John J. Rhodes	93–96	31	259	Mean 93rd–102nd
Executive Committee	Robert H. Michel	97–103	29	472	30%

[a] As ranking member of Ways and Means, Jere Cooper chaired the committee on committees in the 83rd Congress.

TABLE 4.10
Influence committee requests (pre- and postreform Congress)

	Democrats			Republicans		
Prereform	*All*	*First-term*	*Incumbent*	*All*	*First-term*	*Incumbent*
Prereform Congresses	18.0%	9.1%	29.7%	32.0%	19.4%	43.3%
Post reform Congresses	49.0%	26.2%	72.0%	42.1%	34.4%	52.8%
Pre–post difference[a]	$t = 13.00$ ($p = .000$)	$t = 6.11$ ($p = .000$)	$t = 11.75$ ($p = .000$)	$t = 4.43$ ($p = .000$)	$t = 2.91$ ($p = .004$)	$t = 2.36$ ($p = .019$)

Note: Percentages are of members requesting an influence committee (Appropriations, Budget, Rules, or Ways and Means) as their first choice. Data on member requests are drawn from committee-on-committees briefing books and committee request letters. Data for Democrats include all Congresses from the 80th through the 103rd, with the exception of the 85th. Data for Republicans range from the 85th Congress through the 102nd.
[a]Difference-of-means test between pre-and postreform Congresses.

and to a lesser extent, Budget) increased. If an ambitious member of Congress wanted to have influence over policy, having one's hands on the purse strings of the federal government became increasingly important.

We hypothesize that these two factors led to an increase in requests for the influence committees and thus a decline in assignment success. Table 4.10 presents data on requests for influence committees among Democrats and Republicans in the pre- and post-reform eras. The results suggest support for our hypothesis.

Before the reforms, 18 percent of all Democratic members requested assignment to an influence committee; after the reforms, 49 percent sought assignment to an influence committee. The shift was most pronounced among incumbents (29.7 percent before the reforms, and 72 percent after the reforms). Of first-term Democrats, 9.1 percent requested an influence committee assignment before the forms, and 26.2 percent made such a request following the reforms.

A similar pattern is evident among Republicans, though it is less pronounced. Before the reforms, 32 percent of all Republicans requested influence committee assignments, increasing by 10 percent to 42.1 percent in the postreform period. The greatest increase among Republicans is among first-term members. Before the reform period, 19.4 percent of first-term Republicans requested an influence committee; following the reforms, 34.4 percent made such a request, an increase of 15 percent. An increase, albeit smaller, is also evident among incumbent Republicans.

• • •

The findings of this chapter and the previous chapter present significant support for the CAP framework. Members of Congress have multiple motivations for pursuing specific committee assignments. Although constituency concerns are important to congressional members, they also seek committee assignments as a means for pursuing policy influence and institutional influence. In this chapter and in the preceding chapter, we have focused on the linkage between members' motivations and their committee requests. Our findings are contrary to the assertion that members are primarily motivated by a single-minded pursuit of reelection. The findings presented in this chapter provide evidence that suggests only a modest linkage between constituency and request behavior, as the CAP framework posits, and largely fails to support two of the key assumptions of distributive theory. Committee request preferences, on average, are loosely related to constituency characteristics at best, and unrelated at worst. Four committees draw requests from members with well-defined constituency interests: Agriculture, Armed Services, Interior, and Foreign Affairs. Of the remaining committees, the constituency-preference nexus is unclear. A single behavioral assumption can only partly explain the ultimate composition of congressional committees. Members' committee requests are not, on average, routinely granted by their party committee on committees. For some committees, such as Agriculture and Interior, requests are granted with regularity, but for most other committees, demand within the party is an important variable, and many committees remain outside the reach of the majority of requesters.

CHAPTER FIVE

House Members and the Assignment Process

The committee selection process is totally narcissistic and totally egotistical.

SENIOR LEADERSHIP AIDE

G etting a good committee assignment becomes the central task of most new members of Congress upon election to the House. Improving one's committee assignments demands the attention of many incumbent members of Congress. The committee assignment process is a competitive process. One senior leadership aide attributed the source of the competition to the innate ambition of members of Congress; the committee assignment process becomes an arena for their ambition: "They went through grade school and high school, college; they were always achieving, and so they now see another means of achieving."[1] This observation was confirmed by a member of Congress who plotted for years to receive an assignment to the powerful Ways and Means Committee: "From day one I spent the next four years campaigning to get on the Ways and Means Committee. I don't think that a day went by that I didn't think, what do I need to do today, who do I need to talk to, who do I need to work with, who do I need to get credibility with so that I've got a shot at this."[2]

As the CAP framework and our previous discussion suggests, the committee assignment process will be an arena of intense competition among members of Congress who are seeking to pursue their goals within the constraints of a limited number of available committee slots. In considering committee requests and pursuing assignments, their understanding of the committee assignment process is revealing. In this chapter, we use content analysis (see appendix 2 for a discussion of the data) to systematically analyze the letters written by members seeking assignment to specific committees, to examine how members seek to convince their party committees that they should receive a preferred committee assignment. We take advantage of the fact that one dimension of these letters is that they seek to sell the member to the party leadership. In selling themselves, members will focus on the attributes that *they believe* are most important in the decision calculus of party leaders. By focusing on this dimension of the letters, our major goal is to engage in an ethnographic exercise. That is, we try to understand how participants in the assignment process understand the process by concentrating on what these members believe is important in the assignment process. This is consistent with the CAP framework. Members' beliefs about the assignment process may shape their requests and how they seek to influence the assignment process to secure a preferred request.

Christopher H. Achen and John S. Stolarek (1974) analyzed request letters from Democrats during the same congresses that Shepsle (1978) examined. Their results indicate that endorsements from colleagues and interest groups are the most common justification for receiving a desired committee assignment, followed by geographic considerations, electoral needs, and prior experience. Our findings—based on a much larger sample that includes Republican as well as Democratic members—suggest that members believe experience to be the most important factor in the committee assignment process, focusing on their own experience almost regardless of the type of committee they are pursuing. Experience is followed by geography and electoral needs. We find that these factors vary based on party and electoral status. Our discussion then turns to an examination of the relationship between members' background and their committee assignment requests. We conclude the chapter by examining four cases of members campaigning for a committee assignment that illustrate our quantitative findings in this chapter, support the findings of the previous chapters, and highlight the complexity that the CAP framework suggests.

MEMBER JUSTIFICATIONS FOR GETTING AN ASSIGNMENT

Our coding scheme classifies arguments in support of a preferred committee assignment into eight categories. Some members believe that an endorsement from relevant individuals or groups, either inside or outside Congress, may influence the process. Inside Congress, members may seek the endorsement of other influential members, the chair of the committee to which they aspire, their state delegation, or a special interest organization, such as the Congressional Black Caucus (CBC). Members may expend a substantial amount of effort lining up these endorsements. Their belief is that actors outside the committee on committees may sway support in their favor inside the committee. Charles Schumer's (D-NY) request for Banking is illustrative: "Mr. Reuss, the previous Chairman of the Banking Committee, and my state delegation, as well as Mayor Koch and Governor Carey support me in this effort."[3] In his quest for a seat on the Ways and Means Committee, Hank Brown (R-CO) solicited letters of support that were sent to members of the Executive Committee from more than a dozen special-interest groups.

Other members focus on geographic considerations. Some members focus on their claim as a state or regional replacement for a member who has departed from the committee; some members make the case that their state or their region deserves to have representation, or more representation, on a committee. In making this argument, members believe that a major factor in the assignment process is fair representation of states and regions on committees. During the 100th Congress, E. Clay Shaw (R-FL) argued for assignment to the Ways and Means Committee by focusing on regional fairness: "Over the past few years the Southeastern United States has incrementally lost Republican representations on the Ways and Means Committee. . . . [W]ith the loss of John Duncan, the Southeast is left with no representation. . . . I understand and recognize the interests of this region. I am confident that I can appropriately and fairly represent these interests on the Ways and Means Committee."[4]

The third category is arguments that focus on the electoral concerns of the member. These arguments usually center on the electoral vulnerability of the member, with the member arguing that a particular committee assignment is necessary to bolster his or her electoral fortunes. Occasionally members will focus on their electoral prowess. In making the vulnerability argument, the member expresses a belief that a major motivation for assigning members to committees is the desire of the party to maintain the number of seats that it has in the House by providing members with committee assignments that promote their reelection. Citing an impending challenge from the incumbent that he defeated, a newly elected David Drier (R-CA) requested assignment to Banking: "[I]t is . . . important that I be in the strongest possible position to face the 1982 election. This Committee assignment would certainly strengthen this effort."[5] Other members cite their electoral safety as an important an important consideration for the party committee. This is especially true when requesting assignment to the exclusive committees, as Jim Cooper (D-TN) argued to the DSPC: "I have a safe district with no real opposition after my first race in 1982. I can make tough votes without having to look over my shoulder."[6]

At times, members or their supporters may discuss the electoral significance of a committee assignment request in terms that go beyond the boundaries of a single district. Newly elected Congressman George H. W. Bush (R-TX) wrote to Minority Leader Ford on November 25, 1966, requesting a seat on Appropriations, stressing the electoral implications, not only in his district, but for Republicans in Texas and the entire South: "I think a major assignment of this nature would do a lot to encourage qualified people to run in our party not only in Texas but in other southern states. An assignment of this nature could be construed as a major encouragement to people in our part of the country to get active in the political arena—that rapid progress can be made in our party, etc. There is no member of this committee from any Southern State."[7]

Bush quickly altered his first committee request when it became apparent that Texas Democrats would lose representation on the Ways and Means Committee at the beginning of the 90th Congress. Bush again stressed the electoral implications of his assignment in a new letter to Ford, written December 6, 1966:

> It is likely that Texas will not be represented on the Democratic side of this Committee in the 90th Congress. Should this happen, there is tremendous mileage for the Republican Party in Texas, the President's home state, by putting a man on this important committee. It has long been said by the opposition in Texas that the only way to be effective is to be a Democrat. Saving a seat for Texas on Ways and Means would bring great credit to our party. It would, in my opinion, help show that the best bet for the future in Texas lies with the GOP.[8]

Bush was assigned to Ways and Means as a first-term member.

Many members focus their letters on their experience and how that experience can best be used in their committee assignment. These members believe that because the committee system is a division of labor, the party leadership will accommodate the natural talents of each individual by assigning members to the committees that best approximates their talents, promoting the overall ability of committees to produce good policy. Indeed, one newly elected member, Donald Mitchell (R-NY), went so far as to quote a political science textbook as evidence that experience was most important in the committee assignment process, in support of his request for a committee assignment:

> On page 169 of "The Job of a Congressman," by Tacheron and Udall, in discussing the importance of professional background in committee assignments, it states: "But all agreed that holding elective office, particularly a state legislative office, outweighed any other type of professional experience as a qualification for any committee assignment." . . . In the event this information is still relevant I would like to . . . request that I be appointed to the Armed Services Committee.[9]

Partisan loyalty is another factor some members believe to be important in the assignment process. Members who mention their loyalty to the party believe that the leadership rewards prior support of the party when making assignments. Seeking an assignment to Energy, Gerald

Kleczka (D-WI) argued that he understood "the importance of party unity, loyalty and support." He then offered evidence for his assertion: "I have consistently and steadfastly supported the leadership of my party on matters affecting party unity and control."[10]

The sixth category of argument is interest representation. Some members believe that party leaders are responsive to arguments that some interest is not represented on the committee and that their assignment can redress this shortcoming. Some members focus on their desire to support the White House, advancing the president's legislative priorities by serving on a committee. Finally, the eighth category of argument focuses on past requests that have not been satisfied by the party committee.

Distribution of Committee Request Justification

Table 5.1 illustrates the distribution of committee request justifications. Consider first the distribution among all members. About 80 percent of the justifications mentioned in the letters fall into one of three categories: experience, geography, or electoral considerations. Contrary to Achen and Stolarek (1974), endorsement is mentioned by only a small proportion of members (3.5 percent). By far, members mention their experience most often (42.8 percent) as a justification for placing them on a preferred committee. This indicates that many members involved in the assignment process believe that demonstrating expertise in the policy jurisdiction of the requested committee is an important element of the decision calculus. Turning to the aggregate results for the two parties, the distribution is apparent across parties. Regardless of party, the member's prior professional experience, geography, and electoral considerations, in that order, make up the majority of justifications.

There are two interesting interparty differences: Democrats are more likely to mention endorsements in their letters, and Republicans are more likely to focus on the fact that the committee was previously requested and denied. Both of these are consistent with earlier findings. Democrats tend to focus on endorsements because of their highly structured assignment process relative to Republicans during this period. State delegations often endorsed Democrats seeking assignment to a committee in an attempt to increase the likelihood of success. As chair of the Ways and Means Committee (and the DSPC), Wilbur Mills frequently encouraged members to obtain the endorsement of their state delegation. This interparty difference highlights the limits, evident in Achen and Stolarek, of focusing on a single party; inferences about Democratic behavior do not necessarily apply to Republican behavior. Republicans mention having previously made a request for the committee because first-term Republicans had a pronounced tendency to request assignments they are unlikely to get; thus, they later mention their lack of success in previous years. Republicans were also less likely to receive a preferred assignment overall, often having to be satisfied with committees that they did not request; therefore, they are more likely to return to the process with hard-luck stories to convince the leadership to grant their request.

Examining intraparty differences also reveals interesting patterns. First-term Democrats are more likely to mention experience and electoral concerns than are their incumbent colleagues. Of first-term Democrats, 45.2 percent mention experience, compared with 33.3 percent of incumbent Democrats. A decrease of similar magnitude is present among the Republicans. This may reflect a learning process in which some members come to the realization that committee assignments do not necessarily go to the most experienced members, but go instead to members who have other attributes of interest to the party committee. Electoral concerns similarly decline among first-term members of both parties. It is likely that following a successful reelection campaign, members are less concerned about their electoral future. Incumbents of both parties were more likely than their junior colleagues were to point to partisanship as an important attribute, probably because junior members do not have a history of party loyalty in the House, and party loyalty in other capacities may not be considered credible.

Table 5.2 presents data for examining the assertion that members of Congress may engage in making different arguments to their party committees based on the committee they are requesting; members may believe that some arguments are more likely to be persuasive than others. Consider first the results for all members. Several patterns are apparent. Two justifications dominate arguments for constituency-oriented committees: experience and geography, followed by arguments about electoral

TABLE 5.1
Committee request jutifications

Justification	All Members	Democrats			Republicans		
		All	*First-term*	*Incumbent*	*All*	*First-term*	*Incumbent*
Endorsement	23	23	11	12	5	1	4
	3.6%	6.8%	6.6%	7.3%	1.6%	0.7%	2.2%
Geography	159	89	43	46	70	27	43
	24.7%	26.5%	25.9%	27.9%	21.7%	19.5%	23.2%
Electoral concerns	95	50	34	16	45	25	20
	14.8%	14.9%	20.5%	9.7%	13.9%	18.1%	10.8%
Experience	280	130	75	55	150	75	75
	43.5%	38.7%	45.2%	33.3%	46.6%	54.3%	40.5%
Partisanship	48	25	3	22	23	6	17
	7.5%	7.4%	1.8%	13.3%	7.1%	4.3%	9.2%
Interest representation	14	13	5	8	1	1	—
	2.2%	3.9%	3.0%	4.8%	0.3%	0.7%	
White House	5	—	—	—	5	2	3
	0.7%				1.6%	1.4%	1.6%
Previous requests	29	6	—	6	23	—	23
	4.5%	1.8%		3.6%	7.1%		12.4%
Total	644	336	171	165	322	138[a]	185

Note: Justifications found in request letters from the 92nd, 93rd, 97th, 98th, 100th, and 101st Congresses.

[a] One case is excluded from the above classification. The new member argued that there was no dominant interest in his district, making him a good candidate for a seat on an influence committee.

concerns. This is inconsistent with what one might expect of appeals for assignment to a committee aimed at serving constituency interests. It might be argued that members would be reluctant to emphasize their personal electoral interest to the party leadership; however, this is one interest shared by party leaders and members: Both want to see the member reelected. A similar pattern is apparent among the policy committees and the influence committees, but several additional justifications are present in influence committee requests. In particular, party-related arguments are more common when a member requests an influence

committee. Apparently, members believe that assignments to these committees are strongly influenced by party leaders' concerns with controlling
the institutional agenda through these committees.

Among members of the two parties, the justifications cited by members
seeking committee assignments are similar. Experience and geography are
the most common arguments, regardless of committee type. Democrats,
however, are less likely than Republicans are to cite electoral concerns
in their pursuit of an influence committee assignment. Some Republicans
argued that they needed an assignment to an influence committee in
order to shore up electoral support in their district. This seems to indicate
that Republican requesters believe that the RCC tends to be more responsive to electoral arguments than to other arguments (except geography
and experience). Democrats are more likely than Republicans are to cite
the desire to represent a particular group interest on an influence committee; no Republicans mention interest representation as an important
reason for assigning them to a committee. This is not surprising given
the philosophical and electoral differences between the two parties.
Democrats tend to emphasize group representation as a means for
holding together their diverse electoral coalition; Republicans tend to
downplay the importance of individual groups, arguing that party
interests and policies benefit all groups equally. A few Republicans cite
their desire to help the White House to promote its policies as a reason
for assigning them to a committee. During the period covered by our
sample, Republicans held the White House exclusively; what is surprising
is that no Democrats mention their desire to oppose the policies of a
Republican president through their committee assignment. Republicans
are also more likely to justify their request by citing past attempts to be
assigned to the committee. This is especially true of the policy and influence committees.

In sum, members focus their arguments for committee assignments
on their experience and on geographic fairness, followed by electoral
considerations, regardless of committee type. Through these arguments,
we can gain insight into what members of Congress believe to be the
most important factors when party leaders make committee assignments.
Somewhat surprisingly, members seem to believe that electoral factors
do not dominate the decision process, though there is some difference

TABLE 5.2
Committee Type and Request Justification

Committee type	Justification—all members							
	Endorsement	*Geography*	*Electoral concerns*	*Experience*	*Partisanship*	*Interest representation*	*White House*	*Previous request*
Constituency	5	48	31	49	6	5	2	8
	21.7%	32.4%	34.1%	18.7%	13.0%	41.7%	40.0%	26.7%
Policy	8	41	26	103	8	1	1	9
	34.8%	27.7%	28.6%	18.3%	17.4%	8.3%	20.0%	30.0%
Influence	10	59	34	110	32	6	2	13
	43.5%	39.9%	37.4%	42.0%	69.6%	50.0%	40.0%	43.3%
Total	23	148	91	207	46	12	5	30
	Justification—Democrats							
Constituency	3	26	14	29	2	5	—	2
	16.7%	32.1%	29.8%	23.9%	8.3%	41.7%		33.3%
Policy	7	27	19	45	4	1	—	1
	38.9%	33.3%	40.4%	37.2%	16.7%	8.3%		16.7%
Influence	8	28	14	47	18	6	—	3
	44.4%	34.6%	29.8%	38.8%	75.0%	50.0%		50.0%
Total	18	81	47	121	24	12		6
	Justification—Republicans							
Constituency	2	22	17	20	4	—	2	6
	40.0%	32.8%	38.6%	14.2%	18.2%		40.0%	25.0%
Policy	1	14	7	58	4	—	1	8
	20.0%	20.9%	15.9%	41.1%	18.2%		20.0%	33.3%
Influence	2	31	20	63	14	—	2	10
	40.0%	46.3%	45.5%	44.7%	63.6%		40.0%	41.7%
Total	5	67	44	141	22		5	24

Note: Committee type derived from Deering and Smith (1997). Justifications found in request letters from the 92nd, 93rd, 97th, 100th, and 101st Congresses.

between the parties. As we demonstrate in chapter 8, electoral factors are somewhat important in the assignment process—but not as important as intuition might suggest—and the effect of electoral concerns varies between the two parties in ways that are consistent with that analysis.

EXPERIENCE AND COMMITTEE REQUESTS

Perhaps Members of Congress frequently cite past experience as a justification for being placed onto a requested committee because their employment experience is related to the committees they request. Table 5.3 presents the results of statistical analysis of the relationship between occupation and committee requests. Using biographical data on congressional members, we classified them into occupational categories (ICPSR and McKibbin 1997).[11] We matched these categories with committees according to the jurisdiction of the committee. For instance, the occupational thesis would hold that former farmers would be likely to gravitate toward the Agriculture Committee, and former military would be drawn to the Armed Services Committee. This approach betrays at least one potential weakness; members of Congress often gain experience in state and local government before ascending to the House. In many cases, members' references to "experience" relate to experience they have accrued during previous public service that is unrelated to their occupational history.

Shepsle's evidence (1978) indicates a linkage between occupational background for the Agriculture, Banking, Education and Labor, Energy and Commerce, and Judiciary committees in his analysis of Democratic requests. Our results suggest a more complex picture. Two committees evidence a strong linkage between occupational experience and committee requests: Agriculture and Judiciary. Former farmers are more likely to request assignment to Agriculture. The single exception to this general statement is that Republican incumbents who request Agriculture do not tend to be overrepresentative of farmers. Lawyers, regardless of party or electoral status, are likely to request assignment to Judiciary. Evidence for the other three committees is mixed. Though the results are weak, Republican incumbents from financial backgrounds are overrepresented among those who request assignment to Banking. Slightly stronger are the results for Education and Labor. First-term Democrats with labor backgrounds are overrepresented among those requesting this committee, and weaker evidence suggests the same among Democratic incumbents; weak evidence also shows a linkage with those from educational backgrounds. First-term Republicans with teaching backgrounds

TABLE 5.3
Committee requests and previous occupations

Committee • Experience indicator	Incumbent			First-term		
	All	*Democrats*	*Republicans*	*All*	*Democrats*	*Republicans*
Agriculture						
• *Farming*	**.000**	**.021**	.610	**.000**	**.000**	**.000**
Armed Services						
• *Military*	.487	.709	.297	.595	.779	.157
Banking						
• *Finance (business)*	<u>.086</u>	1.0	<u>.054</u>	.176	.191	.168
Budget						
• *Finance (business)*	<u>.079</u>	1.0	.157	.375	1.0	.276
• *Industry (business)*	.244	.850	.303	1.0	.287	.661
Education and Labor						
• *Labor*	<u>.066</u>	<u>.052</u>	1.0	**.000**	**.000**	1.0
• *Education (teaching)*	1.0	1.0	1.0	**.005**	<u>.079</u>	.021
Energy and Commerce						
• *Health*	.128	**.045**	1.0	.101	.118	.623
Foreign Affairs						
• *Military*	.764	1.0	.902	1.0	.504	.353
Interior						
• *Natural resources*	.224	.145	1.0	1.0	1.0	1.0
Judiciary						
• *Lawyer*	**.000**	**.001**	**.004**	**.000**	**.000**	**.000**
Public Works						
• *Labor*	1.0	1.0	1.0	.620	.413	1.0
Science						
• *Military*	.856	.249	.151	.239	.102	1.0
• *Technical*	**.009**	1.0	**.005**	**.031**	.113	.164
Ways and Means						
• *Finance (business)*	.782	.648	1.0	.174	.713	.110
• *Industry (business)*	.824	1.0	.501	1.0	.619	1.0

Note: Data on occupations from ICPSR and Mckibbin (1997). Committees with no relevant prior occupation omitted. Number of simulations = 10,000. Random number see = 2000000. Null Hypothesis: Committee assignment preferences are unrelated to the members' previous occupation.

bold   Monte Carlo p < .05 (one-tailed)
<u>underline</u> Monte Carlo p < .10 (two-tailed)
none   Results fail to support hypothesis at either standard.

are overrepresented in requests for Education and Labor. Among Democratic incumbents, those with a health background are overrepresented among those requesting Energy and Commerce. Given that Shepsle examined only Democrats, these results are somewhat consistent with his findings.

We examine the relationship between occupational experience and committee requests for seven committees not considered by Shepsle: Armed Services, Budget, Foreign Affairs, Interior, Public Works, Science, and Ways and Means. Evidence for these committees does not provide support for the occupation-request hypothesis. The singular exception is Science. There is some evidence that members who formerly held technical occupations were overrepresented among those requesting Science. This seems especially true of incumbent Republicans who requested assignment to the committee.

THE VIEW FROM THE PARTY COMMITTEES

Many members place an emphasis on their experience in letters to the party committees. Our interviews with those who have been a part of the committee assignment process shed some light on what members of the party committees believe are the important factors influencing which members receive committee assignments.[12] There are substantial differences between the responses of members and staff of the two parties, and our interviews suggest there have been significant changes as the parties have reversed fortunes.

Members of the DSPC who served while the Democrats were in the majority generally agreed that electoral concerns were important in making committee assignments. According to one DSPC member, "If the member thinks that [a committee assignment] is important, then we would try to accommodate it if it is necessary for reelection."[13] However, electoral concerns compete with other factors, such as party loyalty, as Speaker Jim Wright claimed: "When the Steering and Policy Committee called on somebody to vote on something that is party policy. That's party policy. That's the second function of the Steering and Policy Committee."[14]

Before becoming the majority party, Republicans who served on the Executive Committee put high value on two variables: experience and geographic representation, with some concern for party loyalty. Republican members' beliefs tend reflect this, as measured in the letters. One long-serving member of the Republican Executive Committee mentioned as "the prime consideration: Is this person good? Is he or she going to be able to do the job?"[15] Experience was followed by a concern for geographic representation. One influential former member of the Executive Committee put it simply: "I felt very strongly about geography, just a good mix."[16] Another senior member confirmed this sentiment, acknowledging that regional accommodation was more of an art than a science: "We did worry about representativeness with respect to regions and states and so forth, and we would like to have the committees be relatively representative of what is out there. . . . We never tried to be perfectly representative with respect to region, or state, or size of state."[17] Members of the Executive Committee also mentioned some concern with party loyalty. Members needed to be "reasonably responsive to the rest of the caucus. . . . They didn't have to be slavishly loyal, but it was a good thing to know that if you really needed a vote, you could get one every once in a while."[18]

Upon becoming the minority in the House, a party weighs these factors differently, and this is true in both parties. According to one Democratic staff member who is well acquainted with the assignment process, while the Democrats were in the majority, geographic considerations were the most important factor in making committee assignments. Electoral considerations are most important now that Democrats are in the minority. Most members of the Democratic Caucus seem to understand that accommodating the electoral concerns of members, to maintain the number of Democratic seats in the House, is an important step toward regaining the majority. Party loyalty, in some respects, is emphasized less in the process than when the Democrats were in the majority. To accommodate the requests of Democrats who represent moderate or Republican-leaning districts, emphasis on party loyalty has been relaxed. As a senior staff member put it, "That is where the conservative Democrats, the Blue Dogs, were most upset. 'We come from . . . a district that votes heavily Republican, and they are going to decide who gets an exclusive committee on party loyalty? I am never going to be able to vote with the party as much as a member from Detroit, or Chicago, or San Francisco.'" The Democratic leadership has moderated demands for party loyalty while in the minority, and has sought to establish quotas for groups like the Blue Dogs, on influence committees in particular.[19] Members on both sides of the assignment process report that raising money for the party has also become an important influence on who receives important committee assignments.[20] A Democratic leadership aide claimed, "the money wasn't [a big factor] up until recently, as big as it is now . . . that's a newer twist in the last eight years."[21]

Conversely, the shift from majority to minority and the party-centered philosophy of the new Republican leadership means that there is now a high premium put on party loyalty, as there was among Democrats while they were in the majority. When asked what he believed was the most important factor in the assignment process, a leadership staff member replied that it was respect for the party agenda; the assignment process is now "more agenda driven. Being able to get things done in the House . . . that probably plays more."[22] A member of the Republican Steering Committee (formerly RCC) after the Republican takeover put it slightly differently: "I would describe it as being more of a team player. You just go on the acknowledgment that everybody has party loyalty, and nobody wants to hurt the party, but here are times when you need to be a team player." The question one asks oneself, she continued, is "has this person been a particular pain-in-the-you-know-what? And that happens very rarely, very rarely; but that is a consideration."[23]

Related to party loyalty, perhaps a part of what this member referred to as being a "team player," is a new consideration for those in party leadership positions: an emphasis on raising campaign funds to promote Republican congressional candidates. One staff member, beaming at the recent appointment of his boss to the Appropriations Committee, emphasized the role of raising money in helping his member to gain a seat on the committee: "He did a lot for party. . . . He raised over $2.3 million for the NRCC [National Republican Congressional Committee]; raised $338,000 for the House-Senate dinner in 1999. He was a good Republican. . . . We did a fundraiser for the state party up in . . . the state senate . . . [and] raised $135,000 for them. I helped congressional candidates that were running, just by giving advice and being able to talk to them on the weekends. . . . We did a lot for the Bush campaign, so you know, that all helps."[24]

The status of the party—whether it is the majority or minority party—appears to have important consequences for the committee assignment process. When a party is in the majority, the assignment process seems to be dominated by two major concerns: protecting the majority by being responsive to the needs of marginal members, and promoting party loyalty so that the party can push its agenda through the House. Some indications of changes in the assignment process in the Republican House are consistent with this finding. Republicans have put a much higher value on "teamwork" (party loyalty) as measured by both support on the floor and party fundraising since becoming the majority, though both Democrats and Republicans report that raising money has become an important criterion for assignment to sought-after committees. The party in the minority is faced with a significant lack of committee seats, which demands that the assignment process be redirected toward the singular goal of "keeping peace in the family." Party committees accomplish this by shifting their assignment calculus toward providing balance within the committees through geographic (such as regional) accommodation within their caucus.

THE COMMITTEE ASSIGNMENT ODYSSEY

As the CAP framework demonstrates, success in the pursuit of a committee assignment is dependent on numerous factors, only some of which are under the control of the member seeking an assignment. The following case studies illustrate the complex interactions of the factors outlined in the framework. Each committee assignment odyssey is unique, and the following examples are used to illustrate how member motivations are only one aspect in the quest for a choice committee assignment.

Butler Derrick and the Quest for Influence

Democrat Butler Derrick was elected to the House in 1974 to represent the Third District of South Carolina. A former state legislator with an intense interest in fiscal matters, he entered the House with seventy-four other "Watergate babies" in the Democratic congressional election landslide. These members entered the Congress on the heels of important reforms, especially in the committee assignment process (see chapter 2), that led them to believe that they would be able to exercise significant influence in the House without having to wait to accrue seniority. With such a major influx of new members, the party leadership was under intense pressure to put new members immediately into influential committees to which they might otherwise have had to wait years to have access. Many of these members made the most of their opportunity by aggressively seeking committee assignments that would allow them to pursue their policy interests. Butler Derrick was no exception, and, ultimately, he became one of the more successful members of the class of 1974.

If constituency concerns had been central to Derrick's motivation for seeking a committee assignment, he likely would have sought an assignment to Agriculture or to Veterans' Affairs, but these committees held little personal interest for him.

> I came from a big farming area, a lot of farm interest, and, I mean, I had no particular interest in being on Agriculture. . . . My district had more veterans' business claims than any other district in the country. . . . . And my predecessor had been there for twenty-six [years], had been on the Veterans' Committee the entire time, and was chairman when he left Congress. When I didn't request the Veterans' Committee, some of my constituents got upset with it, but, you know, they got over it. And that just wasn't an area where I had a particular interest.[25]

He also passed on the opportunity to seek an assignment on Armed Services, despite the significant military presence in his district: "I didn't think that it was necessary for me to be on a military committee. I thought I could serve my constituents better—do a better job and also serve my own personal needs—in approaching it in a different manner."[26]

Instead of pursuing a constituency committee, Butler Derrick sought a slot on Ways and Means, because he believed it would provide him an opportunity to gain broad influence over public policy: "What I was interested in was getting myself into a situation where it is kind of like the blood vessels in your body: If you know where the money is going, you know what is going on."[27] In pursuing an assignment to the committee, Derrick first emphasized his legislative experience in the South Carolina legislature, focusing on his membership on the state Ways and Means Committee, and his four years as chair of a subcommittee responsible for "almost half of the entire state funds." He also emphasized his electoral security: "As you will note, I received approximately 65% of the total vote in a three-man race in the Democratic primary and approximately 66% of the total vote in the general election in November. . . . I would hope that this is an indication that [I] will be in Congress for years to come."[28]

Derrick mounted an aggressive campaign for the Ways and Means slot. He encouraged his brother, who had worked for committee chair Wilbur Mills a few years before, to contact Mills on his behalf. The governor of South Carolina also contacted Mills about Derrick: "We are very proud of Butler and are convinced that he will have a long and successful career in United States House of Representatives. Anything you can do to help him would be personally appreciated."[29] Sapp Funderburk, a mutual friend of Derrick and Mills, also contacted the chair, prevailing on him for a personal favor in helping Derrick to obtain a seat on the powerful committee.[30] Finally, Derrick paid a visit to the chair: "[I] thought that I might have, could have, gotten on [the committee], but this was about the time that [Mills] had his unfortunate battle with [alcohol]," which drove Wilbur Mills from Congress.[31]

Butler Derrick did not receive an assignment to Ways and Means, but his efforts did gain the attention of Speaker Carl Albert, who tapped him for membership on the Budget Committee. Derrick thus became the first first-term member of Congress to serve on the influential committee. It was an assignment that was consistent with Derrick's goal of achieving membership on one of the influence committees in Congress: "I always felt that in order to get the best overview of government, you wanted to be on one of the finance committees."[32] He also received an assignment to Banking: "Probably a leftover," he speculated.

During his first term, Derrick took up the fight against the Humphrey-Hawkins bill, which, he felt, "would make the government an employer of last resort."[33] Richard Bolling, chair of the Rules Committee, who was leading the supporters of the legislation, "went to Tip and said, 'we need him on our side.'"[34] Just two years after achieving an impressive committee assignment, he was approached by Speaker Tip O'Neill to accept a position on the Rules Committee. In explaining his reasons for wanting to be on Rules in a letter to Speaker O'Neill, he expressed his interest in improving the congressional budget process: "I can provide the Rules Committee with expertise on backdoor spending, authorization deadlines, and various other provisions dealing with the Budget timetable, issues which are often resolved in the Rules Committee."[35] Derrick's work on Humphrey-Hawkins, though it was inconsistent with the position of the House majority leadership, likely played an important role in demonstrating his emerging mastery of the legislative process—his expertise— which members often believe important in the assignment process.

Service on Rules is difficult for Democratic members for several reasons. First, because the committee's members are appointed by the Speaker (or Democratic leader, when in the minority) there is an expectation that Rules members will support the legislative goals of the leadership. O'Neill warned Derrick of this when they discussed his appointment: "'Butler,' he said, 'if I put you on the Rules Committee, 99 percent of the time you can do what you want to do. . . . On the floor, that is your business. But if I ever get in a jam and I need your vote, you had better give me a mighty good reason not to vote with me.'"[36] This expectation can put members into the position of supporting positions that are unpopular with their constituency. Derrick was cautioned by other members of the South Carolina delegation about the risks of being on the committee: "Other members of the delegation that I discussed it with said, . . . you are crazy to get on the Rules Committee, because you are going to have to make decisions on so many things that may not be politically compatible."[37]

Rules Committee service is also difficult to explain to constituents in terms of exactly what one does and how it benefits one's constituents. It is "probably . . . the least constituency-oriented committee as far as people back home are concerned."[38] Despite these problems, Derrick sought membership on Rules because, as he explains, "I had not been able to get on the Ways and Means Committee, and I wanted to be on one of the three major committees."[39] In explaining Rules to his constituents, he focused on the influential nature of the committee. Thus, the assignment to Rules allowed Derrick to rationalize the value of the committee to his constituents and justify his quest for influence: "The Rules Committee, if used properly, gives you a lot of leverage. I mean, . . . you are constantly accommodating committee chairmen and subcommittee chairmen, and other members of the Rules Committee. . . . I thought it was one of the three [major committees], in some ways more powerful than the Ways and Means Committee."[40] Using his position on Rules, he was able to deliver significant benefits to his district, including a $155 million appropriation for the Savannah River nuclear waste site.

Butler Derrick served on the Rules Committee from 1977 until he retired in 1994, just before the Republican surge. Before 1994, he had only one close call electorally, gaining only 54 percent of the vote in 1988—in ten elections he had dipped below 60 percent of the vote on only three occasions—despite the trend in his district, like many in the South, toward the Republican Party; his seat was assumed by a Republican. At the time he retired, he had built up enough seniority to be on track to become committee chair and he had ascended to a party leadership position as chief deputy whip. He continued to seek influence over fiscal policy throughout his service on Rules by serving additional terms on the Budget Committee as the Rules representative.

The case of Butler Derrick illustrates several of the themes we have developed. First, Butler Derrick, like many members, was primarily motivated not by constituency concerns but by his personal policy interests and his quest for influence in the House. He served on committees that were consistent with his primary motivations, rather than pursuing assignment to committees that were directly associated with his constituency's interests. Despite his service on committees without direct constituency ties, he was able to convince his constituents of its value, deliver benefits to his district, and satisfy his personal goals.

Lynn Martin's Ambition Meets the Assignment Process

Lynn Martin (R-IL) came to Congress in 1981, having earned a reputation in the Illinois state legislature as a fiscal conservative—her nickname there had been "axe" for her desire to cut government programs

(Churchman 1981). In a letter to Republican Leader Michel, the newly elected representative explained her interest in serving on Appropriations: "I have served on an Appropriations Committee on the County Board, State House and State Senate[;] it is obviously an area of much interest. I am not trying to kid myself that I understand the Congressional appropriations process, or the vastness of its direction, but it is certainly something in which I have much interest."[41] She concluded a letter written a few days later, "I appreciated your information about the Appropriations Committee and, although I know it would be a long shot, would still hope to be appointed."[42]

There were seven Republican vacancies on Appropriations in the 97th Congress, but Martin did not receive one of the seats. In fact, she was not among those nominated during the ten ballots that it took to fill the vacancies. It is not surprising that she did not win an Appropriations seat in her first attempt; before the 1994 elections, the Republicans rarely seated new members on influence committees. Further, Leader Michel supported another member of the Illinois delegation with slightly more seniority (John Porter, who had won a special election in January 1980), which illustrates the role of delegation politics in Martin's case. Porter eventually won a seat on the committee on the eighth ballot.

Martin's consolation prize was assignment to Budget and to House Administration. Neither of these assignments fulfilled Martin's interest in serving on one of the more influential House committees. She gave the credit for her ability to get on Budget to Michel: "Would that have happened had the leader not been elected? Well, you can always argue that you're skilled and wonderful, but there's a lot of people that are skilled and wonderful. Never knock luck."[43] The Budget Committee gave her limited ability to influence policy in Illinois, but Budget at the time was dominated by the Democratic majority, leaving little for a minority member to influence in terms of national policy; neither Democrats nor Republicans have ever viewed House Administration as a plum assignment. In the 98th Congress, Martin sought to improve her committee position by trading in her position on Administration for Ways and Means, Appropriations, or Rules, while remaining on Budget. She admitted to Michel that her task would be difficult this time, not because of her lack of seniority, but because of the seats held by her

Illinois Republican colleagues: "I accept . . . that Illinois Republicans are appropriately represented on both these committees."[44] However, Martin still listed Ways and Means and Appropriations as her two most desired committees.[45] She made her strongest argument for appointment to Rules by playing up her strengths and personal loyalty: "I have given much thought to my capabilities and interests, and since I am a synthesizer rather than a creator, I believe that this will be the best utilization of my abilities. . . . I suspect that there will be a number of requests for [this] assignment and that it might seem strange to put a second term member on the Rules Committee. I do feel, Mr. Leader, that I am well suited for that Committee and could represent your interests very well."[46] Martin again failed to receive an assignment to one of the influence committees; she received her fifth choice, a seat on Public Works.

Still seeking a more prestigious committee assignment, Martin appealed to the RCC for one of the four open slots on Armed Services in the 99th Congress. When asked about her choice of Armed Services, she denied any connection to constituency concerns: "No. Illinois was fiftieth in Armed Services spending and had very little . . . national role. Our district was very kind and let me do whatever I wanted to do." When asked why her constituency was so accommodating, she joked, "I don't know . . . probably to keep me out of there!"[47] In competition with nine other Republicans for one of the four slots, Martin won an outright majority on the first ballot, with ninety-four votes, and she relinquished her seat on Public Works. At the beginning of her third term in the House, Martin had finally found a place on one of the more sought-after committees (especially among Republicans) in the chamber. A less-ambitious politician likely would have gone to work and waited to climb the seniority ladder. Every committee transfer makes the new committee member the low person on the ladder, and Martin, who had changed committees every Congress, had yet to establish seniority on any committee.

Despite her assignment to Armed Services, Martin continued to seek a seat on Appropriations; she was motivated by a desire to have real influence and was not content to remain on any committee other than one of the three major committees: "I was already on Armed Services [and Budget]. . . . I was on major committees. It was hard to argue that I

[was] overlooked."[48] With three vacancies on Appropriations entering the 100th Congress, Martin requested a transfer and had good cause to be optimistic. She was about to enter her fourth term, she had been elected to a position in the leadership (conference vice-chair in 1985), and she now had the strong support of Michel.[49] She had established her credentials as a fiscal conservative, particularly through her three terms on the Budget Committee; her National Taxpayers Union (NTU) score at the close of the 99th Congress placed her in the 92nd percentile of all members of the House and was good enough to earn her a Taxpayer's Friend award from the organization.[50]

Unfortunately for Martin, her request for Appropriations was caught up in a major confrontation between the large and small states in the RCC that was well beyond her control. The Texas representative on the Executive Committee had entered into an alliance with the small-state representatives to gain joint control over the committee assignment process. The first ballot produced victory for Tom DeLay (R-TX). DeLay, who had served as the first-term class representative to the Executive Committee the previous year, was serving as the second-term class representative in the 100th Congress.[51] On the second ballot, Martin was nominated by Michel but received only his nine votes; the winner on ballot two was Conservative Opportunity Society member Vin Weber from Minnesota, one of the small states in the Executive Committee. Weber had been nominated for a slot on Appropriations during the previous committee assignment meeting, at the start of the 99th Congress, but at that time, he was able to get the support of only his own three-member state delegation. In his letter to Michel (and other Executive Committee members) requesting a transfer to Appropriations, Weber emphasized his previous unsuccessful attempt to join the committee.

The final ballot pitted Martin against Jim Kolbe, a second-term member from Arizona, and Barbara Vucanovich, a third-term member from Nevada. Conventional wisdom would seem to favor Martin. She was the more senior member, and she had a place in the formal leadership. In addition, she had a more conservative NTU score than either of her rivals (Martin, 63; Kolbe, 59; and Vucanovich, 53). Martin was also considered a protégé of the Republican leader.[52] How did Jim Kolbe defeat Lynn Martin for the final seat on Appropriations in the 100th

Congress?[53] The answer lies in the process used by the House Republicans to select committee members and in the intraparty cleavages that created conditions in which members of the Executive Committee formed alliances and put the Republican leader in a weak position. Joseph White's study (1989) of the Appropriations Committee includes a passage from an unnamed Appropriations member, familiar with the balloting, who describes the internal politics that led to Martin's defeat in December 1986, when the Executive Committee met to decide assignments to the exclusive committees:

> Two years ago there was the, I think correct, perception that the small states got screwed. This time around, led by [minority whip] Trent Lott, the small states put together a coalition, needed one more state, and it was Texas. Freshmen couldn't get Appropriations, and others were not interested. . . . Some were already on one of them; others had seniority where they were. . . . So that made life very easy in the deal-cutting. For instance the three member states had five people they were trying to accommodate. We said 'we have only one thing we really want; when you are ready to talk, just let us know.' (1989, 136)

According to this member, the one thing that the four-member states wanted from the exclusive committee assignments was a place for Kolbe on Appropriations.[54] The outcome of the final Appropriations battle reflected this coalition: Kolbe received ninety-eight votes; he received every vote from the small-state representatives, and Texan Bill Archer's vote put him over the top. Clearly, the coalition that described by the Republican quoted above did form in the Kolbe-Martin race.[55]

In discussing House leadership in the Democratic Party, Sinclair (1995) found that one measure of a leader's power was his or her ability to place same-state colleagues in desirable committee positions. A leader's success in obtaining good assignments for his or her state colleagues fortifies the leader's reputation, because there is an expectation in the Washington community that he or she will do so and because appearing powerful is an important component of influence. Despite the explicit support of the Republican leader, Martin was defeated in her effort to gain an assignment to Appropriations. This is compelling evidence that the leader (Michel) or even the leadership, more broadly defined if one is to look at formal roles (Martin was a member of the leadership team), by no means controlled committee assignments for the Republicans.[56] Many years later, Martin reflects on the possible reasons she lost to Kolbe:

> It had a lot to do with lots of other things that weren't about Kolbe or me. You are lucky sometimes, and sometimes things are beyond your control. The western states got together, and they were underrepresented, so there were regional differences. But I think if you look back, I could have campaigned differently; you can go through everything you didn't do quite as correctly as possible. But the reality is that Bob Michel was an extraordinarily big help, and he couldn't be—then it almost worked in reverse. No big deal. That's just part of life, really. Some people never get to be on the money committees.[57]

Still seeking influence in the House, Martin requested a seat on Rules in the 101st Congress.

> If I couldn't get Appropriations, . . . I would accept Rules because . . . the House has to be determined by rules. . . . Although in some ways it's a very partisan committee, it's not partisan for the press. You're working on small, terribly uninteresting details to those who don't understand the process, but for the process itself—it meant that I could also have a hand, or at least a finger, in virtually every piece of legislation that hit the floor, including Appropriations, which have to have rules too.[58]

Again she had Leader Michel's support, and this time it mattered. Before the committee assignments for the 101st Congress, the Republican Caucus had invested the power to make Rules Committee assignments in their leader, and Michel, reportedly still fuming about the circumstances surrounding Martin's failure to gain a seat on Appropriations during the 100th Congress, simply appointed her to the position. Never one to rest on her laurels in the House, Martin decided to run for a Senate seat in the 102nd Congress and was defeated and subsequently served as secretary of labor in the first Bush administration.

Martin's odyssey is as instructive as Butler Derrick's. Lynn Martin, like Derrick, was driven by her desire to serve on one of the House's influential committees. She felt that serving on a committee with a direct linkage to her district was unnecessary because constituents were not that concerned with what committees their representatives served on: "If you're from Illinois, being on the Interior Committee probably isn't [that] important. But were you on the Interior Committee . . . *you'd make of it what you could back in your district*" (emphasis added). She continued, "I think most good politicians . . . learn to try to explain to their districts why they are on a certain committee and why they think it's of value, and usually they succeed."[59] Her ambition, however, was significantly affected by conditions within the assignment process that put her at a disadvantage, despite her protégé-mentor relationship with her party's leader, her leadership position, and her credentials as a solid conservative. Unlike many members of the House, Martin was not content, once she received an assignment to a major committee (Armed Services), to simply accumulate seniority and influence within a given policy domain; she continued to seek influence despite the "costs" of "queue jumping." Finally, one cannot help but notice that both these ambitious politicians, Derrick and Martin, found their way onto the Rules Committee, which became, for both, the means by which they would exercise their influence in the House.

B-1 Bob Dornan Does Battle with the Executive Committee

Their ability to get elected is evidence that most members of Congress possess significant political skills. Of all the ambitious politicians who might seek a congressional seat, the winner in an election has either proved his or her political abilities or been extremely lucky. When new members arrive in Congress, others who have demonstrated equal political skills surround them. That is what makes the quest for a committee assignment difficult and competitive. The attributes that make members of Congress popular in their districts, however, may work against them when they make the transition to the campaigning for a committee assignment.

Political style can play an important role in the politics of committee assignments. Also important are the norms observed by those in positions of party leadership, especially those who serve on the Executive

Committee. From mid-century through the early 1990s, "establishment" Republicans, moderates from the Midwest and Northeast who pursued a largely bipartisan strategy in their relationship with the "permanent" Democratic majority, mostly dominated the Republican Party leadership. During the late 1970s and throughout the 1980s, the Republican Party underwent a fundamental transformation (see chapter 2). Slowly the center of gravity in the party shifted to the right ideologically, and toward the South and the West geographically. These new-style conservatives were interested less in collaborating with the Democratic majority than they were in challenging the majority in an offensive aimed at building a Republican majority. The confrontational style of the new conservatives clashed with the accommodating style of the establishment Republicans, who controlled the committee assignment process at the time.

The committee assignment saga of Robert K. Dornan (R-CA) illustrates the role of political style and the significant changes that were occurring in the Republican Conference during much of his tenure in Congress. Dornan exhibited an aggressive and flamboyant conservatism, often taking advantage of one-minute speeches on the House floor to promote his conservative positions and to attack liberal causes and the Democratic majority. For instance, a fervent opponent of President Clinton, Dornan accused the president on the House floor of organizing protests against the Vietnam War while living abroad as a college student, giving "aid and comfort to the enemy." He was banned from speaking on the floor for the rest of the day. In another case, he nearly came to blows on the floor with Democrat Tom Downey during a debate over support for the Nicaraguan Contras in 1985.

The Republican Executive Committee was composed of senior members, establishment Republicans, concerned with traditional House values of decorum and comity, which underpinned their ability to negotiate with the Democratic majority. What Dornan may have perceived as activity supportive of the Republican Party likely was perceived by accommodationists as incompetence, behavior that made their job more difficult. His aggressive style did not sit well with most of the Executive Committee, and this slowed Dornan's progress toward a preferred assignment to Armed Services. Not until there was significant change in the culture of the Republican Conference overall, and in the composition of the Executive Committee, did Dornan finally achieve the committee assignment that he had been seeking for so long.

Bob Dornan, a former radio and television journalist, was narrowly elected to the 95th Congress in 1976 from a conservative Southern California district. A former fighter pilot and Vietnam War veteran, he was a strong advocate of defense programs generally, and the B-1 bomber in particular. Dornan acquired the nickname "B-1 Bob" because of his strong support for the B-1, a new-generation bomber envisioned as a replacement for the B-52. As a newly elected member of Congress, Dornan's request for assignment to Armed Services, and no other committee, emphasized his background and political interests:

> Due to my long U.S.A.F. service as a jet fighter pilot . . . and a very important industrial element in my district, which is the aerospace capital of the world . . . most important Rockwell International (B-1 Bomber) . . . my first, second and third choices would be the Armed Services Committee. . . . My relations with Pentagon people are excellent. Many have expressed hope that I secure an Armed Services Committee position because of my TV/Radio background lending itself to the opportunity to present the B-1 to the American people on national talk shows in a positive, clear presentation.[60]

Dornan did not receive an assignment to the Armed Services Committee. As our previous analysis suggests (see chapter 4), this is hardly surprising; the committee is very popular among Republicans, and the rate of success is quite low. He did receive assignments to Science and Merchant Marine, neither of which he requested.

Reelected to serve in the 96th Congress by a much larger margin, Dornan renewed his attempt to receive an assignment to Armed Services or to Foreign Affairs. Again Dornan referred to his experience as an important factor to consider, and again he was denied assignment to the committee: "As you recall, in my first term I flew the B-1, and the B-52, and seven front-line fighter aircraft. The district I represent in California is the most prominent aerospace and defense industry complex in the entire free world. In any case, I think that my qualifications for such a post, especially my military background, deserves special consideration."[61]

In the 97th Congress, Dornan requested assignment to Appropriations, Armed Services, or Foreign Affairs. Jerry Lewis received the California Republican Delegation endorsement for the Appropriations seat. Dornan highlighted his personal experience and his constituency as major reasons for seeking assignment to the committee in a letter to outgoing Republican leader John J. Rhodes:

> After four hard-fought races, I am sure that you would agree that a third term Member of the House of Representatives should have the opportunity to serve on at least one prestigious Committee that would have a direct, positive impact on people of his district. . . . I have three major choices: Appropriations, Armed Services, and Foreign Affairs. . . . I know that my good friend and colleague, fellow Californian Jerry Lewis . . . wants a position on Appropriations and whatever the outcome of our regional competition, I think it only prudential for me to spell out the case for my second choice: the House Armed Services Committee. . . . First, I have had the honor of serving my country for 23 years as a United States Air Force fighter pilot. . . . Second I . . . represent the biggest aerospace and defense industry complex in a free world. . . . Third, may I please remind you also of my direct experience with sophisticated military equipment, particularly the front line jet fighter aircraft. . . . John, as I mentioned to you previously, there is a division of labor in the House of Representatives just as there is a natural division of labor in society as a whole. In the private sector, a person should be assigned to those labors that best comport with his aptitudes, experience and professional background. That same principle should also apply to our labors in public service.[62]

Despite his seniority and experience, Dornan did not receive the delegation's endorsement for a seat on Armed Services, which went instead to the newly elected Duncan Hunter. A young, handsome, and articulate conservative, Duncan Hunter was easily elected to serve on Armed Services. Dornan was elected to Foreign Affairs by unanimous consent in the Executive Committee, gaining a seat on a sought-after committee.

A thorn in the side of the national and California Democratic Party, Dornan's district was redrawn following the 1980 census, relocating him to the district of a popular moderate Democrat, Jerry M. Patterson. Rather than challenge Patterson in the new district in 1982, Dornan chose instead to run, unsuccessfully, for the California Senate seat. With encouragement from the Republican leadership, Dornan mounted a challenge to Patterson in 1984, defeating him by a slim margin. Upon his return to the House, Dornan again took up his quest for a seat on Armed Services. In his request for a new committee assignment in the 99th Congress, Dornan wrote, "I had a meeting with the Minority Leader and Minority Whip *before* I declared in Feb. to run against a 10 year popular incumbent. Outcome: 'TAKE CARE OF PATTERSON WE TAKE CARE OF (DORNAN).' Thank you my colleagues for remembering."[63] Though Dornan was nominated in the Executive Committee, he again failed to get a significant level of support for one of the four vacancies on Armed Services, one of which went to Republican Leader Bob Michel's protégé Lynn Martin. Dornan won only a relative handful of the roughly ninety votes necessary for a majority—sixteen votes on the first ballot and the eighteen votes from the California representative on the Executive Committee on the last ballot. Two things about the voting in the Executive Committee are interesting to note. First, the California representative voted with the majority on every other vote, except the last ballot, when he cast California's votes for Dornan, the only votes that Dornan got on that last ballot. Second, Jerry Lewis was an establishment Republican, and Dornan, a maverick from the emerging conservative majority. It is possible that Lewis's votes for Dornan were cast only to satisfy his responsibility to the California delegation to support the state's endorsed candidate. Instead of receiving a seat on Armed Services, Dornan found himself on Foreign Affairs once again. Disunity within the California delegation, caused largely by conflict between establishment Republicans focused on accommodation and those taking a more confrontational stance toward the Democratic majority, was a major reason for accommodationist Lewis's) lack of support for Dornan.

By the time the committee assignment process began for the 100th Congress, Dornan was becoming frustrated with his inability to receive an assignment to Armed Services. In a note to the Executive Committee, Dornan expressed his frustration, and countered possible arguments against his assignment to the committee, especially the argument that there were too many Californians on the committee: "May Allah show mercy. This is my fifth try—count 'em—five tries '76, '78, '80, '84 and now . . . I ask two humble questions: 1. Am I not qualified? 2. Am I not finally senior enough with 5 open seats? . . . I served on a smaller committee (17 Rep. Slots on Foreign Affairs 20 on Armed Service) with 2 other Californians, i.e. Zschau, Lagomarsino, so Calif. Status should NOT be an impediment!"[64]

In his letter to Bob Michel seeking an assignment to Armed Services, he explicitly put forward the geographic argument and made a claim for a "California seat" on the committee:

> I am writing to seek your support for a committee change at the 10-year point in my House service. Obviously a very serious decision for me . . . I have sought this assignment every two years since I first took a seat in Congress on January 4, 1977, 12 years ago, . . . With at least three open seats on Armed Services and little change in overall House numbers there is no better opportunity than now to allow me to switch from the prestigious Foreign Affairs Committee to the equally important Committee on Armed Services. (One of those three open seats has, by tradition, belonged to a Californian and the California delegation recently voted to recommend that I replace our California colleague Bob Badham on the committee.)[65]

Following a series of contentious votes in which the committee could not produce a majority candidate, and wherein Dornan did not receive a single vote, they accepted a slate of the four candidates who received the greatest number of votes. The following day the Republicans learned that they would be granted an additional seat on Armed Services to which another candidate was nominated and accepted by unanimous consent. Dornan had again lost his bid for Armed Services and had not garnered a single vote, not even from the California representative who had, in effect, been directed by his California colleagues to support Dornan in the Executive Committee.[66]

As the committee assignment season approached once again in 1988, Dornan again requested reassignment from Foreign Affairs to Armed

Services. Very aggressively seeking the assignment, he made a note on his preference sheet that it was his sixth try to get on the committee. By this time, the Executive Committee had undergone significant changes. Bowing to pressure from a growing conservative insurgency led by Newt Gingrich, the Executive Committee was reformed to provide the party leadership with more influence over the assignment process, with the presumed effect being that party discipline would be increased. As a part of this effort, the party leadership—the Republican leader and the whip—was granted a vote on the committee for the first time since Joseph Cannon was Speaker of the House in 1909. Equally important, a number of establishment Republicans had been replaced on the Executive Committee by members who were more sympathetic to the cause of the insurgent Republicans.

This time, after ten years of trying, Bob Dornan was rewarded with a slot on the Armed Services Committee, receiving votes from the California representative on the Executive Committee as well as the votes of most other large-state representatives and Republican leader Bob Michel. As it turns out, this was an important event, because a short six years later, the Republicans gained a majority in the House, and Bob Dornan found himself in the position of chair of the Military Personnel Subcommittee. Using that position, he was able to promote one of his conservative causes, banning HIV-positive soldiers from combat duty. The policy was never approved or implemented, but the position provided a platform for Dornan.

In 1996 Dornan was defeated for reelection by Democrat Loretta Sanchez, by a scant 954 votes in a district drawn by the California legislature in the hopes of defeating him. As a partial explanation for his loss, Dornan claimed, in the *Wall Street Journal,* "What beat me was more homosexual money than in any race in history, including from a group called Lesbians for Motherhood." Charging vote fraud, he convinced Speaker Newt Gingrich to begin a House investigation into his loss. When the investigation ended a year later with no finding of fraud, Dornan threatened a rematch with Sanchez, saying, "For the next year, 11 months and seven days, I will be on her case" (Georges 1996). In the 1998 rematch, Sanchez soundly defeated him.

Bomb-throwers are often overlooked in the committee assignment processes of both parties, processes that often reward teamwork and coalition building. Contrast the rapid rise of Tom DeLay through the committee process—he represented his class on the RCC during his first and second terms, achieving an appointment to Appropriations during his second term—with the committee fate of Newt Gingrich, who requested Appropriations in his first term and was given an assignment to Public Works and to House Administration, where he remained from 1978 until he was elected Speaker in 1995. Another Republican revolutionary who excelled at the one-minute inflammatory speech but fared poorly in the committee assignment process was Bob Walker (R-PA), who repeatedly sought to change his committee assignments, with little success.

The Political Style of Jim Traficant

Lest one think that only the Republican Party has members not placed on important committees because fellow members fear they would prove embarrassments, we now turn briefly to the case of James A. Traficant, Jr. (D-OH). Traficant came to Congress with a reputation as a brash, bombastic individual who was not a team player. Two years before Traficant was elected to Congress in 1984, the Mahoning County (Ohio) Democratic chair called him "a nitwit, a lunatic, a raving maniac" (Barone and Ujifusa 1988, 952). As Mahoning County sheriff, Traficant had escaped being tried by the federal government for allegedly accepting bribes. In defending himself, he claimed that he was conducting his own sting operation. He was acquitted, even though the FBI had audio tapes of Traficant accepting the bribes, and the person to whom he claimed to have returned the bribe money was never found.

Shortly after being elected to Congress, Traficant sent a letter to Majority Leader Wright, listing his preferences for major, minor, and select committee assignments. In requesting assignment to Public Works as his first choice, with dual service on the Science Committee, Traficant claimed he would be support the party's success: "I want to reiterate that I will be supportive of the Democratic leadership, and I am hopeful of playing a useful role in achieving some successes in the upcoming 99th Congress."[67] In addition, Louis Stokes, dean of the Ohio Democratic delegation, wrote a letter to the Speaker and other members of the DSPC asking for support for Traficant's request for membership on Public Works.[68]

Traficant received both his major and minor committee assignments for the 99th Congress. Neither committee was particularly important to the Democratic agenda, nor did the committees have jurisdiction over any controversial legislation. The Democrats could afford to place a maverick member on these committees with little fear of negative consequences. It soon became apparent that Traficant was not going to serve a quiet apprenticeship in the House, devoting his time to committee business and supporting the Democratic leadership while waiting his turn for seniority to deliver the perks of power. He quickly became known as one of the most flamboyant and demagogic members of Congress. He frequently took to the House floor to decry the abuses of the CIA, FBI, and IRS in speeches that were largely aimed at a devoted C-Span following. Barone and Ujifusa described some other subjects of Traficant's vocal outbursts: "Traficant loves to engage in one-minute tirades, so vivid they're often shown on evening news broadcasts, and even netting him an hour on Phil Donahue's program. He passionately backed measures to help the Mahoning Valley, and in policy terms [was] one of Congress's most flamboyant protectionist and isolationist members. . . . He was a particularly vitriolic opponent of the Gulf War" (1992, 992–93).

After serving two terms on Public Works, Traficant sought a transfer to Appropriations. In a letter to Speaker Wright, Traficant again argued his loyalty: "Since coming to Congress, I have loyally supported the party and have tried to be an outspoken advocate for the positions we have taken. Rest assured that I will continue to assist the leadership and the party in every way I can during the 101st Congress."[69] The DSPC did not grant Traficant's request, and he remained in his initial committee assignments.

By 1992, Traficant had switched his sights to the Ways and Means Committee as a potential forum to do battle with the IRS. He was unsuccessful at the start of both the 103rd and 104th Congresses in garnering support for his bid for Ways and Means membership—his reputation as a vocal maverick certainly diminished his chances of success. Influential Ways and Means chair Daniel Rostenkowski, whose support as chair and as DSPC member was seen as critical for candidates seeking membership to the powerful committee, describes the lengths Traficant went to in his attempts to secure Ways and Means membership:

> Traficant—Traficant, whether you liked it our not, had a following. He'd take those one-minutes—he had all these people in these daycare centers sitting there railing against everybody. He called me and said, "I want to get on Ways and Means." I said, "No damn way." He said, "Danny, you got to do this. I'll be loyal." I said, "You'll be loyal for a week. You're too flamboyant— no way." "Danny, please I promise you, I'll be a damn good worker." "I'm not saying that you won't be a good worker, but I won't be able to give you an idea about how we balance things out, because you shoot from the hip." Mike Ditka calls me and says, "I don't know what I'm asking, but I played football with Traficant in Pittsburgh. He wants to get on your committee." I said, "Mike, do I tell you how to coach your football team?" He said, "No." "Then don't tell me how to run my goddamn business." "I told him I would just ask. I told the guy I would ask." I said, "Mike, he's nuts." He says, "I thought you'd tell me that." But Traficant had a following. He'd get in those one-minutes and he'd have the senior citizens write letters complaining about how evil government was or the FBI. I didn't have too much of an argument with him about the FBI.[70]

An editorial in the *Cleveland Plain Dealer* (1992) claimed that by campaigning for a seat on Ways and Means in 1992, Traficant in effect spoiled any hope that Ohio could retain the committee seat being vacated by retiring representative Donald Pease. The editorialist concluded that the unpredictable and confrontational Traficant had no chance of being chosen to such an important and visible committee.

As time progressed, Traficant became more and more estranged from the Democratic leadership in the House, and his voting became more and more conservative. At the start of the 107th Congress in 2001, Traficant voted for the Republican candidate for Speaker, Dennis Hastert, and was subsequently stripped of his committee assignments and expelled by the Democratic Caucus. He remained in the House without any committee assignments until he was expelled in 2002, following his conviction for ten counts of bribery, racketeering, and tax evasion. He was sentenced to eight years in prison, where he ran unsuccessfully for reelection to Congress in November 2002.

• • •

To gain insight into how members pursue preferred committees, this chapter has focused on the role of member beliefs about the assignment process. The CAP framework suggests that members' beliefs play a role in shaping which committees they request and how they proceed when seeking a committee assignment. Using the request letters as the basis of an ethnographic exercise, we have sought to understand the process from the perspective of both requesters and participants in committee on committees' deliberations. Our findings suggest that many members believe that expertise plays an important role in achieving a committee assignment, as do geographic and electoral concerns. For the most part, members of the committees on committees confirm these beliefs. Although these findings hold generally across the two parties, there are apparent differences between the majority and minority party (at least during the period for which we have data). In the majority party, leaders tend to put a higher premium on protecting their majority and party loyalty; in the minority party, leaders focus on conserving seats and tolerating party defections. Members' beliefs about the assignment process, expressed through the letters, reflect direct participants' understanding of the process. When members' beliefs conflict with those of the leadership (as in the case of Dornan and Traficant), they may find themselves frustrated in their ambitions. Dornan's beliefs about the assignment process, that expertise plays an important role and that his party loyalty would be rewarded, were inconsistent with the stylistic expectations of a party leadership focused on partisan accommodation. Once the party leadership had undergone significant change, his request was accommodated. Traficant simply could not overcome the stylistic concerns that figure into the process.

Chapters 3 through 5 have examined the committee assignment process from the demand side, that is, the individual committee request. Our major findings suggest that members' identify their interests in different ways, consistent with the CAP framework described in chapter 1. Sometimes interests are shaped by district and electoral concerns; more often, they are shaped by the members' personal interests, experience, background, and quest for institutional power. The politics of the committee assignment process injects significant competition and conflict into the quest for committee seats. Members of Congress do not appear overly motivated in their committee request behavior by concerns about reelection; in fact, members of Congress are often motivated to pursue committees that are presumably contrary to their electoral interests because of their policy concerns and their quest for institutional influence. As the case studies in this chapter illustrate, the individual motivations of members and the structure of the committee assignment process influence committee preferences and committee assignments significantly. In the chapters that follow, we explore further the politics of the assignment process that influences committee assignments.

CHAPTER SIX

LEADERSHIP AND COMMITTEE ASSIGNMENTS

Well, it seems that the leader has a dual interest, and sometimes part of his responsibility may conflict with another. He should be interested in what should promote the best results in the House and what would be best for this individual member who is seeking an assignment.

FORMER SPEAKER JIM WRIGHT

In this chapter, we adopt a multiple-motivations framework for understanding the role of party leaders in the committee assignment process. The role of leadership in the process can be best understood by looking at the policy, institutional influence, and electoral motivations of leaders. However, reelection is often meaningless without the leadership position (witness the departure of so many Republican House committee chairs when term limits are reached, four in 2000 alone); therefore, the other two motivations assume greater importance. Leaders try to use assignments to maintain their power base by keeping most of their membership satisfied with the division of committee positions. Leaders also use committee assignments to advance party agendas. This policy motivation is especially true of leaders who are in the majority; minority leaders can afford to be less concerned with the policy consequences of committee assignments.

The influence of party leaders over committee assignments is also a reflection of their personal style and the leadership context within which they operates. Leaders of relatively homogenous parties have greater incentives and abilities to influence the committee assignments of their members, but the style and personality of the leader is also an important factor (Rohde 1991). The historical context of the period is likewise important, and leadership influence over the committee assignment process must be considered within the nature of leadership at the given time (Peters 1997). The process is ultimately a political one, and any contention that a leader has controlled the process completely during the modern period would be a gross exaggeration. Leaders have had different levels of desire and success in influencing the assignment of members to standing committees, but no modern leader has controlled the process in the way that Speaker Cannon did (Lawrence, Maltzman, and Wahlbeck 2001).

CONGRESSIONAL LEADERS AND POWER

Congressional leaders are ambitious; no one would rise to the top of an organization comprising so many overachievers without a strong motivation for power and control. In much of the political science literature on Congress, the electoral motivation is seen as dominant (see chapter 1). For leaders, the electoral motivation is often secondary. Leaders try to use the committee assignment system to advance and preserve their own power, though each has done it in an individual style. Leaders need to create followers who are not only loyal to the goals of the party, but also personally loyal to the leader as an individual. Many members have high party-unity scores, but party-unity voting does not measure the personal loyalty that members may exhibit for a leader. Throughout the period that we are considering (and we believe throughout the entire history of Congress), personal loyalty, a variable that is impossible to quantify, has been a key factor in determining the composition of the exclusive committees in Congress.

Most of the literature on leadership involvement in committee assignments assumes unified leadership, sharing the same goals. However, our work illustrates that both political parties experienced periods when the top party leaders had differing views on committee assignments. In addition, a more broad definition of leadership, one that includes members of the committee assignment panels, reveals a great deal of conflict and disagreement about the organization of Congress. For both parties, for all years considered, committee assignment decisions involved fierce competition among leaders for limited resources. Committee assignment meetings often had to be held over many days (it took nine meetings to assign all the Democratic members of the 94th Congress); voting often went on for many ballots, even for the less popular committees. In addition, the information that we have on committee-on-committees balloting indicates that for both parties, winning coalitions were rarely larger than the minimum required for success.

The appointment power in general is frequently described as one where the leader creates one ingrate (the appointee) and ten enemies (those who sought but did not receive the assignment).[1] Appointment in a system where members gain property rights to committee membership, and party leaders typically do not have the ability to remove members of committees, does not provide the leader with much power to threaten a member, and the gratitude of the assignment may fade and be replaced by a "what have you done for me lately?" attitude. As Richard E. Neustadt (1990) points out when discussing presidential control of bureaucratic decisions, without the removal power, there is little to bind the bureau chief to the president; party leaders are likely to find themselves in a similar strategic position when it comes to their caucus and the satisfaction of committee requests.

A review of literature on leadership involvement in the committee assignment process since the Legislative Reorganization Act of 1946 (P.L. 79-601), a period during which both parties relied on committees to make the committee assignments, reveals no clear answers. "It is difficult . . . to see any consensus in the literature on the susceptibility of the assignment process to the influence of party leaders. On the one hand, several scholars emphasize the routinization of committee assignments. . . . On the other hand, some of the same scholars emphasize the party leadership's important role in the assignment process" (Cox and McCubbins 1993b, 22).

Leaders want to influence the composition of committees, especially during periods when the House is a driving force in setting the policy-making agenda; however, leaders have felt the need to distance themselves from the perception that they alone are the ones responsible for allowing a member to obtain assignment to a key committee. Leaders owe their positions to continued support of their partisans. Party leaders cannot afford to make too many enemies from the committee assignment process. If members feel that the process is not fair and that the leadership has prevented them from advancement within the organization, they are likely to support challenges to the leaders. Just as Nicolo Machiavelli (1950, 70) warned Lorenzo, that "princes should let the carrying out of unpopular duties devolve on others, and bestow favors themselves," modern congressional leaders have sought to distance themselves from the decisions of committee assignment panels that are not favorable to a member, while claiming credit for placing members on the committees of their choice.

This chapter uses archival, interview, biographical, and secondary account data to develop the thesis that leadership behavior regarding committee assignments can best be understood using a multiple-motivations framework. Cases of leadership involvement in the process are discussed in detail to illustrate the multiple, and at times conflicting, goals. The cases discussed are meant to illustrate the various factors that influence leaders in making decisions regarding committee assignments. The best way for leaders to meet all three goals is by minimizing the number of ingrates and enemies and by maximizing the number of personally loyal supporters in key institutional positions. This is best done by ensuring that members on the committees that control policy—Ways and Means, Appropriations, Rules, and Budget—feel a personal loyalty to the leader. In addition, potential enemies and contending factions must feel at a minimum that the process is fair and that they and members close to them have a reasonable shot at assignment success.

REPUBLICAN LEADERS IN THE POSTWAR ERA

We first turn our attention to Republican leaders in the postwar House, an area of research that has been given little attention. We find considerable evidence that leaders have conflicting goals that they try to achieve with the committee assignment process. The Republican Conference assignment method during most of the period (which is the focus of chapter 2) played a large role in determining how successful leaders were in achieving their goals. The system was originally created as a way for a faction comprising members from the larger, northeastern and midwestern states to control the committee assignment process by limiting the number of important decision makers. An aggressive leader could work with this small group of influential Republican Committee on Committees (RCC) members to dominate the process. However, domination of the process has a price, especially for a minority leader. Without sufficient committee slots to placate many members, a party leader who is seen as too dominant is in danger of losing his or her formal position. The revolt against Speaker Cannon is well documented elsewhere, and will not be rehashed here. There is no doubt that opponents of Cannon used his behavior in controlling committee assignments as evidence that he had become too powerful.

This pattern of younger members challenging the Republican leadership using arguments emphasizing the lack of responsible positions for members with less seniority continued throughout much of the modern period. Later Republican leaders, Bob Michel in particular, apparently learned from the mistakes of their predecessors and played a much less domineering role in a much more open process. We now turn to the individual cases of the Republican leaders.

Joe Martin

Joseph W. Martin, Jr. (R-MA) served as the Republican leader in the House from 1939 until 1959, when the Republican Conference narrowly voted to replace him with Charles Halleck (R-IN). Martin served two terms as Speaker of the House (80th and 83rd Congresses, with Halleck assuming the position of majority leader each time), and he returned to the post of minority leader each time his party lost the majority. Martin claimed to have exerted significant control over committee assignments as both minority leader and Speaker: "I was chairman of the Committee on Committees all the time I was leader. We had five states—New York,

Pennsylvania, Ohio, Illinois, and California. I didn't give a damn whether the other states were there, or what they wanted. We would make up a slate and push it through."[2] In his autobiography, Martin, using a more diplomatic tone, maintained, "While the committee on committees may formally select members for committees, for example, the Speaker does in fact exercise a strong influence over these choices from among the ranks of his own party. Thus members must look to him for a chance of advancement. In the four years that I served as Speaker no Republican went on an important committee without my approval" (1960, 181).

Unfortunately, most of the documentary records dealing with committee assignments from Martin's leadership have been lost.[3] However, the limited documents that remain from the period indicate that rank-and-file Republicans perceived Martin to have a large role in the committee assignment process.[4] In a letter to Walter C. Ploesser (R-MO), dated December 7, 1946, Marion T. Bennett (R-MO) claims, "Joe Martin told me at lunch today that he felt I should have any committee I wanted."[5]

Charles Halleck's 1959 defeat of Martin in the race for minority leader was a product of many factors, but the discontent with committee assignments felt by many junior Republicans, particularly those from small states, certainly played a role. If members perceived Martin to be largely responsible for their committee assignment fates, then Martin could be held accountable for the failure of many junior members to be placed on desirable committees, especially those members not from the five large states that controlled the RCC under Martin. Martin apparently believed that the unhappiness of junior members with their committee assignments contributed to his downfall, as he claims in his autobiography:

> The toll of the years had removed a number of my staunchest old supporters from the House, and in the press of affairs I had never become as close to various of the younger and newer members as they and I might have wished. After a couple of years in Congress these men had begun to feel their oats. Many of the "Ivy Leaguers," as we call some of these young fellows, started dreaming of personal advancement through a change of leadership. Encouraged by Halleck and the White House people

and plied with promises of patronage and preferment in committee assignments, they had taken to complaining that I was not displaying enough partisan aggressiveness. (1960, 8)

In addition, Martin did not have a loyal group of close friends in the House who would support him and rally others in his behalf. This is in direct contrast to Samuel Taliaferro Rayburn (D-TX), who cultivated an active and influential following through his "Board of Education" and judicious use of committee assignments as rewards.[6] Martin claims that he never wanted such a following: "A final circumstance that worked to my disadvantage in that first week of January 1959 was that in all my years as Speaker and Leader I had never tried to build a personal faction in the House. I did not want one, and I never believed that it would have been beneficial to the party. Hence, when the showdown approached, there were no particular Martin forces for me to rally" (1960, 9).

Martin's defeat, aided by the active support of Young Turks within the Republican Party and with the tacit support of the White House, appears consistent with other attempts to redistribute power within the Republican Conference.

Charles Halleck

Robert L. Peabody (1966) likewise found dissatisfaction with committee assignments to be one contributing factor in the subsequent defeat of Charles Halleck by Gerald R. Ford (R-MI) in the 1965 race for Republican minority leader. Halleck was supported by younger members who felt they were not sufficiently represented in the committee assignment process in his 1959 defeat of Martin. As leader, Halleck responded by adding a first-term representative to the Executive Committee of the RCC in 1961 and a second-term representative in 1963. However, despite these and other organizational changes meant to give younger members a greater say in party activities, "the continued domination of these organizations by senior members and the continuing frustrations of minority status led to further unrest and dissatisfaction among the more junior members who made up well over a majority of the House Republican party" (Peabody 1966, 4).

This dissatisfaction took the form of the revolt against Halleck in 1965. Peabody claims that some Republican members who were not pleased with their committee assignments blamed Halleck and his leadership: "[A] minority Leader, compared to the Speaker and the Majority Leader, inevitably suffers from fewer choice committee assignments to dispense to promising newcomers and party regulars. . . . Since the rewards are fewer and the competition usually keener, he more often ends up pleasing only one member or one state delegation, at the cost of antagonizing several" (1966, 6).

Conflicts over committee assignments as well as policy were exacerbated under Halleck by his leadership style. His abrasive style of dealing with colleagues as well as opponents did not endear him to his party's rank and file (Peabody 1966).

Additional evidence that first-time Republican members in the 88th Congress were displeased with their committee assignments comes from a memorandum written by Donald Rumsfeld (R-IL), then president of the 88th Club, to newly elected Minority Leader Ford just before the start of the 89th Congress. In the memorandum, Rumsfeld requests that Ford appoint a second-term representative to the Executive Committee, because second term members, "although no longer freshmen, are in large numbers asking [for] new committee assignments, and feel very strongly that this would improve their chances of receiving proper consideration."[7] Rumsfeld goes on to endorse Jack Wydler (R-NY) to serve on the RCC as the representative of the twenty-two members of the 88th Club. Rumsfeld says of Wydler, "He was very much in your corner in the minority leadership contest, is not seeking a new committee assignment for himself, and, we feel would be very much inclined to work closely with you to help solve the dozens of problems relating to committees."

Both Charles Halleck and Joe Martin were turned out as Republican leader, in part because of the perception shared by many younger members, especially those from small states, that they were not receiving sufficient representation on key committees. Halleck's successors in the position were aware of the difficulties associated with the responsibility for making committee assignments and sought to distance themselves from retribution by (1) blaming minority status and unfair distribution of committee ratios by the Democratic majority for insufficient Republican seats; (2) avoiding the perception that they as individuals were responsible for the fate of any individual member, by being careful not to make direct promises and stressing the committee nature of Executive Committee decision making; and (3) repeatedly emphasizing the need for a fair and equitable process.

Gerald R. Ford and John J. Rhodes

Both Gerald R. Ford and John J. Rhodes appear to have learned from the revolts that overthrew the two previous Republican leaders. Throughout the archival records of both minority leaders, considerable evidence shows that both tried to convey to other members that they were supportive of requests for committee assignments but that the process was controlled by the RCC, and demand for committees far outpaced the supply of seats allocated to House Republicans. In responding to letters from members seeking committee assignments, Ford often tried to deflect criticism onto the Democratic leadership for its failure to provide sufficient seats to meet the demands of Republican members. The following excerpt from a letter to Robert V. Denney (R-NE), who was seeking a seat on the Appropriations Committee, is typical of the letters that Ford sent in response to committee assignment requests during the 91st Congress:

> Your motivation in seeking this assignment is fully appreciated, for you certainly have the background and experience which would enable you to make a valuable contribution to the deliberations and work of the committee.
>
> However, in checking over the list of standing committees and reflecting on possible committee vacancies to be filled by the Republicans, you will notice that we have a full membership on the Committee on Appropriations. Even though we have gained 1.26% in our membership in the House, it is highly unlikely that the Democrats will weaken their control of the Committee by releasing any seats for our use without a hard-fought struggle which they

have the votes to win. I am sure you will readily recognize that a committee with fifty or more members can become an unwieldy group. Moreover, I am doubtful that Speaker McCormack and the others in the Democrat leadership would be sympathetic to increasing the size of the Committee to accommodate us.

In any event, you may be sure I will make every effort to get as many seats as possible for Republicans on each of the committees when Speaker McCormack and I meet to negotiate the committee ratios for the 91st Congress.[8]

In other letters, Ford emphasized the excess of demand over supply that limited a member's chances of securing a desired seat. In response to William Dickinson's (R-AL) request for a place on Appropriations in 1967, Ford wrote, "As you may be aware, more than six times as many requests for assignment to this committee have been received as we have any hope of having vacancies to fill. So I am sure that you will readily understand the problem which will confront the Committee on Committees in filling the spots relinquished by Democrats for our use."[9]

Even when Ford was asked to endorse a Republican candidate seeking election to the House for a specific committee slot should that member be elected to Congress, Ford was hesitant to speak for the RCC in anything resembling the bold language used by Martin. In a September 15, 1970, memorandum, the executive director of the National Republican Congressional Committee (NRCC), John T. Calkins, wrote to Ford, asking him to write a letter supporting congressional candidate from Oklahoma Jay Wilkinson (who ultimately was defeated by Thomas Steed) for a seat on Armed Services were he to be elected. Calkins included a proposed draft letter, in which Ford was asked to say, "As Minority Leader, I would like to officially inform you that we in the Republican Leadership will do everything possible to assure you a seat on that Committee." The Calkins draft concludes: "You will receive priority consideration for assignment to the House Armed Services Committee should you be elected to the Congress in November."[10]

The actual letter Ford sent to Wilkinson is a much weaker endorsement, and one that does not come from the Republican leadership, but from Ford personally: "In view of the heavy concentration of military installations in your district, I can readily understand your desire to become involved in the work of the House Committee on Armed Services. Assignment to that committee would enable you to render effective, constructive service to your constituents. Should you be successful in November, I will be glad to do everything I can to help you achieve your desired goal."[11]

The one famous case where Ford took sides in the committee assignment process occurred early in his tenure as minority leader and likely taught him a lesson. Soon after his elevation to Republican leader, Ford tried to advance the interests of some of his supporters—unsuccessfully.

> In 1965, Gerald R. Ford fresh from his victorious campaign against incumbent Republican leader, Charles Halleck, went down to defeat in his effort to get an easterner assigned to the committee [Ways and Means]. James F. Battin (Mont.) defeated Charles Goodell (N.Y.), a leader of the Republican bloc that helped Ford topple Halleck.
>
> Battin's winning coalition included the votes of three large delegations: California, Illinois, and Pennsylvania. He was close to James Utt (a member of Ways and Means who doubled as the California representative on the Committee on Committees) who wanted another westerner on Ways and Means and who was attuned to the voices of some business interests that did not want Goodell to succeed. The votes of Illinois were directed by Leslie Arends who, with a seconding speech from Battin, has just been reelected as the party's whip to the chagrin of those Republicans (Goodell and others) who had defeated Halleck. Luckily, Battin was on the Foreign Affairs Committee and if he left it for Ways and Means then James Fulton of Pennsylvania who wanted to return to Foreign Affairs after having been on it previously, could fill the vacancy. In a classic example of implicit bargaining in the House, without a word between them, Fulton supported Battin for Ways and Means. Fulton then returned, happily, to Foreign Affairs and Goodell remained, unhappily, on the Education and Labor Committee. (Manley 1970, 44)

Rhodes followed Ford's lead by refusing to expend political capital on public endorsements for committee assignments that had the potential to create ingrates and enemies. Frequently, his letters to members as well as to other influential individuals and groups who endorsed a Republican member for a particular committee seat received responses that stress the difficulty of pleasing everyone and Rhodes's desire to ensure that the process was fair. In a letter responding to a supporter of Bob Kasten (R-WI), following the Watergate election of 1974 when Democrats elected so many new members, Rhodes wrote, "I like Bob Kasten, too. He is a real comer and I will do my best for him. It is particularly tough this year, as you know, but we are making every effort to make the appointments as equitable and satisfactory to all as is possible under the circumstances."[12]

Rhodes's response to first-term member Robert W. Davis (R-MI), who expressed "keen disappointment" over his committee assignments, likewise indicates a desire to avoid the fate of Martin and Halleck by stressing how difficult it is in the minority to please everyone, and how Rhodes would do his best to rectify the situation in the future: "I can appreciate your disappointment in the committee assignments which you were given. It just wasn't possible to do all we wanted to do for every freshman Member. Just know that we'll keep your request in mind and, as soon as possible, take better care of you! You certainly deserve the best."[13]

Finally, Rhodes was also asked by the NRCC to endorse Republican candidates for the House and provide these candidates with written support for a particular committee assignment that was viewed as important to his or her district (typically either Agriculture or Armed Services). Like Ford, Rhodes made no overt promises of assignments: "It has always been my belief that the interest of a Congressional District and the Nation as a whole are best served when Members of Congress are assigned to committees which can utilize their talents and expertise to the fullest extent. I can assure you that every consideration will be given to making certain that you are appointed to the House Committee on Agriculture."[14]

As Republican minority leader, neither Ford nor Rhodes controlled the committee assignment process. Both were willing to allow the committee to make decisions, and in doing so, avoid individual blame from the many dissatisfied Republicans. For the minority party, there are never enough seats on important committees to keep everyone happy. The idea that the committee assignment process is routine and simply accommodates the requests of members is inaccurate. The best that the minority leader can do is to promote a feeling that the committee assignment process is fair, and that members have a chance at good assignments.

Bob Michel

Robert H. Michel, who served as Republican leader from the 97th through the 103rd Congress, is another example of a leader who largely allowed the process to operate without much leadership interference. The data obtained from the Michel Papers provide a unique insight into the role that one party leader played in the committee assignment process during a ten-year period. During most of the period covered by this study, the Republican leader served ex officio, without vote, as chair of the RCC and its decision-making subcommittee, the Executive Committee. It was only after the reforms instituted at the start of the 101st Congress that the party leader and whip were given a formal vote in the process. This fact alone seems to raise important questions about the Republican leader's influence over committee assignments. Why would a congressional party give no formal voting role to its *leader* in deciding the composition of committees? Although Republican Leader Michel did not have a vote in committee balloting (97th through 100th Congress), as the representative of the Illinois delegation on the Executive Committee, he did exercise voting authority on behalf of his delegation throughout the period, and therefore we are able to analyze the leader's success in getting members whom he supported assigned to key committees through five cycles of the assignment process.[15]

Table 6.1 is derived from an analysis of all contested ballot elections conducted by the Executive Committee during the 97th through the 101st Congress for all committees. These data were obtained by coding the paper ballot slips cast by Executive Committee members (which are stored in the Michel Papers at the Dirksen Library). As table 6.1 indicates, Republican leader Bob Michel in no way dominated the assignment process for key committees. In 116 contested committee assignment final

TABLE 6.1
Michel support for committee assignment winners

Congress	Final ballots	Michel votes for winner	% Michel votes for winner	Exclusive committee vacancies[a]	Michel votes for winner	% Michel votes for winner
97th	15	9	60.0	11	7	63.6
98th	22	6	27.3	6	2	33.3
99th	45	28	62.2	6	3	50.0
100th	15	7	46.7	11	4	36.4
101st	19	11	57.9	1	0	0.0

Data coded by authors from paper ballots found in the Robert H. Michel Papers.
[a]Appropriations, Energy and Commerce, and Ways and Means.

ballots, Michel's chosen candidate was only successful in winning the committee seat 61 times (about 52.6 percent of the time). Michel was not able to build winning coalitions in support of his candidates; candidates were almost as likely to win places on committees without Michel's voting support as they were if Michel voted for them.

What is even more striking is Michel's inability to get his favored candidates placed on the exclusive committees—Appropriations, Energy and Commerce, and Ways and Means. Michel voted for only sixteen of the thirty-five (45.7 percent) members selected to vacancies on these three committees. Although there were times when Michel supported a defeated candidate who was victorious in a later round of balloting, on eleven separate occasions, the candidate supported by Michel did not receive any of the vacancies on the exclusive committees. Like his immediate predecessors, Bob Michel did not control the committee assignment process when he was minority leader. In an interview, Michel stressed fairness over party or leadership goals: "Well, of course as leader and chairman of the committee, *my whole objective* was to make everybody happy. Pleased with their committee assignment. Pleased with the process, at least, that they got a fair shake" (emphasis added).[16] To Michel, the perception that the process was fair to all members seems to have been much more important than exercising direct control over individual assignments.

Also apparent from the voting data is the lack of consensus among the leadership. Three different whips served the Republican Conference under Michel's leadership—Trent Lott, Richard Cheney, and Newt Gingrich. Although there is evidence that Michel had a better relationship with Cheney than with either Lott or Gingrich, when it came to choosing members for committees in the 101st Congress, Michel and Cheney did not share the same voting criteria. Of the twenty-seven rounds of written ballots for committee assignments filled at the start of the 101st Congress (the only Executive Committee session when both the leader and the whip cast recorded votes), the leader and the whip voted for the same candidate only eleven times (40.7 percent). The whip was no more successful in supporting the winning candidate than was the leader—both supported eleven of nineteen eventual winners.

Newt Gingrich

Much has been written about the degree of control that Newt Gingrich (R-GA) exerted over committee assignments during his time as Speaker. Gingrich certainly exerted a great deal of control, especially during his first year as Speaker—many Republicans felt that Gingrich was largely responsible for their electoral success and allowed him considerable discretion that first year. In the words of Robert Livingston (R-LA), "It was his choice to make. Because I think the conference would have . . . I mean here we were, elated to take over the majority for the first time in forty years, so that any decision that he would have ultimately made would have stuck."[17]

In his first year as Speaker, Gingrich rewarded friends, especially first-term members and members who had belonged to his Conservative Opportunity Society, and punished those who had not been supportive of his revolutionary tactics in the past. His influence on the assignment of committee chairs in particular demonstrated the duality of motives that is central to leadership decision making. Gingrich passed over the senior Republican on three key committees to appoint someone who he felt would be better at furthering the Republican agenda as well as more loyal personally. It should not be surprising if all members who were passed over for committee chairs had supported

Edward Madigan (R-IL) in his 1989 race against Gingrich for Republican whip. The five top Republicans on Appropriations had all voted for Madigan, as had the member whose seniority placed him next in line for chairing both Energy and Commerce and Judiciary.[18]

Gingrich used the Speaker's office and task forces instead of committees to push much of the Republican agenda in the 104th Congress, a move that apparently was not favored by many of the other senior Republicans. Bob Livingston explained his view of Gingrich's motivations: "He never trusted the committee process. In point of fact, he did everything that he could to undermine the committee process. Because he loved task forces, and he loved controversy and almost chaos, because it allowed him to run things in the way that he wanted to."[19]

In addition, he used his influence on the Steering Committee (formerly the RCC) to place first-term members of the 104th Congress on exclusive committees. This was opposed by many senior members. Largely due to the efforts of Gingrich, first-term members received nine of ten Commerce Committee (formerly Energy and Commerce) openings, seven of the eleven available Appropriations seats, and three places on Ways and Means. The decision to break with tradition by placing untested members on key committees led to considerable controversy when first-term Appropriations appointee Mark Neumann (R-WI) refused to follow the leadership's lead in committee voting. Livingston described Neumann with some ambivalence:

> I understood the Appropriations Committee and felt that it was a plum that you gave to tested, tried-and-true individuals who wouldn't be mavericks, and in fact Neumann was about as far from that as you could imagine. It ended up working; we ended up developing a pretty good relationship, but to say that it wasn't rocky would simply be untrue. We had some really knock-down drag-out fights. Neuman was an individual. He was . . . I thought he would have been perfect for the Budget Committee and ultimately got him on the Budget Committee in an effort to encourage him to go elsewhere. But he really did have a sense of the numbers. [He had been] a small businessman and very successful. He analyzed as an incoming freshman the entire federal budget, and he

prepared his own budget. And if you didn't like his choices, he had backup choices for changes. The guy was phenomenal. But he was not a committee person. Certainly wasn't an Appropriations Committee person. And was not what one would call a team ballplayer in the sense of the word. And you know, that could be positive or negative. And in my opinion as the chair of the committee, who was trying desperately to make sure that everyone stayed on the team so that we Republicans could cut the budget successfully and yet fulfill our responsibilities under the Constitution, I thought that he was a hindrance.[20]

As the elation over taking control of the House after forty years in the minority began to wear off, other members of the Republican Conference began to object to the use of task forces instead of committees.[21] As the negative consequences of Gingrich's operating style became apparent, Gingrich no longer could dictate assignments to the conference.

In discussing his role in the process, Gingrich contends that that he could not impose his choices on the Steering Committee: "And we would literally consider every possibility. We would then vote. . . . The speaker had the most votes in the room but did not have anything like a majority by himself" (quoted in Wagner 2001). Like previous Republican leaders, Gingrich was willing to write letters and attend campaign events for Republican candidates, promising to assist successful candidates in their pursuit of a given committee assignment of special interest to the district. Like previous Republican leaders, Gingrich was careful not to overpromise:

> I think generally if you get a letter from the speaker and the majority leader, that's a big step in the right direction. And let's say you're representing an agricultural district and it really matters to your district that you be on Agriculture. Well, the odds are pretty good that you're going to get there anyway. But if it will help you win the election, it's not too hard to get one of the senior leaders to come to your district for a campaign event, and at the campaign event they'll have a press conference and they'll tell the press, "I'm going to do everything I can to get them on the right

committee." And that does have some effect on the election, and usually they keep their word. Usually, that's where [the new members] end up. But the leadership's pretty careful not to say that unless they can do it. (Wagner 2001)

Bob Livingston, who was Gingrich's choice to head the Appropriations Committee, and who chaired the Steering Committee during its committee assignment phase in 1998, when he was selected as his party's candidate for Speaker (he resigned from the House before being elected Speaker), shared his observations on the difficulties of leadership:

> The Steering Committee is a composite of the larger conference. There were factions and alliances. You know, generally speaking, it was the Speaker that guided the show, and he had sufficient votes to force his will on it. But sometimes he didn't, and sometimes he had to make a deal with the other side. Sometimes he was just disinterested—for whatever reason, didn't care one way or the other whether X or Y got the committee slot. You had other members— California might want on a committee, and Texas might want to trade. . . . I mean, that whole process within the Steering Committee is a very intense situation, where there is no guarantee of the outcome. The Speaker has got the edge, but if the majority leader and the whip decide to buck the Speaker and form their own alliances, the Speaker can be left out in the cold. Or you know, maybe a Committee chairman—Ways and Means, Budget, or Appropriations—wants to make sure that he gets his views enforced, and he gets a block of set members. He better have the votes to do it, because if he is short, he could get rolled, and if he makes an ass of himself, he might get rolled disastrously. It is every bit as intense as the big conference.[22]

Gingrich did not make the same enemies as former Republican leaders Martin and Halleck had made; he consciously tried to reward the large and influential class of first-term members elected in 1994. By bypassing the committee system, violating the seniority of members who were in line to be committee chairs, and placing untested, maverick first-term members on key committees, however, he created tensions with the senior members of the conference. Gingrich's place as Speaker was threatened by an abortive coup in the summer of 1997, and he was finally forced to resign in 1998.

Dennis Hastert

The selection of Dennis Hastert (R-IL) as the new Speaker marked a return to a committee-centered form of leadership. In the words of one Republican leadership staff member, "Newt was a much more hands-on Speaker then his predecessors had been. He very much wanted to have his hands on what was going on in the committees. The committees did resent the amount of influence he used over the committees. . . . Speaker Hastert is not. [He] lets the committees work their will. . . . [He] does not interfere as much."[23]

Unlike Gingrich, Hastert does not rely heavily on task forces, preferring instead the "regular order" of committees.

Hastert has also backed away from one of the major innovations of the Gingrich period by drastically reducing the number of key committee assignments that go to first-term members (Bresnahan 2000). This change, which was initiated by Bob Livingston when he briefly chaired the Steering Committee in 1998, has been continued under Hastert.[24]

In the committee assignment process, there is some evidence that the Republican leadership under Hastert has used committee assignments to reward friends and punish those who deviate from the party position (Bolton 2003). However, once given, committee assignments lose their value as tools of future motivation, and leadership PAC money (all the more important under the recently enacted campaign finance laws) is a more potent method currently used by the Republican leadership.

DEMOCRATIC LEADERS IN THE POSTWAR PERIOD

Throughout most of the postwar period, the Democrats were the majority party in the House, and much more has been written about Democratic leaders. Little of this research, however, has focused on the role of the leaders in making committee assignments. The following sections recount the committee assignment influence of the postwar Democratic leaders. As did their Republican counterparts, Democratic leaders balanced competing goals.

Sam Rayburn

Speaker Sam Rayburn's (D-TX) ability to influence committee assignments was the subject of a poem written by a Democratic member, which originally appeared in the *New York Times*:

> I love Speaker Rayburn, his heart is so warm,
> And if I love him he'll do me no harm.
> So I shan't sass the Speaker one little bitty,
> And then I'll wind up on a major committee.

(Goodwin 1970, 73)

Rayburn was House Democratic leader (either Speaker or minority leader) for more than twenty years, longer than anyone else in history. He was able to influence the composition of the Ways and Means Committee (then the Democrats' committee on committees), fill key vacancies with members who were not only loyal Democrats but also personally loyal, and use Ways and Means to exert control over the process of assigning members to other committees. The small size of the Democratic membership on Ways and Means (fifteen when the Democrats were in the majority; ten when in the minority, compared with the forty-six-member DSPC of today) enabled Rayburn to ensure he had influence over a majority of the member's votes. Members of Ways and Means felt they owed Rayburn for their seats and consulted with him before making assignments. Although there will always be rivals for the leadership in an institution comprising many ambitious politicians, Rayburn was able to ensure the personal loyalty of that most Ways and Means members.

Manley (1970) and Shepsle (1978) both make the case that Rayburn stacked the membership of Ways and Means with loyal members as a way to control committee assignments. "By affecting who goes on Ways and Means the leadership affects who goes on other committees and, through this indirect but remarkably effective means, what legislation is reported to the House" (Manley 1970, 25). We have uncovered archival evidence of the methods Rayburn used to manipulate the Ways and Means membership.

The case of Wilbur Mills (D-AR) is illustrative. After serving one term on Banking, Mills sought membership on Ways and Means. Unlike other committee assignment decisions, Ways and Means candidates were voted on by the full Democratic Caucus. Mills was not successful in this first attempt. According to Zelizer (1998, 10), Rayburn subsequently asked Mills, "Why didn't you tell me you wanted on the Ways and Means Committee? I'd have put you on my list. . . . You can have the next vacancy." Mills was elected to the Ways and Means Committee on October 15, 1942; he owed Sam Rayburn for the position.[25] Mills subsequently became a close associate of Rayburn, one of his so-called "boys."[26]

Correspondence in the Mills Papers indicates the degree to which Rayburn and Mills collaborated in making committee assignments, even in the years before Mills's elevation to chairman of the committee.[27] Mills appears to have acted as both an advisor and an envoy for the Speaker, providing detailed advice about which members should be appointed to Ways and Means and contacting the anointed members to encourage them to seek the assignment. The following exchange of letters illustrates the pattern.

On November 11, 1948, Sam Rayburn wrote a brief letter to Wilbur Mills: "I would very much like to have your views on Membership on the Committee on Ways and Means." On November 16, 1948, Mills replied with a long letter to Rayburn:

> You will recall that Tom O'Brien and Cecil King served on the Ways and Means Committee during the 79th Congress, and you perhaps have talked to them during the 80th Congress of their desire to return to the Committee when a vacancy occurred to which they could be assigned. I know that Cecil will desire to return to the Committee, but since Tom is on the Appropriations Committee, I am not certain that he will want to unless you or Mr. McCormack ask him to do so. I had, however, counted these two as possibilities to fill two of the vacancies. Of course Texas will be entitled to a place on the Committee, and I understand during this year while the Congress was in session that Judge [Jesse Martin] Combs would very much like that place. Thus as I analyzed the situation, there may be three vacancies for other members of the Congress. Two freshmen members of the 80th Congress immediately come to my mind as being ideal selections for the Ways and Means Committee, and I think they are properly located geographically. I

am referring to John Carroll of Colorado, and Carl Albert of Oklahoma. These men certainly are loyal as well as men of outstanding ability. Should they be acceptable, that would leave one other place, and for that spot, I had in mind two other members, Hale Boggs of Louisiana or Mike Feighan of Ohio . . . .

These members, plus those of us on the Committee who always go along with the leadership on committee assignments[,] would certainly *leave no doubt as to committee organization being in accordance with the policies and desires of the House leadership.* Furthermore, in my opinion these additions to the Committee will prevent that Committee from being controlled in the future by a coalition of some of our Democrats and the Republicans. I should think that all of them would be interested in increased benefits under Social Security as recommended by the President and that they would likewise, with the possible exception of John Carroll who should be checked on the subject, be for extension of the Reciprocal Trade Agreements Act without amendments and for acceptance of the International Trade Organization Charter if the same is submitted to the House and Senate both for action.

From all reports, the President's program is such that it will be necessary for our Committee to cooperate if important phases of it are to actually be enacted. I have particularly in mind the Social Security program and his recommended changes. It may be that we can obtain some support and cooperation on these matters from the Republicans in view of the recent election, but I think it is safer for us to plan the membership of the Committee on the Democrat side so that we will not need the support of any of the Republicans on the Committee to put through the legislation to which the Democratic Platform commits the Party. (emphasis added)

On November 22, Rayburn replied, "Thank you for your fine letter of November 16th and the suggestions you made in it. I will want to see you at the earliest moment possible when I arrive in Washington on the twenty-eighth of December and I will have your letter before me when we talk."[28]

Apparently, Mills did not think it necessary to consult with Rayburn before encouraging any of his Ways and Means favorites to pursue assignment actively. In letters to each, he discusses the "high regard" that the Speaker and majority leader have for each addressee. The following excerpt from a letter to Hale Boggs dated November 12, 1948, is typical of letters sent to Carroll, Albert, King, O'Brien, Feighan, and Combs before the planned December 28th meeting.

> During the past several days, I have been thinking in terms of vacancies to be filled by the Democrats on the Ways and Means Committee for the 81st Congress. In thinking of prospective members for these vacancies, I have been thinking in terms of you endeavoring to obtain one of the vacancies. As you know, there will be six to be filled by the Democrats. Your loyalty to the party in the past and your basic common sense in approaching legislative problems, as well as the high affection which I have for you, causes me to believe you to be an ideal member for that committee. I know too of the high regard which Mr. Rayburn and Mr. McCormack have for you and I sincerely believe that if your delegation will act immediately in requesting consideration in their assistance in providing such a place for you, that it can be obtained. If you are hesitant yourself in requesting their consideration, which you should not be, and if you are interested, you might let the entire delegation sign a letter to Mr. Rayburn requesting such membership for you. I would also do the same thing in a letter to Mr. McCormack.

Boggs replied on November 16, 1948: "I have naturally given some consideration to the Committee in my own mind but have been hesitant to make any steps in my own behalf. Since receiving your most encouraging letter, however, I have taken the liberty of contacting Eddie Hebert here, and he has contacted the other members of the Delegation, who, I am reasonably sure, will join in a letter to Mr. Rayburn and Mr. McCormack."[29]

Not surprisingly, King, O'Brien, Combs, Boggs, and Carroll were all selected to be members of the Ways and Means Committee (along with Stephen Young of Ohio).[30] Under the leadership of Rayburn, members knew that personal loyalty was important to Ways and Means Committee assignment. Mills was loyal to Rayburn (and to majority leader John McCormack), and he recommended other like-minded members for committee service.[31] The crucial role played by the Rules Committee in the legislative process and the importance for a leader to have members

on Rules who are loyal are well known. Both parties have adopted procedures that place the assignment of Rules members in the hands of the
party leader or Speaker.[32]

The degree to which Rayburn worked with Mills to select Rules
members is likewise apparent from the archival record.[33] In a letter
dated November 16, 1948, Rayburn instructs Mills, "I trust that you will
make no commitments for a place on the Committee on Rules until I have
had the opportunity to talk with you." Mills responded the following
day: "You may be assured that it is my intention to make no commitments
for places on the Committee on Rules until I have had an opportunity to
discuss the matter with you and learn of your wishes. You may be
assured of my complete understanding of the necessity of our Committee
cooperating with you to the fullest in assigning members to the Committee on Rules."[34]

John McCormack and Carl Albert

Shepsle (1978) and others have noted that neither of Rayburn's
immediate successors, John McCormack and Carl Albert, was as influential in the committee assignment process as was Rayburn. As reform-
era Speakers, both McCormack and Albert presided during a time of
considerable turmoil within the Democratic Caucus. As Peters (1997)
points out, this was a time when the Democratic Party leadership was
becoming more democratic, and reforms were made to include more
members in the processes of decision making and leadership. Although
Rayburn could deal almost exclusively with committee chairs, his successors were confronted with a much more empowered rank and file. Both
men appear to have used their influence on committee assignments
sparingly, and typically only to further the careers of members from
their home states.

The McCormack period also coincided with the rise of the Democratic
Study Group (DSG), a major proponent of reform. In 1963 the DSG
was instrumental in defeating the McCormack-endorsed Ways and
Means candidates—Phil Landrum (D-GA) and Wilfred Denton (D-OH).
Landrum apparently supported expansion of the Rules Committee in
exchange for McCormack's endorsement for a position on Ways and

Means; however, at the time the full caucus was responsible for selecting Democratic members for Ways and Means, and Landrum was unacceptable to the increasingly liberal caucus (Shepsle 1978).

In a January 1961 interview with Richard Fenno, McCormack emphasized the personal element (rather than policy) when discussing how members were chosen for the Appropriations Committee:

> Of course, personality enters in. Like any gang of fellas on the corner, like any group. You have different personalities. Some members are more popular than others. They are all different. Some of the members are brilliant but they are lazy. Others are not so brilliant, but they develop what they have, and they work hard. Some men are eloquent speakers; but they don't have that 'it' to make a speech. Others don't speak so well, but they've got the courage to go down and say what they feel. It takes a lot of guts to get up off that chair for the first time and face the House. Other members are there for years and years, and no one even knows they are there. But we know they are there. We know they are doing their job in committee, that they are brilliant men, smart men, and that they are on the job all the time. We're just human beings down here—all different. We take all these things into consideration. You can't help it.[35]

McCormack adopted a largely hands-off attitude toward committee assignments, allowing the Ways and Means Committee under the strong leadership of Wilbur Mills to arrive at results that were acceptable to the majority. There is evidence that the administration of John F. Kennedy tried to influence the placement of Democratic House members to further its agenda during the time of McCormack's Speakership. Responding to a question about Kennedy administration involvement in lobbying for a friendly replacement for John J. Riley (D-SC) on the Appropriations committee, Kennedy aide Lawrence F. O'Brien claimed, "Certainly we had a very great interest in committee assignments, because throughout this period we were walking a tightrope and it was essential for us to take advantage where we could of every opportunity that might give us a little additional strength on the Hill."[36]

Like McCormack, Carl Albert rarely sought to assert his committee assignment preferences as a member of the Democratic leadership. Newly elected members frequently wrote to Albert in his capacity as whip, requesting that Albert assist in their quest for a desired committee. For example, first-term representative John Brademas (D-IN) wrote, "I would like to take the liberty of indicating to you, as one of the leaders of the House, my preferences on assignment to a committee. I hope that it will be possible for me to be assigned to the Committee on Education and Labor."[37] Albert's response to Brademas was the same reply that he sent to many other members seeking his support: "As to Committee appointments, this is a responsibility of the Committee on Ways and Means where the merits of the various applicants are examined, and I feel sure the Leadership and the House would be inclined to go along with whatever conclusions the Committee on Ways and Means reaches. However, I assure you that I will bear your interest in mind and do what I can to assist you."[38]

As whip, Albert was unable to get his Oklahoma colleagues placed on the most desirable committees. His attempts to get an Oklahoman assigned to Ways and Means (first John Jarman, then Ed Edmondson) were unsuccessful.[39] In an interview with Ron Peters, Albert recalled his difficulties placing members of his delegation on key committees: "[I]t took me twelve years as a Whip and as the Dean of our group to get [Rep. Thomas] Steed on the Appropriations Committee. It was almost impossible. Mills didn't want him to go on, [Appropriations Committee chair Clarence] Cannon didn't want him to go on" (1979, 24) Albert told Richard Fenno in March 1963 about his relatively hands-off approach in the assignment process:

> As whip I wasn't consulted at all [about Appropriations committee appointments]. As leader, I talk[ed] about it with the Speaker and with the members of the committee [on committees]. I have candidates, of course, and will talk about them. The Speaker's the man to see on that, really. Many times, the Speaker makes the selection and the committee just goes along. But once in a while the committee goes against the wishes of the Speaker. And I've had candidates of mine rejected. On the whole, I try not to interfere in what the committee does. They are the constituted authority, and once you start meddling with them you get into trouble. They

are set up to do the job. So, I try to stay out of it as much as I can. The only time I say anything is when I think the thing is serious. You may watch the first few selections to see how things are going.[40]

Shepsle (1978) confirms that Albert's increased powers did not lead to increased control over committee assignments.

Although the reform movement further increased the power of the Speaker at the end of 1974 by moving the assignment process from the Ways and Means Committee to the Steering and Policy Committee, or DSPC (which was chaired by the Speaker with a majority of the members appointed by the Speaker), this reform did not dramatically increase the power of the Speaker (Smith and Ray 1983). Shepsle, however, recounts an interview with a member who stated that if Albert (or then Majority Leader O'Neill) spoke out in favor of a member seeking an assignment, that member "had it greased" (1978, 242).

In an extensive interview with Ron Peters, Albert claimed that vesting the powers of committee assignments in the DSPC chaired by the Speaker "enhanced the power of the Speaker enormously." However, when discussing that power, Albert focused solely on how he was able to use it to assist his Oklahoma colleagues in securing desired assignments:

> That showed my power—my power as Chairman of the Com-mittee on Committees and the Steering and Policy Committee was demonstrated the very first day when I appointed the Rules Committee and I appointed Clem McSpadden, the first freshmen ever to be on the Rules Committee, I appointed [James] Jones, one of the first sophomores ever to be on the Ways and Means Committee, I took care of Oklahoma, you know, we had for the first time in many, many years (certainly not in my time) mem-bers on . . . the three most important committees.[41]

The Democratic Caucus enacted a reform at this time that had an important and lasting effect on the power of the subsequent Speakers, vesting in the Speaker (or the minority leader) the power to appoint Democratic members to the Rules Committee. A final piece of evidence from the Albert years indicates that as Speaker, he did not try to domi-nate committee assignments and used his influence sparingly, while allowing for much democratic involvement in the process. Albert made it clear that he was not in favor of a proposal to change caucus rules to make Rules Committee members the direct choice of the Speaker. He told the assembled Democratic Caucus, "I have had such wonderful support from the Committee on Rules that I don't think I can improve it, as long as I am Speaker, by supporting this matter, and I have had tremendous support from this gentleman (Mr. Madden). I want my friend, Dick Bolling, to make clear that this amendment does not come from the Speaker."[42] Albert had witnessed the battle between Rayburn and Judge Howard Worth Smith over the size of the Rules Committee and knew the difficulties that a Speaker could encounter when the Rules Committee failed to cooperate with the leadership. Yet he still did not want to accept complete responsibility for choosing Rules members. There is little evidence that either Speaker—McCormack or Albert—tried to dominate the process. This is consistent with much of the literature on this period, as the fractionated Democratic Caucus struggled with reform.

Tip O'Neill

Carl Albert retired from Congress soon after the reforms were enacted. Thomas P. (Tip) O'Neill (D-MA) assumed the position with greater institutional powers than any of his postwar predecessors, but he also inherited a more empowered Democratic membership. As Speaker, O'Neill had the power to appoint eight members to DSPC and served as chair of the committee. Despite his formal powers, by most accounts, Tip O'Neill continued the tradition of noninterference with the committee assignment process that was characteristic of Carl Albert and John McCormack; however, O'Neill did talk of using the DSPC as his "strong arm in formulating and implementing policy for the House," and at times was influential in securing assignments for desired candidates.[43] He was apparently most concerned that Massachusetts members received their desired assignments, and he would often use his influence for other members of the New England delegation as well. A Democratic leadership staff member, who attended DSPC meetings under O'Neill, confirmed this view of the Speaker:

In most cases, it was a decentralized process. There were certain people Tip wanted and that was it, . . . like [for] a new member from Massachusetts or new member from Connecticut sometimes, if he wanted to go a little beyond, but mostly from Massachusetts. If they wanted something, even if it was a really big thing like Ways and Means, . . . he just insisted that they get it regardless who the competition was or regardless of regional things, regardless of every other possibility, and he got it. In exchange for that he left the process fairly open for everything else.[44]

Although O'Neill had a relatively hands-off attitude toward most committee assignments, as Speaker he had the choice (subject to caucus approval) of the Democratic members of the Rules Committee. In making his selection, it is clear that he valued personal loyalty above even party loyalty. His selection of four Rules members at the start of the 96th Congress is illustrative.

On December 15, 1978, Billie Larsen (O'Neill's staff member responsible for committee assignments) forwarded a memorandum to O'Neill, giving the Speaker background on the party loyalty for all candidates for the exclusive committees (Appropriations, Rules, and Ways and Means) as well as for the Budget Committee.[45] Each candidate had three sets of party-unity scores for each session of the previous (95th) Congress: Speaker's preference, whip, and DSPC.[46]

Two of the seats available on the Rules Committee had belonged to members from California and Texas—Bernie F. Sisk (D-CA), who had retired, and John Young (D-TX), who had been defeated. Although each of those states' delegations took it upon themselves to endorse a successor, in neither case did O'Neill follow the delegation's recommendation.

Californian Jerry Patterson wrote the Speaker on June 5, 1978 (soon after Sisk had announced his intentions), expressing an interest in filling the vacancy to be caused by Sisk's resignation. In a subsequent letter to O'Neill, Patterson wrote of his qualifications for the Rules slot: "My four years in the House have given me valuable experience and a record of delivery and loyalty to the leadership."[47] The California Democratic delegation endorsed Jerry Patterson by a vote of 19–7. Harold T. (Bizz) Johnson wrote to inform O'Neill of California's endorsement of Patterson:

"[H]e is a progressive and dedicated Democrat who would be of complete loyalty to you in the 96th Congress."[48]

Instead, O'Neill selected Anthony Beilenson for the California slot on the Rules Committee. Both Patterson and Beilenson had high party-unity scores, but, according to many observers, O'Neill's decision to select Beilenson over Patterson had its roots in the power struggle between California's Phil Burton on the one hand and the incumbent Democratic leadership (O'Neill and Wright, as well as Rules member Richard Bolling) on the other.[49] Patterson was closely allied with Burton (Sheppard 1985). Before the 96th Congress, Wright had defeated Burton for majority leader by a single vote of the Democratic Caucus, in an election that fostered considerable division among House Democrats. Talk of Burton as a future challenger to Wright (and potentially O'Neill) was common in the media. O'Neill wanted someone who was loyal to him personally on the important Rules Committee, not someone who was ultimately loyal to potential rival Burton.[50]

The Texas delegation endorsed Jim Mattox for the Texas vacancy on Rules. However, in a letter to Speaker O'Neill just before the assignment of Rules Committee members, Mattox revealed some doubt about whether he would ultimately be placed on the committee:

> The Texas delegation has traditionally held a seat on this important Committee and the Dean of the Texas delegation, Mr. Jack Brooks, Majority Leader, Mr. Jim Wright, and the entire Texas delegation support my request for this assignment.
>
> I wish to point out to you that philosophically I am and always have been a loyal Democrat, devoted to the principles of the Democratic Party. I rank in the top four in the Texas delegation in support of the Democratic Party Platform and I'm in the top five in ratings from ADA [Americans for Democratic Action] and organized labor.
>
> I am sure you are aware that I have endeavored to cooperate with the leadership whenever it was possible for me to do so. Whenever you needed a vote, you got it, often times at the expense of heavy criticism in my home district. . . .
>
> I realize that some people have said that the closeness of my recent reelection suggests that I am not from a "safe" enough district to have the independence to support the leadership positions.

I do not believe this to be the case. There is a critical difference between votes on the floor and votes in Committee. I would have considerably more flexibility in Committee than I would have on the floor, but I feel that even on floor votes that I can comfortably support the leadership position whenever it is essential to do so. I do not mind taking hard or difficult positions and I've never avoided an issue simply because it might be politically damaging. I am not foolish enough to throw away votes that I do not have to, but my colleagues know that they can count on Jim Mattox.

If I receive this assignment, I commit to you my unequivocal support on any occasion you see the need to request it. I believe that in the overwhelming majority of the time we will be on the same side regardless.[51]

This plea from Mattox did not have the desired effect; O'Neill chose first-term member Martin Frost for the Texas vacancy on Rules. The leadership team chose someone whom majority leader Jim Wright thought would be personally loyal. In his autobiography, Wright claims to have convinced the Speaker to support Frost:

When Texas colleague John Young was defeated for reelection, I talked Speaker O'Neill in 1979 into appointing freshman Martin Frost to Young's vacated post on the Rules Committee. Tip was at first reluctant. That was the Speaker's personal committee, the one on which he depended to schedule his bills for the floor. But I had watched Martin Frost for several years and was convinced that he'd do an excellent job. I knew his family, had observed his work as a reporter for *Congressional Quarterly*, and had closely followed his campaign in a Dallas district adjacent to my own.

"I'll vouch for him, Mr. Speaker. He can stand the heat, he understands the loyalty that post requires, and he'll be dependable." Tip took a puff on his cigar and stabbed his finger in my chest. "Okay, Jim," he said, "but I'm holding you responsible." I never had occasion to regret that recommendation. (1996, 310)

For one of the two remaining vacancies on Rules, O'Neill chose Butler Derrick (whose case is discussed in chapter 5). The choice of Derrick over members with considerably higher party-unity scores who had also sought a Rules seat (including future committee member and Democratic whip David Bonior) indicates the importance of geography in the Speaker's calculations. O'Neill could not afford to alienate southern Democrats and chose a member he viewed as the safest choice from a region that was generally not supportive of the direction of the national Democratic Party's policy agenda. For the final seat on Rules, a vacancy created by the retirement of Rules Committee chair James Joseph Delaney (D-NY), there were three New York candidates—John LaFalce, Leo Zeferetti, and Jerome Anthony Ambro, Jr. All three Democrats from New York had similar, high party-unity scores, and O'Neill chose Zeferetti.

Jim Wright

The experience of Jim Wright (D-TX) concerning committee assignments provides considerable insight into the competing motivations of party leaders, as well as the often conflicting motivations that members of the same leadership team may have. Much has been written of Wright's aggressive control of the policy agenda and use of committee assignments to further his agenda as Speaker.[52] However, even Wright did not dominate the process, and his experience as majority leader is even more revealing of the combinations of motives.

Jim Wright's efforts to get a second Texan on the Ways and Means Committee during the period when he was majority leader illustrates that in the tug of war between party loyalty and the ties of geography, geography usually wins. Leaders not only do not always pursue committee composition that would be the most favorable to party policy goals, but also sometimes have a hard time getting what they want. As the majority floor leader, the person most responsible for securing positive action for party policy on the House floor, Wright frequently put the interests of the Texas delegation ahead of concerns for party loyalty, and sometimes he lost.

Sam B. Hall, Jr., was nominated by the Texas Democrats as their candidate to succeed Omar Burleson on Ways and Means at the start of the 96th Congress and was supported by Wright. Hall was one of the most conservative Democrats, and one of the least likely to vote with the party leadership on key votes. Hall had voted the Democratic position on key votes only 12.5 percent of the time in the second session of the

95th Congress, compared with Wright, who voted correctly 93.5 percent of the time, and Ways and Means chair Dan Rostenkowski, who had a voting score of 92.8 percent.[53]

Thirteen Democratic members were nominated for one of five vacancies on Ways and Means at the beginning of the 96th Congress. Hall's party-unity scores were worse than those of any other competitor, yet in DSPC voting, he received the most votes on the sixth ballot, and therefore was the third candidate to receive DSPC endorsement. However, in a rare event, the five nominees the DSPC forwarded to the Democratic Caucus for the five open slots—Hall, Tom Downey (NY), Cecil (Cec) Heftel (HI), James Shannon (MA), and Frank Guarini (NJ)—were challenged by three additional members, Ronnie Flippo (AL), Wyche Fowler (GA), and James Oberstar (MN).

During the fourth and final ballot of caucus voting, Hall received the sixth most votes. Receiving the most votes of any candidate on that decisive ballot was Wyche Fowler, whose name had been withdrawn in the DSPC after receiving only five votes in the third round of voting. Another failed candidate was Oberstar, who not only had the highest party-unity scores, but was also thought to be the front-runner (Cohen 1979).

Hall was not deterred from seeking a slot on Ways and Means, and when the next slot opened up (the following summer, when Abner Mikva, of Illinois, was appointed to the bench), he again sought the committee assignment with the assistance of Jim Wright. Again, coalitions formed in the DSPC that worked against placing Hall on Ways and Means.

Hall lost in DSPC balloting to Rostenkowski's favored candidate, Marty Russo, a member of the Illinois delegation.[54] In a letter to Wright written before the vote, Hall claimed to have commitments of support from eight DSPC members, three tentative yes's, three definite no's, and ten members who did not reveal their preference to Hall.[55] The support was not enough. In the end, the majority leader's candidate was defeated. According to Farrell, party loyalty was a decisive factor in Russo's victory:

> As the pace of turnover in the House increased, O'Neill augmented his personal relationships with "the book," a computerized record of the loyalty of each House Democrat that was compiled, refined and maintained by aide Billie Larsen. When Representative

Sam B. Hall of Texas wanted a seat on Ways and Means, the contest came down to Hall and Representative Martin Russo of Illinois. O'Neill said, "Let's have the book," and showed the steering committee how Hall has consistently failed to support the Democratic leadership. Russo got the seat. (2001, 433)

Speaker O'Neill had been listed as an "unknown" on the tally sheet put together by Hall and shared with Wright. Ultimately, by drawing Hall's poor party-unity scores to the attention of DSPC members, O'Neill played a role in defeating the candidate favored by his majority leader.

In isolation, the case of Sam Hall supports the theories that attribute a large role to parties in committee assignment. A Democratic member who tended not to support the party position on key votes was denied placement on a control committee. Even with the endorsement of the leadership, a candidate who was too far from the median voter was rejected by the caucus. However, party-influence theories would not predict that the majority leader would put his political capital behind a candidate who had not demonstrated his loyalty.

The case of Kent Hance is even more difficult to explain from a partisan perspective. Despite the failure of Sam Hall to secure a seat on Ways and Means, Majority Leader Wright still wanted another Texan on the committee, and when the 97th Congress commenced, he agreed to place the name of second-term member Kent Hance in nomination. Hance had proved even less likely than Hall to support the Democratic agenda; his internal party-support score on key votes for the first session of the 96th Congress was 8.6 percent; and thus, he failed to support the leadership 91.4 percent of the time. Only 5 Democrats of 272 ranked in an internal leadership list were less likely to support the agenda during the previous session. Wright recognized that Hance might not receive the assignment and therefore worked hard to assure that Hance would be successful.

[T]here is always a fight among younger members who try to get on Appropriations or Ways and Means. The fellow from West Texas—Kent Hance—1978, he had just defeated the Republican nominee George W. Bush in that race for Congress. He had come upon the retirement of George Mahon. George Mahon had been

the chairman of the Appropriations committee and was therefore
[a] very well-known, prominent member of Congress. After two
years, Hance came to me and said: "Mr. Leader, people in my part
of the country don't understand why I can't be in an important
prominent position like Mr. Mahon was. It's hard for them to realize
that he had a long wait." I said, "Now, Kent, what do you have in
mind?" He said "I'd like to be on the Appropriations Committee
or the Ways and Means Committee so that I could convince them
what an important congressman . . . I can be for them." I said,
"Kent those particular committees are held back in reserve for
those people who have proven their loyalty to the party and to
their colleagues and to the institution. We usually don't, we try not
to put many new people on them. It's going to be a hard sell to the
Steering and Policy Committee to get you on there because you
haven't been voting with us on some of the big issues." "Well," he
said, "that is just the point. I want to be a team player. If I had a
position like this, they would tolerate my voting with the team
because they would understand that I'm part of the team and I
have to stick with them. I could explain it to them." I said, "That
makes sense." But what I had told him was the truth. Without my
advocacy and championing, he couldn't have made it on the committee . . . without demonstrated loyalty.[56]

In contrast to his failed effort to secure a seat on Ways and Means for
Sam Hall, Wright was able to help secure a seat for Hance on the committee. Almost immediately the trouble began for Hance. The second-term
member became the only Democratic supporter of Reagan's first major
tax bill (the Hance-Conable bill) and frequently broke ranks with his
Democratic colleagues on Ways and Means. His behavior infuriated committee chair Dan Rostenkowski: "In the following weeks and months,
Hance became a committee pariah. During a committee trip to Baltimore,
he was assigned a seat in the back of the bus, behind the staff. The
chairman also refused to allow him to travel with the rest of the committee to China. Even during committee meetings, Hance was humiliated. He
was quite literally grounded; Rostenkowski made sure his chair, unlike the
others', did not have wheels" (Birnbaum and Murray 1987, 105).

Hance remained on the committee through the 98th Congress, and in
1984, attempted unsuccessfully to capitalize on the notoriety that he had

won as the Democratic sponsor of Reagan's tax cuts by running for the Democratic nomination for the Texas Senate seat being vacated by John Tower.

Wright was encouraged by Democratic colleagues to consider himself a representative of the leadership rather than the Texas delegation when supporting Ways and Means candidates. Members of the leadership and members of the committee on committees often face the difficult choice between advancing the collective interests of the party, on the one hand, and advancing the interests of their state on the other. Jim Oberstar (D-MN), who also desired one of the two Ways and Means vacancies in the 98th Congress, wrote Wright: "I realize that you may be in a delicate position on this matter since one of the current vacancies results from a departing Texas member—and I appreciate your situation. However, I also know that as Majority Leader, your interest extends beyond Texas to the best interests of our entire Democratic Caucus."[57]

Wright supported another Texan in the race for the Ways and Means seat to replace Hance, Mike Andrews, who was endorsed by the Texas delegation. Wright told journalist Margaret Shapiro, "Mike has given solemn pledges that he will certainly be more of a team player . . . that he will not do what Kent Hance did" (Shapiro 1985). Although Andrews was not as conservative as Hall or Hance, his *Congressional Quarterly* (CQ) party-unity score was still seven points less than the mean for Democrats, and Barone and Ujifusa claim, "he has not always gone along with the Democratic Leadership" (1988, 1190). In spite of Wright's best efforts to secure a place for Andrews, two other members were selected for Ways and Means when the DSPC made its committee assignments on January 22, 1985.[58] At the time, there were allegations of a deal made on the DSPC in which members from Pennsylvania, Massachusetts, and Illinois voted as a bloc in favor of Brian Donnelly (MA) and William Coyne (PA) for Ways and Means and Richard Durbin (IL) for Appropriations (Shapiro 1985; Granat 1985). In an interview, Rostenkowski confirmed that he had a longstanding relationship and made deals with John Patrick Murtha, Jr. (D-PA) on the DSPC.[59]

Another vacancy on Ways and Means was created in July of the following year, and this time Andrews was successful in his bid for membership. Documents located in the archived papers of former Speaker

Wright indicate the level of involvement that Wright played in helping Andrews in 1986. A tally sheet with the names of DSPC members and telephone extensions was found, and next to each name was written either "OK" or nothing. To those members whose names were preceded by a handwritten OK, Wright sent the following note: "Just a word of my personal thanks for your support yesterday of Mike Andrews' placement on the Ways and Means Committee. Your support meant a lot and I want you to know how very much I appreciate it. Warmest personal regards."[60]

Majority leader Jim Wright's efforts to place a second Texan on the Ways and Means Committee run counter to much of our theoretical understanding of the role of parties and leaders in the committee assignment process. The complexities and competing motivations involved in the process of assigning members are evident. Wright knew that support from the Texas delegation was essential for his ultimate elevation to Speaker; he tried to use committee assignments to maintain the loyalty of Texas delegation members. Making sure that Texans were on key committees could also help Wright back home. Finally, personal loyalty of successful Texans not only would be useful to him to ensure his institutional position, but it could be called upon when he needed votes to further the Democratic agenda. Placing Hance on Ways and Means was one of two instances when Wright came to regret his assistance in getting members on committees (the other being Phil Gramm on Budget). Of Hance, Wright said, "Usually people are more prone to show their appreciation."[61]

On the one hand, the leader needs to be concerned with policy and what is best for the party agenda. Party loyalty is stressed, especially for those members assigned to control committees, where many of the major policies are determined. On the other hand, the leadership must be concerned with party maintenance and keeping peace in the family. If Wright had turned his back on his Texas delegation by failing to support Texans for key committees, he would have jeopardized the relationship with his core of institutional support. Unlike their northern, liberal partisans, conservative southern Democrats had some place to turn if they felt that the party leadership was not providing them with a fair share of the plum committee positions. Fear of conservative defection to the Republican Party or to more conservative Democratic candidates in leadership elections was a factor in leadership decisions.

The Democratic leaders, like the Republican leaders, were motivated by a combination of self-preservation, advancement ambition, and the desire to enact good public policy. The defection (or retirement) of too many conservative members unhappy with their committee assignments could threaten Democratic majorities. Although Wright certainly recognized that the three Texas Democrats he supported for Ways and Means were not representative of the national party, to alienate conservatives jeopardized the working majority and risked turning over control of the institution to the Conservative Coalition.

As Speaker of the House, Jim Wright tried to exert more control than any other modern Democrat ever did over the committee assignment process. Even so, in the words of a longtime Democratic leadership aide, "Jim Wright [was] a little bit more aggressive, a little bit more, sort of, concerned about who got what. But again, a lot of it was left to the members themselves."[62] Wright did take measures to try to ensure that the members of the DSPC were loyal to him (rather than to Dan Rostenkowski, his potential rival for control of the House Democrats): "When Wright joined Steering and Policy as majority leader, he seemed lost by contrast. One former O'Neill aide said, "I can't recall him ever being a factor on Steering and Policy." Even at the beginning of the 99th Congress, Wright's last as majority leader, Rostenkowski outmaneuvered him over committee assignments and hoped to use Steering and Policy as a power base against Wright even after he became Speaker" (Barry 1989, 82).

Instead of allowing the groups with representation on the committee on committees to select their own representatives, Wright appointed members who would be loyal to the speaker. He even went so far as to appoint Jim Chapman (D-TX), a member who was actually in his second term (because he had been elected in a special election in the previous Congress), as first-term representative. In addition, "Wright asked Jack Brooks, the dean of the Texas delegation, to run for election from his region, knowing he would win and be loyal. And there was Energy and Commerce chairman John Dingell. . . . Dingell asked Wright for one of the Speaker-appointed seats, promised his support, and guaranteed that the member elected from his region would support Wright as well. . . . In return, Dingell would have Wright's support when naming members to Energy and Commerce" (Barry 1989, 83).

Steering and Policy belonged to Wright.[63]

Wright's desire to use the DSPC as a way to ensure party loyalty was much more apparent when Wright was Speaker than when he was majority leader, as he described in an interview:

> Steering and Policy would specifically enumerate what is going to be party policy, and those were the numbers. A sitting member who wanted another committee assignment would be graded, yes. Within the committee there were a good many people who were interested in party loyalty. They didn't want to have committees entered with folks who would betray a majority of the members. [These folks] get comfortably ensconced on a committee and believe themselves impervious to removal. They get very, very independent of the wishes of the members. So rightly or wrongly, the members on the Steering and Policy, representing a cross-section of new and old members in their respective areas, often wanted to have a member's attention for the record. Now, last Congress, we had eighteen votes, maybe nine in the first session, nine in the second, that were policy votes—usually wouldn't be that, there would be fourteen or sixteen. Now, on how many of these was he with us? And look at how many times he was against us. And if he was against you more than he was with you, well, that old boy is lucky [to have the] assignment that he has. He didn't have much claim on additional assignments. Yes, that came into being, I guess during Tip's term as Speaker. Yes, definitely.[64]

At the suggestion of Butler Derrick (SC), Wright proposed to increase the power of DSPC by creating a one term probationary period for new committee assignments (Barry 1989). Wright appointed a task force to study the proposal, but no action was ever taken on it.

Finally, when asked whether he had a say about someone getting on a committee that he did not want, and whether this ever happened while he was Speaker, Wright responded, "Well, there were times when

I might have had preferences, might have preferred someone else, but generally, I believe that in both Congresses where I served as Speaker, we were able to pretty well get what we wanted."[65]

Jim Wright's downfall as Speaker is typically attributed to his Democratic colleagues' failure to support him when he was faced with ethics allegations brought by Newt Gingrich (Peters 1997; Barry 1989). Wright's aggressive use of committee assignments to further his personal and policy goals likely contributed to his downfall, because he could be held personally responsible by members who failed to get their desired committee assignments. Although other factors, such as personal style, aggressive use of the powers of Speaker, and visibility, likely played a larger role in Wright's political demise, his influence over the committee assignment process might have contributed somewhat to the lack of support that led Wright to resign as Speaker.

Tom Foley

The leadership of Thomas S. Foley (D-WA) is best considered in two distinct phases: an early phase of accommodation before and during the House Bank Scandal, and a more assertive phase following the scandal that coincided with the election of the first Democratic president in twelve years. Before the bank scandal, which surfaced in late 1991, Foley was frequently described using words such as "passive" and "non-confrontational." The contrast between the personalities of Jim Wright and Tom Foley was stark. Wright was aggressive, partisan, and agenda driven; Foley was the opposite.[66]

In the wake of the bank scandal, support for Foley among House Democrats declined. Many Democrats criticized Foley's handling of the situation, and Democrats such as Charlie Rose (NC), George Miller (CA), and Dave McCurdy (OK) began to explore challenges to the Speaker. Democrat John Bryant (TX) decried Foley's passive demeanor and openly called for the Speaker to step down. In an effort to protect his political future, Foley took a number of steps designed to reward loyalists and create new allies. He increased the number of leadership appointments to the DSPC by creating two additional chief deputy whip positions, giving him more supporters on the panel responsible for committee assignments.[67] The increased number of leadership appointments to the DSPC in many ways made the committee look and operate a lot like the old RCC, where a subcommittee (in this case the leadership appointees) put together a slate that was then confirmed by the full committee. Sinclair claims that during the early 1990s, the Democrats adopted much more of a slate approach to filling committee vacancies: "By putting together a slate—a process that involves considerable consultation and bargaining—the leaders can more easily attain a satisfactory balance among the multiple objectives they attempt to satisfy in the assignment process. It is the 'operating control' of the Steering and Policy Committee that makes such slating possible" (1995, 95)[68]

Richard Blow (1993) contends that after the 1992 election, Foley used the slate process to tighten his control on the Speakership in the wake of the bank scandal and opposition to his conciliatory leadership style:

> Foley and his allies put together a slate of 30 candidates for key committee slots and were able to secure [the requested committee] assignment for 29 of those in Steering and Policy. Foley rewarded members who had remained loyal to him, and punished those who had not been supportive. "I'm not some Lyndon Johnson-esque person running around keeping track of slights," Foley claims. "But on the other hand, the people who clearly have been good friends and have supported you very strongly—I think that's an obligation."

Foley also used his power to assign members to select committees—the top Democrat personally appoints Democratic members to the Permanent Select Committee on Intelligence—to stifle potential opposition. In retaliation for McCurdy's aborted challenge to Foley's leadership, the Speaker refused to reappoint McCurdy to chair the Select Intelligence Committee after the 1992 election:

> In one case a committee chairman [David McCurdy of Oklahoma] who had openly talked about running against me for Speaker was also subject to my personal appointment as a chairman [to the Permanent Select Committee on Intelligence]. Even though I felt that he was a very good committee chairman, and I'd appointed him somewhat against the advice of other people, I didn't think I could

ignore his active opposition so I didn't reappoint him. (Biggs and Foley 1999, 120)

In an effort to win the backing of the large class of Democrats elected in 1992, Foley and the other top Democratic House leaders traveled around the country just after the 1992 election to meet newly elected Democrats. During the meetings, committee assignments were discussed, and Foley subsequently told reporters, "freshmen were 'likely' to get some slots on powerful panels" (Cooper 1992). "Altogether, nine freshmen Democrats received appointments to the top three committees—Appropriations, Ways and Means, and Energy and Commerce" (Zuckman 1992, 3785).

Foley began serving as Speaker at a time of considerable partisan strife and made a conscious effort to be a different kind of Speaker than his predecessor had been. When the banking scandal threatened his leadership, he became more aggressive and used the DSPC to show members that support for the Speaker was beneficial to their careers. Unfortunately for Foley, he was defeated in the 1994 election, and we will never know if he would have continued his more hands-on approach.

Dick Gephardt

As minority leader, Richard Gephardt (D-MO) was most concerned with making sure all the diverse factions of the Democratic Caucus felt like they were getting fair representation on the committees. The role of committees in moving a unified Democratic agenda that had been so important under Jim Wright was superseded by concerns about keeping various factions happy (and in some cases, preventing members from switching parties) and keeping Gephardt in power. As the first Democratic minority leader in forty years, Gephardt needed to keep factions happy so that conservatives would not become Republicans to enjoy the fruits of majority status. This shift in tactics is consistent with our findings regarding Republican decision making in the Executive Committee during their time in the minority; protecting the minority and reducing conflict becomes paramount to the minority leader.

One senior Democrat claimed that Gephardt micromanaged the process to ensure that various factions viewed the process as fair. Gephardt was instrumental in splitting the DSPC into two separate bodies: Throughout

Gephardt's leadership period, the Steering Committee was responsible only for making committee assignments and a separate Policy Committee was established to develop and coordinate party positions. The purpose of the split was to compensate for the loss of so many committee seats that accompanies minority status by giving more members a responsible role in the institution. However, the split meant that the explicit link between party policy and committee assignments was separated during Gephardt's tenure as minority leader.

The slate procedure that originated under Tom Foley was institutionalized during the Gephardt years. Before the formal meetings of the Steering Committee, Gephardt would meet with leaders of the various factions—the Blue Dog Democrats; the New Democrat Coalition; and the Congressional Black, Hispanic, and Women's caucuses—and put together a slate of candidates. The goal of that slate, according to one senior leadership aide, was to balance numerically the number of members on the key committees with the proportion of each group represented by Democratic House members.

> It's almost scientifically mathematical. We have a number of caucuses in our party, which represent virtually the whole body of the party and people . . . strongly identify with that little part of the caucus that they're talking about. What we've done is, almost, we've taken over as a leadership the selection of, not giving it to a broader group, just maybe the ten to twelve people . . . and we have slated our people for vacancies on [Energy and] Commerce, Ways and Means, Appropriations, and Budget, and their slates have over time pretty much evened out except for a little bit of a problem, which we will correct the next time around, having almost percentage-wise what their percentage in the caucus was. . . . Since we've been in the minority no one has gotten the three approved committees—Ways and Means, Appropriations, and Commerce—without it being decided by the leadership.[69]

The role of the full Steering Committee has been altered from one of "horse trading" (to use the words of Henry Waxman) to a "rubber stamp" on the decisions made by Gephardt along with factional leaders. Minority status is difficult for a leader, since there are very few plums to give out. Unhappiness with institutional position naturally breeds discontent. When Gephardt decided to step down as Democratic leader at the beginning of the 108th Congress, a backlog of members felt that he had pledged support for their bid for an exclusive committee and they were waiting for the next round of committee assignments. Although many of these pledges were general (similar to the pledges of support issued by Gerald Ford and John Rhodes discussed earlier), some were apparently explicit promises, for example, a pledge to Bernie Sanders (I-VT) of a seat on Appropriations in exchange for Sanders's promise not to leave the House to run for a seat in the Senate. Nancy Pelosi refused to honor these commitments when she assumed the leadership.

Although the leadership aide quoted above claimed that the mathematical quota system for assigning members to committees was meant to keep peace, our interviews revealed two types of objections to Gephardt's balanced-slate approach. One complaint was that some groups did not feel they were getting their fair share, as a member of the New Democrat Coalition explained:

> It is unfortunate that, you know, part of the membership on committees is driven by fundraising, and . . . by caucus politics to some extent, and I'll be very honest—because some of us are willing to challenge the leadership and some of the traditional constituencies, it doesn't necessarily endear [us] to a lot of our Democratic colleagues. And there are examples of that, where that has made it probably more difficult for some of our members of the more centrist New Democrats to secure assignments to some committees, especially the exclusive committees.[70]

A second criticism of the slate method was leveled by a former member of the DSPC. He claimed that the process had become a popularity contest, in which the most popular, rather than the most qualified, member of each caucus was given the next exclusive opening.

Nancy Pelosi

Upon her selection as Democratic leader in November 2002, Nancy Pelosi (D-CA) moved quickly to make the committee assignment process more of a policy leadership tool. In March 2003, Pelosi altered the function of the Steering Committee, giving it a role in policy formulation as well as committee assignments and restoring the name Steering and Policy Committee (Billings 2003). She has displayed a willingness to use committee assignments as a tool for party unity and has been criticized for her willingness to reward loyalists instead of vulnerable members from difficult districts, who often feel the need to vote against the party (Billings 2004). Pelosi displayed her willingness to link party loyalty with institutional position by engineering a change in Democratic Caucus rules designed to give the DSPC greater leverage over members of exclusive committees. In March 2004, the Democratic Caucus approved a proposal to subject all subcommittee ranking members (or subcommittee chairs) on exclusive committees to approval by the DSPC. This move was designed to give the committee the ability to remove members from desirable positions if they vote against party policy. A similar effort, led by Leslie Byrne in the 104th Congress after a number of subcommittee chairs voted against President Clinton's first budget reconciliation, was defeated when the Democratic leadership (Foley and Gephardt) failed to support the maneuver (see Burger 1993).[71] At the time, Gephardt defended the leadership's position, claiming that the move would "violate normal advancement within the team" (Smith 1996).

Although it is too early in Pelosi's tenure as minority leader for anyone to make any definitive conclusions, she has adopted a much more aggressive position in general and has demonstrated a willingness to use committee assignments to promote party unity in the Democratic Caucus in a way that only Jim Wright has done previously. Pelosi's more aggressive use of committee assignments in promoting party unity indicates the stylistic differences that also enter into the committee assignment process. Whether such a strategy can be sustained is an open question.

PARTY SUPPORT AND ASSIGNMENT
TO INFLUENCE COMMITTEES

Leadership is a difficult concept to explain. Personalities, skills, contexts, and goals differ among individuals and over time. We now turn to a quantitative approach to explore questions of the relationship among leadership, party unity, and committee assignments. The core argument of the party-cartel theory is that party leaders seek to appoint party

TABLE 6.2
Democratic Party loyalty and committee assignments (by institutional era)

Committee requested	Institutional era	
	Prereform 80th–93rd Congresses	Postreform 94th–103rd Congresses
Success (all committees)	.145	.789
Appropriations	.247	.201
Budget	—	.405
Rules	.812	.413
Ways and Means	.562	.279

Note: Committees chosen are the committees most closely associated with party loyalty in the literature. Significance levels (*p*) for Monte Carlo difference-of-median tests. Number of simultaions = 10,000. Random number seed = 2000000.
Null Hypothesis: Committee assignment success is unrelated to party support.
bold   Monte Carlo $p < .05$ (one-tailed)
none   Results fail to support party-support hypothesis at either standard.
n/a   No or too few cases to draw a conclusion.
+   Appointed members are significantly overrepresentative of party supporters.
−   Appointed members are significantly underrepresentative of party supporters.
Sign omitted if critical *p* is not significant.

regulars to committees, especially influence committees, so that they can promote the party agenda. As our discussion above suggests, party leaders often have difficulty influencing committee assignments, and their involvement and success is dependent on a number of political variables. To test the party-cartel hypothesis, we use a similar approach to that used in chapter 4. We examine the median party-unity scores of members who are successful in achieving assignment to an influence committee to determine whether they exhibit party-loyalty behavior that is significantly different from those who fail to gain the same requested assignment. According to party-cartel theory, the median member selected for committee membership should be significantly different from those who are denied assignment. As our analysis above demonstrates, however, additional political factors may attenuate such a result.

Table 6.2 provides the results of difference-of-median tests on party-unity scores for Democrats. We perform the analysis separately for the pre- and postreform eras. In the postreform era, the party leadership could more directly influence committee assignment through its control

TABLE 6.3
Democratic Party loyalty and committee assignments (by leadership era)

Committee requested	Leadership era				
	Rayburn	*McCormack*	*Albert*	*O'Neill*	*Wright/Foley*
Success (all committees)	.066	.148	.616	.766	.643
Appropriations	**.668**	**.885**	.138	.102	**.662**
Budget	—	—	—	.474	**.066**
Rules	1.0	—	.855	.412	—
Ways and Means	.786	1.0	.764	.605	.326

Note: Committees chosen are the committees most closely associated with party loyalty in the literature. Significance levels (*p*) for Monte Carlo difference-of-median tests. Number of simultaions = 10,000. Random number seed = 2000000.
Null Hypothesis: Committee assignment success is unrelated to party support.
bold Monte Carlo $p < .05$ (one-tailed)
none Results fail to support party-support hypothesis at either standard.
n/a No or too few cases to draw a conclusion.
+ Appointed members are significantly overrepresentative of party supporters.
− Appointed members are significantly underrepresentative of party supporters.
Sign omitted if critical *p* is not significant.

over the DSPC. Our analysis suggests that the median member selected to serve on the influence committees during both periods are representative of all requesting members in terms of party loyalty. These findings do not support the expectations of party-cartel theory.

Table 6.3 displays the results of the same analysis, this time performed within leadership eras. The results suggest the same general conclusion. However, there are several interesting findings. First, with all committee assignments, successful committee requesters in the Rayburn and McCormack eras tended to have higher levels of party support than did those who were unsuccessful. During the Albert and O'Neill eras, this finding disappears, but party loyalty appears to be rewarded with assignments to the Appropriations Committee. Finally, during the Wright and Foley era, the median member successfully placed on the Budget Committee tended to have higher levels of party support than did the unsuccessful applicant. Results of the analysis of Republican requesters (table 6.4) evidence a similar pattern: The party-unity scores of members chosen to the influence committees are likely to be similar to those who are not selected for the committee.

TABLE 6.4
Republican Party loyalty and committee assignments (by leadership era)

Committee requested	Leadership era			
	Halleck	*Ford*	*Rhodes*	*Michel*
Success (all committees)	.999	.451	.448	.705
Appropriations	.638	.393	.555	.285
Budget	—	—	.514	.388
Rules	—	.497	.171	.280
Ways and Means	.774	.866	.823	.508

Note: Committees chosen are the committees most closely associated with party loyalty in the literature. Significance levels (p) for Monte Carlo difference-of-median tests. Number of simultaions = 10,000. Random number seed = 2000000.
Null Hypothesis: Committee assignment success is unrelated to party support.
bold   Monte Carlo $p < .05$ (one-tailed)
none   Results fail to support party-support hypothesis at either standard.
n/a   No or too few cases to draw a conclusion.
+   Appointed members are significantly overrepresentative of party supporters.
−   Appointed members are significantly underrepresentative of party supporters.
Sign omitted if critical p is not significant.

Politically, it makes sense for the party leadership not to overplay its party-loyalty hand when making assignments to the influence committees. First, significant sections of the party caucus are politically unable to be highly responsive to the party leadership. In particular, southern Democrats and northeastern Republicans would have great difficulty voting the party line on a consistent basis for fear that they would be subject to electoral defeat. If the party leadership insisted that all members assigned to these committees observe strict party loyalty, sectors of the caucus would never have representation on these committees. Second, leadership members must consider their ability to muster winning coalitions on the floor. If the control committees are solely composed of party loyalists, their legislative vehicles may not be acceptable to the median voter on the floor, thus threatening the ultimate success of the party agenda.

Control over the party agenda likely depends on a slightly less blunt instrument than stacking the influence committees with party loyalists. Effective control appears to have two elements. First, leaders create the impression that assignment to highly sought-after committees is dependent on party loyalty. This encourages members to consider their votes on agenda items closely, especially if they covet influence committee seats. Second, leaders assign a cross-section of the caucus to the influence committees while stressing the need for more moderate members to support the party, especially in *committee*, when necessary, and allowing them to use their judgment and vote their constituency on the floor, when necessary.

· · ·

Our analysis suggests that leadership influence in committee assignment varies tremendously. None of the leaders discussed in this section, with the possible exception of Gingrich in the 104th Congress, can be described as controlling the process unilaterally. Despite wielding significant new powers over the last three decades, Democratic leaders did not and *could not* (according to most members we interviewed) dictate committee assignments. To the degree that they could assert influence, they often evidenced competing impulses, at times seeking to advance the interests of the party, but often influenced by state or regional concerns. Within the committees on committees, significant maneuvering and coalition building (as we demonstrate in more detail in the next chapter) competed with the interests of the leadership.

CHAPTER SEVEN

INSIDE THE BLACK BOX

The way the committee on committees worked, which became very obvious very quickly, was through horse-trading; you vote for my guy, I'll vote for your guy.

JUDD GREGG (R-NH)

In the large body of literature on committee assignments in the U.S. House of Representatives, no study has yet examined the process using data on voting patterns within the committees responsible for making assignments. The best empirical studies of the congressional assignment process to date have looked at the input of the system (individual members' rank-ordered requests for positions on committees) and the output of the process (actual committee assignments) without peering inside the "black box" that is the ballot-by-ballot voting history of each committee member.[1] There is good reason for this: The process by which congressional parties assign their members to committees is shrouded in secrecy. Neither party allows outsiders to attend committee assignment meetings; both parties rely on secret ballots to choose their committee representatives; and members and staff are uniformly unwilling to discuss the inner workings of committee voting in detail.

In this chapter, we take advantage of newly discovered data on Republican committee assignments under the leadership of Robert Michel to look inside the black box. We have collected the votes of each individual member of the Executive Committee of the RCC for every contested ballot between the 97th and the 101st Congress. These data allow us to test numerous hypotheses about committee assignments in the modern Congress with much greater precision than has been previously achieved. We use Executive Committee voting data to explore the formation of coalitions in the assignment of aspirants to committees.

As we have shown, House leaders did not systematically control the committee assignment process for purposes of ensuring party loyalty. House leaders have limited political capital; when they influence the process too frequently, they run the risk of weakening their hold on the leadership. Leaders choose when to involve themselves in the process and often have multiple and at times conflicting motivations regarding committee composition. In addition, different party leaders have different skills; the context of leadership is dynamic as well. If the party leader (or leaders) does not control the process, than how does the process work?

Based on our statistical analysis; interviews with congressional members, former members, and staff; and a systematic review of qualitative accounts of the committee assignment experience, we conclude that, contrary to the expectations of Shepsle (1978), the Republicans' committee assignment process was characterized by long-term coalitions, vote swapping, and large-scale deal making. We find evidence to suggest that the process used by Democrats (though varying by time period and degree) also encouraged the formation of coalitions and vote trading, and that even in the period after the Republicans gained control of the House, coalition building was common in committee-on-committees politics. In short, the process is much more political than the self-selection perspective suggests.

According to Shepsle's formulation, the party committees operate as neutral referees among competing individual claims on committee slots, pursuing what he refers to as a "strategy of accommodation" (1978, 108). Shepsle maintained that "large coalitions that hold together over several votes and several committees appear quite unlikely" (182). Smith and Ray (1983) present evidence regarding the internal deliberations of the Democrats' assignment process that supports the expectations of Shepsle and distributive theory. Using *aggregate* vote totals received by candidates for Democratic committee positions, they conclude that the committee assignment process is largely without significant factional strife. Unfortunately, Smith and Ray did not have access to *individual* votes in the DSPC, which impeded any effort to identify voting patterns within the committee.

Based on previous research that has identified and discussed factions within the Republican Party during the period from the end of World War II until the Republican capture of the House in 1994, we posit three broad factions within the Republican Party that influenced the committee assignment process and suggest an additional factional cleavage unique to decision making in the RCC: a large state–small state cleavage. The Republicans' committee assignment process was characterized by the formation of multiple factions, with identifiable cleavages that prompted factions to vote together as blocs to select new committee members. Our analysis suggests that the large state–small state competition within the Republican Executive Committee had a significant influence on factional conflict and coalition building in the committee. Among House Democrats, coalition formation and vote trading seem more common than has been previously suggested.

REPUBLICAN FACTIONS, CLEAVAGES, AND COALITIONS

Before beginning our discussion of political conflict within the RCC, we must define three terms used extensively throughout the remainder of this chapter: factions, cleavages, and coalitions. Factions are relatively loose associations of political actors who share significant political interests and persist over time. Cleavages are lines of political demarcation that simultaneously divide some factions, discouraging cooperation between factions, while encouraging cooperation between other factions. Coalitions are short-term arrangements among factions aimed at achieving the shared goal of two or more factions at a given point in time.

Factions in the House Republican Party

Studies of the House Republican Party were rare during the party's forty years in the minority. Only recently, since the Republicans took control of the House in the 1994 election, has research on the House Republican Party begun to flourish. Scholars often ignored divisions within the House Republican Party. In part, this was due to the minority status of the party. Largely, however, these divisions were ignored because of the seeming ease with which the Republicans organized its opposition to Democratic initiatives in the House. Consequently, House Republicans were often wrongly depicted as homogenous (Koopman 1996).[2]

Howard Reiter (1981) depicts a party divided into three clusters: the liberal, moderate northeastern "misfits"; the conservative party "regulars," who came from areas of traditional Republican Party strength; and the "realigners," a group of equally conservative party members who believed in a different strategy and new tactics—"that the Republicans should make an all-out effort to attract white Southerners, ethnics, blue-collar workers and suburbanites by capitalizing on their racial fears and dislike of antiwar protestors, psychedelic drugs, street crime and the counter-culture" (293).[3] Reiter points out that although the two largest clusters—the regulars and the realigners—shared a similar level of conservatism, they differed sharply on the question of tactics. The regulars were willing to work with the Democrats and wanted the Republican Party open to all, including the northeastern liberals. The realigners favored confrontation and wanted to exclude in the party those who did not share their strong conservative convictions.

Rohde (1991) similarly divides the House Republicans of the period into three factions: traditional conservatives (Reiter's regulars), new conservatives (Reiter's realigners), and moderates and liberals (Reiter's misfits).[4] Rohde argues that during much of the period under examination, factionalism plagued the House Republicans, until significant events in the 99th and 100th Congress created increased animosity toward the Democrats, which increased unity within the Republican Conference.

More recently, Connelly and Pitney (1994) have identified seven sources of cleavage, suggesting overlapping factional membership within the

House Republican Party. These sources of cleavage can be placed in two categories. Fundamental cleavages are due to geography (western and southern members versus northeastern and midwestern members), seniority (junior versus senior members), ideology (conservative versus moderate members), and institutional loyalties (congressional loyalists versus presidential loyalists). Stylistic cleavages describe elements of political modality: supporters of national strategy versus supporters of local strategy; party activists versus the "district guys" and "committee guys"; and bombthrowers versus responsible partners.

The cleavages Connelly and Pitney identify mostly define the factional divisions described by Reiter and Rohde. Supporters of a national strategy were most closely related to the realigners' faction, and supporters of the local strategy are drawn from the regulars and the misfits. Realigners tended to be from the western and southern wings of the party and were more junior, conservative, and loyal to the White House; misfits tended to be supporters of the local strategy and were from the northern, more senior, and less conservative wings of the Republican Conference. Although the misfits and the regulars tended to have common origins (more northern and more senior than the realigners were), regulars shared the more conservative ideology of the realigners, which was a potential source of cooperation between the two factions.

Party activists tended to be from that section of the party that sought to form a viable congressional Republican Party (realigners), while district and committee guys tended to focus on institutional service and service to their constituency (misfits and regulars). Republican bomb-throwers focused their strategy on characterizing the Congress as a corrupt institution and laying blame for corruption at the feet of the Democratic majority (realigners); responsible partners focused their efforts on working with the Democratic majority to moderate majority policy and advance fundamental Republican policies (misfits and regulars).

We contend that during the period under consideration, the House Republican Party is characterized by three broad factions: misfits, regulars, and realigners (to borrow Reiter's terminology). Connelly and Pitney's discussion puts a finer point on the factional structure of the party, emphasizing an important ideological commonality between the realigners and the regulars. We suggest that the substantial stylistic division between the realigners and regulars, coupled with an important institutional cleavage in the composition of the Executive Committee (the large state–small state representational arrangement), prevented cooperation between these two factions, promoting coalitions between the misfits and the regulars within the committee.

LARGE STATES VERSUS SMALL STATES

Our discussion to this point has centered on the factional structure of the entire Republican Conference. Although we believe that existing factions within the Republican Conference are important for understanding conflict within the committee assignment process, we contend that the representational arrangements that segregated representation into large-state and small-state groupings in the Executive Committee (see chapter 2) created an additional cleavage in the party and played an important role in the development of conflict within the party.

The limited literature on the Republicans' committee assignment process alludes to a domination of the process by the states with historically large Republican delegations, typically states of the Northeast and Midwest: "This [process] concentrates the power over committee assignments in the hands of the senior members from the large state delegations" (Masters 1961, 348).[5]

CLEAVAGE STRUCTURE IN THE EXECUTIVE COMMITTEE

Conflict within the Republican Party over this period is characterized by three broad factions—consistent with Reiter (1981) and Rohde (1991)— and with three major cleavage lines. Borrowing Reiter's terminology, we refer to the three factions as misfits, regulars, and realigners. Figure 7.1 illustrates the factional structure within the RCC that we suggest was present during this period. The three cleavage lines between these factions are institutional cleavage (the solid line) due to the structure of the committee, pitting large states against small states in the RCC; ideological cleavage (the thickly dashed line), dividing moderate and conservative members; and stylistic cleavage (the thinly dashed line),

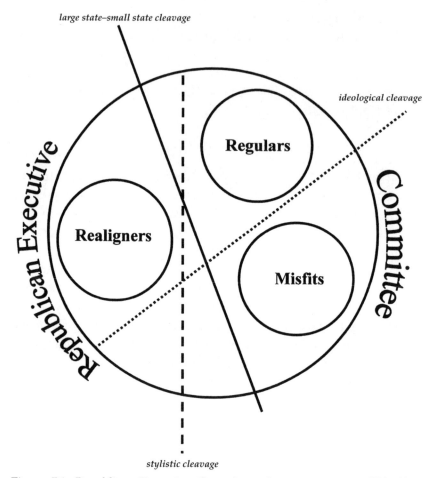

Figure 7.1. Republican Executive Committee cleavage structure, 97th–101st Congresses.

dividing bomb throwers and responsible partners. On one side of the institutional cleavage, misfits and regulars tend to be representatives who come from the large-state groupings within the RCC and generally share a nonconfrontational style within the House; the main cleavage between these two groups is ideological, with the misfits leaning toward moderate positions and the regulars toward conservative positions. Ideologically, the regulars have more in common with the realigners than with the misfits; however, two cleavages prevented a successful partnership between these two factions: differences of political style, with the realigners being too confrontational for the regulars, and, more important, the fact that the realigners were mainly represented in the small-state groups, often by representatives who did not share their views, and rarely had an opportunity to influence the committee assignment process because of the advantage given to the large states in the process. Thus, we contend that the structure of the RCC encouraged coalitions that involved the misfits and regulars.

Given these cleavage and coalition tendencies, we expect that the factional structure of RCC voting will primarily reflect the large state–small state split that is encouraged by the representational structure of the Executive Committee. In the presence of a large-state faction, ideological cleavages will be muted as moderates and conservatives from the large-state groupings combine their votes to promote the interests of their states. As the large state–small state cleavage wanes, we expect to see more obvious ideological conflict that would otherwise be muted by large state–small state conflict.

DATA AND METHODOLOGY

To identify factions within the Republican Executive Committee we analyze individual ballots cast in the committee in the 97th through the 101st Congresses. Unlike Smith and Ray (1983), who examine the vote *totals* in the DSPC in the 95th through the 97th Congresses, we draw our data from *individual votes.* This enables us to examine the committee assignment process at a level unique in the congressional literature. Specifically, we can examine the degree to which voting factions emerge within the Executive Committee and describe the cleavage structure within the committee.

Paper Ballot Data

The Republican Executive Committee began its deliberations during this period with committee assignments to the "major" committees. Assignments to Appropriations, Energy and Commerce, Rules, and Ways and Means were made first, because members assigned to the major committees are likely to surrender assignments on less sought-after committees and free up committee seats for other—especially new—members. When the number of requesters for a preferred committee exceeded the number of committee slots available, the Executive Committee voted on each slot. Each member of the Executive Committee cast the number of votes, by secret ballot, to which he or she was entitled.[6] If no candidate garnered a majority of the total number of votes cast, those nominees receiving no votes, and the nominee with the least number of votes, were dropped from the voting, and the balloting continued. Once a nominee received a majority of the votes cast, he or she became the Executive Committee's nominee for the committee slot.[7] This process was repeated until all slots on a given committee were filled.

We use data collected and coded from the actual paper ballots used in the Executive Committee during deliberations, obtained from the Robert H. Michel Papers at the Dirksen Congressional Center in Pekin, Illinois. On each ballot, the Executive Committee representative indicated his or her name, representative grouping, nominee, and the number of votes cast in support of the nominee.

Table 7.1 depicts the membership of the Executive Committee from the 97th through the 101st Congresses. Committee staff carefully placed these ballots in envelopes, grouped by committee and ballot number. This information allows for certain identification of voting members and their preferences.

Table 7.2 presents the distribution of these votes by committee over the five congresses included in this study.[8] As the distribution of votes indicates, the committees that regularly generated the level of competition that necessitated a vote are the committees that are well established in the literature as attractive.[9] Those committees that generate the most competition within the Executive Committee are Appropriations, Armed Services, Banking, Energy and Commerce, and Ways and Means. Together these committees account for 114 of the 192 votes taken in the Executive Committee over this ten-year period (59.1 percent).

Because of the changing structure of the Executive Committee, we have chosen to refrain from combining Congresses in this analysis. Although a single member may consistently represent his or her state for many years, this is not always the case. Furthermore, RCC membership is not stable from Congress to Congress, especially compared with

TABLE 7.1

Republican Executive Committee annual rosters (97th–101st Congresses)

Representative Unit	97th Congress	Votes	98th Congress	Votes	99th Congress	Votes	100th Congress	Votes	101st Congress	Votes
California	Clair Burgener	21	Jerry Lewis	15	Jerry Lewis	17	Jerry Lewis	18	Jerry Lewis	18
Florida	n/a	—	Bill Young	6	Bill Young	6	Bill Young	7	Bill Young	11
Illinois	Bob Michel	14	Bob Michel	10	Bob Michel	10	Bob Michel	8	Dennis Hastert	8
Indiana	n/a	—	n/a	—	John Myers	5	n/a	—	n/a	—
Michigan	Bill Broomfield	7	Bill Broomfield	6	Bill Broomfield	6	Bill Broomfield	7	Bill Broomfield	9
New Jersey	Jim Forsythe	7	Jim Courter	4	Jim Courter	4	Jim Courter	6	Jim Courter	6
New York	Frank Horton	17	Frank Horton	14	Frank Horton	14	Frank Horton	15	Frank Horton	13
Ohio	Del Latta	13	Del Latta	11	Del Latta	11	Del Latta	10	Ralph Regula	10
Pennsylvania	Joe McDade	13	Joe McDade	10	Joe McDade	10	Joe McDade	10	Joe McDade	11
Texas	n/a	—	Bill Archer	6	Bill Archer	6	Bill Archer	10	Bill Archer	8
Virginia	Bill Wampler	9	William Whitehurst	6	William Whitehurst	6	Stan Parris	6	Stan Parris	5
Five-member states (A)	Bill Frenzel (MN)	15	n/a	—	n/a	—	n/a	—	n/a	—
Five-member states (B)	n/a	—	n/a	—	n/a	—	n/a	—	n/a	—
Four-member states (A)	Jim Broyhill (NC)	24	n/a	—	Eldon Rudd (AZ)	—	Bob Stump (AZ)	11	Bob Stump (AZ)	12
Four-member states (B)	n/a	—	n/a	—	Tom Petri (WI)	—	Tom Tauke (IA)	11	Jim McCrery (LA)	11
Three-member states (A)	Bill Dickinson (AL)	15	Bill Frenzel (MN)	15	Bill Frenzel (MN)	18	Bill Frenzel (MN)	15	Arlan Stangeland (MN)	12
Three-member states (B)	n/a	—	Floyd Spence (SC)	—	Floyd Spence (SC)	18	Hank Brown (CO)	15	Rod Chandler (WA)	12
Two member states (A)	Henson Moore (LA)	24	Bill Dickinson (AL)	24	Bill Dickinson (AL)	10	Bill Dickinson (AL)	9	Bill Dickinson (AL)	10

TABLE 7.1 (*continued*)
Republican Executive Committee annual rosters (97th–101st Congresses)

Representative Unit	97th Congress	Votes	98th Congress	Votes	99th Congress	Votes	100th Congress	Votes	101st Congress	Votes
Two-member states (B)	n/a	—	Henson Moore (LA)	10	Henson Moore (LA)	9	Mickey Edwards (OK)	9	Mickey Edwards (OK)	10
One-member states (A)	Don Young (AK)	13	Don Young (AK)	13	Don Young (AK)	11	Don Young (AK)	13	Don Young (AK)	13
First-term members	Hal Rogers (TX)	1	Bobbi Fiedler (CA)	1	Tom DeLay (TX)	1	Jim Bunning (KY)	1	Chuck Douglas (NH)	1
Second-term members	Tom Loeffler (TX)	1	Ed Zschau (CA)	1	Dan Burton (IN)	1	Tom DeLay (TX)	1	Jim Bunning (KY)	1
Republican leader	n/a	—	n/a	—	n/a	—	n/a	—	Bob Michel (IL)	12
Republican whip	n/a	—	n/a	—	n/a	—	n/a	—	Dick Cheney (WY)[a]	6

Note: When membership in a state grouping exceeded eighteen, conference rules called for the group to be broken in two (A and B) and to be given two members on the Executive Committee.

[a]After Cheney was appointed secretary of defense in March 1989, he was replaced by Newt Gingrich (GA). Committee assignments for the 101st Congress were in place by the time Gingrich joined the Executive Committee.

the relative stability of the standing committees. In fact, during this period, large-state representatives on the committee served an average of three terms, while small-state representatives served an average of only two terms.

Executive Committee Factions

Factions are groups of representatives on the Executive Committee who tend to vote in unison when allocating committee assignments to Republican members. Each member of the committee will have multiple interests that he or she seeks to satisfy with committee votes. Executive Committee members are agents of the state or state-group caucus that elected them to the committee and must respond to the interests of their constituency by pursuing representation for their members on committees. Executive Committee representatives who are perceived as ineffective may be removed from committee membership by their state or state-grouping caucus in a subsequent election.[10] Each member of the Executive Committee also has individual ideological interests, a personal vision of the policies that should be pursued by Republican members of House committees, and beliefs about the role and direction of the party within the House. To the extent that members of the committee shared these and other interests with other committee members, we expect to observe the emergence of factions within the committee, as indicated by systematic voting patterns within the committee.

FACTOR ANALYSIS

To identify factions quantitatively, we rely on the methodological approach advanced by Glenn R. and Suzanne Parker (1979, 1985).[11] In their study of House committee factions, they use factor analysis to identify groups of committee members who tend to vote together on legislation before their committee. Each voting member of the Executive Committee is coded as a "variable," and each ballot is considered as a "case" in the dataset. In our study, the factor analysis indicates the degree to which members of the Executive Committee were voting together in support of a nominee for a committee seat. Again following the Parkers, we have chosen the varimax rotation for its ease of interpretation.[12]

TABLE 7.2
Republican Executive Committee vote distribution
(by committee, 97th–101st Congresses)

Committee	97th Congress	98th Congress	99th Congress	100th Congress	101st Congress	Committee Totals
Agriculture	6	3	5	—	—	14
	13%	7.3%	8.5%			7.3%
Appropriations	10	3	3	4	—	20
	21.7%	7.3%	5.1%	20.0%		10.4%
Armed Services	8	5	4	4	4	25
	17.4%	12.2%	6.8%	20.0%	14.8%	13.0%
Banking	4	5	11	2	10	32
	8.7%	12.2%	18.6%	10.0%	37.0%	16.7%
Budget	3	2	6	—	3	14
	6.5%	4.9%	10.2%		11.1%	7.3%
Energy and Commerce	9	4	3	4	2	22
	19.6%	9.8%	5.1%	20.0%	7.4%	11.4%
Foreign Affairs	3	4	6	—	3	16
	6.5%	9.8%	10.2%		11.1%	8.3%
Interior	1	—	—	—	—	1
	2.2%					.5%
Public Works	—	5	9	—	4	18
		12.2%	15.3%		14.8%	9.4%
Rules	1	—	—	—	—	1
	2.2%					.5%
Science	—	4	4	—	1	9
		9.8%	6.8%		3.7%	4.7%
Small Business	—	—	5	—	—	5
			8.5%			2.6%
Veterans' Affairs	1	—	—	—	—	1
	2.2%					0.5%
Ways and Means	—	6	3	6	—	15
		14.6%	5.1%	30.0%		7.8%
Congress totals	46	41	59	20	27	193
	23.4%	23.4%	30.7%	10.4%	14.1%	

Note: Data from paper ballots found in the Robert H. Michel Papers indicate the number of ballots conducted before all seats on the committee were filled.

Factor scores may be interpreted in much the same way that correlation coefficients are interpreted, though the substantive meaning of negative factor scores is a matter of some dispute (Kim and Mueller 1978). Members are considered allied with a faction in the committee when the factor analysis indicates a tendency for the member to vote with that faction regularly, as indicated by the factor score.[13]

IDENTIFYING CLEAVAGES

In addition to identifying factions, we are interested in determining whether these factions reflect systematic cleavages within the Republican Conference, those cleavages that systematically cause members to vote with one another, resulting in observed factional behavior. To identify the cleavage structure in the RCC, we correlate the factor scores generated by the factor analysis with individual level indicators of committee members' traits (Parker and Parker 1979, 1985). Table 7.3 lists the quantitative measures we use in our analysis, and the cleavages that divide these factions. We also examine the large state–small state cleavage discussed above. Correlations between these indicators and the factor scores are interpreted as indicative of the salience of that cleavage in the formation of factions within the Executive Committee (Parker and Parker 1979, 1985).

In using more than one indicator, we seek to improve the substantive conclusions we reach; when two or more of indicators suggest a salient cleavage, we can have more confidence that a cleavage is substantively meaningful. Furthermore, in using multiple measures of ideology, we intend to explore whether fine-grained measures of ideology can improve our ability to describe cleavages. For instance, the most reliable measure of ideology available to congressional scholars is the Poole and Rosenthal DW-NOMINATE scores (1997). The primary weakness of DW-NOMINATE is that it indicates ideology over a broad array of policies at the expense of identifying narrower policy preferences. Thus, in addition to the DW-NOMINATE scores—and despite the weaknesses associated with interest group scores—we include interest group scores, which rely on a narrower set of policy interests that may be influencing the choices of Executive Committee members.

ANALYSIS AND DISCUSSION

There was always some chicanery. People ganging up, you know, . . . people leaving the room and coming back in, and it just used to gall my hide. . . . I would have to admonish them: "Hey, I know what is going on here, and what I'm trying to do is make this as fair as possible." . . . The big states were entitled just about automatically to

one seat on Ways and Means or Rules or something like that. . . .
Some small state has to have some kind of a chance.

                         REPUBLICAN LEADER BOB MICHEL

Smith and Ray (1983) have argued that the structure of the Democrats' committee assignment process inhibited the active formation of coalitions. In the Democrats' complex assignment process, each member of a large (currently forty-six members) committee on committees casts one vote for each vacancy on a committee. Only one committee slot is filled per ballot, and a winner must receive a majority of votes cast. There are term limits placed on committee-on-committees membership. Smith and Ray contend that these arrangements promote consensus within the committee on committees. The most comprehensive studies of the Democrats' committee assignment process (Shepsle 1978; Gertzog 1976) de-emphasize the contentious and political nature of the process, characterizing it as self-selective and routine.[14]

Smith and Ray's interpretation of the Democratic process does not seem to apply to the House Republicans' process, which was anything but routine (we also challenge the application to the Democrats, later in this chapter). Multiple ballots were frequently required, and coalitions were often of the minimum winning variety. The Republicans' process during the period under consideration was much more prone to cleavage formation than Smith and Ray suggest. The weighted voting system distributed power unevenly, concentrating power in the hands of relatively few key players. Executive Committee members voted for a single choice per ballot, and as balloting progressed, names were eliminated so that the final ballot was often a contest between two or three members. No limit was placed on the number of consecutive terms a member could sit on the RCC. All in all, the Republican system was conducive to political deal making. Although we are more concerned with the resulting coalitions that formed and what they say about the factional divisions within the party, it must be noted that the possibility of a skilled politician or politicians orchestrating a winning coalition was not out of the question.

Figure 7.2 depicts the size of winning coalitions in Executive Committee votes on the most widely requested committees (Appropriations,

TABLE 7.3
Cleavage indicators used in faction correlation analysis

Cleavage category	Indicator(s)	Source
Intraparty		
Partisanship	Presidential opposition or support in preceding Congress	*Congressional Quarterly Almanac*, various editions
	Party-unity score in preceding Congress	*Congressional Quarterly Almanac*, various editions
Ideology	Conservative Coalition score in preceding Congress	*Congressional Quarterly Almanac*, various editions
	DW NOMINATE score in preceding Congress	Poole and Rosenthal (1997)
	Interest group scores in preceding Congress: ADA[a] COPE NSI CCUS	Barone and Ujifusa (various years)
Seniority	Year elected to the U.S. House	*Barone and Ujifusa* (various years)
Regional	Regional dummy variables	ICPSR regional classifications
RCC Representational	Large state–small state dummy variable	Large states have a single representative on the RCC; small states are grouped together.

[a]ADA (Americans for Democratic Action); COPE (Committee on Political Education of the AFL-CIO); NSI (National Security Index); COCUS (Chamber of Commerce of the United States).

Armed Services, Banking, Energy and Commerce, and Ways and Means) during the period of Michel's leadership. Fifty nine percent of the coalitions were small majorities—less than 60 percent of the Executive Committee votes. Only 4 percent of the coalitions were nearly unanimous, with greater than 80 percent of the Executive Committee votes for the same candidate. In four of the five committees covered in this part of the analysis, a majority of the Executive Committee winning coalitions fell in the 50 to 59 percent range, indicating considerable competition within the Executive Committee. For the remaining committee, Ways and Means, not a single winning coalition exceeded 69 percent of the Executive Committee votes. It may be concluded, therefore, that members of the Executive Committee did not all think alike in making committee assignments and that the level of competition for choice seats was very high. The picture of committee assignments painted by figure 7.2 resembles a divided voting body rather than a decision-making unit that is characterized by consensus.

EVOLUTION OF EXECUTIVE COMMITTEE FACTIONS

Table 7.4 reveals the factional structure of the Executive Committee during the 97th through the 101st Congresses. This analysis indicates a party and Executive Committee divided largely along the lines suggested by Reiter (1981). The Executive Committee was divided into three main factions: misfits (faction 1), realigners (faction 2), and regulars (faction 3). An additional faction (faction 4), composed of the first- and second-term representatives, had formed as well. Faction 1's more liberal *misfits* (ADA score, $r = .520$; COPE score, $r = .572$) were largely from the Northeast ($r = .604$). These members were from some of the largest state delegations as well and accounted for eighty-four votes in Executive Committee balloting. Included in this faction were Frank Horton of New York (one of the most liberal members of the Republican Conference at the time) and Joseph McDade of Pennsylvania. As misfits, these powerful members were more likely to vote against their party majority (party unity, $r = -.417$).

Faction 2 comprised the realigners, southern members ($r = .516$), mostly from states with small Republican delegations ($r = -.358$), who were more conservative (DW-NOMINATE score, $r = .541$; Conservative Coalition, $r = .576$), and who were active in opposing President Carter in the previous Congress (presidential opposition, $r = .469$). Participating in this coalition were Henson Moore (LA) and Bill Dickinson (AL). Faction

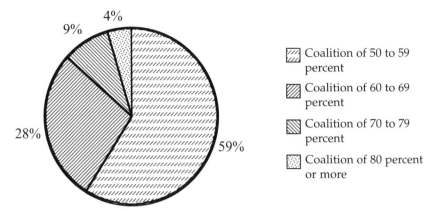

Figure 7.2. Winning coalition size in the Republican Executive Committee, 97th–101st Congresses.

3 represents the regulars, who were conservatives, but who tended to be more likely to support the president, regardless of party (presidential opposition, $r = -.395$). Frequently these members represented areas of the country, the Midwest in particular, that had long been a bastion of Republican support (midwestern districts, $r = .407$). Bob Michel and Bill Broomfield (MI) were included in this voting bloc.

The image of the 97th Executive Committee voting factions fits the schematic developed above (figure 7.1). In contrast, analysis of the Executive Committee voting in the 98th Congress does not reflect the factions, though the large state–small state cleavage persists (see table 7.5). Our analysis reveals five factions, with none retaining any of the appearance of the factional divide in the 97th Congress. This is likely due to a shake-up of the old party factions that had been present in the 97th. The election of Ronald Reagan in 1980 and the assumption of Republican control of the Senate meant that all House Republicans had to pull together (in cooperation with conservative southern Democrats) if they were to enact Reagan's programs.

Notice the lack of importance of virtually all the intraparty cleavages in the Executive Committee voting at the start of the 98th Congress. The 1982 midterm elections resulted in a net loss of twenty-six seats for the House Republicans, including many formerly held by liberals and moderates

TABLE 7.4

Republican Executive Committee factional structure
(97th–101st Congresses)

Representative	Factions (factor scores)				Explained variance
	1	2	3	4	
Pennsylvania	.854	.306	.359	−.060	.953
New Jersey	.821	.038	(.441)	.095	.884
Ohio	.811	(.425)	−.242	.091	.906
California	.795	.239	.359	−.061	.822
New York	.730	.278	(.517)	.178	.911
Two-member states	.142	.930	.146	.112	.919
Virginia	.248	.893	.108	−.022	.871
Three-member states	.106	.836	.168	.355	.864
One-member states	(.630)	.708	−.135	−.025	.917
Four-member states	.402	.631	.262	−.403	.791
Illinois	.036	−.007	.898	−.006	.808
Five-member states	.263	.242	.838	−.062	.834
Michigan	(.436)	.202	.729	.248	.824
Second-term members	.371	.284	.305	.709	.814
First-term members	(.417)	.005	(.429)	−.514	.623
Summary statistics					
Eigenvalue	7.82	2.41	1.43	1.09	
Variance explained (%)	52.11	19.91	12.24	11.52	92.29

Correlates of factional structure				
Intraparty cleavages				
Presidential opposition, 96th	−.437*	.469**	−.395*	.273
Party unity, 96th	−.417*	.268	−.253	.300
Conservative Coalition, 96th	−.226	.576**	−.513**	.240
DW NOMINATE score	−.205	.541**	−.454	.311
Member seniority	.037	−.026	.133	.048
ADA score	.520**	−.182	,073	−.113
COPE score	.572**	−.223	.068	−.052
NSI score	−.224	.437*	−.374*	.168
Regional cleavages				
Northeastern member	.604***	−.312	.149	.052
Southern member	−.566**	.516**	−.285	−.008
Midwestern member	−.186	−.360	.407*	.055
Western member	.346*	.092	−.294	−.121
Large-state member	.471**	−.358*	.173	.060

Note: Date from Executive Committee paper ballots found in the Robert H. Michel Papers. Principal component analysis using varimax rotation. Factor scores in boxes indicate high levels of attachment to the voting faction; scores in parentheses indicate marginal levels of attachment to the voting faction. Correlations are Pearson's r between variable in the left column and the factor scores in the top part of the table. All votes included for Appropriations, Armed Services, Banking, and Energy and Commerce committees.
*$p < .10$ (one-tailed)
**$p < .05$ (one-tailed)
***$p < .01$ (one-tailed)

(misfits) who had nonetheless supported Reagan's conservative agenda. The party had become a more uniformly conservative party. The cleavages that are apparent in the 98th Congress are nonideological, based more on geography and the large state–small state distinction within the RCC. Northeasterrn members tend to gravitate toward factions 2 and 4 (r = .411 and .285, respectively), with more liberal members of the RCC also gravitating toward faction 4 (ADA score, r = .312). Although southern members trend *away* from northeastern faction 2 (r = -.211), they do not coalesce in a single faction. The single most prominent split in the RCC is associated with the large state–small state split. Large states tended to associate most with faction 5, while small states gravitated toward faction 1.

In the 99th Congress, there is *strong* evidence of the large state–small state conflict. Table 7.6 depicts Executive Committee voting on all major committee ballots in the 99th Congress. Faction 1, which is the most prominent faction, comprises the large-state members (r = .710). The seven states in this faction come from the traditional areas of strong Republican representation (California, New York, Florida, New Jersey, Pennsylvania, Michigan, and Ohio) and had a combined voting strength in the RCC of seventy-three votes during the 99th Congress.

The remaining members are grouped into four additional factions; however, there is no large faction of small-state members to challenge the large-state faction. In the 99th Congress, both members representing three-member states vote in the same faction, and both members representing two-member states likewise vote with each other, but the pairs are in different factions—two-member states do not vote with three-member states. Faction 2 is the only other reasonably sized faction in the analysis. We were unable to find any statistically significant correlates with this factor, indicating that there was no organized opposition to the large states, and when similar actors voted together, they were split between the large and small states.

Kennedy attributes the development of a large-state coalition in the 99th Congress to the political skills of Jerry Lewis (CA).[15]

> In his first year of sitting on the Republican Committee on Committees, his sole assignment from his delegation being to hold the Appropriations seat of a retiring California member for her successor,

TABLE 7.5

Republican Executive Committee factional structure (98th Congresses)

Representative	Factions (factor scores)					Explained variance
	1	2	3	4	5	
First-term members	.911	.277	−.009	.009	.018	.908
One-member states	.900	−.125	−.039	−.059	.015	.830
Ohio	.778	.139	.183	(.443)	.297	.942
Texas	.707	(.513)	.189	.289	.015	.883
Florida	.678	−.202	.081	(.456)	.273	.791
Three-member states (B)	.677	.348	.413	(.446)	.029	.953
Threemember states (A)	.666	.381	(.448)	.342	.060	.908
Second-term members	.592	.312	(.516)	.399	.264	.944
California	.215	.897	.202	.212	.137	.956
New Jersey	.301	.829	.229	.283	.109	.929
Illinois	−.101	.784	.131	−.192	.129	.696
Pennsylvania	.301	.705	(.475)	.317	.124	.930
Two-member states (A)	.043	.686	(.532)	−.354	−.189	.918
New York	.274	.465	.408	.389	.329	.719
Two-member states (B)	.030	.320	.925	.109	−.046	.973
Michigan	.134	.192	.917	−.014	.135	.915
Wisconsin	−.173	−.071	−.021	−.916	.064	.878
Indiana	.024	.124	−.018	−.033	.938	.896
Virginia	(.567)	.169	.218	.076	.653	.829
Summary statistics						
Eigenvalue	9.71	3.29	1.41	1.23	1.16	
Variance explained (%)	51.09	17.31	7.42	6.49	6.09	88.41

Correlates of factional structure

Intraparty cleavages						
Presidential support, 97th	−.058	.103	−.041	−.065	−.113	
Party unity, 97th	.058	−.002	.015	−.026	−.065	
Conservative Coalition, 97th	.023	−.042	.002	−.097	.016	
DW NOMINATE score	−.008	−.146	−.023	−.214	−.043	
Member seniority	.375**	−.013	−.233*	.167	−.150	
ADA score	−.023	.128	.038	.312*	.178	
COPE score	.013	.020	.016	.187	.183	
NSI score	−.104	.036	−.042	−.221*	−.296*	
COC score	.137	−.097	−.145	−.209	−.242*	
Regional cleavages						
Northeastern member	−.220*	.411**	.048	.285*	.125	
Southern member	−.025	−.211*	.138	−.047	−.045	
Midwestern member	−.136	−.035	.158	−.096	.029	
Western member	.362**	−.096	−.358**	−.106	−.091	
Large-state member	−.227*	.216	−.171	.206	.537***	

Note: Data from Executive Committee paper ballots found in the Robert H. Michel Papers. Principal component analysis using varimax rotation. Factor scores in boxes indicate high levels of attachment to the voting faction; scores in parentheses indicate marginal levels of attachment to the voting faction. Correlations are Pearson's *r* between the variable in the left column and the factor scores in the top part of the table. All votes included for Appropriations, Armed Services, Banking, and Energy and Commerce committees. When membership in a state grouping exceeded eighteen, conference rules called for the group to be broken in two (A and B) and to be given two members on the Executive Committee.
*p < .10 (one-tailed)
**p < .05 (one-tailed)
***p < .01 (one-tailed)

he lined up enough support early to secure the assignment. Or so he thought. When the Committee on Committees met, someone else got the seat. "I was not happy with that," Lewis says, by all accounts an understatement. "I went about putting together a coalition that would make sure that wouldn't happen again." Two years later, in the next round of committee assignments, Lewis' big-state coalition got the seat back. He paid the price: resentful small states organized against him, in the Committee on Committees and elsewhere, and mounted a stiff challenge to his bid for the policy chair. (1989, 6–7)

Table 7.7 illustrates the analysis for all studied committees in the 100th Congress. Faction 1 is again clearly the large-state faction (r = .628), and again with a significant northeastern membership. As northeastern large-state members have gained seniority, the variable measuring terms is now significant. Often congressional conflict is placed in the context of generational turnover, and voting on the Executive Committee seems to reflect this. A Republican member described the process to John Barry in 1986, "Michel's like the old bull in the caribou herd; all the young bulls are going to give him the horn. Trent's the leader. Trent's slick. I want leaders who are slick. Let's say 'skilled.' Michel's not as Machiavellian as Trent or Wright, or Gingrich" (1989, 160)

Also apparent is the emergence of a large competing faction (faction 3) that represents the small states' interests. This coalition of more partisan (r = .272) and conservative members (Conservative Coalition, r = .371) represents a group that Reiter terms realigners. Included in this group are future senators Jim Bunning (KY) and Hank Brown (CO).

The power of this voting faction becomes more apparent when we look at voting patterns for a specific committee. Table 7.8 contains results of an analysis of voting for vacancies on the Appropriations Committee in the 100th Congress. In the voting, there were two competing factions, one consisting mostly of large-state members, the other consisting of small-state members. An anonymous member of Appropriations describes this small-state "cabal" in White (1989): "Two years ago there was the, I think correct, perception that the small states got screwed. This time around, led by [minority whip] Trent Lott, the small states put together a coalition, needed one more state, and it was Texas" (136).

Table 7.6
Table 7.6
Republican Executive Committee factional structure (99th Congresses)

Representative	Factions (factor scores)					Explained variance
	1	2	3	4	5	
California	.950	.285	−.125	.032	−.040	.987
New York	.948	.297	−.082	.041	−.032	.996
Florida	.948	.297	−.082	.041	−.032	.996
New Jersey	.947	.292	−.095	.035	−.039	.994
Pennsylvania	.939	.315	−.065	.052	−.021	.989
Michigan	.935	.299	−.065	.029	−.018	.970
Ohio	.932	.319	−.053	.055	−.109	.989
First-term members	.245	.863	.006	.364	−.074	.943
Texas	(.465)	.816	.027	−.054	−.042	.887
Illinois	(.436)	.789	−.037	.017	−.072	.820
Second-term members	(.464)	.784	−.049	.040	−.074	.840
Two-member states (B)	.363	.719	−.082	(.470)	−.128	.893
Indiana	(.603)	.685	−.067	.089	−.050	.848
Twomember states (A)	.345	.642	−.097	(.577)	−.110	.887
Three-member states (B)	−.199	−.119	.954	−.029	−.128	.965
Three-member states (A)	−.199	−.119	.954	−.029	−.004	.965
One-ember states	.313	.311	.614	−.206	−.265	.685
Virginia	−.081	−.013	−.037	.952	−.025	.915
Four-member states (A)	−.048	−.088	−.056	−.054	.989	.995
Four-member states (B)	−.048	−.088	−.056	−.054	.989	.995
Summary statistics						
Eigenvalue	7.72	5.04	2.28	2.25	2.09	
Variance explained (%)	36.76	23.99	10.85	10.72	9.99	92.32

Correlates of factional structure

	1	2	3	4	5	
Intraparty cleavages						
Presidential support, 98th	−.140	.199	−.139	.337*	−.080	
Party unity, 98th	−.320*	.099	.025	.104	.143	
Conservative Coalition, 98th	−.300	.274	−.002	.177	−.013	
DW NOMINATE score	−.140	−.060	−.101	.102	.238	
Member seniority	−.328*	−.003	.068	−.009	.284	
ADA score	.230	−.245	.082	−.119	−.071	
COPE score	.330*	−.151	−.024	−.206	−.069	
NSI score	.068	.293	−.121	.195	−.241	
COC score	−.061	.222	−.049	−.031	−.045	
Regional cleavages						
Northeastern member	.489**	−.080	−.208	−.121	−.095	
Southern member	−.292	.208	.039	.593***	−.232	
Midwestern member	−.030	.038	.019	−.271	.120	
Western member	−.059	−.249	.130	−.310*	.244	
Large-state member	.710***	.224	−.479**	.052	−.328*	

Note: Data from Executive Committee paper ballots found in the Robert H. Michel Papers. Principal component analysis using varimax rotation. Factor scores in boxes indicate high

TABLE 7.6 (*continued*)
Republican Executive Committee factional structure (99th Congresses)

levels of attachment to the voting faction; scores in parentheses indicate marginal levels of attachment to the voting faction. Correlations are Pearson's r between variable in the left column and the factor scores in the top part of the table. All votes included for Appropriations, Armed Services, Banking, and Energy and Commerce committees. When membership in a state grouping exceeded eighteen, conference rules called for the group to be broken in two (A and B) and to be given two members on the Executive Committee.
*$p < .10$ (one-tailed)
**$p < .05$ (one-tailed)
***$p < .01$ (one-tailed)

Notice in table 7.8 that Texas is no longer part of the large-state coalition but is instead associated with the small-state (mostly southern) coalition.[16] These results confirm the following account:

> Trent Lott, from Mississippi, tall, dark-haired, with glasses and a TV anchorman's haircut, was the whip, Michel's elected deputy. His relationship with Michel was not that of a loyal follower. Lott had his own power base, regularly hosted luncheons to plan leadership strategy without inviting Michel. When the Republicans were making committee assignments for the 100th Congress, Lott organized a coalition of members from small states which deprived Michel of the assignments he wanted for two Illinois protégés, Lynn Martin and Jack Davis. (Barry 1989, 160)

The most important conclusion to be drawn from this analysis is that in December 1986 (when the committee assignments were determined for the exclusive committees), a new faction emerged within the Executive Committee that rivaled the old large-state order. Before this, the committee assignment process had been controlled largely by the party regulars, often in alliance with the moderate northeastern misfits, who took advantage of the tilt in the process toward the large states. In 1986, the realigners gained control of the process through active cooperation and were able to place their members on important committees. The Executive Committee voting process used during the period was weighted in favor of the party regulars (and the misfits) at the expense of the realigners. Regulars were common in the large industrial states of the Northeast and Midwest. Realigners were more common in the smaller but more numerous states of the South and West. Large states were guaranteed a seat at the Executive Committee table; small states

TABLE 7.7
Republican Executive Committee factional structure (100th Congresses)

Representative	Factions (factor scores)				Explained variance
	1	2	3	4	
New York	.946	.188	.103	.209	.986
New Jersey	.943	.181	.107	.209	.978
Florida	.943	.184	.100	.194	.972
Pennsylvania	.931	.201	.129	.191	.961
Illinois	.916	.275	.151	.169	.966
Ohio	.847	.041	(.490)	.068	.964
Virginia	.592	(.495)	.054	−.405	.763
Michigan	.583	(.498)	.183	.087	.629
Four-member states (B)	.151	.960	.064	.158	.974
California	.059	.909	.069	−.212	.879
Texas	.352	.707	.366	.255	.822
Four-member states (A)	.398	.683	.298	.296	.802
Second-term members	(.472)	.563	.123	(.484)	.789
Three-member states (A)	.135	.015	.978	.052	.978
Two-member states (A)	.145	.115	.962	.051	.962
First-term members	−.002	.312	.801	−.080	.746
Three-member states (B)	(.455)	.355	.653	.395	.916
One-member states	.398	.010	.542	(.461)	.665
Two-member states (A)	(.497)	.115	.036	.730	.962
Summary statistics					
Eigenvalue	6.97	3.99	3.84	1.74	
Variance explained (%)	36.69	21.05	20.22	9.15	87.11

Correlates of factional structure

Intraparty cleavages					
Presidential support, 99th	−.249*	.206	.121	.128	
Party unity, 99th	−.402**	.242*	.272*	.154	
Conservative Coalition, 99th	−.065	−.211*	.371**	.469***	
DW NOMINATE score	.248*	−.043	−.207	.251	
Member seniority	.504***	−.358**	.003	.036	
ADA score	.305*	−.290*	−.031	.023	
COPE score	.443**	−.312*	−.191	−.083	
NSI score	.107	−.199	.056	.010	
COC score	−.375**	.333**	.184	.115	
Regional cleavages					
Northeastern member	.575***	−.254*	−.300*	.050	
Southern member	−.203	.001	.055	.003	
Midwestern member	.024	−.001	.090	−.163	
Western member	−.300*	.227*	.106	.127	
Large-state member	.628***	.077	−.539***	−.467**	

Note: Data from Executive Committee paper ballots found in the Robert H. Michel Papers. Principal component analysis using varimax rotation. Factor scores in boxes indicate high

TABLE 7.7 (*continued*)
Republican Executive Committee factional structure (100th Congresses)

levels of attachment to the voting faction; scores in parentheses indicate marginal levels of attachment to the voting faction. Correlations are Pearson's *r* between variable in the left column and the factor scores in the top part of the table. All votes included for Appropriations, Armed Services, Banking, and Energy and Commerce committees. When membership in a state grouping exceeded eighteen, conference rules called for the group to be broken in two (A and B) and to be given two members on the Executive Committee.
*$p < .10$ (one-tailed)
**$p < .05$ (one-tailed)
***$p < .01$ (one-tailed)

were placed in groups without regard to their regional and ideological composition.

In the 101st Congress, Republicans reformed the committee assignment process to increase the influence of the party leadership in the assignment process. The Lagomarsino Report, which served as the basis for the reforms, proposed that the Republican leader be granted twelve votes in the Executive Committee, and the Republican whip, six votes in the committee.[17] Among other things, this reform was aimed at making party loyalty a more prominent consideration in the assignment process.

Several things are worth noting in Executive Committee voting in the 101st Congress (see table 7.9). First, despite the assumption that the party leadership would vote as a bloc in the committee, Michel and Cheney were clearly voting with different factions in the committee (factions 2 and 3, respectively). Furthermore, neither of these factions reflects partisanship considerations; the correlation coefficients fail to achieve significance. Second, the large state–small state cleavage is no longer apparent. Third, a generational split is now apparent, with faction 2 representing a group of more senior members and faction 4 comprising the representatives of the two newest classes, along with future Speaker Dennis Hastert. This faction represents the young conservative activists who were elected in such large numbers in the elections leading to the Republican takeover of the House in 1994.

DEMOCRATIC COALITIONS

As Shepsle (1978) has pointed out, identifying coalition forming and vote trading without ballot results is virtually impossible. However, in

TABLE 7.8
Republican Executive Committee factional structure
(100th Congresses, Appropriations Committee assignments)

Representative	Factions (factor scores)		Explained variance
	1	2	
First-term members	.935	.354	1.0
One-member states	.935	.354	1.0
Two-member states (A)	.935	.354	1.0
Two-member states (B)	(.484)	−.875	1.0
Three-member states (A)	.935	.354	1.0
Three-member states (B)	.935	.354	1.0
Four-member states (A)	.935	.354	1.0
Four-member states (B)	.935	.354	1.0
Second-term members	.935	.354	1.0
Texas	.935	.354	1.0
Virginia	.996	.086	1.0
California	.404	.915	1.0
Florida	.404	.915	1.0
Illinois	.491	.871	1.0
Michigan	.392	.920	1.0
New Jersey	.404	.915	1.0
New York	.404	.915	1.0
Ohio	.404	.915	1.0
Pennsylvania	.404	.915	1.0
Summary statistics			
Eigenvalue	15.23	3.77	
Variance explained (%)	80.17	19.83	100

Correlates of factional structure

Intraparty cleavages			
Presidential support, 99th	.367*	−.301	
Party unity, 99th	.518**	−.345*	
Conservative Coalition, 99th	.359*	−.256	
DW NOMINATE score	.058	−.117	
Member seniority	.524***	−.478**	
ADA score	−.218	2.61	
COPE score	−.330*	.346*	
NSI score	−.101	−.057	
COC score	.358*	−.286	
Regional cleavages			
Northeastern member	−.482**	.403**	
Southern member	.318*	−.507**	
Midwestern member	−.145	2.38	
Western member	2.12	−.018	
Large-state member	−.652***	.640***	

Table 7.8 (*continued*)
Republican Executive Committee factional structure
(100th Congresses, Appropriations Committee assignments)

Note: Data from Executive Committee paper ballots found in the Robert H. Michel Papers. Principal component analysis using carimax rotation. Factor scores in boxes indicate high levels of attachment to the voting faction; scores in parentheses indicate marginal levels of attachment to the voting faction. Correlations are Pearson's *r* between variable in the left column and the factor scores in the top part of the table. When membership in a state grouping exceeded eighteen, conference rules called for the group to be broken in two (A and B) and to be given two members on the Executive Committee.
*$p < .10$ (one-tailed)
**$p < .05$ (one-tailed)
***$p < .01$ (one-tailed)

our interviews, Democratic members and staff were just as likely as Republicans to discuss vote swapping and lasting coalitions. Democratic members perceive the system as one that is fundamentally political and susceptible to coalition building and politics. The names of several Democratic members are frequently repeated in the popular accounts of Congress as being influential in building coalitions during the period under examination. These members include John Breaux, John Murtha, Dan Rostenkowski, Phil Burton, and Frank Thompson.

Howard Berman (D-CA) described coalition building among the Democrats that developed over the position of first-term-member representative to the DSPC, and subsequently, over the assignment of members to committees:

> At that time, Phil Burton was alive, and my closest political allies . . . were Henry Waxman and Phil Burton. Well, Jim Wright, who was the majority leader, always thought of Phil Burton as a potential future opponent, just as he had been his opponent—he had defeated him by one vote back in 1976. . . . So Jim Wright was very wary of my candidacy and went out and, oh, in addition to that he got Murtha and Rostenkowski and John Dingell, who was always fighting Henry Waxman. So these old bulls, and Tony Coelho to some extent too—he viewed Phil as a potential rival; he wanted to be sort of the rising star of California and didn't want to see Phil coming back and sort of crowding him out. And they all opposed me, and they actually went out and sought a candidate against me, and when that candidate turned out to be sort of a dud,

TABLE 7.9

Republican Executive Committee factional structure (101st Congresses)

Representative	Factions (factor scores)				Explained variance
	1	2	3	4	
Four-member states (B)	.963	.109	.083	.135	.964
Four-member states (A)	.962	.109	.082	.135	.962
Florida	.928	.147	.088	.298	.979
Virginia	.968	.331	.309	.078	.801
Pennsylvania	.751	.394	(.480)	−.154	.974
New York	.752	.393	(.498)	−.148	.976
New Jersey	.718	.358	(.478)	−.292	.957
Texas	−.144	.890	.344	.182	.964
Two-member states (A)	.367	.883	.052	.037	.919
California	.306	.878	.233	.134	.937
Ohio	.305	.867	.328	−.081	.960
Leader	.337	.850	.139	−.037	.856
Three-member states (A)	.368	.288	.848	.026	.939
Three-member states (B)	.368	.288	.848	.026	.939
Whip	−.031	.121	.820	.315	.788
Michigan	.355	.243	.741	.231	.788
Two-member states (B)	.056	.444	.733	.062	.741
One-member states	.154	(.605)	.679	−.226	.902
First-term members	−.093	−.226	.121	.876	.842
Illinois	.356	.255	.010	.800	.832
Second-term members	.211	.352	.381	.564	.632
Summary statistics					
Eigenvalue	5.99	5.45	4.95	2.26	
Variance explained (%)	28.54	25.96	23.56	10.76	88.82

Correlates of factional structure

Intraparty cleavages

	1	2	3	4	
Presidential support, 100th	−.247	.125	−.348*	.450**	
Party unity, 100th	−.260	−.116	−.168	.557***	
Conservative Coalition, 100th	−.296	−.077	−.255	.613***	
DW NOMINATE score	.062	−.032	−.116	.174	
Member seniority	−.089	−.463**	−.111	.504***	
ADA score	.252	.064	.290	−.538***	
COPE score	.332*	.024	.245	−.561***	
NSI score	−.173	.007	−.174	.271	
COC score	−.361*	−.027	.011	.424**	

Regional cleavages

	1	2	3	4	
Northeastern member	.369**	−.206	−.248	−.007	
Southern member	−.099	.219	−.173	.134	
Midwestern member	.059	.076	−.083	.081	
Western member	−.108	−.079	.273	−.121	
Large-state member	.070	.156	−.217	.157	

TABLE 7.9 (*continued*)
Republican Executive Committee factional structure (101st Congresses)

Note: Data from Executive Committee paper ballots found in the Robert H. Michel Papers. Principal component analysis using varimax rotation. Factor scores in boxes indicate high levels of attachment to the voting faction; scores in parentheses indicate marginal levels of attachment to the voting faction. Correlations are Pearson's *r* between variable in the left column and the factor scores in the top part of the table. All votes included for Appropriations, Armed Services, Banking, and Energy and Commerce committees. When membership in a state grouping exceeded eighteen, conference rules called for the group to be broken in two (A and B) and to be given two members on the Executive Committee.
*$p < .10$ (one-tailed)
**$p < .05$ (one-tailed)
***$p < .01$ (one-tailed)

they then switched their support to a really good guy, who I ran against, and we had our own little campaign for four or five days during the orientation and a little bit before, and I think I beat him by one vote, a guy by the name of John Bryant, from Texas, . . .

Phil was on the committee, he was California's representative on the committee, and I was the freshman representative on the committee. . . . [In] the 1982 election, the Democrats picked up twenty-six seats, and there were something like fifty-five or fifty-six freshmen Democrats. Eight of them were from California for the Democrats, and our goal was to try to get those eight the best possible assignments. Those eight were all people who were close to Phil, and they had all come through the reapportionment of 1981, which Phil and I were both heavily involved with—me in the legislature and him as the guy who always sort of coordinated the reapportionment for the delegation. And there were tensions on things like Energy and Commerce and on some of the other assignments. There were Jim Wright's candidates versus Phil's candidates.[18]

• • •

Analysis of voting patterns in the Executive Committee of the RCC provides congressional scholars with their first opportunity to peer inside the black box of the committee assignment process. Previous studies of the process have focused on the Democrats exclusively and emphasized the consensual nature of the process. Distributive theory suggests that the party leadership will behave like a neutral arbiter among competing individual claims on committee slots, resulting in a generally consensual process (Shepsle 1978). Previous studies used aggregate vote tallies to confirm this assertion (Smith and Ray 1983). By contrast, we have access to the individual votes within the RCC, enabling our analysis of the development of factions within the Republican assignment process. The findings suggest that the Republicans' committee assignment process during this period was anything but consensual and was marked by significant factional conflict as RCC representatives sought to promote the interests of their protégés and their factions. Conflict within the Executive Committee is also likely a function of the minority status of the Republican Party. Absent the ability to exercise restrained manipulation of committee ratios, the Republicans were unable to create committee slots to accommodate increased demand; this likely increased the value of each committee seat and, in turn, increased the level of conflict within the committee.[19]

Our analysis also yields valuable insights into the evolution of factions within the Republican Party throughout this period. To some degree, our results support the factional alignments suggested by Reiter (1981), Rohde (1991) and Connelly and Pitney (1994). Early in this period, RCC factions tended to develop in ways that were broadly consistent with the work of these scholars. In the first year covered in the study, the ideological cleavages within the Republican Party were especially apparent in voting coalitions on the Executive Committee. However, in subsequent years, as the Republican congressional delegation became more uniformly conservative, other cleavages became more apparent. The large state–small state cleavage, which had plagued the process for many years, became pronounced in the 99th and 100th Congresses. As the Republican electorate has shifted to the less densely populated (small) states of the South and West, power has moved as well. This is evident in the emergence of a rival small–state coalition in the 100th Congress, which controlled many of the key committee assignments and forced leadership to rethink the rules for making committee assignments.

CHAPTER EIGHT

WHO GETS WHAT AND WHY

Most requester characteristics are irrelevant to the goals and objectives of CC [Committee on Committees] members.

SHEPSLE, *THE GIANT JIGSAW PUZZLE*

T he CAP framework suggests that the assignment process will be characterized by significant conflict caused by members seeking to promote partisan, individual, and group interests through persuasion and bargaining both outside and inside the committee assignment process. As a former member of the DSPC pointed out, the assignment process is hardly routine; if the committee on committees had "a united view, . . . it wouldn't go through five or six ballots, eliminating candidates and arguing about the merits of the people involved, with the proponents each trying to emphasize a different argument as to why their person should be elected."[1] Another long-time member of the DSPC described the jockeying that goes on within the committee:

> I'd make sure that whoever came on in that zone would work with me and harness votes. . . . "Can you get this vote? Can you get that vote?" I had a situation in Steering and Policy when one of my membership was not voting for a candidate out of our area but voting for a candidate out of California. Finally, a member came

over to me and said to me, . . . "This person isn't voting for your guy." I went over to see him, and I said to him, "You don't vote for him this time, he doesn't get on this time, you're not coming back to Commerce. I'll go back to_____ and tell him what you've done." Next time he voted with us.[2]

From the distributive theory point of view, party leaders and each committee on committees is "concerned solely with satisfying requester demands. . . . [I]t acts as an 'impersonal' preference aggregation device in an effort to keep requestors happy" (Rohde and Shepsle 1973, 899). Routinized self-selection, as Gertzog (1978) describes the committee assignment process, is aimed at accommodating the committee requests of members, constrained only by the supply of available committee slots. According to this view, the assignment process largely ignores the individual characteristics of the requesters. According to Gertzog, the "Committees on Committees simply match preferences with vacancies . . . giving less and less attention to resolving contest between two or more aspirants for the same vacancy" (1978, 708).

Despite the intuitive appeal of the routinized self-selection perspective, members and former members of the committees on committees acknowledged in interviews that several political factors beyond simple supply and demand shaped the assignment process. Both committee representativeness and party loyalty were considered important when choosing among requesters. One long-time RCC member explained the role of party loyalty: "The criteria that I think we all used, either consciously or subconsciously, is to be reasonably responsible to the rest of the caucus. [A member] doesn't have to be slavishly loyal, but the good thing to know is that if you really need a vote, you can get one every once and a while."[3] Another Republican put it in slightly different terms:

> [P]eople who are always bucking, who are not cooperative, who are not team players, who are not all for one, one for all, probably are not going to be on the good committees. [Assignment] is also given as sort of a— I don't want to say it—thank you, but an acknowledgment, because in fact, the bigger, more highly profiled political fights will take place on those committees, and you do need to make sure from a partisan standpoint that you have the

army that you need on the frontline of defense. . . . You're lineup is important. You have to be able to trust your lineup in a lot of ways.[4]

A number of Democrats we interviewed agreed. One summed it up succinctly: "Party support plays a big part."[5]

Loyalty is only one personal characteristic that may affect a member's request success. By exploring the bivariate relationships between personal characteristics, we can examine several hypotheses about the influence of personal characteristics on the committee request success of Democratic and Republican members. The resultant findings, in the context of a multivariate model that incorporates variables representing each of the three committee models, challenge the behavioral basis of distributive theory. Broadly speaking, we have three major expectations for this analysis. First, because committee assignments are a function of political conflict and bargaining, personal characteristics will play a role in the success or failure of individual members to receive requested assignments. Second, as we have argued repeatedly, the factors that influence success within the two parties will reflect differences between the two political parties. Finally, because political leadership and political context matter, there will be significant differences in request success over time within the parties. Far from being a routinized process, committee assignment is a function of politics.

ASSIGNMENT CONTEXT

The most fundamental difference in the committee assignment process is a difference in the levels of information that committee-on-committees members have about first-term and incumbent members. Except in those rare cases when a celebrity (such as entertainer Sonny Bono, actor Fred Grandy, college football coach Tom Osborne, or former Seattle Seahawk football star Steve Largent) is elected to the House, committee-on-committees members have relatively limited amounts of information about first-term members; and with celebrities, the available information is often useless. Even first-term members who are well known in their district or state and have significant political experience arrive in Washington, D.C., as relative unknowns. The lack of reliable information about new members' ideology, or their partisan loyalty (other than the members' own claims), which may be legitimately based on previous service in a state legislature, makes it difficult to distinguish among these new members. Some factors, however, do set some first-term members apart from their colleagues. The circumstances of a member's election, whom the new member is replacing, experience in the House as a staff member, and family ties may all distinguish new members from one another. Many new members engage in campaigns for committee slots, lobbying members of the committee on committees, and seeking thereby to distinguish themselves from other incoming members.

Committee-on-committees members have a great deal more information about incumbents who wish to alter their committee assignments. Incumbents have served some time in Congress, allowing their colleagues insight into their work ethic, personal style, committee participation, voting behavior, policy predilections, and so forth. In some cases, this information is informal, based on impressions about members' behaviors. In some cases, the party may provide systematic analyses of members' voting behavior to the committee on committees for consideration. For instance, the archival record suggests that in considering committee assignments, both parties would occasionally use more or less sophisticated measures of party loyalty based on "key votes." Voting with the DSPC policy position was often considered important for future consideration for committee assignments, as former Speaker Jim Wright explained,

> Maybe eight times in a year, the Speaker and the leadership will ask Steering and Policy to pass a resolution calling on the members to vote for this bill, or for this amendment, or against that amendment . . . party regularity votes. These are counters. In those days, we would try to enforce the idea that if you expect to get on a committee, if you expect consideration of that nature from the leadership— and you are free to vote any way your conscious dictates; we would never ask you to vote against the wishes of your constituency—but when the Steering and Policy Committee called on somebody to vote on something that is party policy, that's party policy.[6]

In the presence of both anecdotal and systematic information about incumbent members, generic personal characteristics might be less important than other personal characteristics for differentiating first-term members from one another. These other characteristics, such as ideology and party loyalty, might assume a more prominent role in the assignment process.

Incumbents have an additional advantage in the committee assignment process: their current committee portfolio. Under most circumstances, incumbents who receive new committee assignments are required to surrender, or exchange, some or all of their current committee assignments in return for the new assignments. The purpose of this party rule is to ensure a sufficient supply of committee seats for all partisans and to prevent members from dominating the most sought-after committee slots. We suggest that the members' existing committee portfolios, that is, the value of their committees to other members who might want those slots, are taken into consideration in the assignment process. Simply put, we suggest an *exchange theory* of committee assignments.[7]

This occurs in two interrelated ways. First, when awarding committee assignment to a member who already holds a slot on a desirable committee, the committee on committees will create an additional slot for another member on a sought-after committee. For instance, consider two hypothetical members pursuing a seat on the Ways and Means Committee. One member serves on Banking and on Government Operations, and the other serves on Merchant Marine and on Post Office. By awarding the seat to the first member, the committee on committees will free a seat on the Banking Committee, for which they are likely to have several requests, but awarding the seat to the second member will simply create slots on committees that are difficult to fill in the first place. Second, a member's current committee portfolio might be considered a "leading indicator" of a member's *future* performance. For instance, some first-term members receive more valuable committee portfolios than do others. In favoring these members, the committee on committees is, in effect, signaling which of the first-term members have promise for the future. When that more successful first- or second-term member returns to the committee on committees, he or she has an advantage, because the exchange value of the existing committee portfolio presents additional opportunities for the committee on committees.

PERSONAL CHARACTERISTICS AND REQUEST SUCCESS

Political parties have a collective interest in the electoral fortunes of their members. The proximate interest of political party organizations, the party in the electorate, is to promote the election of enough of their members to Congress so that they constitute a majority in the House and Senate. Political parties in Congress have resources that may help members get reelected. The proximate interest of party leaders in Congress is to maintain the number of seats the party holds in the chamber. The minority party cannot become the majority if the party is losing seats in the chamber; the minority must maintain existing seats and hope to win more in a future election. For the majority party, maintaining the majority relies on the ability of incumbents to be reelected. The proximate interest of members of Congress is in being reelected. Shaping public policy or exercising political power depends on this ability. Party leaders in Congress and individual partisans thus have a shared interest: reelection.

The Marginality Thesis

Recognizing the shared interest of congressional parties and their members, political scientists have explored the relationship between the electoral fortunes of individual members and one of the resources that the party leadership can distribute to members that may promote their reelection: committee assignments. Drawing on interviews with both Democrats and Republicans in the House, Nicholas Masters (1961, 357) argued, "[a]lthough a number of factors enter into committee assignments . . . the most important single consideration . . . is to provide each member with an assignment that will help to ensure his reelection." Similarly, Charles Clapp (1964, 207) found that "[w]here competition for vacancies exists, choice assignments are often given to members representing 'marginal' congressional districts as opposed to those from districts firmly held by the party." A House member put a fine point on Masters' and Clapp's findings: "When I first came to Congress, our party went from the majority to the minority. Though I waged a strong campaign for a good committee assignment, I couldn't get one. *What few decent openings were available were given to those elected from marginal districts*" (quoted in Clapp 1964, 234, emphasis added).

Dan Burton (R-IN) made the same point when he wrote Bob Michel at the start of the 99th Congress: "Because I enjoyed a large plurality in 1982 I was passed over for every committee assignment I requested. Please, I need your help this time!"[8] According to the Masters' and Clapp's hypothesis, one would expect members elected by slim margins, often considered to be winning percentages of less than 55 percent, to be more successful in achieving a preferred committee assignment as a means for helping them shore up their electoral fortunes and maintain seats for the party.

There are important theoretical reasons to believe that party leaders may not influence the committee assignment process (Shepsle 1978). Maintaining seats in the House is a public good; all members of the congressional party benefit from their collective number. As Mancur Olson (1965) demonstrates, individuals are often unwilling to use their personal resources to promote a public good. Partisans involved in the committee assignment process may not be willing to sacrifice their ability to use their role to accrue political capital that can be used later to promote their own political interests. However, there may be powerful incentives for participants in the assignment process to be responsive to the collective interests of the party. Being involved in the committee assignment process provides the committee-on-committees member with a private good, the ability to accrue political capital; members whose continued service in the process depends on the support of the party leadership may conclude that it is in their interest to support the creation of a public good. Further, party leaders exercise a great deal of influence in the policy process. By cooperating with the party leadership in the party committee on committees, the member may be able to promote his or her policy interests in the future.

Examining Masters' and Clapp's hypothesis, Charles S. Bullock (1972) used quantitative data to consider the relationship between electoral marginality and the receipt of "good" committee assignments, that is, assignments to more highly sought-after committees. Using actual committee assignments, he demonstrates that marginal representatives receive committee assignments that are equivalent to the assignments of safe members. In the absence of committee request data, however, it is impossible to know which committees the members from marginal districts are requesting and whether party leaders are more responsive to their requests relative to more electorally safe members. With Democratic committee requests in hand, Shepsle reexamined Masters' and Clapp's thesis and concluded, "there are strong grounds for rejecting this hypothesis" (1978, 197). Smith and Ray (1983) modeled Democratic committee assignments in the 95th to 97th Congresses using committee-on-committees ballot data that reflected which members were actually nominated for committee seats. They found that, contrary to the expectations of Masters' and Clapp's hypothesis, electoral marginality actually disadvantages both first-term and incumbent requesters. Based on the weight of the accumulated evidence, Eulau concluded, "the reelection hypothesis has been shattered" (1985, 211).

Table 8.1 displays the results of our comparative analysis of Masters' and Clapp's hypothesis for first-term Democrats and Republicans. Our results suggest mild support for Masters' and Clapp's hypothesis applied to Democrats, and *significant* support when applied to Republicans. First, consider the findings for all requested committees. Among first-term Democrats, 57 percent of the marginal members were granted their preferred committee assignment compared with 51.8 percent of those elected with more than 55 percent of the vote; the result is mildly significant ($p = .10$). First-term Republican marginal members are much more successful in their quest for a committee assignment (43.9 percent of their requests granted) relative to their nonmarginal colleagues (34.1 percent request success), and the result is quite robust ($p = .02$).

Next, consider the findings by type of committee request. The relationship between marginality and success disappears among Democrats. Yet support for Masters' and Clapp's hypothesis persists for Republicans, especially those Republicans requesting a constituency committee; 74.4 percent of Republican marginal members requesting a constituency committee have their request granted compared with about 58 percent of nonmarginal Republicans. As expected, our analysis of marginal incumbents (table 8.2) suggests no relationship between marginality and request success. One exception is that Democratic marginal incumbents who request influence committees are significantly less likely to receive their request than are their colleagues who come from safe districts. The committee on committees may fear giving such a slot to a marginal

TABLE 8.1
Electoral marginality and first-term request success

Committee type		Democrats		Republicans	
		Nonmarginal district	*Marginal district*[a]	*Nonmarginal district*	*Marginal district*[a]
All committees	Request denied	173 48.2%	138 43.0%	141 65.9%	125 56.1%
	Request granted	186 51.8%	183 57.0%	73 34.1%	98 43.9%
		Tau-b = .05 (*p* = .10)		*Tau-b* = .10 (*p* = .02)	
Constituency	Request denied	31 29.5%	43 29.9%	30 42.3%	20 25.6%
	Request granted	74 70.5%	101 70.1%	41 57.7%	58 74.4%
		Tau-b = −.004 (*p* = .50)		*Tau-b* = .18 (*p* = .02)	
Policy	Request denied	84 48.0%	61 47.7%	59 67.0%	51 58.6%
	Request granted	91 52.0%	67 52.3%	29 33.0%	36 41.4%
		Tau-b = .003 (*p* = .50)		*Tau-b* = .09 (*p* = .14)	
Influence	Request denied	58 76.3%	33 75.0%	52 96.3%	54 93.1%
	Request granted	18 23.7%	11 25.0%	2 3.7%	4 6.9%
		Tau-b = .02 (*p* = .50)		*Tau-b* =.07 (*p* = .34)	

Note: Analysis for "all committees" includes service committee requests. Separate analysis of marginality and service committee requests is omitted because of the small number of such requests. The *p* is the one-tailed Monte Carlo value based on 10,000 simulations, using a random number seed of 2000000.

[a]Marginal districts are those in which the winner received less than 55% of the two party vote.

member who will feel constituency pressure to vote against the leadership on important committee and floor votes, or who will bend to leadership pressure only to be defeated in a subsequent election.

Further support for Masters' and Clapp's hypothesis comes from members' committee request letters.[9] In our sample of letters, 77 percent of first-term Democrats who mentioned future electoral challenges as a

TABLE 8.2
Electoral marginality and incumbent request success

Committee type		Democrats		Republicans	
		Nonmarginal district	Marginal district[a]	Nonmarginal district	Marginal district[a]
All committees	Request denied	278 51.7%	42 47.7%	377 69.4%	77 74.0%
	Request granted	260 48.3%	46 52.3%	166 30.6%	27 26.0%
		$Tau\text{-}b = .03$ $(p = .28)$		$Tau\text{-}b = -.04$ $(p = .18)$	
Constituency	Request denied	39 37.5%	6 31.6%	82 67.2%	16 51.6%
	Request granted	65 62.5%	13 68.4%	40 32.8%	15 48.4%
		$Tau\text{-}b = -.04$ $(p = .40)$		$Tau\text{-}b = .13$ $(p = .07)$	
Policy	Request denied	69 61.1%	10 41.7%	91 65.5%	17 73.9%
	Request granted	44 38.9%	14 58.3%	48 34.5%	6 26.1%
		$Tau\text{-}b = .15$ $(p = .06)$		$Tau\text{-}b = -.06$ $(p = .25)$	
Influence	Request denied	156 53.1%	26 57.8%	196 73.4%	42 87.5%
	Request granted	138 46.9%	19 42.2%	71 26.6%	6 12.5%
		$Tau\text{-}b = -.03$ $(p = .32)$		$Tau\text{-}b = -.12$ $(p = .02)$	

Note: Analysis for "all committees" includes service committee requests. Separate analysis of marginality and service committee requests is omitted because of the small number of such requests. The p is the one-tailed Monte Carlo value based on 10,000 simulations, using a random number seed of 2000000. Percentages are row percentages.

[a]Marginal districts are those in which the winner received less than 55% of the two party vote.

concern were successful in achieving their preferred committee assignment compared with a 55 percent success rate among those who did not mention electoral challenges ($p = .055$). A similar pattern is apparent among first-term Republicans; 52 percent of these members who mentioned future electoral challenges received their preferred assignment compared with 29 percent of those members who did not mention their electoral safety concerns ($p = .051$). In short, it appears that the party

WHO GETS WHAT AND WHY

committees on committees are responsive to the electoral concerns of first-term members.

Our results are mostly consistent with Shepsle's (1978) findings for Democrats: Marginal Democrats are not given preferential treatment in the assignment process. However, our findings among Republicans provide support for Masters' and Clapp's hypothesis. Why the differences in findings? Recall that Masters and Clapp drew their interview data from members of both political parties; Shepsle analyzed Democratic members only. Masters and Clapp may have conflated statements made by members of the two distinct political parties, reaching the conclusion that both parties treated marginal members in the same way. Shepsle, on the other hand, used systematic, quantitative data relating to a single party and inferred, at least implicitly, that his conclusions would hold for both parties. Our results suggest that his conclusions do not hold for both parties. Our approach and findings highlight the importance of combining systematic data analysis with the analysis of qualitative data that encompass both parties.

A more important question is, why the difference between the parties? Throughout the period considered here, the Democrats were the majority party (except during the 81st and 83rd Congresses), and the Republicans were the minority party (our Republican data begin with the 86th Congress). The differences in findings between the parties may be attributable to the differential value of preserving seats. Nominally speaking, the goal of the parties is to control the House, which is achieved by holding 218 seats, a minimum winning coalition for organizing the chamber. In a formal sense, each additional seat beyond 218 diminishes in value such that—given the sizeable majorities House Democrats had throughout most of this period—assisting marginal members has less value to the party than does pursuing policy-oriented goals. For the minority, on the other hand, maintaining seats is the sine qua non for achieving majority status; thus, protecting seats by favoring marginal members may be highly valued. When the minority achieves majority status, the party will attempt to consolidate the victory by providing attractive committee assignments to newly elected members. Following the period of consolidation, once majority status appears to be assured, the party will then be less responsive to claims of marginality.

The opposite of electoral marginality occurs when a member runs unopposed for a House seat. Table 8.3 presents the relationship between possessing an uncontested seat and request success for both first-term and incumbent Democrats.[10] These results suggest that first-term Democrats who run unopposed are significantly *more likely* to be granted their preferred assignment than other first-term Democrats (67.4 percent versus 53.4 percent, respectively); a significant pattern is not in evidence among incumbent Democrats. When we control for the type of committee requested, two interesting results emerge. First, a newly elected Democrat who runs unopposed and requests a constituency committee is virtually assured of success. Second, a Democratic incumbent who runs unopposed is significantly more likely to receive a requested transfer to a policy committee than is a Democrat who faced opposition.

In summary, we have provided significant new support for Masters' and Clapp's hypothesis. Party committees on committees apparently do weigh the electoral vulnerability of members when deciding committee assignments. This finding is more robust for the Republican Party, which may be a function of the party's minority status throughout this period. For Democrats, running unopposed for election tends to be a more powerful consideration in the assignment process: First-term Democrats who ran unopposed had a greater probability of receiving a preferred committee assignment. Among incumbent members, however, electoral considerations seemed mostly unimportant in the assignment process. This is the case because incumbents have established a record in the House—a voting record, a reputation for their committee work, and so forth—providing the committee-on-committees members with more information on which to base their committee assignment decisions. This finding is consistent with our results in chapter 5, which highlighted the role of electoral considerations in the minority party's committee assignment process.

Predecessor's Committee Status

The only personal characteristic that Shepsle finds to be significant in the committee assignment process is the committee assignment of the member's predecessor, the person that the new member is replacing

TABLE 8.3
Electoral opposition and Democrats' request success

Committee type		First-term Democrats		Incumbent Democrats	
		Opposed	*Unopposed*	*Opposed*	*Unopposed*
All	Request	297	14	278	42
committees	denied	46.6%	32.6%	51.7%	47.7%
	Request	340	29	260	46
	granted	53.4%	67.4%	48.3%	52.3%
		Tau-b = .07 (*p* = .02)		*Tau-b* = −.03 (*p* = .29)	
Constituency	Request	73	1	39	6
	denied	31.5%	5.9%	37.5%	31.6%
	Request	159	16	65	13
	granted	68.5%	94.1%	62.5%	68.4%%
		Tau-b = −.14 (*p* = .02)		*Tau-b* = .04 (*p* = .40)	
Policy	Request	137	8	69	10
	denied	48.1%	44.4%	61.1%	41.7%
	Request	148	10	44	14
	granted	51.9%	55.6%	38.9%	58.3%
		Tau-b = .02 (*p* = .41)		*Tau-b* = .15 (*p* = .06)	
Influence	Request	86	5	156	26
	denied	76.8%	62.5%	53.1%	57.8%
	Request	26	3	138	19
	granted	23.2%	37.5%	46.9%	42.2%
		Tau-b = .08 (*p* = .20)		*Tau-b* = −.03 (*p* = .32)	

Note: Analysis for "all committees" includes service committee requests. Separate analysis of electoral opposition and service committee requests is omitted because of the small number of such requests. The *p* is the one-tailed Monte Carlo value based on 10,000 simulations, using a random number seed of 2000000.

in Congress. It is common—but by no means standard operating procedure (because the format of the briefing book varies with each new chair of the committee)—for information about the committee assignment of the new member's predecessor to be included in the committee on committees' briefing book. This informational cue may influence committee-on-committees decision making. Among the first-term Democrats in our sample, 10 percent requested a seat on the committee of their predecessor—slightly lower than the 15 percent in Shepsle's study—and 8 percent of first-term Republicans made such a request. Similar percentages of members made claims on the committee seats of their predecessors in their request letters to the committees on committees.[11]

Table 8.4 shows the relationship between predecessor status and request success among first-term Democrats and Republicans. First-term Democrats requesting any committee on which their predecessor held a seat are significantly more likely to receive their request than those who do not have a prior claim on the seat (62.5 percent versus 52.3 percent respectively), a statistically significant difference. Similarly, first-term Republicans who have a prior claim on a seat are significantly more likely to receive the requested assignment than those who cannot exercise a prior claim (57.6 percent versus 34.4 percent).

When we control for the type of committee requested, the relationship persists, with some interparty differences. For Democrats, a prior claim on a committee assignment seems to extend to policy-oriented committees and to constituency committees; a prior claim on an influence committee seems, for the most part, to have little influence on success. For Republicans, however, the prior claim on a committee seat seems to extend only to constituency committees; the status of one's predecessor does not significantly influence success when the first-term Republican requests a policy or influence committee.

One dimension of this relationship that we are unable to address is whether the predecessor becomes involved in the new member's campaign for the committee seat that is being vacated. When Richard Bolling (D-MO) retired from the House, he vacated a seat on the influential Rules Committee, a committee that he chaired for many years. His successor, Alan Wheat (D-MO), requested to fill the seat being vacated by Bolling. Under most circumstances, it would be highly unusual for a first-term member to fill a seat on Rules, not only because it is an influence committee, but because the leadership generally likes to have time to take the measure of members who might fill a seat on such a powerful committee, to be assured that the member will support the leadership when necessary. Prior to Wheat's request for Rules, only two first-term House members had ever been assigned to the Rules Committee. Like many members, Wheat engaged in a campaign for the seat: "I told everyone, call Tip O'Neill and tell him you think I'd be a good person to be on the Rules

TABLE 8.4
Predecessor's committee status and first-term request success

Committee type		Democrats		Republicans	
		Predecessor did not hold seat	Predecessor held seat	Predecessor did not hold seat	Predecessor held seat
All committees	Request denied	278 47.7%	48 37.5%	236 65.6%	39 42.4%
	Request granted	305 52.3%	80 62.5%	124 34.4%	59 57.6%
		Tau-b = .08 (p = .02)		Tau-b = .19 (p = .00)	
Constituency	Request denied	65 32.5%	13 21.0%	39 37.1%	12 23.5%
	Request granted	135 67.5%	49 79.0%	66 62.9%	39 76.5%
		Tau-b = .11 (p = .06)		Tau-b = .14 (p = .05)	
Policy	Request denied	135 49.1%	15 37.5%	99 65.6%	15 53.6 %
	Request granted	140 50.9%	25 62.5%	52 34.4%	13 46.4%
		Tau-b = .08 (p = .09)		Tau-b = .09 (p = .15)	
Influence	Request denied	77 77.0%	20 76.9%	98 95.1%	12 92.3%
	Request granted	23 23.0%	6 23.1%	5 4.9%	1 7.7%
		Tau-b = .00 (p = .50)		Tau-b = .04 (p = .50)	

Note: Analysis for "all committees" includes service committee requests. Separate analysis of predecessor's committee status and service committee requests is omitted because of the small number of such requests. The *p* is the one-tailed Monte Carlo value based on 10,000 simulations, using a random number seed of 2000000.

Committee."[12] The difference in Wheat's case is that a long-time member of the leadership seemed to throw his weight behind his successor with Speaker Tip O'Neill, who controlled appointments to the committee. When asked whether Bolling helped him get the assignment, Wheat replied, "Absolutely. He appreciated the fact that I wanted to be on the committee and that I understood the influence it could have on the House of Representatives, and I think he lobbied for me also."[13] Wheat knew that he had been successful when he heard from Speaker O'Neill:

"The Speaker told me that if one more person called him telling him I should be on the Rules Committee, . . . I wasn't going to get appointed to anything!"[14]

Former Staff and Request Success

House staff members commonly run for seats in the House. During the period covered by our data, fifty-four members reported that their last federal job before serving in the House was on congressional staff. Of these fifty-four, thirty-seven were Democrats and seventeen were Republicans. Among the representatives included in our data who previously served on congressional staff are very successful members, including Barbara Boxer (D-CA), Anthony Coelho (D-CA), Tom Daschle (D-SD), John Dingell (D-MI), Tom Foley (D-WA), Trent Lott (R-MS), Bob Michel (R-IL), Bill Richardson (D-NM), Donald Rumsfeld (R-IL), and David Stockman (R-MI). Former staff members may have insight into the importance of committee work and the committee assignment process that helps them be successful in receiving a preferred committee assignment in their first term. Perhaps as staff members, they had significant interaction with their new colleagues or gained a high level of trust from members of the committee on committees. Former congressional staff members can call upon their former patrons for endorsements. Finally, because staff members are often seen as extensions of particular members of Congress, additional information (voting cues) about the likely behavior of former staff is available when the members are newly elected.

Table 8.5 illustrates the relationship between status as a former staff member and committee request success. The relationship is particularly strong for Democrats. More than 80 percent of first-term Democrats who were former staff members were granted their preferred committee assignment compared with 52.7 percent of first-term Democrats who had not been on staff. This relationship is fairly robust across committee type, including influence committees. By contrast, being a former staff member did not seem to carry any particular cache within the Republican assignment process. It appears that, at least for Democrats, having served on the congressional staff gives a new member a leg up in the committee assignment process.

Tom Daschle (D-SD) made his request for Agriculture known to the committee on committees nearly a year before he was elected to the House. He wrote to O'Neill, seeking the Speaker's support: "I am writing, admittedly very early, to seek your support for a position on the House Agriculture Committee should I be elected to the Congress from South Dakota's First district next November. . . . While it is early, I believe my prospects for election are good, and I know having a congressman on the Agriculture Committee is important to South Dakota."[15] The letter concludes, "Should you seek further information on me or my campaign, I'm certain that Senator Jim Abourezk, for whom I worked for four years, would be happy to answer any questions."

Daschle continued to convey to the Speaker and to others, in meetings and through letters, the importance of an assignment to Agriculture until his goal was achieved. In a letter to majority leader Jim Wright, Daschle argued, "I made a major campaign issue of the fact that Republicans representing my District have not served on that Committee and [I] pledged repeatedly to seek a seat on the Agriculture Committee. It would be a distinctly poor start to follow a long, messy recount with a failure to achieve what the last two Democrats before me achieved, namely a seat on Agriculture."[16] Daschle received a seat on the Agriculture Committee as a first-term member.

A second Democrat in our sample who had previously served on congressional staff is Norman Dicks (D-WA), who had been a legislative assistant for senator Warren Magnuson (D-WA). Like Daschle, Dicks made his committee assignment preferences known early and relied on his experience as a staff member in making the case for an assignment to the Appropriations Committee as a first-term member. Dicks visited Washington in September 1976 (before his election to the House in November 1976) to meet with House leaders. Candidate Dicks spelled out his committee choices in part of a letter to O'Neill that September: "I enjoyed our meeting today in the Capitol and wanted to let you know my choices for Committee assignments as rapidly as possible. My first choice is the House Appropriations Committee; second, the House Armed Services Committee and, third, the House Ways and Means Committee."[17]

In a letter to newly elected majority leader Jim Wright, Dicks supports his request for placement on Appropriations with reference to his staff experience: "As appropriations assistant to Senator Warren Magnuson for eight years prior to my election to Congress, I learned a great deal about the appropriations and budget processes. I hope I can put this experience to good use as an effective member of this important House Committee."[18] Wright's reply acknowledges the importance of Dicks' experience to obtaining the assignment: "It was my special pleasure to have a hand in insuring your nomination to the vitally important Appropriations Committee. I know you will find that assignment stimulating and fascinating and certainly your long service with Warren Magnuson in the Senate will serve you in good stead."[19]

Dicks originally considered requesting membership on the Armed Services Committee as his first choice but was urged to request Appropriations by senior Washington State colleagues (Davis 1991, 25). Dicks was able to enlist support for his Appropriations bid from a well-respected former member of the House, Julia Butler Hansen, who wrote to O'Neill: "[I have] a favor that I would like you to consider. . . . I would like to urge your consideration of our new Member from the Sixth District, Norm Dicks, as member of the House Appropriations Committee. Norm is extremely capable. He was in Senator Magnuson's office and handled many of his appropriations matters when I was a member of the House. He is a top flight person, and anything that you can do would be sincerely appreciated by the State of Washington."[20] Dicks was assigned to the Appropriations Committee as a first-term member.

Family Ties

Politics tends to run in the family. To see this, look no further than the Kennedy and Bush families. Although these two families represent political dynasties, there are many more obscure political families. In fact, over the period covered in this research, 111 first-term members of Congress, 61 Democrats and 50 Republicans, had immediate family who had prior congressional experience. Similar to congressional staff members, those who are related to members or former members of Congress may have access to important insights into the assignment process, and they may enjoy a higher level of trust among members of the committee on committees than do other members of Congress. For instance, when

TABLE 8.5
Former congressional staff's first-term request success

Committee type		Democrats		Republicans	
		Not former staff	*Former staff*	*Not former staff*	*Former staff*
All committees	Request denied	319 47.3%	7 18.9%	263 60.5%	12 70.6%
	Request granted	355 52.7%	30 81.1%	172 39.5%	5 29.4%
		Tau-b = .18 (p = .001)		Tau-b = −.04 (p = .38)	
Constituency	Request denied	78 32.0%	0 0%	49 32.0%	2 66.7%
	Request granted	166 68.0%	18 100%	104 68.0%	1 33.3%
		Tau-b = .18 (p = .001)		Tau-b = −.10 (p = .13)	
Policy	Request denied	146 48.2%	4 33.3%	110 64.0%	4 57.1%
	Request granted	157 51.8%	8 66.7%	62 36.0%	3 42.9%
		Tau-b = .06 (p = .20)		Tau-b = .03 (p = .50)	
Influence	Request denied	94 79.0%	3 42.9%	104 95.4%	6 85.7%
	Request granted	25 21.0%	4 57.1%	5 4.6%	1 14.3%
		Tau-b = .19 (p = .03)		Tau-b = .10 (p = .17)	

Note: Analysis for "all committees" includes service committee requests. Separate analysis of former staff and service committee requests is omitted because of the small number of such requests. The p is the one-tailed Monte Carlo value based on 10,000 simulations, using a random number seed of 2000000.

Susan Molinari (R-NY) was elected to Congress, she had unusual insight into the committee assignment process; her father, Guy Molinari (R-NY), had served before her in the House. Molinari replaced her father, who advised her on how to be successful in the assignment process:

> My dad was in Congress before I was, and he gave me the talk when I got in, and said, 'OK, here's the different routes you can go. . . . I didn't even think of asking for major committee assignments . . . but my dad was always on Transportation, and that's a big issue in New York City, and that was something that I was

interested in. . . . I definitely wanted on Transportation, which was not a problem because I succeeded my dad, and it's especially easy for [family] members to hop into that committee assignment and fill out the term.[21]

Albert Gore, Jr. (D-TN) followed his father into politics, and like his father, he was an ambitious southerner with moderate views. Gore initially requested a seat on Appropriations, but when it became apparent that he would be unsuccessful, he switched his sights to Energy and Commerce. Gore was successful in his quest for a seat on Energy and Commerce during his first year in Congress, something that only about 37 percent of first-term Democrats were able to attain. Majority Leader Wright describes Gore's early ambition and success:

> Now I spotted talent in a young Tennessean, Albert Gore Jr., whose parents I knew and admired. My own advice was sometimes less than perfect, I discovered. Al, not yet twenty-nine, wanted to go for a spot on the Commerce Committee in his first term. I tried to dissuade him. "First termers are hardly ever considered for assignment to that committee," I told him. "To make a big run this year might irritate folks. They might think you too brash. Why not bide your time and get better known?" The youngster thanked me for my advice but ignored it. He worked every member of the Steering Committee diligently and won the assignment he sought. He exceeded my expectations and I was delighted. I've never again underestimated Al Gore. (1996, 311)

But Gore was not satisfied with just a seat on Energy and Commerce. After learning of his successful placement, Gore wrote a letter to Speaker O'Neill seeking a second assignment, an extremely unusual request: "Thank you for your favorable action in assigning me to the Interstate and Foreign Commerce Committee. I appreciate it very much. I understand that you have completed filling the vacancies on the major committees and will now begin work on the non-major committees. I am now asking for your vote to secure an assignment to the Government Operations Committee."

Gore's letter concludes: "P.S. My second preference would be to serve on the Science and Technology Committee, and my third would be Interior and Insular Affairs."[22] Although Gore did not receive a seat on Government Operations, he was placed on Science in addition to Energy and Commerce.

Table 8.6 presents our analysis of the relationship between family ties and request success. Once again, interparty differences are immediately apparent. Among Democrats, there is a significant relationship between having family ties and request success. Seventy percent of first-term Democrats with family ties received their preferred committee assignment, while 53.5 percent of first-term Democrats without family ties were successful. The relationship persists for constituency committees and, weakly, for policy committees, but not for influence committees; committee-on-committees members generally require sufficient information about a representative before awarding such an assignment. The results for Republicans indicate no significant support for the hypothesis.

• • •

Over the last three decades, the political science literature has marginalized the degree to which the personal characteristics of individual members, and committee politics, influence the assignment process. Our results to this point suggest that perhaps too much has been made of the "routine" nature of the committee assignment process in two ways. First, our results indicate that personal characteristics influence request success. We have found significant support for Masters' and Clapp's hypothesis; confirmed the importance of a prior claim on a committee slot based on the member's predecessor; and shown that factors such as congressional family ties and experience on congressional staff may influence the success of members who request specific committee assignments. Second, our results demonstrate important differences between the two parties that we would not expect to observe if the process were, in fact, routine.

MULTIVARIATE MODELS OF REQUEST SUCCESS

Our multivariate models involve two broad classes of variables. On the one hand are indicators of individual members' personal characteristics: electoral variables (marginality, lack of opposition), predecessor's

TABLE 8.6
Family ties and first-term request success

Committee type		Democrats		Republicans	
		No family ties	Family ties	No family ties	Family ties
All committees	Request denied	317 46.5%	9 30.0%	266 60.6%	9 69.2%
	Request granted	364 53.5%	21 70.0%	173 39.4%	4 30.8%
		Tau-b = .07 (p = .05)		Tau-b = .03 (p = .30)	
Constituency	Request denied	77 30.8%	1 8.3%	49 32.5%	2 40.0%
	Request granted	173 69.2%	11 91.7%	102 67.5%	3 60.0%
		Tau-b = .10 (p = .06)		Tau-b = −.03 (p = .50)	
Policy	Request denied	145 48.3%	5 33.3%	113 63.8%	1 50.0%
	Request granted	155 51.7%	10 66.7%	64 36.2%	1 50.0%
		Tau-b = .06 (p = .15)		Tau-b = .03 (p = .50)	
Influence	Request denied	94 76.4%	3 100%	104 94.5%	6 100%
	Request granted	29 23.6%	0 0%	6 5.5%	0 0%
		Tau-b = −.09 (p = .30)		Tau-b =.05 (p = .50)	

Note: Analysis for "all committees" includes service committee requests. Separate analysis of family ties and service committee requests is omitted because of the small number of such requests. The p is the one-tailed Monte Carlo value based on 10,000 simulations, using a random number seed of 2000000.

committee status, congressional staff experience, family ties, ideological proximity to the party median, and partisan loyalty. On the other hand are indicators of committee seat supply and demand. Table 8.7 lists the variables and the hypothesized relationship of each to request success according to the three committee models. The self-selection hypothesis predicts that the personal characteristic variables will mostly wash out in the presence of supply-and-demand indicators. Party-cartel theory suggests that party loyalty will be a major factor in request success.

Informational theory expects ideological proximity to the party median to increase a member's chance of preferred assignment.

As we have argued, the personal characteristics most likely to influence the assignment process will be significantly different for first-term members than for incumbents. In the absence of reliable information about new members' ideological or partisan behavior, committees on committees will focus on more easily distinguishable factors such as electoral safety. Incumbents' ideology and party loyalty are the personal characteristics most likely to be relevant to committees on committees. We also contend that the committee on committees considers the member's current committee portfolio and makes strategic decisions based on the slots that will be freed up for other members when awarding new committee assignments.

First-Term Members

Table 8.8 displays the results of our analysis of request success for first-term Democrats. Model one lists both personal characteristics and supply and demand variables. Model two includes both variables and dummy variables for each of the Speakers during the period (excluding Speaker Albert, for statistical reasons).[23] Contrary to the predictions of the routinized self-selection model, most of the personal characteristics continue to demonstrate a significant effect on the request success of first-term members when analyzed in a multivariate context. The already weak relationship between electoral marginality and request success for first-term Democrats evaporates in a multivariate context; however, the other relationships we report above remain robust in a multivariate model. First-term Democrats who run unopposed increase their probability of request success by 119 percent. If a member requests a seat held by his or her predecessor, the member is 93 percent more likely to receive the request than are those without this prior claim. Former staff members and those with family ties are significantly more likely to receive a preferred assignment than are new members without the experience or family connection. All of these findings buttress the bivariate relationships illustrated above.

Table 8.7
Hypothesized relationship of model variables to request success
(by committee theory)

Variable	Hypothesized relationship		
	Self-selection/ distributive theory	Informational theory	Party-cartel theory
Personal characteristic			
Marginality	no relationship	no prediction	no prediction
Electoral opposition	no prediction/ no relationship	no prediction	no prediction
Prior claim (predecessor on committee)	increased success	no prediction	no prediction
Congressional staff experience	no prediction/ no relationship	no prediction	no prediction
Family ties	no prediction/ no relationship	no prediction	no prediction
Ideological proximity	no relationship	increased success	no prediction
Party loyalty	no relationship	no relationship	increased success
Exchange value of current committee assignments	no prediction	no prediction	no prediction
Supply-and-demand			
State member on requested committee	decreased success	no prediction	no prediction
Number of party vacancies on requested committee	increased success	no prediction	increased success
Number of party requests for requested committee	decreased success	no prediction	no prediction
Geographic competition for requested committee	decreased success	no prediction	no prediction
Senior geographic competition for requested committee	decreased success	no prediction	no prediction
Value to other members of requested committee	no prediction	no prediction	no prediction

Consistent with the routinized self-selection model, five of the six sup-ply-and-demand variables are significantly related to request success in the predicted direction. Increased supply of committee slots increases the likelihood that a first-term Democrat will receive a requested committee assignment; increased competition for a limited supply of committee slots reduces the likelihood that a first-term Democrat will receive a requested committee. Favoring the first-term Democrat during this period are a larger number of party vacancies on the committee, with each additional vacancy increasing the probability of success by 9 percent. If a representa-tive from the member's state is already on the committee, the probability of success increases by 69 percent, a finding that is somewhat counter-intuitive; however, it likely reflects the fact that first-term Democrats will request a committee on which their state has a member only if they are confident that an additional state member will be tolerated on the committee.[24] Working against a first-term Democratic requester are geo-graphic competition for a committee slot and the competition among all members if the requester seeks a slot on a sought-after committee.

Model two adds dummy variables for each of the Democratic Speakers during the period that we examined. Consistent with our discussion in chapter 4, request success varies within leadership eras, independent of other model variables. In particular, first-term Democrats were at a sig-nificant disadvantage during the Wright and Foley Speakerships, with the probability of success during those two eras reduced by more than 50 percent. Parameter estimates for the other variables in the model remain unchanged by the addition of these variables.

Model results for first-term Republicans (table 8.9) provide interesting contrast to the findings for first-term Democrats. First-term Republicans elected by slim margins are significantly (52 percent) more likely to receive a requested committee relative to their more electorally safe colleagues. Consistent with our findings in a bivariate context, first-term Republicans who are former staff members or who have family ties to the institution have no advantage in the Republican assignment context. Similar to first-term Democrats, Republicans who have made a previous request for a committee seat are significantly more likely to receive their request. As with the findings for first-term Democrats, personal characteristics matter, contrary to the routinized self-selection model.

TABLE 8.8
First-term Democrats' request success (multivariate)

Variable	Model 1 β (Wald)	Log odds	Model 2 β (Wald)	Log odds
Marginality	.12 (.39)	—	.11 (.34)	—
electoral opposition	.79 ** (3.01)	2.19	.86 ** (3.55)	2.37
Prior claim	.66 *** (6.16)	1.93	.69 *** (6.69)	1.99
Congressional staff experience	1.51 *** (6.60)	4.54	1.34 *** (5.16)	3.86
Family ties	1.14 ** (4.65)	3.14	1.07 ** (4.03)	2.91
State member on committee	.52 *** (25.52)	1.69	.52 *** (24.36)	1.69
Party vacancies (#)	.09 ** (3.41)	1.09	.08 * (2.81)	1.09
Party requests (#)	−.04 ** (7.14)	.714	−.04 ** (4.59)	.965
Geographic competition	−.74 ** (3.68)	.478	−.82 ** (4.35)	.438
Senior geographic competition	−.75 (1.20)	—	−.75 (1.16)	—
Request value	−.49 *** (30.49)	.611	−.52 *** (31.83)	˙597
Rayburn	—		−.26 (.65)	—
O'Neill	—		−.15 (.18)	—
Wright	—		−.85 *** (3.43)	.429
Foley	—		−.77 *** (3.46)	.461
Constant	.31 (1.16)		.62 * (2.11)	
Psuedo R^2		.29		.29
Predicted (%)		72.1		72.8
−2 x LLR		678.07		671.37
N		603		603

Note:
*$p < .10$ (one-tailed)
**$p < .05$ (one-tailed)
***$p < .01$ (one-tailed)

Consistent with the expectations of the routinized self-selection model, however, several of the supply-and-demand variables influence request success. Unlike first-term Democrats, first-term Republicans gain no advantage from an increased number of party vacancies on their requested committee. Similar to Democrats, increased numbers of requests and geographic competition decrease the likelihood of request success for first-term Republicans; requests for more valuable committees also decrease the likelihood of request success for these Republican members.

As with the first-term Democrats, model two includes dummy variables for each of the Republican leaders during this period (excluding Halleck, for statistical reasons). Although the estimates for the other variables remain consistent, first-term Republicans requesting committees under the leadership of John Rhodes (AZ) were less likely to receive a preferred committee assignment.

Incumbents

As we have argued, we expect that different variables will influence the request success of incumbent members seeking changes in their committee assignments. We expect members' behaviors while in office, as measured by ideological proximity to the party median and by party loyalty, to be important considerations in the assignment process. We also include in the model a measure of the exchange value of the members' current committee assignments. Our indicator is the value of each member's committee assignments in the previous Congress—the Grosswart score. Status as a former staff member or family ties, which may have been important in the first term, become unimportant in the second term and are thus excluded from the analysis. Electoral considerations continue to be potentially important considerations and are thus included in the model. Finally, we retain all supply-and-demand variables.

The results for model one in table 8.10 indicate the importance of personal characteristics in the committee assignment process for incumbent Democrats. Increased party loyalty and proximity to the ideological median of the party both significantly increase the probability that incumbent Democrats will be successful in receiving a preferred committee assignment. This finding is important for the informational and

TABLE 8.9
First-term Republicans' request success (multivariate)

Variable	Model 1 β (Wald)	Log Odds	Model 2 β (Wald)	Log Odds
Marginality	.42 * (2.49)	1.52	.42 ** (2.41)	1.52
Prior claim	.68 ** (4.55)	1.97	.65 ** (4.15)	1.93
Congressional Staff experience	−.36 (.19)	—	−.13 (.03)	—
Family ties	−.43 (.18)	—	−.48 (.23)	—
State member on committee	.89 *** (22.08)	2.44	.92 *** (22.85)	2.52
Party vacancies (#)	.02 (.69)	—	.09 * (1.79)	1.09
Party requests (#)	−.03 ** (1.97)	.969	−.03 (1.11)	.975
Geographic competition	−.69 * (1.81)	.502	−.64 (1.50)	—
Senior geographic competition	−.32 (.18)	—	−.32 (.18)	—
Request value	−.77 *** (27.66)	.462	−.79 *** (23.99)	.450
Ford	—		.08 (.04)	—
Rhodes	—		−.62 * (3.76)	.539
Michel	—		−.16 (.15)	—
Constant	.14 (.15)		.14 (.09)	
Psuedo R²		.42		.43
Predicted (%)		77.6		76.8
−2 LLR		364.59		361.58
N		366		366

Note:
*p < .10 (one-tailed)
**p < .05 (one-tailed)
***p < .01 (one-tailed)

party-cartel theories, especially given the robustness of the findings in the presence of the supply-and-demand variables. There appears to be support also for the exchange theory: Incumbent Democrats who had valuable committee portfolios were significantly advantaged in the assignment process. Electoral marginality does not influence the likelihood of a successful request, though running unopposed does increase the likelihood of success, both findings that are consistent with our findings among first-term Democrats.

The supply-and-demand variables do not perform as well, relative to the findings for first-term Democrats, in predicting the request success of incumbent Democrats. Of the four variables included in the model, only one is statistically significant: the more requests received for the committee being requested by the incumbent Democrat, the lower the likelihood of success, reducing the probability of success by 6 percent. These findings do not support the routinized self-selection model; rather, they support the contention that, at least where requests from incumbent Democrats are concerned, the committee assignment process is heavily influenced by personal considerations.

Model two, which again includes dummy variables for each of the Democratic Speakers through this era (excluding the Wright and Foley periods) indicates that incumbents fared better under the Rayburn, Albert, and O'Neill Speakerships relative to the Wright Speakership. However, there is evidence of variation among these leadership eras. Incumbent Democrats were at a much greater advantage during the Rayburn and Albert eras than they were during the O'Neill and Wright eras. This may be due to increased reliance on partisan loyalty as a criterion for committee assignments. Under Speaker O'Neill, the use of party-unity scores in the assignment process became more common, and this use intensified under Wright. In fact, the impact of party loyalty on success in model two doubles when the leadership era variables are included in the equation.

As shown in table 8.11, we find evidence for a somewhat different set of dynamics among incumbent Republicans. Model one indicates that, as with the Democrats, party loyalty is an important consideration for incumbents seeking new committee assignments; in fact, the magnitude

TABLE 8.10
Incumbent Democrats' request success (multivariate)

Variable	Model 1 β (Wald)	Log Odds	Model 2 β (Wald)	Log Odds
Party loyalty	.02 ** (2.84)	1.02	.03 *** (8.29)	1.04
Ideological proximity	1.52 ** (2.95)	4.56	2.74 *** (7.97)	15.41
Exchange value$_{t-1}$	.30 *** (8.22)	1.36	.29 *** (7.36)	1.35
Marginality	.36 (1.02)	—	1.73 (.22)	—
Electoral opposition	.57 ** (3.19)	1.78	.44 ** (2.72)	1.72
State member on committee	1.16 *** (42.77)	3.19	1.18 *** (42.85)	3.25
Party vacancies (#)	−.01 (.03)	—	−.09 (1.59)	—
Party requests (#)	−.06 *** (6.01)	.944	−.02 (.74)	—
Geographic competition	−.68 (1.36)	—	−.81 ** (1.83)	.446
Senior geographic competition	.34 (.17)	—	−.74 (.73)	—
Rayburn	—		1.98 *** (11.92)	7.24
Albert	—		2.06 *** (8.54)	7.88
O'Neill	—		1.09 ** (3.79)	2.98
Constant	−2.46 *** (6.53)		−5.40 *** (18.52)	
Psuedo R^2		.26		.31
Predicted (%)		73.3		74.7
−2 x LLR		412.47		395.34
N		356		356

Note:
*$p < .10$ (one-tailed)
**$p < .05$ (one-tailed)
***$p < .01$ (one-tailed)

of the effect is the same as for incumbent Democrats. Ideological proximity, on the other hand, is statistically insignificant in contrast to the
observed effect for incumbent Democrats. Neither the exchange theory
nor Masters' and Clapp's marginality hypothesis is supported in the
multivariate model. It appears that party loyalty was the prime personal
consideration for the RCC during this period for incumbents.

Supply-and-demand variables perform well in model one, indicating
that competition for committee seats plays an important role for incumbent Republicans. Increased numbers of party vacancies on a committee
significantly increase the probability of request success for these members,
and geographic competition for a requested committee significantly
reduces the likelihood of success. When we include the leadership era
variables, the results are similar, though ideological proximity edges
into statistically significant territory. There is also some evidence that
incumbent Republicans were less likely to receive requested assignments under the leadership of Bob Michel.

• • •

Routinized self-selection suggests that the committee assignment
process is largely a function of the supply of committee slots and the
demand for open slots. The party committees on committees, from this
point of view, simply attempt to accommodate requests and "keep peace
in the family." According to this model, the personal characteristics of
Democratic members are largely irrelevant to the process. Though Republican requests, to this point, were never examined, the implicit assumption
was that the same was true of the Republican assignment process.

Our framework suggests that the committee assignment process will
be competitive among members and subject to an array of forces within
the process, including attention to personal characteristics, significant
conflict and bargaining within the secretive process, supply-and-demand
considerations, and the differential influence of party leaders. Our interview evidence suggests support for this view. Our quantitative analysis
suggests several other conclusions (our findings are summarized in
table 8.12). First, contrary to the routinized self-selection perspective,
personal characteristics matter in the committee assignment process.
Second, it is risky to generalize across parties; the assignment process in

TABLE 8.11
Incumbent Republicans' request success (multivariate)

Variable	Model 1 β (Wald)	Log Odds	Model 2 β (Wald)	Log Odds
Party loyalty	.02 * (2.25)	1.02	.02 ** (3.02)	1.02
Ideological proximity	−1.38 (1.46)	—	−1.49 * (1.65)	.224
Exchange value$_{t-1}$	.51 (.33)	—	.05 (.19)	—
Marginality	−.004 (.000)	—	−.16 (.19)	—
State member on committee	1.59 *** (60.14)	4.94	1.60 *** (60.31)	5.00
Party vacancies (#)	.11 * (2.52)	1.11	.11 ** (2.98)	1.12
Party requests (#)	.007 (.13)	—	.02 (1.32)	—
Geographic competition	−1.48 ** (3.05)	.228	−1.52 ** (3.19)	.219
Senior geographic competition	−.89 (.59)	—	−.92 (.62)	—
Ford	—		.27 (.42)	—
Rhodes	—		−.19 (.20)	—
Michel	—		−.52 * (1.86)	.59
Constant	−3.90 *** (12.10)		−4.19 *** (11.33)	
Psuedo R²		.31		.32
Predicted (%)		71.4		74.0
−2 x LLR		412.48		406.87
N		416		416

Note:
*$p < .10$ (one-tailed)
**$p < .05$ (one-tailed)
***$p < .01$ (one-tailed)

TABLE 8.12
Summary of multivariate request success findings

Variables	First-term members		Incumbent members	
	Democrats	*Republicans*	*Democrats*	*Republicans*
Personal Characteristics				
Marginality	n.s.	+	n.s.	n.s.
Electoral opposition	+	N/A	+	N/A
Prior claim	+	+	N/A	N/A
Congressional staff experience	+	n.s.	N/A	N/A
Family ties	+	n.s.	N/A	N/A
Ideological proximity	N/A	N/A	+	n.s./+
Party loyalty	N/A	N/A	+	+
Exchange value of current committee assignments	N/A	N/A	+	n.s.
Supply and demand				
State member on requested committee	+	+	+	+
Number of party vacancies on requested committee	+	n.s.	n.s.	+
Number of party requests for requested committee	-	-	-	n.s.
Geographic competition for requested committee	-	-	n.s./-	-
Senior geographic competition for requested committee	n.s.	n.s.	n.s.	n.s.
Value to other members of requested committee	-	-	N/A	N/A

Note:

n.s.   not significant
+   significant positive relationship
-   significant negative relationship

the parties emphasizes different characteristics as important. Which personal characteristics matter is dependent upon the political party and the electoral status of the requesting members. For instance, electoral marginality is an important consideration for first-term Republicans, but not for Democratic requesters or Republican incumbents. Democratic members who run unopposed are advantaged in the assignment process.

Third, consistent with the self-selection hypothesis, supply-and-demand variables provide broad parameters for the committee assignment process. However, within those parameters, personal characteristics, party structures, and politics help to determine which members will be successful. For instance, first-term Democrats and incumbent Republicans gain an advantage from increased vacancies on requested committees, but incumbent Democrats and first-term Republicans do not. Finally, different leaders can affect the assignment process in different ways. Our findings provide some support for the contention that several of the reforms instituted in the Democratic Party in the early 1970s had repercussions for the committee assignment process. In particular, party loyalty became an increasingly important criterion for incumbents seeking to improve their committee assignments.

CHAPTER NINE

GENDER, RACE, AND REQUEST SUCCESS

Probably one of the last areas in which prejudice remains fashion-able is with regard to the equal rights of women. My appointment to the Judiciary Committee would certainly give all Republican women as well as all lady lawyers a great boost.

MARGARET M. HECKLER (R-MA)

Over the last several decades, the number of women and racial minorities elected to Congress has increased. An institution that was once almost exclusively male and white now looks more like America than it ever has (though it has a long way to go to be completely representative of the diversity of the country). Perhaps because these changes in the composition of Congress are relatively recent, little research has focused on the committee experiences of women and minorities in the House. In this chapter, we specifically address the request behaviors, and request success, of women and African Americans in the House.[1] In so doing we adapt the insights of the previous chapter, and incorporate some of the unique contextual factors that these two groups have confronted in the House.

A PLACE AT THE TABLE

Numerous authors contend that women legislators have a special interest in policies that differentially affect women; women legislators may choose to pursue committee assignments that are consistent with those policy interests (Carroll 2002; Dodson 1998; Rosenthal 1998; Swers 2002a, 2002b). Amplifying these arguments, other scholars have argued that the committee assignments of women significantly affect their ability to influence public policy outcomes (Barrett 1997; Bratton and Haynie 1999; McGlen and O'Connor 1998; Norton 1995, 1999, 2002; Schroedel and Corbin 2002). Despite the large body of research on House committee assignments in general, few studies have analyzed the committee assignments of female legislators.[2]

Two notable exceptions to the paucity of systematic studies of women's committee assignment experience are the studies by Sally Friedman (1996) and Irwin N. Gertzog (1995). Friedman examines the prestige associated with the committee assignments of women and minority members of the House in the period after 1965, finding that "women and minorities are not simply stereotyped into lower prestige or selective committees but are represented on committees of varying prestige in similar proportions to the average legislator" (78).[3] Gertzog likewise found that "women elected to the House since the mid-1960s have been more successful than their predecessors in securing prestigious assignments, and they have fared better as a group than the males whose House careers began when theirs did" (1995, 137). Gertzog bases his conclusion on an analysis of the percentage of females serving on exclusive committees by term compared with that of their male counterparts.[4] Both Friedman and Gertzog rely on *observed* committee assignments, not the members' preferences for committee assignments; that is, they look at what these members *got* rather than what these members *wanted*. Since members of the House often do not receive their preferred committee assignment, it is impossible to infer from data on actual assignments whether women's committee assignments are a function of the choices they make or of a committee assignment process that is unresponsive to the policy preferences and political styles of women members.[5] In addition, both Friedman and Gertzog lump together Democratic and

Republican women. As we demonstrate below, the failure to look at partisan differences allows the gains made by Democratic women members to compensate for the less attractive assignments received by the smaller number of Republican women legislators.

In contrast to these studies, we employ request data to assess how gender and party affiliation influence women's committee assignments. First, we consider whether women's committee requests indicate committee preferences that are distinct from those of their male counterparts. Second, we examine whether party affiliation influences the success of women members in receiving their preferred committee assignment.

Women's Representation in the Committee Assignment Process

We describe the mechanics of the committee assignment process in detail in chapter 2, and we do not reprise those descriptions here.[6] Instead we focus on an important difference in the representative structure of the Democratic and Republican committees on committees during the Congresses for which we have data, a difference that had important implications for women's committee assignments: female representation on the party committees on committees.

The DSPC included at least one female member from the 88th Congress through the end of the period under consideration—the 103rd Congress. From the 88th Congress through the 93rd, Martha Griffiths (MI) served on the Ways and Means Committee, which then served as the Democratic committee on committees. After the reforms of 1974 that vested the Democratic committee assignment function in the newly reconstituted Democratic Steering and Policy Committee (DSPC), women were *guaranteed* a seat at the table; one of the Speaker's appointments to the DSPC was set aside for a woman, specifically to represent the interests of women members.[7] In addition, late in 1980, the secretary of the caucus, a position reserved for a woman member (Gertzog 1995), was also included as an ex officio voting member of the DSPC (Sinclair 1995), which guaranteed women at least two seats on the DSPC until the position of caucus secretary was eliminated in 1987.[8]

The Executive Committee of the RCC did not ensure that women were included in the committee assignment process. Indeed, only one woman served on the Executive Committee during the Congresses covered by this research, Bobbi Fiedler (CA), and she served as a representative of the first-year Republican members of the 99th Congress, not of women legislators. Furthermore, the weighted-voting system used in the Executive Committee generally marginalized these representatives because they controlled one vote out of the total number of House Republicans (out of 180 votes in Bobbi Fiedler's case).[9] Thus, the interests of women members were much less likely to be directly represented in the Republicans' committee assignment process in contrast to the process used by House Democrats.

We hypothesize that the representational structure of the RCC negatively affected the ability of Republican women to receive their preferred committee assignment. In the absence of an advocate within the Executive Committee, women would be less likely to receive a desirable committee assignment and, further, would find it difficult to improve their committee assignments, especially through assignments to the more powerful and prestigious committees of the House. The importance to goal attainment of significant female representation within a group is a consistent theme in the literature.[10] Sue Thomas has argued that the institutional environments most likely to support women's policy priorities are "those environments in which higher proportions of women are present" (1994, 86). Additional support for this assertion can be found throughout the literature on women and politics, for example, Noelle Norton (2002) on women's participation in congressional committees; Michael B. Berkman and Robert E. O'Connor (1993) on state-level abortion policy; Kathleen A. Bratton and Kerry L. Haynie (1999) on agenda setting in state legislatures; and Jean Reith Schroedel and Tanya Buhler Corbin (2002) on mifepristone policy in Congress.

As additional support for the assertion that female membership on the Committees on Committees matters, we offer the following qualitative evidence. A task force led by Robert Lagomarsino (R-CA) was formed by the Republican leadership during the 101st Congress to recommend changes in the committee assignment process. One of the recommendations proposed by the task force (but not adopted by the Republican Conference) was to include a women's representative, with a single vote on the Executive Committee. An internal memorandum in the archived papers of Lagomarsino quotes Claudine Schneider (R-RI), the lone female member of the task force: "Republican Women in the House . . . wouldn't mind being treated as a token [on the Executive Committee], as long as it got them in the door."[11] In interviews, female Republican members confirmed that the lack of a woman on the Executive Committee made a difference: "Very much so," emphasized one former member, and another explained why: "Decisions are made privately, and there were generally, at that time, not women in the room, and so part of the key to being in leadership and being on certain committees was to make sure there's someone in the room [to advocate]."[12]

By contrast, we expect that Democratic women would be more successful in receiving desirable committee assignments due to the presence of women on the committee assignment panel who could advocate for equal treatment. When asked whether she saw herself as a representative of women while participating in the committee assignment process, a retired member who had served on the DSPC explained, "I always did. If we didn't look out for ourselves, then who would? In fact, I ended my career with really and truly giving all my influence. I was leaving the Ways and Means Committee, and by leaving it, I was leaving the Democrats without a woman. So that year I spent my entire time pushing to get a woman to take my place when I left."[13] Women in both parties felt that without female representation on the committees on committees, the interests of women members would not be served.

Women's Committee Requests

Several authors suggest that women will prefer committees that have jurisdiction over issues that differentially impact women and women's interests (Carroll 2002; Dodson 1998; Rosenthal 1998). The broad jurisdictions of many committees complicate empirical examination of this expectation. Many congressional committees have at least partial jurisdiction over the many public policies that are of interest to women. Despite the difficulty of identifying specific committees that women stereotypically "should" request—or stereotypically might avoid—some interesting patterns emerge. Table 9.1 contains data on the committee assignment requests of first-term and incumbent members broken down by gender and political party.

It might be argued that Education and Labor is a stereotypical "woman's committee" because of its jurisdiction over education issues and the conventional belief that education is the responsibility of women. Among Democrats, more first-term and incumbent women than men listed Education and Labor first among their committee preferences (11.4 percent of women versus 5.8 percent of men among first-term members; 5.9 percent versus 1.0 percent among incumbents). No Republican women, however, listed Education and Labor as a preference, and Republicans overall were less likely to pursue assignment to Education and Labor.

Armed Services and Foreign Affairs are among the committees that women might stereotypically avoid because of these committees' jurisdiction over the male-dominated worlds of military and diplomatic affairs. First-term Democratic women were almost equally likely to prefer the Armed Services Committee (9.1 percent) compared with first-term male Democrats (9.7 percent). No Republican woman requested Armed Services first, and the committee was as popular among first-term Republican men (9.7 percent) as it was among first-term Democrats. Among incumbent legislators, this pattern is nearly reversed. Democratic women did not request the committee but 11.9 percent of Republican women did; incumbent Democratic and Republican men requested the committee at similar levels, 5.2 percent and 8.2 percent, respectively. When it comes to the Foreign Affairs committee, women and men requested the committee in similar proportions.

A second approach to identifying differences in women's committee preferences is to consider their request behavior relative to the influence committees—Appropriations, Budget, Rules, and Ways and Means—and the noninfluence committee with the broadest jurisdiction, including jurisdiction over many issues of potential interest to female legislators—Energy.[14] No clear pattern emerges when comparing the committee preferences of men and women for membership on influence committees.

Identifying specific committees that women House members might gravitate toward is difficult because of the overlapping jurisdictions of

TABLE 9.1

Gender differences in committee preferences

	Democrats				Republicans			
	First-term		Incumbent		First-term		Incumbent	
	Female	Male	Female	Male	Female	Male	Female	Male
Agriculture	2	77	—	14	1	58	1	17
	4.5%	11.5%		2.3%	5.6%	13.4%	2.4%	2.7%
Appropriations	4	71	12	125	4	64	14	118
	9.1%	10.6%	35.3%	20.1%	22.2%	14.7%	33.3%	19.0%
Armed Services	4	65	—	32	—	42	5	51
	9.1%	9.7%		5.2%		9.7%	11.9%	8.2%
Banking	3	68	—	4	1	22	2	12
	6.8%	10.2%		0.6%	5.6%	5.1%	4.8%	1.9%
Budget	—	5	8	111	1	4	—	41
		0.7%	23.5%	17.9%	5.6%	0.9%		6.6%
District of Columbia	—	1	—	13	—	—	—	3
		0.1%		2.1%				0.5%
Education and Labor	5	39	2	6	—	10	—	3
	11.4%	5.8%	5.9%	1.0%		2.3%		0.5%
Energy and Commerce	9	116	2	62	5	79	5	41
	20.5%	17.4%	5.9%	10.0%	27.8%	18.2%	11.9%	6.6%
Foreign Affairs	2	41	1	31	1	31	3	78
	4.5%	6.1%	2.9%	5.0%	5.6%	7.1%	7.1%	12.6%
Government Operations	1	3	1	23	—	2	—	13
	2.3%	0.4%	2.9%	3.7%		0.5%		2.1%
House Administration	—	1	1	10	—	—	1	8
		0.1%	2.9%	1.6%			2.4%	1.3%
Judiciary	—	28	—	9	2	26	—	8
		4.2%		1.4%	11.1%	6.0%		1.3%
Merchant Marine	1	4	1	16	—	5	—	7
	2.3%	0.6%	2.9%	2.6%		1.2%		1.1%
Interior	1	30	2	31	1	17	—	30
	2.3%	4.5%	5.9%	5.0%	5.6%	3.9%		4.8%
Post Office	—	6	—	6	—	1	—	2
		0.9%		1.0%		0.2%		0.3%
Public Works	6	56	—	12	1	16	4	7
	13.6%	8.4%		1.9%	5.6%	3.7%	9.5%	1.1%
Rules	1	3	1	20	—	3	1	43
	2.3%	0.4%	2.9%	3.2%		0.7%	2.4%	6.9%
Science	—	14	—	13	—	14	3	15
		2.1%		2.1%		3.2%	7.1%	2.4%
Small Business	—	1	—	—	—	—	1	9
		0.1%					2.4%	1.5%
Ethics	—	—	—	—	—	—	—	3
								0.5%
Veterans' Affairs	—	1	—	5	—	1	—	3
		0.1%		0.8%		0.2%		0.5%
Ways and Means	5	37	3	78	1	39	2	108
	11.4%	5.5%	8.8%	12.6%	5.6%	9.0%	4.8%	17.4%
N	44	667	34	621	18	434	42	620

Note: Data on member requests are drawn from committee-on-committees briefing books and committee request letters. Data for Democrats include all Congresses from the 80th through the 103rd, with the exception of the 85th. Data for Republicans range from the 85th Congress through the 102nd.

TABLE 9.2
Female members' request success

| | First-term | | Incumbent | |
	Democrats	Republicans	Democrats	Republicans
	Female members			
Request granted	20	4	15	11
	45.5%	22.2%	44.1%	26.2%
Request denied	24	14	19	31
	54.5%	77.8%	55.9%	73.8%
N	44	18	34	42
	Tau b = −.216 (−1.84)**		Tau b = −.188 (1.65)**	

Note: Data on member requests are drawn from committee-on-committees briefing books and committee request letters. Data for Democrats include all Congresses from the 80th through the 103rd, with the exception of the 85th. Data for Republicans range from the 85th Congress through the 102nd. Percentages are calculated by column. Number in parentheses is the asymptotic t-value.
*$p < .10$ (one-tailed)
**$p < .05$ (one-tailed)
***$p < .01$ (one-tailed)

congressional committees; however, there is little evidence in these data to suggest that women gravitated toward or away from committees that they might be "expected" to prefer or to avoid, with the possible exception of Education and Labor for Democratic women.

Nothing is more important to members' pursuit of individual goals than the committees to which they are assigned. Our data allow us to examine the success of women House members in achieving assignment to their preferred committee. Our primary argument leads us to expect that Democratic women will have a greater likelihood of receiving a preferred committee assignment relative to Republican women. Table 9.2 presents request success data for female members, by party and electoral status.

The results in table 9.2 suggest a significant difference between women of the two parties regardless of electoral status. Democratic women, whether incumbents or first-term members, are more likely than their Republican colleagues are to receive a preferred committee assignment. Democratic women receive their preferred assignment, on average, about

45 percent of the time, but Republican women are successful only about 24 percent of the time. These differences are statistically significant.

As we demonstrate in the chapter 8, request success is dependent on a combination of personal characteristics and supply-and-demand variables. To confirm the effects of party and gender on the assignment process, we estimate three multivariate models, the results of which are presented in table 9.3. In the first model, we consider the requests of all female House members. Our primary hypothesis leads us to believe that party affiliation will have a significant negative impact on request success for Republican women. We control for various factors that are important to the success of all members (as we show in chapter 8), including both personal characteristics and supply-and-demand variables. The results in model one suggest a significant negative impact of party on request success for Republican women. A Republican woman, other factors held constant, is 10 percent less likely than a Democratic woman is to receive a preferred committee assignment.

Models two and three estimate a similar model among all members of the Democratic Party and the Republican Party. In these models, we include a gender term. Our expectation is that the gender term in the Republican model will be negative, indicating that Republican women are at a significant disadvantage in the assignment process because of their lack of representation in the committee assignment process. We expect that the gender term in the Democratic model will be equivalent to zero, indicating that Democratic women are not at a disadvantage, receiving preferred assignments with the same likelihood as their male party counterparts.

The results indicate that Democratic women were, in fact, equally likely to get a preferred committee assignment as their male colleagues were. Republican women, on the other had, were at a severe disadvantage. Other things held constant, Republican women were 45 percent less likely to receive their requested assignment than were Republican men.

Gender, Party, and Committee Assignments

Congressional committees are pivotal to a member's ability to pursue her policy goals in the House. The success of women in achieving preferred

TABLE 9.3
Gender and request success probabilities

Independent variables	Model 1 All female members	Odds ratio	Model 2 All Democrats	Odds ratio	Model 3 All Republicans	Odds ratio
	Successful First Committee Request[a]					
Gender[b]	—		−.26 (1.01)	—	−.60 ** (3.28)	.548
Party[c]	−.01** (4.94)	.990	—		—	
First term	−.69 * (1.84)	.503	−.17 * (1.76)	.842	.19 (1.52)	—
Marginality	.67 (1.24)	—	.09 (.52)	—	−.005 (.001)	—
Cong. staff experience	.727 (.36)	—	.51 ** (3.85)	1.67	−.34 (.95)	—
Family ties	.53 (.33)	—	.22 (.56)	—	−.09 (.06)	—
Geographic competition	.68 (.63)	—	−.22 (.77)	—	−.43 * (1.67)	.65
Senior geographic competition	−1.94 (−1.88)	.144	−.43 (1.42)	—	−.79 ** (2.62)	.454
Request value	−.39 (11.39)	.677	−.21 (35.16)	.811	−.29 *** (52.41)	.747
Constant	1.77 (4.88)		.71 (28.14)		.448 (.43)	
N	136		1205		511	
Predicted (%)	66.9		59.7		66.3	
Pseudo R^2	.26		.06		.06	
−2 x LLR	152.33		1606.55		621.96	

Note: Figures in parentheses are t_{wald}. The odds ratio is not reported when the associated coefficient is not significant.

* $p < .10$ (one-tailed)
** $p < .05$ (one-tailed)
*** $p < .01$ (one-tailed)

[a]Dependent variable is 1 if member received requested assignment, 0 if member did not receive requested assignment.

[b]Gender is coded 1 if the member is female, 0 if member is male.

[c]Party is coded 1 if the member is a Republican, 0 if the member is a Democrat.

committee assignment might powerfully shape their ability to pursue their individual policy interests; there are few opportunities outside the committee hearing room to influence public policy significantly. Prior to this study, it was impossible to fully appreciate female House members' committee assignment experiences and how they might differ from those of their male colleagues. Previous studies have had to focus on women's actual committee assignments to draw conclusions about how the committee assignment process responds to women's interests. Our extensive database of committee requests enables us to identify what women members of the House *wanted* and what they *got* when the committee assignments were made.

Our results shed significant light on several puzzles in the literature. First, contrary to arguments that suggest that women will gravitate toward committees with jurisdiction over "women's issues," our results suggest that the committee requests of women did not significantly differ from those of men. This does not suggest that female House members' interests are identical to those of male House members. Rather, this result suggests that women (like men) can pursue their interests through membership on various committees.

Second, our results suggest that party has a significant influence on the ability of women to achieve committee positions. At least in the case of Republican women, women were not being treated equally, as previous studies suggested. One explanation for this discrepancy is that the Republicans' committee assignment process had a built-in gender bias; that is, Republican women were unlikely to have a place at the table from which to advocate the interests of women. A woman who had been a member of the Republican Conference during this time described this reality: "Does it make sense that the Republicans should not support women? No, that does not make sense. Is it the truth? Yes. . . . Not only do they traditionally not help women to get elected, but once the women are elected, they don't do much to help further their careers."[15]

A female member who sought membership on the Armed Services Committee alluded to the bias confronted by Republican women in the assignment process:

> One of the Steering Committee members said, "Let me give you a piece of advice: The best thing you can do is you talk to these

people on . . . the committee on committees and the Armed Services Committee and convince them you are not a Pat Schroeder." She was the only woman on the [Armed Services] Committee, and they didn't like her. "You've got to convince them that you are not like her." I think that was the best advice, 'cause they just see [a] woman—"Oh god, don't be another, you know, feminist who's not for a lot [of] defense things we are for." I made sure I tacked my approach that way.[16]

Another member, asked whether Republican women were actively discriminated against in the assignment process, described what she saw in Congress:

I can tell you that there have been quite a few women in my ten years in Congress who completely mimicked the votes of the men and did not participate in the Congressional Women's Caucus or any of the meetings that the women sometimes put together . . . so the fact of the matter is that they voted like the men—they did what the men wanted—the only difference is that they wore a skirt and they were not advanced.[17]

Evidence for the role of gender in the committee assignments of Republicans occasionally appears in members' request letters. Claudine Schneider was a moderate Republican from Rhode Island, first elected to the House in 1980 with 55 percent of the vote in a district that had not elected a Republican since 1938. Her committee preference was Energy and Commerce. Being a first-term member, elected by a relatively slim margin, it is unsurprising that she was assigned instead to two minor committees, Merchant Marine and Science. Schneider was reelected in 1982 and in 1984 with substantially larger margins, each time requesting Energy and Commerce or Appropriations.

Requesting a transfer to Energy and Commerce in 1986, Representative Schneider reflected on her position as a moderate within a conservative conference, and her role as a representative of issues important to women. Citing a "recent poll" suggesting that the national Republican Party needed to evidence more "openness, a broader perspective on the issues, and [to reach out] to a more diverse constituency," she argued to Republican leader Bob Michel,

I believe that I represent much of this broader perspective. I hang tough on budget cutting, but I am also an activist on the environment, women's equity, and regaining America's competitive edge in world markets. At the same time I fear that these attributes are some of the very reasons that the Republican leadership has not assigned me to the committee of my choice. . . . Bob, it is not in the interests of the future of the party to alienate Republicans like myself. We are crucial to the future success of Republicanism. The Party will be counting on Republicans like me if it is to continue gaining strength in the East and the Midwest.[18]

In a final attempt to transfer to the Appropriations Committee, Schneider eloquently voiced her frustration with her predicament: "After eight years of toiling in the vineyards, I feel that the time has come to let me taste the wine. . . . I have served loyally and steadfastly on the lesser committees to which I have been assigned, knowing that my turn would eventually come. I honestly feel that time is now."[19] Schneider served two more terms in the House, on the same two committees to which she was originally assigned, before unsuccessfully running for the Senate.[20]

As the Republicans took control of Congress in the 104th, Republican women appeared to become more successful at achieving more valuable committee assignments (Arnold and King 2002; Norton 2002). Republicans taking over the majority undoubtedly helped the cause of Republican women; majority status created more committee slots into which women could be placed. However, another event may be more significant in Republican women's committee success: the appointments of Tillie Fowler (FL) and Susan Molinari (NY) to the Executive Committee (renamed the Steering Committee), the first women included on the committee since Bobbi Fiedler in the 99th Congress, and the first time in history *two* women were present during the Republicans' committee assignment process.

According to a very senior male member of the Republican leadership involved in the committee assignment process, the resurgent party consciously made an effort to be inclusive, especially of women: "I would say that we didn't try to exclude them. We were conscious of the image that we were projecting. By and large, I think that women got a pretty good break."[21] In fact, another member of the Steering Committee stated that gender helped to determine some committee assignments once the Republicans came into the majority: "[T]hen all of a sudden Judiciary started handling some issues, like abortion, et cetera, and both political parties decided that they needed to have more women on, so now you have Mary Bono, who wasn't a lawyer, on the Judiciary, a) because she wanted to be, and b) because she was articulate—[she]got the issues—but also because they needed women there."[22]

That women began receiving more prestigious committee assignments in the wake of the Republican takeover does not necessarily mean that women were becoming more successful in achieving preferred committee assignments. Without knowledge of what the women requested, we do not know whether they were getting what they *wanted*. Republican women may still be subject to the same discrimination that we identify in earlier Congresses; however, now that Republican women have assumed a place at the table, their interests are more likely to be addressed in the committee assignment process in the future.

COMMITTEE POLITICS IN BLACK AND WHITE

Until recently, very little research had been done on the committee assignments of African American members of Congress.[23] All previous studies of African American members' committee assignments have relied on evidence of the committee assignments that these members received; none of the scholars had access to the committees that members requested and pursued. These scholars are nearly unanimous in reaching the conclusion that African Americans do as well as or better than whites in the quest for important committee assignments; however, without information regarding the committees that African American members *request*, this conclusion can not be substantiated. Indeed, our analysis shows that the committee request behavior of African American members does not always reflect the scholarly wisdom; assignment success is variable, and the committee assignments of African American members are subject to changes in the internal politics of the House. These studies, like so many others, focused on what members got rather than what they wanted, but the committee assignment process cannot be accurately characterized as pure self-selection.[24] Committee assignment data are not an adequate surrogate for members' interests, and focusing on assignment data will lead to erroneous conclusions. Using interview data, combined with our request data, we explore key questions about the committee assignment experience of members of the Congressional Black Caucus (CBC): 1) On what types of committees do African American members seek membership? 2) How have African American members fared in the committee assignment competition; in particular, how does their rate of committee assignment success compare with that of white members? and 3) How has request success varied over time? Our analysis in this section focuses only on Democratic House members; there was only one African American Republican in the House during this period.

The history of African American House member committee assignments in the modern era can be broken into three periods.[25] The early period (the period of emergence, pre-1971) was characterized by small numbers of African American members who sought membership on a limited number of committees of particular interest to African American members (particularly Education and Labor, Banking, and Judiciary) and did not seek or receive membership on the most important committees in the House.[26] The middle period (the period of empowerment, 1971–1990) coincides with the formation of the CBC and increasing African American influence in the House. During this period, African American members were increasingly placed on highly valued committees and gained status within the House. The final period (the period of expansion and retrenchment) encompasses the large influx of African Americans elected to Congress, especially after redistricting created many new minority districts for the 1992 congressional election. During this period, African Americans have not done as well in the hunt for top committee assignments as in the previous period, in part because of their lack of seniority (and the loss of Democratic control of the House).

Period of Emergence (pre-1971)

During the early period under consideration, African Americans typically requested committees of perceived importance to the national African American community. These committees, Education and Labor, Banking, and Judiciary, dealt with matters of importance to all African

Americans, and members who may have seen themselves as representatives of a race rather than of a geographic district would understandably select these committees.

Most assuredly, getting onto important committees was a struggle for African American members in the early years. The case of Shirley Chisholm is emblematic of the struggle during this early period. Shirley Chisholm was elected in 1968 to represent a Brooklyn district with a large African American majority. Chisholm requested a seat on Education and Labor (a committee that had a tradition of African American membership and was important to the African American community for its educational and antipoverty programs), but she was placed on the Agriculture Committee instead. To make matters worse, she was given slots on the Forestry and Rural Development Subcommittees. Chisholm argued against the inappropriate assignment:

> I understood that geography and seniority make it difficult for a first-term representative to get his first choice of a committee assignment. But I think it would be hard to imagine an assignment less relevant to my background or to the needs of the predominantly black and Puerto Rican people who elected me, many of whom are unemployed, hungry, and badly housed, than the one I was given. I pointed out that there were only nine black members of the House, although in terms of the percentage of the population that is black there should be more than forty (I underestimated—I should have said fifty-five). So, I said, the House leadership "has a moral duty to somewhat right the balance by putting the nine members it has in positions where they can work effectively to help the nation meet its critical problems of racism, deprivation, and urban decay." (1970, 84)

Violating the norms of first-term member behavior, Chisholm challenged her committee assignments before the Democratic Caucus. She was subsequently reassigned to Veterans' Affairs, a very low influence committee, but one that Chisholm found more suitable for her constituency.[27] During this early period, the small number of African American members did not organize to press their demands, and they were excluded from the influence committees—Appropriations, Rules, and Ways and Means. "In the history of the Congress, no black ever sat as a member of these committees. We were not in the system. . . . Essentially we had no power in Congress" (Louis Stokes, quoted in Cohodas 1985, 676).

Shortly after Shirley Chisholm challenged the Democratic Party leadership, the African American members of Congress began meeting as a group, first as the Democratic Select Committee, and in 1971, as the Congressional Black Caucus (CBC).[28] According to Marguerite Ross Barnett, the CBC had a demonstrable effect on African American request success:

> CBC ability to demand and get better committee assignments has been one of the few clear achievements of black representatives organizing as a caucus. Three reasons account for their improved assignments in the Ninety-fourth Congress: negotiations conducted with the House leadership by Charles Rangel, CBC chairman; CBC lobbying for better committee assignments through their network of colleagues in the DSG [Democratic Study Group] and in their state delegations; and the greater opportunity for committee mobility in the Ninety-Fourth Congress because of the large number (103) of representatives who lost in the 1974 elections. (1975, 46)

Early in the development of the CBC, chair Louis Stokes (OH) appointed a task force, headed by Ron Dellums (CA), to examine the role of CBC members in the House. The Dellums task force argued in its report that African American members of Congress had been elected as "legislators, not Civil Rights leaders." In an interview, Stokes explained the task force's recommendations for African American members:

> [We could] best utilize our ability as *legislators* to address problems related to black Americans in the Congress, and toward that end we should stop trying to be all things to all black people, because we had neither the resources nor the abilities to be able to continue that process. So instead it was recommended that what we try to do was to spread our influence throughout the Congress, under the committee system, in such a way that we would be effective and be able to put a black perspective on any legislation moving through those committees in the Congress, the realization being that

where you really effect legislation is in the committee process, not on the floor after a bill has been reported out of committee.[29]

At this point, the CBC established a policy of attempting to increase their policy influence by spreading their members throughout the committee system. The first objective, Stokes explained, was to get caucus members onto the power committees.

> [W]hen we looked at the committee system, we realized that the three power committees in the Congress—Appropriations, Ways and Means, and Rules—had never had a black member of Congress on [them], and so we realized that if we were to be effective, and effect change, and be able to put a black perspective on legislation, we had to break into the power in the Congress. And so the first move was made with me on Appropriations, and the second move was to put Charlie Rangel on the Ways and Means Committee and Shirley Chisholm on the Rules Committees. So once that had been accomplished, we had effectively broken into the power in the Congress.[30]

To be sure, these gains were not made without a struggle, but the CBC used its collective muscle to influence committee assignment decisions. As a second-term member, Louis Stokes, of Cleveland, sought to become the first African American member of the powerful Appropriations Committee in December 1970. Charles A. Vanik, who was then Ohio's representative on the Ways and Means Committee (which at that time made committee assignments for Democratic members), originally pledged to nominate Stokes for Appropriations. Vanik subsequently withdrew his pledge under pressure from the Cuyahoga County Democratic Executive Committee, which objected to Stokes's tactics in local Ohio politics.[31] The nine African American members of Congress cosigned a letter to Vanik, asking him to reconsider:

> [L]et us also be candidly mindful of another dimension to this issue. Louis Stokes is black; the prospects of what would be an historic appointment to the Appropriations Committee has been publicized, as a result of leaks by you, in the black press and other communication media across and outside of the country. It would be extremely difficult now to explain that the racial factor was not

involved even though we know from your record and personal philosophy that this has no bearing on the matter.

We fervently hope, therefore, that you will reconsider and nominate Louis Stokes based on his merit.[32]

Despite the pressure, Vanik refused to nominate Stokes when the Ways and Means Committee met to decide committee assignments. Under existing Democratic Caucus rules, only the designated representative on Ways and Means (Vanik) could nominate a member for a committee vacancy. However, the caucus voted to change the rules to allow a member's state delegation to overrule the decision of its representative on Ways and Means and nominate a member. Stokes was subsequently nominated and won a place on the committee, becoming the first African American to serve on the House Appropriations Committee.

In another case, Ron Dellums (D-CA) was initially placed on the Foreign Affairs and District of Columbia committees rather than on Education and Labor as he had requested. Instead of seeking a transfer to Education and Labor at the start of his second term in the 93rd Congress, Dellums requested a seat on Armed Services. He offers the following rationale for this decision in his autobiography:

> Lou Stokes had often observed that the strength of the Congressional Black Caucus resided in its diversity, and the members of the CBC decided to implement that observation by seeking placement on all of the committees. We would be able to widen our influence and share information, and in theory we would be missing no opportunity to advocate on behalf of our agenda. The CBC already had outstanding members on Education and Labor, I reasoned, and I was available to them to the degree that they would find my expertise useful. Perhaps I could make my contribution to reordering national priorities and to covering CBC's agenda in another context.
>
> I went to our next meeting and discussed my interest in a seat on the House Armed Services Committee. None of the other Caucus members expressed an interest or felt inclined to seek an assignment to that committee, so the group as a whole agreed to send a letter to the Democratic leadership in behalf of my appointment even though we understood that this was going to be a difficult, uphill battle. In fact, nobody in the CBC really believed I had a

chance of securing the appointment to the Armed Services Committee, because of my high-profile activities in opposition to the Vietnam War and in favor of reducing military spending. (Dellums and Halterman 2001, 100)

Dellums was not given a place on the Armed Services during the DSPC's initial consideration of the committee's vacancies, even though there were three vacancies, and only one other returning incumbent sought membership on Armed Services. Upon learning of the committee vote against him (and that the chair of Armed Services, conservative F. Edward Hebert of Louisiana, had conducted a campaign against Dellums's assignment to the committee, alleging that Dellums was a security risk), Dellums decided to try to overturn the decision. Accompanied by Louis Stokes (chair of the CBC) and William Clay (D-MO), Dellums confronted Speaker Carl Albert and Ways and Means chair Wilbur Mills about the decision. Stokes recounted the basic arguments of both sides:

Albert and Mills told us they could get any black member of the caucus onto the Armed Services Committee except Ron Dellums. And we told them that he was the member of the caucus that the caucus had selected, and that we select our own leaders, and that we wanted him on the committee. So they said, 'We'll see what we can do,' and they went back into the committee, and they came out ten minutes later, and they told us that he was on the Armed Services Committee.[33]

Dellums's account portrays a slightly different picture of the situation:

Clay said, "If you don't put Ron on the committee, the CBC will call a press conference and denounce the party and the Congress as racist. There's no other possible explanation for excluding this brother from service on the committee."

Stokes finished up. "Mr. Speaker, Mr. Leader, Mr. Chairman, this is a matter of principle."

Looking back and forth between us, Speaker Albert said, "I'll go back in and see if we can't get the committee to reconsider." At that moment I knew we had won. (Dellums and Halterman 2001, 103)

Dellums received the seat, becoming the first African American member of the Armed Services Committee and, ultimately, the first African American chair of the committee.[34]

The CBC was influential in the committee assignment process and the success of its members by consciously trying to distribute CBC members across all committees. "There was never any thought of trying to pack a committee," one CBC member recalled.[35] Another judged this strategy to be "extremely successful—*extremely successful.*"[36]

Period of Empowerment (1971–1990)

During the 1970s and 1980s, African American members seemed to fare much better in their committee assignments than they had in earlier decades. At roughly the same time, in 1974, the power to make Democratic committee assignments was taken away from the Ways and Means Committee and given to the DSPC.[37] The Speaker of the House was made the DSPC chair and was given a number of appointments, including one reserved for an African American member to look out for the interests of other African American members. According to former Speaker Jim Wright (D-TX) "A bunch of young Watergate babies . . . came to Congress wanting more representation. They wanted somebody from their class to have a chance to be on Steering and Policy and so forth. They wanted racial balance on it."[38]

It is clear from an internal Democratic Party briefing book that a seat on the DSPC was designated an African American seat beginning with the 94th Congress.[39] CBC representation on the Democratic Steering Committee (as it is now called) has grown steadily; as of this writing, eight African Americans are on the forty-five-member committee responsible for assigning Democratic House members to standing committees.[40] Pressure from the CBC along with active African American member participation in the committee assignment process apparently improved the assignment prospects of CBC members. This is consistent with our finding above that the inclusion of women on the committee assignment panel improves the fortunes of women seeking committee assignments (see also Frisch and Kelly 2003b).

No member exemplifies the impressive success achieved by African American members within the Democratic Caucus more than William H. Gray III (PA). Bill Gray requested seats on Banking and on Budget as a first-term member of Congress in 1979. Not only was he placed on both committees, but ballot data indicate that on the Budget Committee, Gray was the first ballot selection of DSPC members, receiving eighteen votes, more than any other member received during the seven rounds of balloting that it took to fill the committee vacancies.[41] In his second term, Gray requested a transfer to the powerful Appropriations Committee and was again successful. By 1984, Gray was running for Budget chair, which he also won. He was successful in getting Speaker Tip O'Neill to oppose any waivers to the three-term limit on consecutive Budget Committee membership, thereby eliminating potential competition from outgoing chair James Jones (D-OK) and future chair Leon Panetta (D-CA).

Gray's success was not limited to committee assignments; his string of successes carried over into Democratic leadership races. As a first-term member, he was selected to represent his class on the DSPC. He was elected chair of the Democratic Caucus at the start of the 101st Congress, and then was chosen Democratic whip on June 14, 1989, after the previous whip, Tony Coelho (D-CA), resigned from the House. Gray had an uninterrupted string of progressively more important positions during his House career, which lasted until he left the House September 11, 1991. Clearly, progress had been made from a time when Louis Stokes could accurately claim that African Americans were not in the system.

Period of Expansion and Retrenchment (1990–Present)

By 1975, there were African American members on all the influence committees, and until the mid-1980s, African American members seemed to fare as well as or better than white members. What could account for the apparent decline in CBC members' committee success compared with white members in recent years? Three explanations, not mutually exclusive, are possible. Two have already been mentioned; first, an infusion of new African American members in the 102nd and particularly 103rd Congresses reduced the seniority of the African

American contingent. Although seniority is not the only determinant of committee prestige, there is a relationship between the two variables. Second, African American first-term members tending to overreach by requesting assignments to influence committees may affect committee prestige. The third explanation is more controversial but must be considered as well: A backlash against African American members by some white members who feel that African Americans have been given "too many" plum assignments.

Former representative William Lehman makes a candid statement in his published journal:

> September 26, 1987:
> Back in Washington, at the Sheraton Hotel Tennis Club Bill Gray won in straight sets at tennis. We talked about his campaign for Chair of the Democratic Caucus, and I mentioned the *Wall Street Journal* article in Friday's paper on the surge of blacks toward leadership positions in the House, and Gray's statements regarding the increase in leverage of the Black Caucus. I told him that I thought it could adversely affect his candidacy because some of the members feel there are too many blacks in prominent House positions. (2000, 278–80)

Though Gray was ultimately elected caucus chair, garnering 146 of the 259 votes cast, at least one inside observer felt that some white members of the Democratic Caucus resented the institutional positions that African Americans had attained.[42]

One case from the 103rd Congress illustrates some of the difficulties that the CBC faced following the landmark 1992 election. CBC member Carrie Meek (D-FL) was the only one of sixty-three newly elected Democrats (seventeen of them African Americans) to win a seat on the Appropriations Committee. The campaign that Meek undertook to secure that seat has been well documented (Zuckman 1992, which is reprinted in Deering and Smith 1997). However, her situation also illustrates the difficulties that confronted the CBC in December 1992. In addition to Meek, three other African American first-term members and three returning CBC members sought a slot on Appropriations. When Louis Stokes had sought a place on Appropriations, it had been easy for the CBC to rally around a single candidate. With increased numbers, however, comes competition from within the caucus for limited resources.

Following the Republican capture of the House majority in the 1994 election, Democrats were confronted with a new reality. The new majority abolished three standing committees (Post Office, Merchant Marine, and District of Columbia) and created committee ratios favorable to a working Republican majority. These changes resulted in a dramatic loss of committee seats for House Democrats that had a disproportionate impact on African American members. The Democrats used seniority to determine which members lost committee slots, and the lack of seniority of the CBC membership (which averaged 7.67 years of service in 1995 compared with an average of 10.49 years for white members) hurt African American members. Carrie Meek lost her hard-won seat on Appropriations for the entire 104th Congress.[43]

When combined with the current minority status of the House Democrats, proper committee representation of African Americans and other groups within the Democratic Caucus presents an even stickier problem. As a senior leadership aide explained, the Democrats have essentially chosen to use a quota strategy to keep the peace in the caucus:

> So what we've done, and it's almost scientifically mathematical . . . if the Black Caucus [is about] 10 percent of the caucus, they have gotten about 10 percent of the vacancies on these committees which people consider important. The New Democrats are sort of a more moderate group, but it has sort of popped up over the last few years; they get 30 percent of the caucus and they ended up with 30 percent of the assignments. Women, Hispanics, blacks— and that's sort of the way we've approached things so that people see that amongst this very little group of goodies that we have, and we're no longer in a situation where we can create any more for them, that at least what little we have we're trying to hand out . . . in an equitable way.[44]

African American Members and Representation

There is considerable confusion about the types of committees requested by African American members of Congress. Carol M. Swain sees an assimilation trend:

African-American representatives are assimilating, just as other ethnic representatives have. One does not have to be a prophet to see the direction of the changes that are happening. Black representatives are increasingly becoming more like white liberal Democrats. They no longer automatically seek the traditional constituency committees such as Education and Labor, Public Works, and Post Office. They have taken part in a range of committees, including Rules, Ways and Means, and Appropriations. (1993, 44)

David T. Canon describes a pragmatic strategy of redistribution: "The pattern changed dramatically in the 103rd Congress. First, Black members increased their representation on nearly every committee. . . . [S]econd, the distribution of committee assignments shifted. Newer members showed their pragmatism by choosing constituency committees over some of the more traditional Black committees" (1995, 174). Both authors see a shift away from "traditional black committees," but their interpretations of that shift are vastly different. Canon maintains that after the influx of new members that accompanied the 1992 election, African American members adopted a strategy of broad placement on committees by pursuing constituency committees upon which African Americans had been underrepresented. He bases his conclusion on the actual committee assignments that African American members received in the 103rd Congress. Canon claims that "[a]lthough there is not a perfect correspondence between member preferences and actual assignments, the Democratic leadership and the Steering Committee make every effort to accommodate member requests" (1995, 186) Therefore, he interprets committees that members served on as a reflection of "committees on which Blacks elected to serve" (174). To support his assertion that members of the CBC dramatically changed direction, he points out that one-half (nineteen of thirty-eight) of the initial assignments given to first-term CBC members in the 103rd Congress were to constituency committees.

However, examination of the committee request data tells a different story. Of the sixteen members whose requests were listed in the DSPC's briefing book for the 103rd Congress, only four members (25 percent) requested assignment to a constituency committee as their first choice.[45] Three of the four sought membership on Public Works, and the fourth requested Agriculture. Of the remaining twelve new members, eight requested assignment to influence committees, and four requested the most powerful policy committee, Energy and Commerce. Seventy-Five percent of the newly elected members sought placement on an influence or a key policy committee. Of the nine incumbent CBC members who sought changes in their committee assignments at the outset of the 103rd Congress, not one sought placement on a constituency committee. In addition, several CBC incumbents who were serving on constituency committees in the 102nd Congress sought transfer to influence committees, which would have meant terminating service on other committees.

As other scholars have noted, African Americans may see themselves more as representatives of a racial group rather than of a geographic district, and therefore may avoid requesting constituency committees that provide targeted benefits to the residents of the geographic district but are of little use in improving the larger societal problems encountered by African Americans throughout the country.[46] David T. Canon, Matthew M. Schousen, and Patrick J. Sellers (1996), on the other hand, claim that African American members of Congress can be divided into two groups based on style: "traditional style" African American politicians, who practice the politics of difference and see themselves as representatives of African Americans rather than of a particular district; and "new style" African American politicians, who practice the politics of commonality and appeal to white residents as well as to African Americans. These "new style" politicians, they argue, are more likely to seek seats on constituency committees because these seats provide district-specific tangible benefits; however, of the nine first-term CBC members elected in 1992 and identified by Canon, Schousen, and Sellers as "new style" politicians, only one (11.1 percent) sought a seat on a constituency committee as his or her first choice.[47] However, contrary to expectations, three of the seven "traditional style" members sought placement on constituency committees.

The finding that African Americans typically avoid requesting constituency committees is more consistent with Swain's assertion that CBC members were seeking places on policy and influence committees. However, Swain's assertion that request behavior of African Americans mirrors that of white members lacks support. Table 9.4 summarizes the committee requests of African American and white members of Congress. Several interesting patterns are apparent. First, white members are more likely to request constituency committees than are African American members, regardless of electoral status. First-term white members are noticeably more likely to request a constituency committee than are first-term African American members (36.3 percent versus 18.6 percent, respectively). The most popular constituency committees among first-term white members are Agriculture, Armed Services, and Public Works; among African Americans, the few constituency committee requests are spread between Public Works, Armed Services, Agriculture, and Science. Incumbent white members are more than five times as likely as their African American counterparts are to request constituency committees, with Interior and Armed Services being the most favored committees.

In contrast, first-term African Americans are more likely than their white colleagues are to request policy and influence committees. More than half of first-term African Americans request policy committees, with Energy and Commerce being the favorite of these members, followed by Banking and Education and Labor. Somewhat less than half of first-term white members request policy committees (44.8 percent), though like their African American colleagues, they favor Energy. First-term African American members are much more likely than their white classmates are to request an influence committee (27.9 percent and 18.1 percent, respectively). Regardless of race, however, Appropriations is the favorite of those who choose to request an influence committee. African American and white incumbents' request behavior relative to policy and influence committees is similar, with about 20 percent of both requesting policy committees and just over half of each group requesting influence committees. Among those African American members who request influence committees, half request Appropriations, whereas white members are more likely to request Budget than Appropriations.

Taken together, these results suggest several things. African American members are more likely to gravitate toward policy and influence committees. The behavior of first-term white members is more consistent with the conventional wisdom in the literature than is the behavior of first-term African American members. It appears that first-term African American members are more likely than first-term white members are to pursue highly sought-after committees. "New style" African American

TABLE 9.4
Differences in committee preferences of African American and white Democrats

Committee type	Committee	African American		White	
		First-term member	Incumbent member	First-term member	Incumbent member
Service	District of Columbia	—	1 3.1%	1 0.2%	11 2.2%
	House Administration	—	3 9.4%	1 0.2%	8 1.6%
	Post Office	—	1 3.1%	2 0.4%	4 0.8%
	Ethics	—	—	—	—
Consitutency	Agriculture	2 4.7%	—	59 12.1%	3 0.6%
	Armed Services	2 4.7%	1 3.1%	47 9.7%	25 5.0%
	Interior	—	—	16 3.3%	25 5.0%
	Merchant Marine	—	—	—	15 3.0%
	Public Works	3 7.0%	—	43 8.8%	9 1.8%
	Science	1 2.3%	—	11 2.3%	9 1.8%
	Small Business	—	—	1 0.2%	—
	Veterans' Affairs	—	—	—	4 0.8%
Policy	Banking	6 14.0%	—	52 10.7%	2 0.4%
	Education and Labor	6 14.0%	1 3.1%	24 4.9%	5 1.0%
	Energy and Commerce	8 18.6%	3 9.4 %	96 19.7%	55 11.0%
	Foreign Affairs	1 2.3%	2 6.3%	24 4.9%	12 2.4%
	Government Operations	—	2 6.3%	3 0.6%	18 3.6%
	Judiciary	2 4.7%	—	19 3.9%	5 1.0%

TABLE 9.4 (*continued*)
Differences in committee preferences of African American and white Democrats

| Committee type | | African American | | White | |
		First-term member	Incumbent member	First-term member	Incumbent member
Policy	**Appropriations**	8	9	47	101
		18.6%	28.1 %	9.7%	20.1%
	Budget	—	5	5	113
			15.6%	1.0%	22.5%
	Rules	1	1	2	14
		2.3%	3.1%	0.4%	2.8%
	Ways and Means	3	3	34	64
		7.0%	9.4%	7.0%	12.7%
	Totals	43	32	487	502

Note: Data on member requests are drawn from committee-on-committees briefing books and committee request letters. Data for Democrats include all Congresses from the 80th through the 103rd, with the exception of the 85th. Republicans excluded due to small number of African American Republican members. Typology from Deering and Smith (1997). Percentages are column percentages. $N = 1,064$.

members do not appear to be more likely to request constituency committees. Further, there is no clearly typical African American committee, since requests tend to be spread out within committee types.

Among all requesting members, 42.7 percent of African American members receive their first committee request compared with 48.8 percent of white members, a difference that is not statistically significant (see table 9.5). The small gap between white and African American request success appears larger among first-term members: 37.2 percent of first-term African American members receive their first committee request compared with 57.5 percent of first-term white members. After the first term, however, the gap narrows, with 50 percent of African American incumbents receiving their first committee request, and 55 percent of white incumbents receiving theirs, a difference that is not statistically significant.

Several explanations for the discrepancies in request success shown in table 9.5 are possible. First, the party leadership may take into account the racial makeup of committees when making committee assignments.

TABLE 9.5
Request success of African American and white Democrats

| | All | | First-term | | Incumbent | |
	African American	White	African American	White	African American	White
Request granted	32	483	16	280	16	226
	42.7%	48.8%	37.2%	57.5%	50.0%	45.0%
Request denied	43	506	27	207	16	276
	57.3%	51.2%	62.8%	42.5%	50.0%	55.0%
N	1,064		530		534	
	Tau-b = -.04		Tau-b = -.11***		Tau-b = .02	
	(1.42)		(2.49)		(.54)	

Note: Data on member requests are drawn from committee-on-committees briefing books and committee request letters. Data for Democrats include all Congresses from the 80th through the 103rd, with the exception of the 85th. Republicans excluded due to small number of African American Republican members. Number in parentheses is the asymptotic t-value.
*p < .10 (one-tailed)
**p < .05 (one-tailed)
***p < .01 (one-tailed)

Three race-specific scenarios suggest themselves. The leadership may impose a negative quota on the number of African Americans on a committee, refusing to add African Americans as the number of African Americans on the committee increases. At least one African American member suggested that perhaps this was the case: "I did have one experience where it was clear to me that race was limiting my experience to participate on a committee, when I tried to serve on the Budget Committee and I was told by the Speaker at that time [that] there was already sufficient African American representation on the committee. . . . It was his very clear view that [additional representation] ought not to happen, and he didn't support me."[48] Another member denied that there were quotas on African American committee membership: "I don't think that's true. I don't think that's true at all. . . . No, never heard that at all."[49]

The leadership may also impose a positive quota, reserving African American seats on committees and seeking to replace departing African

American members with new African American members. Finally, it is possible that significant competition between African American members for the same committee slot or slots inflates the likelihood of African American members being denied a seat when another African American actually receives an open slot.

Several other hypotheses warrant attention. Our analysis suggests that the value of a requested committee may play an important role in the ultimate success of members. African American members often hail from electorally safe districts.[50] It has long been argued that the party leadership is more willing to devote scarce committee slots to members who are electorally secure and can be counted on to support votes on party agenda items that may be unpopular in many Democratic districts; we describe modest support for this in chapter 8.

Table 9.6 presents estimates of the influence of race on the committee assignments of members, controlling for other possible influences on success. These results suggest that African American members, specifically first-term members, are less likely than their white counterparts are to receive preferred committee assignments, other influences being equal. Indeed, African American members are ninety-five percent less likely to receive their requested committee than are their white colleagues.

Several other results in table 9.6 are worth mentioning. party leadership apparently does not impose a negative quota on African American members; it is *not* the case that the more African Americans on a committee, the less likely another African American will be assigned to the committee. It *is* the case, however, that the party leadership is likely to replace a departing African American committee member with the appointment of another African American member, if a first-term member requests the committee. Indeed, an African American vacancy increases the likelihood of a successful request more than one and a half times for a first-term member. African American members are not failing to receive seats because of increased competition among African American members; in no case is this variable significant. Finally, the more valuable the committee requested by first-term members, the less likely the member will be successful in achieving the assignment, at least among first-term members.

TABLE 9.6
Request success probabilities for African American and white Democrats

Independent variables	Successful First Committee Request[a]				
	First-term			Incumbents	
Af. American member[b]	-2.94***	.053		-.79	
	(6.72)			(.54)	
Af. Americans on req. cmte.[c]	.05	—		45	—
	(.05)			(1.18)	
Af. American vac. req. cmte.[d]	1.26**	3.53		-.06	—
	(3.29)			(.01)	
Af. American czompetition[e]	.06	—		-.23	—
	(.06)			(1.06)	
Marginality	-.02	—		-.30	—
	(.01)			(.99)	
Electoral opposition	.08	—		.14	—
	(.02)			(.24)	
Prior claim	.75 ***	2.12		—	
	(6.75)				
Cong. staff experience	1.59 ***	4.89		—	
	(7.04)				
Family ties	.46	—		—	
	(.69)				
Ideological proximity				-.44	—
				(.86)	
Request Value	-.64	.528		-.02	—
	(65.81)			(.09)	
Constant	2.56***			-.04	
	(12.73)			(.004)	
N	467			448	
Predicted (%)	67.0			55.8	
Pseudo R²	.28			.01	
-2 x LLR	533.17			611.01	

Note: Figures in parentheses are t_{wald}; signs are omitted.
*p < .10 (one-tailed)
**p < .05 (one-tailed)
***p < .01 (one-tailed)
[a] Dependent variable is 1 if member received request, 0 if member did not receive request.
[b] African Americans are coded 1; whites are coded 0.
[c] Number of African Americans on the committee requested by the individual; white members are coded as –1.
[d] Number of African American vacancies created by termination of service on the committee requested by the individual; white members are coded as –1.
[e] Number of African American competitors for the requested committee assignment; white members are coded as –1.
[f] Based on Groseclose and Stewart (1998). Range of individual values: –.31 to 5.0.
[g] Total years of service.

We expect that the request success of African American members will vary according to the political dynamics of the time. In the period of empowerment, during which the CBC was formed and the group developed a strategy to maximize the influence of its members in the House, we expect African American requesters to be more successful. During the period of expansion and retrenchment, in which there is an influx of African American members into the House and, at least on the part of some, a perception that African Americans were developing influence that outstripped their numbers in the Democratic Caucus, we expect that African Americans pursuing committees will meet with reduced success.

Table 9.7 presents the results of our analysis for the most recent periods (of empowerment and of expansion). The results suggest that, in fact, African American House members were significantly less likely to receive their requested assignment during the period of expansion than they were during the period of empowerment. During the period of empowerment, the probability of request success for African Americans relative to other members, other factors held constant, was reduced by 86 percent. During the period of expansion, the probability of success for African American members relative to other members was reduced by 93 percent. The results do not show, however, that African American members were harmed by the presence of other African American members on a requested committee, a negative quota; during the period of empowerment, the number of African American members already seated on the requested committee had no effect on request success, and during the period of expansion, the same variable indicates that African Americans were *more* likely to be granted seats on which African Americans are already serving.

• • •

Committee seats are important resources for members of Congress. Nothing underscores this point better than the simple fact that members compete so intensely for committee seats when they enter the institution and when committee slots become available. As the number of African American representatives in the House has grown over the last five decades, it is useful to examine their experiences in pursuit of committee assignments.

Table 9.7

Request success of African American and white Democrats
(by historical period)

Independent Variables	Success First Committee Request [a]			
	Period of Empowerment		Period of Expansion	
Af. American Member [b]	−1.99	.136	−2.66 ***	.070
	(2.05)		(3.69)	
# Af. Americans on Req. Cmte. [c]	.001	—	.65 ***	1.92
	(.000)		(5.37)	
Af. Amer. Comp. Req. Cmte [e]	.76 **	2.14	−.15	—
	(2.79)		(.65)	
Marginal District	−.18	—	.49 *	1.64
	(.66)		(2.56)	
Unopposed	.178	—	.20	—
	(.30)		(.27)	
Predecessor held seat	.39	—	1.59	4.90
	(1.59)		(8.59)	
First Term Member	.30	1.35	.01	—
	(2.12)		(.001)	
Value of First Req. Cmte. [f]	−.26***	.772	−.17 ***	.847
	(25.78)		(5.14)	
Constant	1.32***	.01		
	(4.15)		(.001)	
N	549		327	
Predicted (%)	60.3		69.7	
Pseudo R²	.09		.14	
−2 X LLR	716.97		389.62	

Note: Figures in parentheses are t_{wald}; signs are omitted.
* p < .10 (one-tailed)
** p < .05 (one-tailed)
*** p < .01 (one-tailed)
[a] Dependent variable is 1 if member received request, 0 if member did not receive request.
[b] African Americans are coded 1; whites are coded 0.
[c] Number of African Americans on the committee requested by the individual; white members are coded as − 1.
[d] Number of African American vacancies created by termination of service on the committee requested by the individual; white members are coded as -1.
[e] Number of African American competitors for the requested committee assignment; white members are coded as −1.

The conventional wisdom in congressional studies suggests that as African American members have become more commonplace in the institution, their behavior has come to mirror that of their white counterparts. Contrary to the arguments of Cannon (1995) and Swain (1993) in particular, African Americans' committee requests do not appear to mirror those of their white colleagues. Indeed, most African American members pursue policy and influence committees. This may be a reflection of a significant difference in conceptions of representation. African American members of Congress may consider themselves representatives of a racial group rather than of a geographic constituency, thus pursuing committee assignments that enable them to influence policies of import to a national African American constituency rather than their narrow electoral constituency. This is not to suggest that these members will be inattentive to the interests of their constituents—reelection continues to be an important part of the decision calculus of these members—but they may construe their constituents' interests much more broadly than white members do.

Differences in committee requests may also reflect the feeling among small groups within the Democratic Caucus that they deserve seats on powerful committees. One leadership staff member suggested that because women, Hispanics, and African Americans have relatively small numbers of members in the caucus that all should have important committee assignments. This view is consistent with the sentiments of one African American member quoted by James B. Johnson and Philip E. Secret: "[A] black congressperson does not have the luxury that a white congressperson has of coming to congress and just representing their congressional district. Black people all over America expect that you understand . . . that you have a responsibility to Black people all over the country who feel they have no representation in the United States Congress" (1996, 258).

African American members tend not to be as successful in achieving preferred committee assignments, at least in their first term. Part of the explanation may lie in these members' tendency to gravitate toward highly sought-after committees. However, holding this variable—and various other race-specific variables—constant, a first-term African American member appears to be at a disadvantage. More senior members, however, do not seem to be at a disadvantage.

Finally, requests and request success must be understood within the context of the African American experience in the House. We suggest three periods within which the committee assignment experience was very different. During the period of emergence, there were few African American members in the House, and they were not organized as a group. These members were forced to fight for positions on committees that were not "traditional black committees." During the period of empowerment, African American members coalesced into the CBC and asserted organized pressure on the Democratic leadership and within the Democratic Caucus to force proportionate representation on House committees. Finally, in more recent years (the period of expansion), as the number of representatives has grown, and as the Democrats became the minority party, African American members have found themselves in more traditional committee assignments. These committee assignments are not by choice, as Canon suggests, but by circumstance. During the 103rd Congress, the large influx of new members, and African American members in particular, created a logjam of requests that the leadership could not immediately accommodate. Now in the minority, the Democrats no longer have the flexibility to create new committee slots to accommodate additional demand for committees. Furthermore, there is some evidence of a possible backlash against the perceived influence of the CBC over the Democratic leadership.

GENDER, RACE, AND COMMITTEE POLITICS

The results of this first ever look into the committee requests and assignment experiences of women and African American House members suggest several generalizations. First, these members, by and large, make committee requests that are very similar to those of their white male colleagues. This does not mean that women and African American members have the same policy preferences as their colleagues; rather, it suggests that the committee system in Congress allows members with different interests to pursue their interests through committees with broad policy jurisdictions. Second, these members often have committee assignment experiences that are distinct from those of their white male colleagues. Women, especially Republican women, over the period examined here often have difficulty being assigned to preferred committees. African American members have at times experienced significant difficulties in receiving their preferred committee assignments.

More broadly, this chapter provides further illustration of a major theme of this work: Committee assignments are not governed by a neutral self-selection process; "routinized self-selection" is a poor description of the assignment process. Party matters, as illustrated by our analysis of women members in this chapter; race matters, as illustrated by our examination of African American members; other personal characteristics and politics matters, as demonstrated throughout this and the previous chapter. Although there is evidence of structural variables that shape the assignment process, consistent with our CAP framework, politics plays a large role—a much larger role than the extant literature suggests.

CHAPTER TEN

COMMITTEE ASSIGNMENT
POLITICS RECONSIDERED

We tried to get, I remember, two of our [California] freshmen members on the Banking Committee—Rick Lehman and Esteban Torres. Lehman got on, but Esteban didn't. The next day, in the Washington Post, . . . there was an article that said Buddy Roemer, who was then a Democrat, had said that "if the Democrats don't put me on Banking, the Republicans will." At a California delegation breakfast that morning, I showed that article to Phil [Burton], and he just got red, and he walked over to the Steering and Policy meeting. . . and told Gillis Long, who was chairman of the caucus, . . . "I'm going to take this to the caucus, this is outrageous, the guy gets to be on the Banking Committee," and Gillis Long goes, "Please, Phil, he's from Louisiana. Please don't do that, please, please," and Phil says, "Well, then, put Esteban Torres on the Banking Committee also." And Gillis said, "You've got a deal." And Phil just backed off. So [the leadership] increased the size of the committee because the Democrats were in control, and they added Esteban.

REPRESENTATIVE HOWARD BERMAN (D-CA)

The underlying assumption of this work is that in committee assignments, *politics matters.* Far from being the routine process often depicted in the literature, committee assignments are the result of individual behaviors in the context of a collective process that is complex and often unpredictable. Committee assignment politics is borne of individuals pursuing their individual interests; thus, our descriptive framework is grounded in discovering and understanding both members' motivations for pursuing specific committee assignments and the political forces that shape their successes and failures. However, individual choices play out in a collective context, the assignment process, in which other political actors are pursuing their own interests, which militates against routine accommodation because members of the assignment committee also seek to advance their own interests. The case studies presented throughout this work, and our empirical findings, highlight this simple but important assumption. The story that begins this chapter is one of many we encountered while researching this book that illustrates the essentially political nature of the committee assignment process in the U.S. House of Representatives.

Not only does politics matter, but *partisan politics matters* in the realm of member behavior and the committee assignment process. There are significant interparty differences in committee assignment politics, and members of the two political parties, and the party organizations themselves, are different. Party labels represent something more than symbolic differences; they represent meaningful distinctions. Interparty differences are reflected in the internal operation of the political parties. In short, our design and our expectations led us to believe that Republican members of Congress would not behave exactly the same way as Democratic members. Many Republican members have different ideas about the appropriate role of representatives and the appropriate role of government in society, ideas that shape their behavior. Further, the Republican committee on committees does not function in the same way as the Democratic committee on committees or make decisions based on the same criteria. Republican Party politics unfolds in ways that are somewhat particular to that party, as we illustrate in chapter 2.

Within the context of our assumption that politics matters, our descriptive framework suggests that members of Congress will pursue committee assignments for various reasons: constituency concerns, individual policy interests, and their desire for political influence. Members' requests compete for a scarce resource, committee seats, within an assignment process that is subject to individual members' lobbying of committee-on-committees members, attempts by party leaders to influence assignments, intraparty conflicts, and coalitions that form within the assignment committees. Successful appointment to a requested committee is the result of the individual characteristics of requesters, committee-on-committees politics, and supply-and-demand considerations. Competition among individual members, coupled with competition within the committees on committees, will produce committees that are relatively heterogeneous. Thus, heterogeneous committees will result as a function of committee assignment politics.

Politics matters in the context of the committee assignment process, and committee assignment politics has important implications for committee politics in the U.S. House of Representatives. House committees are integral to the internal functioning of the institution; they are the primary mechanism for policy making in the House. As a result, committees have drawn significant attention from political analysts. Traditional analysts have mostly viewed committees with suspicion, fearing that committees would service the narrow interests of committee members and their constituencies, who were united by common interests addressed by the committee. Many of these analysts pointed toward committee-based logrolling as the means through which these small minorities of members could produce majority support for their narrowly cast policy proposals. We contend that the politics of the committee assignment process, and the resulting composition of committees, will result in policy output that is significantly different from that predicted by many; political competition within and between committees produces a committee structure capable of performing its task of providing the chamber with legislation that, for the most part, serves the interests of the majority on the floor and of the nation.[1]

CONSTITUENCIES AND COMMITTEE REQUESTS

The CAP framework posits a central role for individual member motivations to better understand individual committee requests. Members of Congress were motivated by constituency and public policy concerns, and by the desire for influence within the institution. Individual motivations are shaped by perceived district constraints and by representatives' predispositions and attitudes about the appropriate role of a member of Congress. Motivations, personal experience, and beliefs about the assignment process combine in a complex manner to influence the committee requests of individual members. Our focus on multiple motivations acknowledges an important role for constituency-oriented motivations. The CAP framework predicts that some members will pursue committee assignments for constituency reasons, primarily on committees that can readily respond—either materially or symbolically—to a well-organized constituency interest. However, our framework also predicts that other motivations will play an important role in the request process, leading many, if not most, members to pursue committee assignments as a means of achieving goals other than reelection. Our view is in contrast to the dominant model in the literature, which posits that constituency concerns motivate members to pursue committees that will allow them to improve their chances of reelection by addressing issues of special importance to their constituents and to deliver particularized benefits to their districts.

Our content analysis of member request letters in chapter 3 supports the view that members are motivated to pursue committee assignments for various reasons and casts some doubt on the degree to which members seek committee assignments because of constituency concerns. Several committees do attract members who are concerned about addressing constituency-centered issues, though in many cases, constituency concerns coexist with substantive policy interests. For instance, many members who request the Armed Services Committee seek to address military issues in service of their constituents but also to pursue a policy interest based on prior military service or concerns about preparedness and other policy issues. The case of Bob Dornan (see chapter 5), who

TABLE 10.1

Committee assignment politics summary of findings

Study	Agriculture	Appropriations	Armed Services	Banking	Budget	Education and Labor	Energy and Commerce	Foreign Affairs	Government Operations	Interior	Judiciary	Merchant Marine	Post Office	Public Works	Rules	Science	Small Business	Veterans' Affairs	Ways and Means
Constituency motivation	+	–	+	–	–	+	?	–	–	+	–	+	+	+	–	–	?	+	–
Constituency characteristics	+	n/a	+	–/?	n/a	–/?	–/?	+	–	+	–	–	–	–	n/a	–	–	?	n/a
Self-selection	+	–	–	+	–	+	–	–	+	+	–	+	?	+	–	–	?	?	–

Notes: Committees with few requests are omitted from this summary.

Constituency motivation: Do two-thirds or more of requesting members mention constituency concerns as a reason for pursuing an assignment to this committee? Source: Table 3.4

Constituency characteristics: Do the Monte Carlo results suggest a relationship between district characteristics and committee request? Source: Table 4.4.

Self-Selection: Do two-thirds or more of members requesting this committee gain membership on the committee? Source: Table 4.8.

+   Support
–   No support
+/–   Mixed support leaning positive
–/?   Mixed findings leaning negative
?   Findings are inconclusive
n/a   Not applicable

repeatedly sought an assignment to the Armed Services Committee, is illustrative of mixed motivations. Committees that have narrow jurisdictions and allow members who have significant district constraints to be responsive to constituency concerns will attract members who are primarily motivated by constituency. Among those committees that attract these members are Agriculture, Armed Services, and Interior, as a summary of our analysis indicates (see table 10.1).

Making good public policy and achieving institutional influence rank highly as motivations for members seeking committee slots. Lynn Martin, a first-term member, immediately gravitated toward Appropriations because of her personal policy interests and past experience in Appropriations at other levels of government; her experience and our other findings are consistent with our contention that members of Congress have multiple motivations. Committees such as Banking, Budget, and Government Operations often draw members who are primarily interested in shaping public policy, and Appropriations, Rules, and Ways and Means often draw members who are motivated by a quest for institutional influence. Even a committee like Armed Services, which is often held up as an example of a constituency-oriented committee, may attract members whose primary interest is policy, not constituency. As our discussion in chapter 3 demonstrates, members like Pat Schroeder and Ron Dellums may pursue a committee such as Armed Services because of policy considerations and may exercise significant policy influence within the committee; as Lynn Martin admits, her desire to serve on Armed Services had little to do with her constituency.

Our examination of the relationship between objective district characteristics and committee requests (chapter 4) supports the expectations of the CAP framework: District considerations are only one component of the request calculus of individual members. Again, this view is somewhat different from the dominant view in the literature, which holds that district interests will directly influence committee requests because members' motivations are singularly motivated, or at least predominantly motivated, by reelection concerns. Coupling our request data with district-level census data over most of the postwar period, we find support for our contention that district characteristics will only modestly influence the committee requests of members. Our results support the constituency-request linkage for four committees: Agriculture, Armed Services, Foreign Affairs, and Interior. The positive results for Agriculture, Armed Services, and Interior are consistent with the findings from the analysis of member motivations. The linkage in these committees between constituency and committee requests makes sense; agriculture and military are two of only a handful of interests that are capable of dominating the interests of a constituency, and the committees that service these interests have sufficiently narrow jurisdictions to be able to do so well. These three committees are the ones most often cited as prototypical constituency committees for good reason. For other committees, the linkage between constituency characteristics and requests is weak to nonexistent, as our framework predicts.

The assumption that the party committees on committees mostly *accommodate* members' committee requests seems supported by high rates of request success for Agriculture, Banking, Education and Labor, Government Operations, Interior, Merchant Marine, and Public Works, but consider this support in the context of the two previous findings. Success at receiving a committee assignment is only important relative to member interests. If requesting members have similar constituency interests, self-selection may result in homogeneous committees. If, on the other hand, members are successful at achieving an assignment, but those members have heterogeneous policy preferences, then the high level of success is irrelevant. Thus, from the perspective of the self-selection hypothesis, the finding that most members who request Agriculture and Interior receive the assignments is important; it suggests that members who pursue membership on these two committees have homogeneous constituency interests, and those interests, in turn, are highly likely to achieve representation on these two committees.

THE POLITICS OF THE ASSIGNMENT PROCESS

Our framework posits a committee assignment process that, for the most part, is anything but the routine accommodation of individual committee requests, as it is often portrayed. Members who are seeking assignment to a committee have beliefs about how the assignment process works, and they develop strategies for pursuing assignments that are consistent with those beliefs. Member lobbying of the party committee on committees will figure as one element of the assignment process, as will other individual attributes, but members' success will also hinge on factors that are out of their control. The structure of the assignment process, attempts by party leaders to advance their own interests or the interests of the party policy agenda, internal party cleavages and coalitions that may form in the structure of the assignment process or in response to leadership efforts, and the representative structure of the committee on committees all can influence the success or failure of an individual member.

Members' beliefs about the factors that create success in the assignment process and the considerations likely to be most important to committee-on-committees members evidence two important patterns (see chapter 5). First, Democrats and Republicans stress different justifications in their appeals for a particular committee assignment. Democrats were more likely than Republicans to cite group endorsements; Republicans, especially first-term Republicans, were more likely to cite experience and to appeal to a merit standard as important considerations for their assignment. Second, appeals varied according to the type of committee being sought; members clearly believe that their committee on committees has different standards for each committee when making assignments. For instance, members seeking assignment to an influence committee overwhelmingly cite their party loyalty, but members seeking an assignment to a policy committee cite their experience.

Our framework suggests that the committee assignment process will be subject to intense internal political competition as multiple actors seek to advance their interests. Party leaders in particular will compete to advance their personal and party policy agendas by attempting to control the assignment process. Internal party cleavages may add another layer of conflict within the assignment process; the structure of the assignment process may make these cleavages all the more apparent (see chapter 6 and 7). Party leaders who seek to control the committee assignment process have faced difficulties. Party heterogeneity may be one part of the puzzle: The more heterogeneous the party, the less control a leader can exert over the process (Rohde 1991). But even during periods of relative homogeneity, leaders have had great difficulty imposing themselves on the process (see, for example, the discussion in chapter 6 of Jim Wright and Newt Gingrich). A major internal party cleavage in the Republican assignment process was the conflict between the large states and the small states over the structure of the assignment process (see chapter 7 and also chapter 2), which reached its apex between the 97th and 101st Congresses. These state groups increasingly voted against each another in awarding highly sought-after committee assignments. More than one Republican was probably harmed, through no fault of their own, by this intraparty conflict.

The routinized self-selection view of the assignment process suggests that personal characteristics are ignored in favor of more objective assignment criteria within the context of supply constraints. Our framework, by contrast, posits significant roles in committee assignment for personal characteristics and partisan differences and suggests interparty differences in these roles. These characteristics *are* important in the assignment process, and their import varies by party (see chapter 8, especially table 8.12). For instance, electoral marginality was an important consideration in the RCC, but lack of opposition in the prior election carried more weight in the DSPC. Although supply-side constraints are important, so are political factors, both of which are consistent with the CAP framework yet are ignored by the routinized self-selection perspective.

Gender and race are important personal characteristics within the assignment process. The representative structure of the committee assignment process can have significant implications for the committee requests of women and African Americans in the House (see chapter 9). Because the DSPC generally included at least one woman in the committee assignment process (at least, one was guaranteed after the reforms of the 1970s), Democratic women in the period we studied were more likely to receive a preferred committee assignment than were Republican women, who were disadvantaged because women were not represented in the Republican process. Our findings show that regardless of party, women were less likely than men to receive their preferred committee assignment in their first term. Following the first term, Democratic women were as successful as men at transferring to a preferred committee, but Republican women continued to languish in less desired and less desirable committees.

The committee assignment experience of African American members is even more complex. Committee assignment success among African American members has varied over the course of three eras: emergence, empowerment, and expansion and retrenchment. During the first period, African American members were few and lacked organization, resulting in assignments that were less prestigious, on committees that dealt with "black issues." During the era of empowerment, African American members formed the Congressional Black Caucus and successfully pressured the DSPC to place CBC members on powerful and prestigious committees. Finally, during the period of expansion and retrenchment, a large influx of African American members collided with supply constraints, and with a possible backlash among other members, and many African Americans had to settle for less prestigious committee assignments.

COMMITTEE ASSIGNMENT POLITICS
FROM A THEORETICAL PERSPECTIVE

In some respects, our results appear to support the informational theory advanced by Keith Krehbiel (1990, 1991), who argues that committees will be heterogeneous with respect to policy preferences. Unlike Krehbiel, we argue that some committees will be homogeneous. We are confident that at least the Agriculture and Armed Services committees demonstrate some of the hallmarks of homogeneity predicted by distributive theory. Consistent with Krehbiel, however, we argue that *most* committees will be heterogeneous, a prediction that is supported by our analysis, but that heterogeneous committee composition results from committee assignment politics rather than from the majoritarian principle and exogeneity of preferences. At the most fundamental level, we differ from Krehbiel because our framework focuses on politics, an inductive result of the complex interplay of multiple actors pursuing multiple goals, and Krehbiel focuses on deducing conclusions about committees through simple rational assumptions. A weakness of his model is his agnosticism on the issue of individual motivations (beyond assuming individuals are rational); in much the same way, the fragility of distributive theory can be related to its reliance on a theoretical world in which members of Congress are solely motivated by constituency concerns and reelection.

Supporters of party-cartel theory will also find some support in our results. The strengths of party-cartel theory are the recognition of multiple motivations and the emphasis on the importance of jurisdiction in determining which committees will be constituency oriented, policy oriented, and influence oriented. A number of the committees that the theory suggests will have a constituency focus, for the most part, behave in that fashion. The theory also predicts that some committees will be more policy oriented, and our results seem to support the broad contention. However, party-cartel theory posits an important, perhaps dominant, role for party leaders in the assignment of members, for influence committees in particular. Our evidence for the influence of party leaders in the assignment process is mixed at best. The party leadership is cross-pressured in the assignment process, especially with regard to the control committees. At least three competing forces limit the ability and willingness of party leaders to dominate the assignment of members to the control committees. First, party leaders seek to promote policies that they believe will help them maintain and expand the number of seats in the House; by putting partisan loyalists into seats on the control committees, the majority party could virtually assure success. Leaders must also be cognizant, however, of their need to build majority support on the floor, and majorities begin with one's own partisans. Therefore, party leaders must be responsive to the needs of all party members by being broadly inclusive. Second, under most circumstances, the party leadership does not control all votes in the committee on committees; the leadership can, and does, lose in the committee. Committee-on-committees members forge alliances to promote their interests over those of the party leadership. Third, party leaders seek to promote the interests of their state, and that may mean compromising party loyalty when necessary to achieve that personal goal. Under specific conditions, which may include relative homogeneity within the party (Rohde 1991), party leaders may be able to exercise additional influence, though their influence will likely be limited by these other factors.

Attempts to understand committee requests and assignments have generally fallen into one of two categories: those that stress theoretical parsimony and predictive power, and those that forgo parsimony and prediction in favor of descriptive and explanatory power. This study falls into the second category. In opting for this approach, we hope to push formal theorists toward models that are more descriptively, and therefore theoretically, defensible. For instance, these theories cannot assume away political parties; the parties exist, and they make a difference in the behavior of legislators. More than pushing the more theoretically minded among us to construct better models, we hope to stimulate additional consideration of congressional committees in congressional studies, not the least of which would be closer attention to how committee assignment politics influences the internal politics of specific House committees and the implications for the House as a policy-making unit.

Measuring Voting Power

One of the characteristic features of the RCC is the reliance on weighted voting in the committee assignment process. In a weighted-voting scheme, actors have unequal numbers of votes in an effort to reflect their relative power within the institution. Although weighted-voting schemes are common in international organizations (Strand 1999), they are far less common in domestic American politics. Throughout our political culture, there is broad consensus regarding the value of functional equality in voting, that is, for the value of one person–one vote. The most visible example of weighted voting in American politics is the Electoral College, in which votes are distributed to states according to the number of congressional seats apportioned to each state.

In the presence of a one-person–one-vote system, actors have an equal probability of affecting the outcome of an election, and their voting power is equal. Voting power in a one-person–one-vote system is easily calculated as one divided by the number of voters in the electorate ($\frac{1}{n}$). Calculating voting power in a system using weighted voting is slightly more complex, because voters' abilities "to influence outcomes do not derive straightforwardly from their percentage share of the total votes" (Strand 1999, 269–70).

Several measures of voting power are available to analysts.[1] One of the most widely used measures is the Banzhaf Power Index (BPI) (Banzhaf 1965). BPI measures the proportion of coalitions (c) in which the actor (p) is a critical member; that is, in the absence of p, the coalition does not prevail.

$$BI_i = \sum_{sev} c(p)$$

BPI_i is a whole number. Calculating a relative measure of voting power for each actor requires dividing BPI for each actor (w) by the voting power of all other voters in the electorate. Thus, Total Banzhaf Power (TBP) for each actor is expressed as

$$TBP_{wi} = BI_{wi} \bigg/ \sum_{k=1}^{n} BI_{w}$$

TBP_{wi} has a value between zero and one, and the sum of all values of TBP_{wi} is one.

The Johnston Power Index (JPI) modifies the Banzhaf Power Index by taking into account the *degree* to which an actor's vote is critical to the success of a given coalition (Johnston 1978). JPI assigns more importance to those players whose participation in a coalition is "uniquely critical"; that is, if the defection of a single actor from a coalition would lead to a coalition failure, that actor is considered more important to the coalition. If two players are critical to the success of a given coalition, each receives half the weight, and so forth. Total Johnston Power (TJP) is calculated as

$$TJP_i = \sum_{sev(i)} \frac{1}{c(p)}$$

TJP_i is a whole number. Calculating a relative measure of voting power for each actor requires dividing TJP_i for each actor (w) by the voting power of all other voters in the electorate. Thus, TJP for each actor is expressed as:

$$J_{wi} = TJP_{wi} \bigg/ \sum_{k=1}^{n=1} TJP_{w}$$

J_{wi} has a value between zero and one, and the sum of all values of J_{wi} is one.

Analysis of weighted-voting schemes often produces nonintuitive results. Assume an electorate of size three: Using a simple majority rule and a one-person–one-vote voting scheme, the voting power of each actor would be ⅓ or .33; each actor in this scenario has equal voting power. Now assume an electorate of size three in which we seek to increase the power of some actors by manipulating voting weights. Actor one is assigned 99 votes, actor two, 98 votes, and actor three, 2 votes. In this case, there are a total of 199 votes, and a majority is 100. These weights seem patently unfair to actor three; actors one and two control the bulk of the votes, and actor three will never have any influence on the outcome of votes under these circumstances. Furthermore, the simple arithmetic calculation of voting power ($\frac{1}{n}$) indicates that actor three has a voting power of .010 (see table A1.1). However, the calculation of BPI and JPI indicate a counterintuitive finding: Despite the differences between the first two actors and actor three in the number of votes they control, all three have exactly the same values of BPI (.333) and JPI (.333). What is the cause of this paradoxical finding? All three actors require one other actor to constitute a majority, providing the smallest actor with unusual leverage despite a lack of votes.

To counteract actor three's unusual amount of power with two votes, intuition suggests that we cut the number of votes from two to one to neutralize the influence of actor three. In this case, there are a total of 198 votes, and a majority is 100. Again, the simple arithmetic calculation of voting power ($\frac{1}{n}$) indicates that actor three has near-zero voting power (.005). However, the calculation of BPI and JPI indicate another counterintuitive finding: Although actor three's voting power is diminished, so is the voting power of actor two, despite a slight increase in the proportion of the vote; and actor one's voting power almost doubles, despite a slight increase in the proportion of the vote.

What is the cause of *this* paradoxical finding? All three actors require one other actor to constitute a majority, providing the smallest actor with unusual leverage, despite a lack of votes. Quite simply, *either* actor two or actor three provides actor one with the votes necessary to reach a majority, regardless of the 97-vote advantage that actor two has over actor three. Further, the difference between values of JPI for each actor indicates the dominant role of actor one as the only voter capable of

TABLE A1.1
Hypothetical voting schemes

Actor	One person one vote (votes)	Voting power Indices	Weighted voting (votes)	Voting power indices	Weighted voting (votes)	Voting power indices
1	1	1/n = .333 BPI = .333 JPI = .333	99	1/n = .497 BPI = .333 JPI = .333	99	1/n = .500 BPI = .600 JPI = .667
2	1	1/n = .333 BPI = .333 JPI = .333	99	1/n = .492 BPI = .333 JPI = .333	98	1/n = .495 BPI = .200 JPI = .167
3	1	1/n = .333 BPI = .333 JPI = .333	2	1/n = .010 BPI = .333 JPI = .333	1	1/n = .005 BPI = .200 JPI = .167

Note: BPI = Banzhaf Power Index JPI = Johnston Power Index

providing the basis for a majority. In short, seemingly meaningless changes in voting weights can produce significant changes in the structure of voting power.

Using BPI or JPI requires a normative judgment regarding the appropriateness of the measure; both provide measures of voting power that help us to understand the underlying voting structure in a weighted-voting scheme. BPI is the more widely used and understood of the two measures. On the other hand, the strength of JPI is that it weights the criticalness of actors within a coalition, thus allowing us to measure and observe some of the attributes of "negative power," that is, the ability of an actor to block the formation of certain coalitions. In this book, we report both indices. Although our findings do not change substantively according to the measure we use, this practice provides some measure of confidence that our findings are not an artifact of the measure employed.

CONTENT ANALYSIS OF
COMMITTEE REQUEST LETTERS

The data used in chapters 3 and 5 are derived from the letters submitted by members requesting committee assignments to the DSPC and the Executive Committee of the RCC. In these letters, House members seeking committee assignments express their preferences, often stating their motivations for seeking a committee assignment and arguing in support of their assignment to a particular committee, which enables us to analyze how requesting members understand the assignment process. The committee request letters submitted by members of Congress are a potentially rich data source. To tap into the potential of the letters, we employed content analysis, the systematic examination of texts or transcripts to translate textual information into "data" that enable qualitative and quantitative analysis of these sources. This approach provides the potential for a marriage between qualitative and quantitative methodologies: "The best content analytical studies utilize both qualitative and quantitative operations on texts. Thus, content analysis methodology combines what are usually thought to be antithetical modes of analysis" (Weber 1985, 10). Creating a content analysis instrument is aimed at ensuring that the coding of the textual data is consistent from letter to letter. The value of presenting this instrument is that it lays bare for scholarly scrutiny the coding rules that were used, and it allows for replication and extension of this research using the same coding scheme.

Bullock (1976), Fenno (1973), Gertzog (1976), Smith and Deering (1984), and Deering and Smith (1997) rely on interviews with members of Congress or their staff to understand the motivations of members. A number of concerns lead us to question this approach. First, research based on interviews relies heavily on *staff* to explain the motivations of each member's pursuit of a given committee assignment. Less than half of Bullock's (1976) interviews (twenty-three of fifty-two) and just over half of Smith and Deering's (1984) interviews (thirty-three of sixty-three) were conducted with members of Congress. It is seems unlikely that all staff members, or even most of the staff, who were interviewed would have access to their member's complete committee preferences and the rationale for those preferences. As Heinz Eulau argues: "It is difficult to accept that one person can serve as a surrogate or agent for another when it comes to a psychological variable like 'motivation'" (1985, 234).

Second, reliance on recall and retrospective judgments contaminates interview data. Members and their staff might provide incomplete or inaccurate recall of which committees the member requested. Another confounding problem with the use of interview data is the possibility that a member or their staff members might rationalize committee assignments that were not requested initially, that is, they might attempt to explain why the member's committee assignments are good assignments before they will admit that the member did not get a requested assignment. In at least one case during our interviews with members of Congress, a member denied seeking to transfer off a committee on which he or she was sitting, but we possessed written requests for transfers to two other, more prestigious, committees. At the beginning of the 102nd Congress, *Congressional Quarterly* canvassed first-term members about their requested committee assignments. When we compared their reported requests with the committee on committees' briefing book, which contains their actual requests, we found that only nine of the fifteen members (60 percent) who responded reported their *actual* request to the reporter; it is hard to believe that the "veil of anonymity" offered by an academic would result in much different results.

We systematically examined the letters submitted by House members to their party committees requesting committee assignments. The letters often reveal the motivations for a member requesting a particular committee, that is, why a member is pursuing membership on a requested committee. Using committee request letters to measure motivations is not without its critics. Deering and Smith argue that committee request letters are unreliable because they represent a member's "attempt to sell himself or herself to party leaders as a candidate for a particular committee assignment, instead of reflecting his or her genuine personal motivation for interest in a committee" (1997, 114), though they offer no support for this assertion. We turned to the letters as a data source for several compelling reasons. First, the letters are a contemporary record of the members' expressed motivations, without the problem of inaccurate recall that is often present in interviews. Further, members are likely to compose the letters themselves, and thus the letters are likely to represent their own thinking, not the thinking of a staff member (and recall that past research depends heavily on interviewing staff).

Second, given the extent of our data collection effort, we were able to increase significantly the number of cases for consideration. Our data are not limited to those members willing to grant an interview; we have access to data on all members who requested a committee or committee transfer. Interview data limit analysis to a single Congress or a few Congresses. Our extensive data collection enables analysis over an extended period. We coded letters for the 92nd, 93rd, 97th, 98th, 100th, and 101st Congresses for both Democrats and Republicans. These Congresses represent a reasonable sample of the period that our entire collection of letters covers, enabling us to explore changes over time, intraparty changes caused by changes in the assignment process, changes in the party leadership, and interparty comparisons. Further, these Congresses include several used by Bullock and by Deering and Smith, providing for a comparison of findings among studies. As the results in chapter 3 suggest, using the letters produces results that are similar to those of interview-based studies and presents an opportunity to expand vastly the number of cases and the historical time frame available for analysis.

TABLE A2.1
Content analysis coding scheme

Motivations		Justifications	
Code	Mention	Code	Mention

Motivations

Electoral
___10 Electoral
___11 District interests
___12 Constituency interests

Policy
___20 Experience
___21 Personal interest in subject of committee
___22 Policy interest in subject of committee
___23 Expertise in subject of committee
___24 Need for policy change
___25 Ideas for policy change

Influence
___30 Influence
___31 Desire to be spokesperson for the party/agenda
___32 Desire to be spokesperson against opposition party
___33 Desire to promote party's positions in House
___34 Desire to counter opposition positions in House
___35 Desire for more responsibility
___36 Need for party-oriented policy change

Justifications

___10 Endorsement
___11 Reported by member (colleague)
___12 Reported by member (e.g., state caucus)
___13 Reported by member (interest group)
___14 Reported by member (other influential)

___20 Geographic
___21 District replacement on committee
___22 State replacement on committee
___23 Regional replacement on committee
___24 State deserving of representation on committee
___25 Region deserving of representation on committee

___30 Electoral
___33 Future electoral challenges (threats)
___34 Electoral safety

___40 Experience
___41 Personal background (private sector)
___42 Personal background (state legislative service)
___43 Personal background (local government service)
___44 Special training or education
___45 Congressional experience
___46 Personal background (other)
___47 Other governmental service (e.g., executive branch)
___48 Military service

___50 Party
___51 Prior service to party (general)
___52 Prior service to party (spokesperson)
___53 Prior service to party (fundraising/campaigning)
___54 Prior service to party (leadership)
___55 Party loyalty (general)

TABLE A2.1 (*continued*)
Content analysis coding scheme

Motivations		Justifications	
Code	Mention	Code	Mention
Influence			
		___56	Party loyalty (party voting record)
		___57	Service to party on other committee(s)
		___60	Interest representation
		___61	Gender
		___62	Race
		___63	Ideology (conservative/liberal wing of party)
		___70	White House
		___71	Promote president's agenda
		___72	Oppose president's agenda
		___80	Other
		___81	Previously sought committee
		___82	No dominant interest in district
___-9	Missing/none mentioned	___-9	Missing/none mentioned

Using content analysis, we coded the members' stated motivations and, in turn, examined whether there is evidence to support the multiple-motivations hypothesis advanced by Fenno (1973), and whether members' motivations are systematically related to the committees that they request. Table A2.1 illustrates the categories we used in the content analysis. We sought to measure two dimensions in the letters. First, we used the letters sent by a member to determine the motivation of the member for pursuing assignment to the committee. In coding motivation, we built on the multiple-motivations approach suggested by Fenno (1973), that is, that members of Congress are motivated to seek committee assignments by constituency concerns, their interest in making public policy, and their quest for influence within the institution. The codes for motivation are restricted to those reasons why a member was seeking membership on the committee. In coding motivation, we sought to determine whether the letter contained an equivalent answer to the question used in interviews of members: "Why did you seek assignment to the _____ committee?"

The second dimension we sought to identify was the member's argument (or justification) for why the member believed he or she should be assigned to the committee being requested. This is distinct from motivation in that the justification is an attempt to sell the party committee on making the desired appointment. As Table A2.1 illustrates, the range of potential justifications for a committee assignment is broad. In the case of both coding exercises, we coded only for the first requested committee.

One potential criticism that arises directly out of the critique of request letters is that it is impossible to make an analytical and quantitative distinction between motivations and justifications in these letters. If the letters are only an attempt to sell the member to the committee on committees and party leaders, then our analytical distinction is meaningless, and the two measures will simply reflect the single dimension of justification. This criticism can be addressed by looking at the correlation between the two measures, which is low: The correlation between the first stated motivation and the first stated justification is .26, and the correlation between the second stated motivation and the second stated justification is .16. Though the correlations are significant ($p < .01$), the correlations are not in the .70+ range that we would expect to observe if the measures were duplicative.

NOTES

CHAPTER 1

1. Although this account of Waxman's career rests heavily on a telephone interview conducted by the authors (June 2003), other published accounts include Jacobs (1995) and Kluger (1996).

2. Waxman to Albert, December 5, 1974, box 219, folder 11, Committee Assignments, 94th Congress, Legislative Files, Carl Albert Papers, Carl Albert Center Congressional Archives, University of Oklahoma.

3. Waxman attributes his success in obtaining the coveted committee assignment in his first term to the influence of Phillip Burton (D-CA). Waxman claims that when he made his request, he did not realize how unusual it would be for a first-term member to gain a seat on Energy and Commerce.

4. Listing from the biography section of representative Henry Waxman's website: http://www.henrywaxman.house.gov/. Accessed March 2005.

5. Rhodes to Thomas, August 15, 1978, box 76, folder 9, MSS-3, John J. Rhodes Minority Leader Papers, 1968–1980, Arizona Collection, Arizona State University Libraries.

6. Wampler to Thomas, August 16, 1978, MSS-3, Rhodes Papers.

7. "Congressman Bill Thomas Reports from Washington." Undated postal patron newsletter, page 1, obtained from Representative Thomas's office.

8. Robert H. Michel, interview by the authors, August 2000, Washington, D.C. See also Amy Keller (1997, B-22), who quotes Michel as stating: "That's the lousiest whole job in the Congress, serving on the darned Ethics Committee. . . . It's a miserable job to perform on Ethics. You get no credit for it. You have to get

some reward." First-term Republican James Sensenbrenner (R-WI) tried (unsuccessfully) to use the leverage of a seat on Ethics to gain membership on the Rules Committee: "Recognizing that the Committee on Committees has a difficult time recruiting 'volunteers' to sit on the Ethics Committee, I would be willing to remain there should I receive your support for a seat on the Rules Committee, thus necessitating the recruitment of one less 'volunteer' for Ethics Committee service in the next Congress." Sensenbrenner to Michel, December 3, 1980, 97th Congress, Leadership Series, Robert H. Michel Papers, Dirksen Congressional Center, Pekin, Illinois.

9. Thomas to Michel, February 10, 1982, 98th Congress, Leadership Series, Michel Papers.

10. "Congressman Bill Thomas, Spring Report from Washington, 1983." Postal patron newsletter, page 3, obtained from Representative Thomas's office.

11. Listing from the issues (trade) section of representative Bill Thomas's website: http://billthomas.house.gov/. Accessed April 2005.

12. Eulau (1984) criticizes Fenno for equating goals and motivations. Goals are strategic; they refer to the ends that politicians aspire to attain. Motivations are predispositions that shape the way politicians pursue their goals. See chapter 3 for additional discussion of the distinction between goals and motivations. Fenno's typology can best be understood as one of multiple motivations.

13. In addition to their legislative function, congressional committees are of interest for other reasons. They are the primary institutional means through which the congressional parties seek to shape policy outcomes consistent with their partisan agendas (Cox and McCubbins 1993b). Committee assignments are also important to individual members of the House. These assignments are the primary means by which institutional influence is distributed to individual members and the assignments influence members' ability to pursue their multiple goals of achieving reelection, making good public policy, and wielding influence within the House (Fenno 1973; Mayhew 1974).

14. James Madison, in *Federalist* #10, defined a faction as "a number of citizens, whether amounting to a majority or a minority of the whole, who are united and actuated by some common impulse of passion, or of interest, adverse to the rights of other citizens, or to the permanent and aggregate interests of the community."

15. Shepsle did not portray the committee assignment process as entirely the result of self-selection or suggest that only constituency-related reelection motivations lead to committee assignment requests; from a public policy perspective, however, the major contribution of Shepsle's 1978 book, as well as several pieces Shepsle later co-wrote with Barry R. Weingast, is the claim that most members select themselves for committees for constituency reasons and then use their positions to further local geographic interests at the expense of the national interest. The following paragraph from Shepsle and Weingast (1985)

summarizes this argument: "There is a second important consequence of the electoral connection. Committees and subcommittees are instrumental to legislators grappling with the pressures of geography. When a legislator arrives in Congress he finds a complex division-of-labor system consisting of over 20 standing committees and nearly 150 subcommittees. Each of these units has a well-defined policy jurisdiction in which it occupies a commanding position in originating new legislation and monitoring and overseeing existing statutes implemented by executive-branch agencies. If a legislator expects to have some impact on new and existing policies that are especially important to his constituencies, he must seek an appropriate niche in the division of labor. And the evidence on committee assignments is quite conclusive: he does! Most legislators gravitate to the committees and subcommittees whose jurisdictions are most relevant to their geographic constituencies" (119). The quotation is followed by a citation to Shepsle's *Giant Jigsaw Puzzle* (1978). See also Shepsle (1983a, 1983b, 1984) and Shepsle and Weingast (1984, 1985).

16. Both parties have used various terms for the committees responsible for making committee assignments, including "steering committee" and "committee on committees." For consistency and clarity in this book, we have chosen to use "committee on committees" as a general term for this decision-making body throughout the period under study.

17. The interplay between "district activity" and "Washington work" is the focus of much of Richard Fenno's outstanding work on congressional politics, from *Home Style* (1977) to *Congress at the Grassroots* (2000) and *Going Home* (2003). In these and other works, Fenno has wisely counseled students of Congress to consider the interplay between constituency and congressional behavior. In-depth analysis of each member's district context is impossible in a work such as this; however, from a heuristic perspective, we mean to do more than simply tip our hats to Fenno's advice: We believe that constituency is important in various ways that influence committee request calculations. In our interviews with members, we sought to understand their district context and understand this complex interplay. Subsequent research should explore in greater depth the relationship between the two in much greater depth than we can accomplish here.

18. Official committee names have been altered over time. We use the shortened name with most common usage hereafter; note, however, the following official names for certain committees: Banking, and Housing and Banking, Finance, and Urban Affairs (Banking); Interstate and Foreign Commerce (Energy and Commerce); and International Relations (Foreign Affairs).

CHAPTER 2

1. For convenience, we will use RCC to represent the decision-making body used by the Republicans to assign members to standing committees. At various

times, the Republicans have used the terms subcommittee, executive committee, and steering committee to refer to the key decision-making body.

2. Until the revolt against Speaker Joseph G. Cannon in 1910, the power to make committee assignments had rested with the Speaker. From 1911 until 1917, the Republicans relied on their floor leader (James R. Mann) to assign members to standing committees. In 1917, a seventeen-member Republican committee on committees was first established as criticism of Mann grew. On the early evolution of the Republicans' committee assignment process, see Brown (1922/1974), Chiu 1928, Hasbrouk (1927), Margulies (1996), and various issues of the *New York Times* (especially February 28, 1919).

3. See chapter 7 for a discussion of the role of committee assignments in the Martin-Halleck contest.

4. Masters (1961) should be viewed as a snapshot of the process during the 86th Congress. The process was dynamic, changing frequently as new actors were added to the decision-making body; due to the lack of study of the Republicans' committee assignment process, however, Masters is still frequently cited to describe the structure of the RCC.

5. Our regional classifications in the text and figures are based on those of the Interuniversity Consortium for Political and Social Research (ICPSR). Northeast: Connecticut, Maine, Massachusetts, New Hampshire, Rhode Island, Vermont, Delaware, New Jersey, New York, and Pennsylvania. Midwest: Illinois, Indiana, Michigan, Ohio, Wisconsin, Iowa, Kansas, Minnesota, Missouri, Nebraska, North Dakota, and South Dakota. South and border: Virginia, Alabama, Arkansas, Florida, Georgia, Louisiana, Mississippi, North Carolina, South Carolina, Texas, Kentucky, Maryland, Oklahoma, Tennessee, and West Virginia. West: California, Oregon, Washington, Alaska, Hawaii, Arizona, Colorado, Idaho, Montana, Nevada, New Mexico, Vermont, and Wyoming.

6. Ford to John D. Taylor, March 27, 1970, subgroup I-7, Republican Committee on Committees (hereafter cited as RCC File), Legislative Assistant (Josephine Wilson) File, 1965–1973, Gerald R. Ford Congressional Papers, 1949–1973, Gerald R. Ford Library, Ann Arbor, Michigan.

7. Resolution included in Executive Committee Notebook I, 92nd Congress, subgroup I-9, RCC File, Ford Papers.

8. Mallary to Ford, January 23, 1973, subgroup I-9, RCC File, Ford Papers.

9. Stangeland et al. to Republican colleague, February 26, 1979, box 80, folder 7, MSS-3, Rhodes Papers. The letter is cosigned by Trent Lott, Jim Johnson, Bill Frenzel, Tom Kindness, Joel Pritchard, Manuel Lujan, Gene Synder, and John Myers.

10. One former member from a small New England state told us that the southern members of his small-state grouping formed an alliance and selected a group representative from the south. In Executive Committee voting, that

member then favored southern members, even at the expense of members from his own small-state grouping.

> The four southern states took control of the group, elected the person to the committee on committees, and he appointed people from the southern states. That's what happened the first time around to me. There was a guy from Alabama that was the representative of our group, and I remember going to his office—I was so naïve—I remember going to his office: "I want to be on Ways and Means." "Oh yeah, sure, sure." And there was a deal struck with the southern states and [my state], which was a two-member state at the time. We just got hammered because my group representative could have cared less, because he was representing the southern bloc. (Anonymous congressional member, interview by the authors, June 2002, Washington D.C.)

11. The claim continued, "Even though Republicans constituted 44.14% of the House and Democrats 55.86%, Republicans were given only 40% of the seats on the Budget Committee and Appropriations Committee, only 34.29% of the Ways and Means Committee sears and only 31.25% of the Rules Committee seats." See *Guy Vander Jagt et al., Appellants v. Thomas P. O'Neill, Jr., et al.,* 226 U.S. App. D.C. 14, 699 F.2d 1166 (D.C. Cir. 1982). See also 524 F.Supp. 519 (1981) and 464 S. Ct. 91 (1983).

12. In internal staff notes taken at a leadership meeting where a discussion of altering the committee assignment process was held, Tom DeLay (R-TX) is quoted as referring to Texas as a middle state, neither large nor small. Box RJL 1-1, folder 19, Committee on Committees Files, 1986–1988, RG 5, Robert Lagomarsino Collection, California State University, Channel Islands.

13. Lott to Michel, January 9, 1987, 100th Congress, Leadership Series, Michel Papers.

14. Bob Stump to Michel, January 29, 1987, 100th Congress, Leadership Series, Michel Papers.

15. Lott to Michel, January 9, 1987, 100th Congress, Leadership Series, Michel Papers.

16. See chapter 7 for an analysis of Michel's votes as minority leader in the 101st Congress. Michel certainly did not dominate the voting.

17. Michel, interview by the authors, August 2000, Washington, D.C.

18. Ibid.

19. Committee assignments for the 101st Congress were made before the election of Gingrich as whip. Dick Cheney (R-WY) was still whip. In spite of the close relationship between Cheney and Michel, the two leaders frequently voted differently in RCC elections. (See Chapter 7.)

20. See, for example, Shepsle (1978), Sinclair (1995), and Maltzman (1999).

21. See Sheppard (1985) and Shepsle (1978). The caucus also voted to place the assignment of Democratic members of the Rules Committee in the hands of

the Speaker (subject to caucus confirmation). It is clear from the transcripts of the Democratic Caucus meeting held on December 3, 1974, that this change, which was proposed by Richard Bolling (D-MO), was not supported by Speaker Albert. (Democratic Caucus meeting transcript, December 3, 1974, box 219, folder 46, Designation of a Committee on Committees, Legislative Files, Albert Papers.) Albert told the Democratic Caucus: "I have had such wonderful support from the Committee on Rules that I don't think I can improve it, as long as I am Speaker, by supporting this matter, and I have had tremendous support from this gentleman (Mr. Madden). I want my friend Dick Bolling to make clear that this amendment does not come from the Speaker" (204). Majority leader Tip O'Neill, however, supported the change: "I believe the Committee on Rules should be the tool and the power of the Speaker of the House. I honestly believe that the Committee on Rules should each year be challenged" (222).

22. This description is premised on the makeup of the DSPC in the 94th Congress.

23. This discussion is pursued for illustrative purposes only. There are many potential problems associated with making assumptions about these kinds of voting blocs. For instance, the Democratic Speaker or leader may appoint members to represent interests within the caucus (e.g., women, first-term members) who will not necessarily vote with the leadership on committee assignments.

24. Although the Democrats' committee on committees had different specific names at various times, for consistency and clarity, we are using DSPC (Democratic Steering and Policy Committee) throughout this book.

25. See chapter 7 for a discussion of the emergence of this process.

26. Anonymous congressional member, telephone interview by authors, June 2003. (All anonymous interviews were confidential; names withheld by mutual agreement.) This member stated that Gephardt's successor as Democratic leader, Nancy Pelosi, has continued the voting system used by Gephardt.

CHAPTER 3

1. Anonymous congressional member, telephone interview by the authors, June 2002.

2. Following Deering and Smith (1997), we use the term "constituency" to refer to committees that are selected for their relationship to a key interest of the members of the constituency, "policy" to refer to committees that provide the member with opportunities to influence specific areas of public policy, and "influence" to refer to committees that are especially powerful in the House.

3. Anonymous staff member, interview by the authors, September 2000, Washington, D.C.

4. Anonymous staff member, interview by the authors, June 2002, Washington, D.C.

5. Durbin to James Wright, November 12, 1982, unprocessed file, Speaker Jim Wright Collection, Special Collections, Texas Christian University Library.

6. Franklin to Michel, November 24, 1982, member preference sheet, 98th Congress, Michel Papers.

7. Smith to Ford, January 27, 1971, subgroup I-9, RCC File, Ford Papers.

8. Mallary to Ford, January 23, 1973, subgroup I-9, RCC File, Ford Papers.

9. Cohen to Ford, December 4, 1972, subgroup I-9, RCC File, Ford Papers.

10. Savage to Thomas S. Foley, December 8, 1980, committee request letters, 97th Congress, Leadership Series, Thomas S. Foley Congressional Papers, Manuscripts, Archives, and Special Collections, Washington State University Libraries, Pullman.

11. Wyden to Foley, December 22, 1980, committee request letters, 97th Congress, Leadership Series, Foley Papers.

12. Bilbray to Foley, November 23, 1986, committee request letters, 100th Congress, Leadership Series, Foley Papers.

13. Engel to Foley, December 7, 1986, committee request letters, 101st Congress Leadership Series, Foley Papers.

14. Zablocki to Wilbur D. Mills, January 4, 1949, Ways and Means committee assignments, Foreign Affairs (2), Wilbur D. Mills Papers, Hendrix College.

15. Smith to Robert H. Michel, April 28, 1981, committee request letters, 97th Congress, Leadership Series, Michel Papers.

16. Swindall to Michel, December 11, 1986, committee request letters, 99th Congress, Leadership Series, Michel Papers.

17. Buechner to Michel, December 19, 1986, committee request letters, 99th Congress, Leadership Series, Michel Papers.

18. Panetta to James Wright, December 6, 1978, unprocessed file, Wright Collection.

19. Pashayan to Michel, December 1, 1982, committee request letters, 97th Congress, Leadership Series, Michel Papers.

20. Hastert to Michel, October 24, 1988, committee request letters, 101st Congress, Leadership Series, Michel Papers.

21. Both Fenno (1966) and White (1989) have studied the members of the Appropriations Committee, finding multiple motivations but an emphasis on chamber influence.

22. Akaka to Tip O'Neill, December 14, 1978, box 11, folder 10, Speaker's Office—Appointments, Party Leadership/Administrative Files, Thomas P. O'Neill Papers, John J. Burns Library, Boston College.

23. Hall to James Wright, November 8, 1982, unprocessed file, Wright Collection.

24. Pelosi to Thomas S. Foley, December 5, 1988, committee request letters, 101st Congress, Leadership Series, Foley Papers. Certainly in retrospect, the

election of Nancy Pelosi as the House Democratic leader in 2002 might lead one to wonder whether policy concerns were in the forefront of her mind, whether what she really wanted was power. It is hard to imagine, however, that as a relatively junior Democrat, she could possibly have imagined this assignment as a stepping stone to leadership; after all, the Democratic Speaker had begun his rise from Public Works, and the majority leader had spent his entire career on Agriculture. A seat on Appropriations did not guarantee her eventual future.

25. Coughlin to Gerald Ford, December 18, 1972, subgroup I-9, RCC File, Ford Papers.

26. Abdnor to Ford, February 27, 1973, subgroup I-9, RCC File, Ford Papers.

27. Bereuter to John J. Rhodes, November 18, 1980,MSS-3, Rhodes Papers.

28. Slaughter to Robert H. Michel, August 12, 1988, committee request letters, 100th Congress, Leadership Series, Michel Papers.

29. A sixth category is possible, mixed constituency and influence. Only three of the 289 members of our sample fell into this category; excluding them from the analysis does not change the substantive conclusions of this section.

30. Hunter to Michel, December 3, 1980, committee request letters, 97th Congress, Leadership Series, Michel Papers.

31. Dellums to James C. Corman, January 5, 1973, Congressman James C. Corman Collection, California State University, Northridge.

32. Hebert had actively opposed the appointment of Dellums to his committee, but Dellums was eventually placed on Armed Services over his objections. Dellums's case is recounted in chapter 7.

33. Schroeder to O'Neill, November 16, 1982, box 12, folder 2, Speaker's Office—Appointments, Party Leadership Administrative Files, O'Neill Papers.

34. Ibid.

CHAPTER 4

1. This complexity is illustrated in the epigraph, which was taken from Macdonald to Mills, January 6, 1955, Committee on Committees, Ways and Means Files, Wilbur D. Mills Papers. In the letter, Macdonald claims, "The district runs from the urban slums of Somerville through the gamut of each and every economic and social group (including farmers) . . . up to millionaires in the City of Melrose."

2. Edwards to Robert H. Michel, November 17, 1980, committee request letters, 97th Congress, Leadership Series, Michel Papers.

3. Hollenbeck to Michel, December 3, 1980, committee request letters, 97th Congress, Leadership Series, Michel Papers.

4. Anonymous leadership aide, interview by the authors, September 2000, Washington, D.C.

5. Following Shepsle (1978), influence committees are not included in the analysis because they do not have a clear jurisdiction that can be linked with district characteristics.

6. Siljander to Robert H. Michel, September 24, 1982, committee request letters, 98th Congress, Leadership Series, Michel Papers.

7. Zschau to Michel, December 3, 1982, committee request letters, 98th Congress, Leadership Series, Michel Papers.

8. Kemp to Gerald R. Ford, November 25, 1971, subgroup I-7, RCC File, Ford Papers.

9. Schumer to Thomas S. Foley, December 11, 1980, committee request letters, 97th Congress, Leadership Series, Foley Papers.

10. Not to mention the problem of using interest group scores as measures of members' policy-specific interests. A cottage industry has arisen in recent years examining the bias of interest group scores. Congressional scholars have advanced methodological "fixes" for the scores and replacement of the scores with other measures altogether (Poole and Rosenthal 1997). Our purpose here is to reexamine Krehbiel's findings in the light of these new data.

11. Data are available at http://www.polsci.indiana.edu/faad/. For additional discussion, see Bickers and Stein (1991) and Stein and Bickers (1995).

12. See Cox and McCubbins (1993b, 21–23) for a review of works that make this claim.

13. For example, Frank McCloskey (D-IN) told Steven Roberts of the *New York Times* that his first choice for a committee assignment was Armed Services (Roberts 1983b). Less than a month earlier, McCloskey had written to Majority leader Jim Wright requesting his support for a seat on the Appropriations Committee, and this request was likewise included in the Democratic Steering and Policy Committee briefing book that was used in the committee assignment meeting. It can be assumed that McCloskey did not reveal his true preference to the reporter for fear of the implied lack of power that could be associated with the failure to be placed on the desired committee. There is little reason to believe that a member (or staff member) would be more forthcoming with a scholar. McCloskey to Wright, December 17, 1982, unprocessed file, box 3-211, Steering and Policy Committee Members, Wright Papers.

14. Although both studies report success of Democratic members in receiving their first request as well as any request, the emphasis in the analysis is on receiving any request. For example, in discussing their results, Weingast and Marshall (1988, 150) claim: "[T]he probability of a freshman's gaining one of his top three is .8."

15. Although this example may at first appear overstated, note that the mean length of assignment request lists from first-term Republicans included more than seven committees for both the 100th and 101st Congresses (See Frisch and Kelly 2001).

16. We use the 93rd Congress strictly for convenience, as a means to accommodate the transition from Ford to Rhodes.

CHAPTER 5

1. Anonymous senior leadership aide, interview by the authors, June 2002, Washington, D.C.

2. Anonymous congressional member, interview by the authors, June 2002, Washington, D.C.

3. Schumer to Thomas S. Foley, December 11, 1980, committee request letters, 97th Congress, Leadership Series, Foley Papers.

4. Shaw to Robert H. Michel, June 22, 1988, committee request letters, 99th Congress, Leadership Series, Michel Papers.

5. Drier to Michel, April 7, 1981, committee request letters, 97th Congress, Leadership Series, Michel Papers.

6. Cooper to Foley, September 11, 1986, committee request letters, 100th Congress, Leadership Series, Foley Papers.

7. Bush to Ford, November 25, 1966, subgroup I-3, RCC File, Ford Papers.

8. Bush to Ford, December 6, 1966, subgroup I-3, RCC File, Ford Papers.

9. Mitchell to Ford, December 21, 1972, subgroup I-10, RCC File, Ford Papers.

10. Kleczka to Thomas S. Foley, November 6, 1986, committee request letters, 100th Congress, Leadership Series, Foley Papers.

11. Occupational categories are as follows: agriculture (business—agriculture/farming); education (secondary school teacher, high school administrator, college administrator, college professor, librarian, educational administrator, public school guidance counselor); finance (business—investments, baking, real estate, insurance, accountant/economist); health (physician, dentist, veterinarian, hospital administrator, pharmacist, medical office manager); industry (business—transportation, contractor, manufacturer); labor (laborer, union officer); natural resources (business—mining/petroleum); technical (architect, urban planner, engineer, surveyor); military; and lawyer.

12. In our interviews, we routinely asked those who had served on the party committee, or staff who were intimately involved in the process, what they believed were the most important factors in awarding a particular assignment to a member. This section relies on those interviews.

13. Anonymous congressional member, interview by the authors, June 2002, Washington, D.C.

14. Wright, Interview by the authors, March 2001, Fort Worth, Texas.

15. Anonymous congressional member, telephone interview by the authors, August 2002.

16. Anonymous congressional member, interview by the authors, August 2000, Washington, D.C.

17. Anonymous congressional member, telephone interview by the authors, August 2002.

18. Anonymous congressional member, telephone interview by the authors, August 2002.

19. Anonymous senior staff member, interview by the authors, June 2002, Washington, D.C.

20. Much has changed since Henry Waxman (D-CA) was scolded by Richard Bolling (D-MO) for making campaign contributions to fellow Democrats who would be in a position to vote for Waxman for chair of the Commerce Subcommittee on Environment and Health in 1979. On the increased importance of campaign contributions in committee assignment decisions, see Eric S. Heberlig (2000) and Eric S. Heberlig and Bruce Larson (2002).

21. Leadership aide, telephone interview by the authors, June 2002.

22. Anonymous leadership staff member, interview by the authors, September 2000, Washington, D.C.

23. Anonymous congressional member, interview by the authors, June 2002, Washington, D.C.

24. Anonymous congressional staff member, interview by the authors, January 2001, Washington, D.C.

25. Derrick, interview by the authors, June 2002, Washington, D.C.

26. Ibid.

27. Ibid.

28. Derrick to Wilbur Mills, November 18, 1974, box 219, folder 7, Committee Assignments, 94th Congress, All Member Requests (C-E), Legislative Files, Albert Papers (hereafter cited as All Member Requests, Albert Papers).

29. Governor John C. West to Wilbur Mills, November 14, 1974, All Member Requests, Albert Papers.

30. Funderburk to Mills, November 21, 1974, All Member Requests, Albert Papers.

31. Derrick, interview by the authors, June 2002, Washington, D.C.

32. Ibid.

33. Ibid.

34. Ibid.

35. Derrick to O'Neill, November 16, 1976, box 11, folder 10, Speaker's Office—Appointments, Party Leadership/Administrative Files, O'Neill Papers.

36. Derrick, interview by the authors, June 2002, Washington, D.C.

37. Ibid.

38. Ibid.

39. Ibid.

40. Ibid.

41. Martin to Michel, November 12, 1980, committee request letters, 97th Congress, Leadership Series, Michel Papers.

42. Martin to Michel, November 18, 1980, committee request letters, 97th Congress, Leadership Series, Michel Papers.

43. Martin, telephone interview by the authors, October 2002.

44. Martin to Michel, October 15, 1981, committee request letters, 98th Congress, Leadership Series, Michel Papers.

45. Martin to Michel, November 24, 1981, committee request letters, 98th Congress, Leadership Series, Michel Papers.

46. Ibid.

47. Martin, telephone interview by the authors, October 2002.

48. Ibid.

49. Both Gertzog (1976) and Shepsle (1978) found that by members' fourth term, most were seated on their desired committee.

50. Fenno (1966, 27) found that in assigning members to Appropriations, Republicans wanted people who were not "too liberal with other people's money." White (1989) confirms this and provides evidence (using *Congressional Quarterly's* Conservative Coalition measure) that during the time period under study, Republicans replaced Appropriations Committee members with members who were much more conservative.

51. Current and former members of Congress and leadership staff repeatedly emphasized to us in interviews that membership on the Executive Committee was extremely helpful to members seeking a change in their committee assignments.

52. Both David M. Kennedy (1989) and John M. Barry (1989) refer to Martin as Michel's protégé.

53. As a newly elected representative, it was already apparent that Jim Kolbe understood the political nature of committee assignments. After being placed on Banking (not his original first choice but a position that he requested), Kolbe told *Congressional Quarterly*: "There's a lot of things at play here. . . . There are states that make trade-offs with each other, all kinds of deals that get made all the way down the line. So many considerations outweigh whether Jim Kolbe is a nice guy. It's very limited what you can do to really lobby for yourself" (Granat 1985, 172).

54. William F. Connelly, Jr., and John J. Pitney, Jr. (1995) and John M. Barry (1989) support the claim that Michel wanted Martin on Appropriations. Barry likewise supports the claim that Lott was able to construct the winning coalition. Connelly and Pitney believe that Michel was so disappointed by this failure that he appointed member Robert Lagomarsino to study the committee assignment process in order to make recommendations that would enhance the leader's power over the process.

55. The strong large-state coalition that was present in the 99th Congress may have resulted from the efforts of Jerry Lewis (Kennedy 1989). Kennedy claims that

Lewis reacted to his failure to get a Californian elected to the Appropriations Committee in the 98th Congress by building a large-state coalition in the 99th Congress. (See the quotation in Kennedy, page 1.)

56. A second member of the Illinois delegation, Jack Davis, was supported by Michel for a place on Armed Services and was likewise unsuccessful in spite of the leader's support. Michel later made a special plea to Speaker Wright, who in turn enlarged Armed Services to include Davis.

57. Martin, telephone interview by the authors, October 2002.

58. Ibid.

59. Ibid.

60. Dornan to John J. Rhodes, n.d., 1976, box 79, folder 22, MSS-3, Rhodes Papers.

61. Dornan to Rhodes, November 28, 1978, box 76, folder 8, MSS-3, Rhodes Papers.

62. Dornan to Rhodes, November 20, 1980, committee request letters, 97th Congress, Leadership Series, Michel Papers.

63. Dornan to Robert H. Michel, November 28, 1984, committee request letters, 99th Congress, Leadership Series, Michel Papers.

64. Committee preference sheet, November 26, 1986, committee request letters, 100th Congress, Leadership Series, Michel Papers.

65. Dornan to Michel, November 22, 1988, committee request letters, 101st Congress, Michel Papers.

66. Executive Committee meeting minutes, January 8, 1987, 100th Congress, Committee on Committees, Leadership Series, Michel Papers. For information on vote tallies, see chapter 6.

67. Traficant to Wright, December 3, 1984, unprocessed file, Wright Collection.

68. Stokes to Wright, December 5, 1984, unprocessed file, Wright Collection.

69. Traficant to Wright, December 3, 1984, unprocessed file, Wright Collection.

70. Rostenkowski, interview by authors, July 2002, Chicago, Illinois.

CHAPTER 6

1. The ingrate-enemy description has been attributed to Louis XIV, John Adams, Thomas Jefferson, Abraham Lincoln, William Howard Taft, Herman Talmadge, and former Boston Mayor James Michael Curley.

2. Martin, interview by Fenno, March 1963. Research Interview Notes of Richard F. Fenno, Jr., with Members of the U.S. House of Representatives, 1959–1965. Internet copy, Special Collections, Records of Congress, National Archives, Washington, D.C. (http://www.archives.gov/records_of_congress/oral_histories/fenno/interview_notes.html)

3. Nicole Tourangeau, archivist for Stonehill College Library, explained: "At some point during Martin's career there was talk of a central depository of

speaker's papers and 30 boxes were packed up and sent into storage. The depository was never built and the boxes have never been found. As a result there are some large gaps in the collection." Tourangeau, e-mail message to the authors, December 12, 2002.

4. Martin served as Speaker and Republican leader during a time of strong committee chairs (and ranking members), and those chairs certainly tried to influence assignments of Republican members to their committees. For example, incoming Appropriations Committee chair John Taber (R-NY) wrote to Martin prior to the 83rd Congress: "The following is a list of some of the names that I would be satisfied with on the Appropriations Committee. . . . There undoubtedly are others who would do well, but these are names that I have had checked on and I get a good report on all of them." Taber to Martin. December 16, 1952, Joseph W. Martin, Jr. Papers, Special Collections, Stonehill College, Easton, Massachusetts.

5. Bennett to Ploesser, December 7, 1946, Martin Collection. (Original in the Joint Collection University of Missouri Western Historical Manuscript Collection–Columbia and State Historical Society of Missouri Manuscripts.)

6. Rayburn typically met informally with a hand-picked group of House leaders each day after the House adjourned. The Board of Education, as the group was called, would discuss the business of the House over drinks in a small hideaway room on the first floor of the Capitol.

7. Memorandum from Rumsfeld to Ford, January 7, 1965, subgroup I-3, RCC File, Ford Papers.

8. Gerald R. Ford to Robert V. Denney, November 26, 1968, subgroup I-5, RCC File, Ford Papers.

9. Ford to Dickinson, January 12, 1967, subgroup I-5, RCC File, Ford Papers. It was not just the exclusive committees for which Ford stressed excess demand over supply. He wrote to John H. Buchanan, Jr. (R-Al) regarding the Foreign Affairs Committee: "[M]ore than five times as many requests have been received as we have any hope of having vacancies to fill." Ford to Buchanan, Jr., January 12, 1967, subgroup I-5, RCC File, Ford Papers.

10. Memorandum from Calkins to Ford, September, 15 1970, subgroup I-7, RCC File, Ford Papers.

11. Ford to Wilkinson, September 29, 1970, subgroup I-7, RCC File, Ford Papers.

12. Rhodes to Ody Fish, December 17, 1974, box 51, folder 3, MSS-3, Rhodes Papers.

13. Rhodes to Davis, January 22, 1979, box 76, folder 9, MSS-3, Rhodes Papers.

14. Rhodes to Ron Marlenee, September 13, 1976, box 79, folder 22, MSS-3, Rhodes Papers.

15. As far as we can tell, Michel is the first Republican leader to vote in committee assignment decisions. Although Michigan was represented on the Executive

Committee while Ford was leader, Alfred Cederberg represented the Michigan delegation on the committee on committees.

16. Michel, interview by the authors, August 2000, Washington, D.C.

17. Livingston, interview by the authors, June 2002, Washington, D.C.

18. Thanks to Douglas Koopman for providing a whip count of the 1989 Republican whip race.

19. Livingston, interview by the authors, June 2002, Washington, D.C.

20. Ibid.

21. Anonymous leadership aide, interview by the authors, August 2000, Washington, D.C.

22. Livingston, interview by the authors, June 2002, Washington, D.C.

23. Anonymous leadership staff member, interview by the authors, June 2002, Washington, D.C.

24. The situation of Michael Forbes (R-NY), who switched parties despite being given a seat on the Appropriations Committee in his first Congress, is cited, in addition to the case of Mark Neumann, as a contributing factor in the decision to return to traditional assignments for first-term Republicans.

25. A letter in the Mills Papers reveals that majority leader John W. McCormack was also supportive of Mills's bid for membership on Ways and Means. Mills had circulated a letter on October 9, 1942, to all Democratic members, soliciting support for his bid to be on Ways and Means. There are numerous copies of the letter, typically with comments of support written by the original recipient (one of whom was a young Texas congressman by the name of Lyndon Baines Johnson). McCormack scrawled at the top of the letter addressed to him (and on which Mills had handwritten that he was sending a similar letter to all Democrats): "Dear Wilbur: I am with you. John McCormack." Box 530, file 1, Ways and Means (Mills Personal) 1942, Wilbur Mills Papers, Hendrix College, Conway, Arkansas. An earlier note from McCormack included in the same file instructs Mills: "I received a wire from [caucus chair] Dick Duncan that it is all right to go ahead with the Democratic caucus for next Wednesday, so go ahead and do your lobbying and get the votes." McCormack to Mills, October 8, 1942.

26. When asked whether he considered himself to be "one of Rayburn's boys," Mills responded "I am always honored when anybody says that." Mills was also a participant in Rayburn's "Board of Education" meetings. Mills, interview by Joe Frantz, November 2, 1971, Wilbur D. Mills Interview I (http://www.lbjlib.utexas.edu/johnson/archives.hom/oralhistory.hom/Mills-w/MillsW.asp), Oral History Collection, Lyndon Baines Johnson Library and Museum, Austin, Texas.

27. Letters from the Rayburn Papers indicate that the Speaker relied more heavily on Mills's advice than on the advice he received from Ways and Means Committee chair Robert L. Doughton (D-NC), who often sided with committee

Republicans to defeat Democratic initiatives. In contrast with Mills's desire to select members who would help enact president Harry S. Truman's agenda, Doughton wrote Rayburn: "I am anxious to work with the Administration but not under it in matters about which our Committee has heavy responsibility. I am hoping we can all pull together in carrying our heavy load, but as you know the work of our Committee is so very heavy we need men who are best qualified for service and whose decisions will not be made by certain groups. In my opinion one of the worst dangers to our Republic is group pressure." Doughton to Rayburn, November 12, 1948, 3R341, Committee Assignments, Sam Rayburn Papers (1913–1961), the Center for American History, University of Texas, Austin.

28. Rayburn to Mills, November 11, 1948; Mills to Rayburn, November 16, 1948; and Rayburn to Mills, November 22, 1948. Ways and Means committee assignments, Ways and Means 1948, Mills Papers.

29. Mills to Boggs, November 12, 1948, and Boggs to Mills, November 16, 1948, Ways and Means committee assignments, Ways and Means 1948, Mills Papers.

30. The Mills Papers also reveal the influence of the Democratic leadership in discouraging members from pursuing assignment to Ways and Means. For example, Don Magnuson (D-WA) wrote to Mills: "I originally had hoped to be considered for the Ways and Means Committee. However, after talking with the leadership, I did not press for it. They were not hostile to my candidacy, but I saw the wisdom and justice of their suggestions that I seek some other spot, there being other candidates who obviously deserved priority for Ways and Means." Magnuson to Mills, January 6, 1955, box 298, file 13, Ways and Means, Committee on Committees 1955, Mills Papers.

31. Many letters in Mills's archives reveal a relationship of personal loyalty between McCormack and Mills. One interesting exchange occurred when McCormack wrote Mills seeking his support for committee assignments for three New England members—Thomas P. (Tip) O'Neill, Edward Boland, and Torbert MacDonald. Mills responded: "Thanks for your letter of January 8 in regard to Tom O'Neill for Rules, Eddie Boland for Appropriations, and Torbert MacDonald for Interstate and Foreign Commerce. It looks as if Massachusetts will have a pretty good batting average on Committee assignments. Certainly it is always a pleasure for me to cooperate with you in the matter of assignments to the various Committees." Mills to McCormack, January 11, 1955, box 298, file 13, Ways and Means, Committee on Committees 1955, Mills Papers.

32. The Democratic Caucus empowered the Speaker (or minority leader) to make assignments to the Rules Committee in 1975; the Republicans made a similar change in 1989.

33. Tip O'Neill's account of his Rules Committee experience similarly captures Rayburn's influence: "I recall in my second term there I had not applied for it, I

had applied for Public Works and I was called by Mr. Rayburn. He said, 'I understand that you were a former Speaker of the House and know about things of this nature.' He said, 'I'm going to recommend that you be on the Rules Committee.' The system through the years of getting on the Rules Committee is that the Speaker of the House named to the Committee on Committees chair the name wanted and the chair of the Committee on Committees never once to my knowledge refused the Speaker the name he wanted on that committee." Democratic Caucus meeting transcript, December 3, 1974, box 219, folder 46, Designation of a Committee on Committees, Legislative Files, Albert Papers.

34. Rayburn to Mills, November 16, 1948, and Mills to Rayburn, November 17, 1948, Ways and Means Committee Assignments, 81st Congress, Mills Papers. In response to numerous letters from individual members seeking assignment to Rules, Mills responded by emphasizing the important role that leadership played in determining who was successful.

35. Fenno Research Interview Notes.

36. O'Brien, interview by Michael L. Gillette, December 4, 1985, Lawrence F. O'Brien Oral History Interview IV (http://www.lbjlib.utexas.edu/johnson/archives.hom/oralhistory.hom/obrienl/obrienl.asp), LBJ Oral History Collection, LBJ Library. There is more archival evidence that the Kennedy administration attempted to influence committee assignments from the other side of Pennsylvania Avenue than there is for any other presidential administration. According to Senator George A. Smathers:

> What happened to me was that after Kennedy got to be president, he called me and said, "Old pal, I want you to do me a favor," always giving you the "old pal, I'm counting on you." "I want you to give up one of your committees and go on the Foreign Relations Committee, because I need some hawks on the committee. We've got too many pacifists on the committee." Wayne Morse and Bill Fulbright and Frank Church, these guys, they were just for giving away everything in the view of Kennedy and me and others. They had their beliefs and we had our beliefs, and I was a sort of a militarist and a strong defense man, and these people were always seeking ways to resolve problems through peaceful methods, which is not wrong, but anyway there are more that are more militant than others, and I was one of the more militant. Kennedy talked me into giving up my position on the Commerce Committee and moving to the Foreign Relations Committee of the Senate, which automatically caused me to give up my seniority on the Commerce Committee and have to move and start at the bottom of the ladder on the Foreign Relations Committee, but that's what I did for my friend Jack Kennedy. And he talked Russell Long into doing the same thing. (Smathers, United States Senator, Oral History Interviews, Senate Historical Office, Washington, D.C.)

However, when asked about pressure from the administration in an interview with Richard Fenno in 1963 (Fenno Research Interview Notes), committee on committees member James Burke (D-MA) responded that there was no White House interference at all.

37. Brademas to Albert, November 30, 1958, box 13, folder 4, General Files, Albert Papers.

38. Albert to Brademas, December 5, 1958, box 13, folder 4, General Files, Albert Papers.

39. See Albert to Wilbur D. Mills, November 24, 1954, and Mills to Albert, November 29, 1954; box 298, file 15, Ways and Means Committee Assignments, Mills Papers.

40. Fenno Research Interview Notes.

41. Albert, interview by Ronald M Peters, Jr., May 9, 1979, tape 1, side 1 (pp. 23–24 of transcript). Oral History Collection, Albert Papers.

42. Democratic Caucus meeting transcript, December 3, 1974, box 219, folder 46, Designation of a Committee on Committees, Legislative Files, Albert Papers.

43. O'Neill to Steering Committee members, May 2, 1977, committee request letters, Foley Papers. Perhaps the best-known case of O'Neill using his influence over the DSPC concerns the appointment of first-term member Robert Mrazek (D-NY) to the Appropriations Committee. According to several sources (see Farrell 2001, 595–96, for example), O'Neill was greatly appreciative that Mrazek had defeated John LeBoutillier, who had been O'Neill's personal nemesis. LeBoutillier had referred to Tip as "big, fat and out of control—just like the federal government" and led a campaign to unseat the Speaker, called "repeal O'Neill" (2001, 595–96). This form of intervention (the appointment of Mrazek) was rare for O'Neill, according to several members who served with him on DSPC.

44. Anonymous leadership staff member, interview by the authors, June 2002, Washington, D.C.

45. Memorandum from Larsen to O'Neill, re: Vote percentages for the 95th Congress, December 15, 1978, box 11, folder 10, Speaker's Office—Appointments, Party Leadership/Administrative Files, O'Neill Papers.

46. Speaker's preference votes included a total of 237 votes during the 95th Congress. They were defined as "[v]otes on critical amendments counted; votes reflecting the 'party line' are included. Also included are veto override votes and some close votes on final passage." Whip votes included 56 votes during the 95th Congress "where Whip Count was taken on important issues." There were 21 DSPC votes "where special task forces were used. No amendments—shows final passage support (i.e. Humphrey Hawkins—does not show where Member was on 'crippling amendments[,]' only whether Member supported final passage)." Memo to Speaker O'Neill from Billie [Larsen], December 15, 1978, re: "Vote Percentages for 95th Congress," box 11, folder 10, Speaker's Office—Appointments, Party Leadership/Administrative Files, O'Neill Papers.

NOTES TO PAGES 203–204

NOTES TO PAGES 203–204   369

47. Patterson to O'Neill, June 5, 1978, and December 7, 1978, box 11, folder 10, Speaker's Office—Appointments, Party Leadership/Administrative Files, O'Neill Papers. Patterson made an interesting abrupt change of strategy between his June letter and his December request. In June, Patterson had emphasized the importance of a Rules assignment to retaining his seat: "As you are aware, my district is considered marginal in terms of my retaining my seat. I believe that my assignment to the Rules Committee would be most beneficial in illustrating to my constituency an ability to work with my colleagues and impact Congressional deliberations in a positive manner." By December, Patterson apparently had come to realize that marginality is not an asset for Rules assignment—members are often expected to make tough party votes that may not coincide with their district's views, and therefore, safe members are usually preferred. In December, Patterson wrote: "[M]y district is a safe Democratic District having been held by my predecessor for 12 years before me. Any district that has been in the Democratic column for 16 years, can, I think, be considered as safe as any."

48. Johnson to O'Neill. December 12, 1978, box 11, folder 10, Speaker's Office—Appointments, Party Leadership/Administrative Files, O'Neill Papers.

49. See Jacobs (1995, 326, 386–87), Cohen (1979), and Farrell (2001). Jacobs claims: "Democrats were badly split between the O'Neill-Wright-Bolling faction and Burton. Virtually every contest, no matter how trivial or how much a sideshow, was viewed through that filter" (387). The depth of the hard feelings surrounding the Wright-Burton split can be seen in a handwritten message from L. H. Fountain (D-NC) to Jim Wright included at the bottom of a letter Fountain wrote announcing his retirement from the House: "You are the best and most capable Majority Leader we've had in my 30 years here. I was happy to be among the first few (you may have forgotten) to urge you to run. Phil [Burton] has hardly spoken to me since. But I'd do the same thing again." Fountain to Wright, December 21, 1982, unprocessed file, Wright Collection. On the Wright-Burton feud, see also chapter 7.

50. Jacobs claims: "A few Burton supporters believed that Freshman Tony Beilenson of Beverly Hills, no friend of Waxman or Berman, voted for Wright [for Majority Leader in 1976]. Subsequent behavior gave them more grist for their suspicions. Beilenson approached Bolling and O'Neill directly and won a coveted spot on the Rules Committee after the 1980 [sic] elections, and Burton 'rearranged' Beilenson's district following the 1980 census. Like Mineta, Beilenson vehemently denied voting for anyone but Burton on all ballots. He liked and respected Bolling, he said, and 'told him flat out who I voted for.' When Bolling chose him for the Rules Committee, Beilenson said, he did so because he wanted 'thoughtful people' on it" (1995, 326).

B.F. Sisk, the Rules Committee member whose retirement created the vacancy, had a slightly different take on the situation. Sisk believed that O'Neill was antagonistic toward the West and wanted to retain power for the eastern states. According to Sisk: "Tip, in my opinion, has never been a good friend of ours in that sense. He is simply a New Englander who resents the power of the West. . . . O'Neill flatly slapped the delegation in the face—a terrible blow politically—by taking another man on Rules. This is almost unheard of with a large state delegation" (1980, 204). Sisk's claim that his offer to resign from Rules before the election so that O'Neill could appoint his replacement (thereby giving the California candidate the highest seniority position of the new members) was flatly rejected by the Speaker. Henry Waxman told us that he believed O'Neill resented the audacity of Californians for trying to dictate the appointment, when the caucus rules now gave the power directly to the Speaker.

51. Mattox to O'Neill, January 1979, box 11, folder 10, Speaker's Office—Appointments, Party Leadership/Administrative Files, O'Neill Papers.

52. See for example Barry (1989); Rohde (1991); and Sinclair (1995). David E. Price, a political scientist who was elected to the House when Wright was Speaker, maintained: "Wright was not inclined to leave Steering and Policy decisions (or much of anything else) to chance" (1992, 48).

53. Percentages are from internal leadership documents, Party Leadership/Administrative Files, O'Neill Papers.

54. See Strahan (1990) on the influence of Chair Rostenkowski on the assignment of Democratic members to the Ways and Means Committee.

55. Listed as yes's were Jim Wright, Bill Alexander, Charlie Rose, Morgan Murphy, Kika de la Garza, John Breaux, W. G. Bill Hefner, and Fernand St. Germain; tentative yes's were George Danielson, Robert Duncan, and Robert Roe; definite no's were Gladys Spellman, Dan Rostenkowski, and Henry Waxman; and unknowns were Tip O'Neill, Tom Foley, John Brademas, Ben Rosenthal, Bill Gray, Bill Ford, Mario Biaggi, Charles Rangel, Dick Bolling, and John Seiberling. The leadership voting as a bloc does not appear likely; other caucus leaders failed to endorse publicly the majority leader's choice. Sam B. Hall, Jr. to Wright, July 26, 1979, unprocessed file, Wright Collection.

56. Wright, interview by the authors, March 22, 2001, Fort Worth, Texas.

57. Oberstar to Wright, November 28, 1984, unprocessed file, Wright Collection.

58. Andrews handwrote a letter to Wright that same day, thanking the majority leader for his "hard work for my candidacy for the Ways and Means Committee and your loyal support and counsel over the past many months." Andrews to Wright, January 22, 1985, unprocessed file, Wright Collection.

59. Rostenkowski, interview by the authors, August 2002, Chicago, Illinois.

60. Wright to Norman Dicks, July 17, 1986, unprocessed file, Wright Collection. The same letter was sent to Claude Denson Pepper (FL), Thomas Foley (WA), Vic Fazio (CA), Marty Russo (IL), Tom Daschle (SD), Tony Coelho (CA),

Paul E. Kanjorski (PA), Barbara Bailey Kennelly (CT), Charles Bennett (FL), Steny Hamilton Hoyer (MD), Mary Rose Oakar (OH), John Murtha (PA), Robert García (NY), Joseph Early (MA), Bill Alexander (AR), Wyche Fowler, Jr. (GA), James Jones (OK), and Cardiss Collins (IL).

61. Wright, interview by the authors, March 22, 2001, Fort Worth, Texas.

62. Henry Waxman, who served on the committee on committees under three separate leaders, used almost identical words to describe Wright's influence as Speaker. Waxman, telephone interview by the authors, June 2003.

63. In describing his attempt to gain a seat on the Commerce Committee as a first-term member, David Price (D-NC) claims: "I did not receive any encouragement from Wright; this suggested to me that the rumors were probably true that he and chairman Dingell, who was also on the Steering and Policy Committee, were prepared to endorse 3 members, none of whom was a freshman for the available Energy and Commerce slots" (Price 1992, 45).

64. Wright, interview by the authors, March 2001, Fort Worth, Texas.

65. Ibid.

66. On the contrast between Wright and Foley, see Rohde (1991, 184–85).

67. The change brought the total of chief deputy whips to three. The positions were used to give leadership positions to three factions of the Democratic Caucus—women, African Americans, and southerners.

68. When asked whether there had ever been a slate under his leadership, Jim Wright responded: "One slot at a time. That was the business of the Steering and Policy Committee. I would never have really presumed to go in there with [a] list, and I don't think that Tip would. Why have the committee? I mean somebody could sit down unilaterally and decide the committees" (Wright, interview by the authors, March 2001, Fort Worth, Texas.) On the use of a leadership slate under Speaker Foley, see also Price (1992) and Brown (1999).

69. Anonymous staff member, interview by the authors, June 2002, Washington, D.C.

70. Anonymous congressional member, interview by the authors, October 2002, Bakersfield, California.

71. Reportedly, this proposal so alienated five southern Democrats that they cited it as one reason for switching to the Republican Party in 1995. Mike Parker (MS), one of the switchers, said contemptuously of Byrne: "That woman. Who did she think she was?" (Smith 1996).

CHAPTER 7

1. Smith and Ray (1983) include the total votes received by candidates for Democratic committee positions, but they were unable to obtain individual voting results within the Democratic Steering and Policy Committee (DSPC). The term "black box" is theirs.

2. One former member told us of the overemphasis on Republican unity during their years in the minority: "When you are a tiny minority as the Republicans were, there is no big deal. You get abused so much, you just naturally hold together." Anonymous congressional member, interview by the authors, June 2002, Washington, D.C.

3. In Reiter's typology, Gerald Ford is "a quintessential Regular." (Another example is George H. W. Bush). Nelson Rockefeller is the prototypical liberal northeastern misfit, and Barry Goldwater was an early "spokesman for the emerging Realigners." Realigners come from the new areas of Republican growth, the South and West (Reiter 1981, 293–95).

4. On the internal divisions of the Republican Conference also see Kolodny (1999) and Koopman (1996).

5. See chapter 2. Additional evidence of a bias in assignments toward large-state members can be found in Kiewiet and McCubbins (1991). D. Roderick Kiewiet and Matthew McCubbins demonstrate that during the 1960s and 1970s, the Republican contingent on the Appropriations Committee overrepresented midwesterners and underrepresented members from the South and border states.

6. Splitting votes among several candidates was allowed under the rules of the Executive Committee during this period, however, such vote splitting was rare.

7. Formally, the Executive Committee made only "recommendations" for committee assignments to the RCC for approval. During this period, the RCC accepted all recommendations of the Executive Committee.

8. There are no ballot slips in the Michel Papers after the 101st Congress.

9. On the attractiveness of various committees, see Malcolm E. Jewel and Chu Chi-hung (1974) and Ray (1982b).

10. Jerry Lewis, who served as the California representative throughout most of this analysis, for instance, was removed from his position on the RCC by the California delegation, apparently for being too willing to cooperate with the Democratic leadership. There were also apparently some bad feelings between Lewis and conservative California member Bill Dannemeyer, who may have held Lewis responsible for his failure to earn a seat on the Budget Committee (Connelly and Pitney 1994).

11. Parker and Parker in turn relied heavily on John G. Grumm (1963).

12. The dominant expectation in the literature is that coalitions are unlikely to form in the party committees on committees (Shepsle 1978) because the primary role of the committee is to accommodate member requests. Thus, the driving question behind our analysis is whether coalitions form; our secondary interest is the nature of these coalitions. For this reason, we adopt an inductive approach through the use of explanatory rather than confirmatory factor analysis, which

requires the researcher to impose specific theoretical expectations on the data. Confirmatory factor analysis might be more appropriate in the context of a different research question.

13. Generally speaking, a factor score of greater than .50 is considered to be of substantive significance.

14. Journalistic and biographical accounts of the Democrats' process often paint a different picture. See, for example, Barry (1989), Jacobs (1995), Dellums and Halterman (2000), and Farrell (2001). Barry contends that former Ways and Means chair Dan Rostenkowski (D-IL) sought membership to the Ways and Means Committee not because of any policy interest, but because Ways and Means then served as the Democrats' committee on committees.

15. In a letter to Hank Brown, Executive Committee member Bill Frenzel gave Frank Horton (R-NY) credit for forging the big state coalition: "When Frank's coalition dumped us, they still gave us a seat on Appropriations and two on Ways and Means. When we returned the compliment, you will remember that we had to make adjustments to keep the committee from flying apart." Frenzel to Brown, July 31, 1987, box 1-8, Committee on Committees Files, 1986–1988, RG 5, Lagomarsino Collection.

16. In a telephone interview by the authors, Bill Frenzel (then a member of the Executive Committee) attributed the participation of Texas in the small-state coalition to the efforts of Tom DeLay (R-TX), who at that time served on the committee as the second-term representative. Frenzel also downplayed the role of Lott, saying: "I will say, he was not the driver, but he's a good politician. He understood how the thing worked, and he got right into it. He was one of the major players. He didn't begin the war, but he was one of the major players." Lott's role in forming a small-state coalition is confirmed by Barone and Ujifusa (1987, 374). See also Hook (1987).

17. The report also suggested creating more geographically compact state groupings while maintaining the weighted-voting scheme that has been a feature of the Republican process since 1919. The Republican Conference did not adopt this reform.

18. Berman, interview by the authors, August 2003, Van Nuys, California.

19. Examination of this hypothesis would benefit from closer examination of Democratic conflict over committee seats, given the party's shift from majority to minority. If this argument holds, one would expect to see increased levels of conflict within the DSPC as the party lost control of the ability to manipulate the available number of committee seats. To a lesser extent, close attention to changes in conflict patterns in the Republican process would also yield insight into how the supply of committee slots influences conflict. However, upon becoming the majority party, Republicans significantly changed the composition of the RCC in a manner that would likely reduce conflict regardless of majority status.

CHAPTER 8

1. Anonymous congressional member, telephone interview by the authors, March 2003.

2. Anonymous congressional member, interview by the authors, August 2002, Chicago, Illinois.

3. Anonymous congressional member, telephone interview by the authors, August 2002.

4. Anonymous congressional member, interview by the authors, June 2002, Washington, D.C.

5. Anonymous congressional member, interview by the authors, October 2002, Bakersfield, California.

6. Wright, interview by the authors, March 2001, Fort Worth, Texas.

7. Groseclose and Stewart (1998) have developed a quantitative measure of the value members place on different committees, known as the "Grosswart" ranking. Because members typically serve on more than one legislative committee, the value of the set of assignments, known as the portfolio, is used in our analysis.

8. Preference sheet for the 99th Congress, Committee on Committees, Leadership Series, 99th Congress, Michel Papers.

9. For discussion of how we coded the request letters, see chapter 3 and appendix 2.

10. The number of Republican seats that were uncontested was so small that it was impossible to generate reliable results.

11. In the sample, 7.6 percent of Democratic members and 9.4 percent of Republican members mention their predecessor's committee status.

12. Wheat, telephone interview by the authors, March 2003.

13. Ibid.

14. Ibid.

15. Daschle to O'Neill, November 30, 1977, box 11, folder 7, Speaker's Office—Appointments, Party Leadership/Administrative Files, O'Neill Papers.

16. Daschle to Wright, December 20, 1978, unprocessed file, Wright Collection.

17. Dicks to O'Neill, September 28, 1976, box 11, folder 7, Speaker's Office—Appointments, Party Leadership/Administrative Files, O'Neill Papers.

18. Dicks to Wright, December 10, 1976, unprocessed file, Wright Collection.

19. Wright to Dicks, January 14, 1977, unprocessed file, Wright Collection.

20. Butler Hansen to O'Neill, December 10, 1976, box 11, folder 7, Speaker's Office—Appointments, Party Leadership/Administrative Files, O'Neill Papers.

21. Interview by the authors, June 2002, Washington, D.C.

22. Gore to O'Neill, January 6, 1977, box 11, folder 7, Speaker's Office—Appointments, Party Leadership/Administrative Files, O'Neill Papers.

23. Including dummy variables in the model for all leaders makes it impossible to find a unique solution to the equation. The Wright and Foley Speakerships are excluded for statistical reasons, becoming the "reference" category for the period variable. Data on party loyalty were not available for the 102nd and 103rd Congresses.

24. Wilbur Mills frequently counseled members against seeking assignments to committees on which the members' state was already represented. For example, Mills responded to a letter from John E. Moss, Jr. (D-CA), who was seeking a position on the Appropriations Committee, with the following warning: "You may encounter some difficulty in obtaining a position on the Appropriations Committee of the House in view of the fact that Harry Sheppard from your Delegation already has a place on the Appropriations Committee. . . . Many members of the Committee on Committees desire to offer assignments such as the ones on the Appropriations Committee to as many states as possible and to avoid two from the same state except in those rare instances where there are more Democrats from the state involved than there are separate committees." Mills to Moss, November 26, 1954, box 298, file 15, Committee on Appropriations, Ways and Means Committee Assignments, Mills Papers.

CHAPTER 9

1. Of the racial minorities represented in Congress, only African Americans are represented in numbers sufficient for meaningful statistical analysis.

2. The research includes mostly anecdotal evidence that early women members of Congress were routinely given poor committee positions; accounts of Shirley Chisholm's (D-NY) refusal to be seated on the Agriculture Committee are common (see, for example, Bingham 1997; Chisholm 1970; and Foerstel and Foerstel 1996). Chisholm argued to the Democratic Caucus that her urban constituency would be poorly served by a seat on the Agriculture Committee and was given a seat on the Veterans' Affairs Committee instead.

3. Adopting a similar approach (but using a different measure of prestige), Arnold and King (2002) examine the value of women senators' committee assignments. They similarly conclude: "[T]he committee system is fairly representative given the small number of women in the Senate itself" (10).

4. Gertzog includes Appropriations, Rules, and Ways and Means in his definition of exclusive committees but unexplainably includes Budget as well. Although the Budget Committee is certainly important, it is by no means exclusive; in fact, members often wish to avoid service on Budget because the limitations placed on consecutive service restrict opportunities for accumulation of the seniority that matters for career advancement. Lynn Martin, a woman whom Gertzog singles out as a success story for her early assignment to

the Budget Committee, did not seek Budget as her initial assignment and viewed the assignment as in some ways an obstacle to institutional influence. Referring to the requirement that members rotate off the committee, Martin told Kennedy (1989) "[N]ot only was that choice going to limit my rise on that committee, it was going to limit my chances for seniority on other committees: because once off Budget I was going to be coming in, in effect, after both my [elected] class and the class to follow" (3). In terms of committee prestige, the most accurate index of committee values (Groseclose and Stewart 1998) ranks Budget well below the exclusive committees and below both Armed Services and Commerce.

5. The assertion that the House committee assignment process is one of self-selection has been refuted by others. See for example Cox and McCubbins (1993b) and Krehbiel (1991). In terms of broad theory, the research reported herein on the committee assignments of women likewise fails to support distributive theory and the self-selection thesis.

6. Shepsle's (1978) description of the post-reform Democratic process is still mostly applicable. Sinclair (1995) discusses the changes that have occurred in the composition of the DSPC. Masters (1961) is a source for understanding the Republicans' committee assignment process, but see chapter 2.

7. The Speaker appointed three members to the DSPC, each to look out for the representational interests of a single group: women, African Americans, and first-term members. When Carl Albert asked Jim Wright for suggested appointees from the Texas delegation to represent these groups, Wright replied, "I tell you what you can do, Carl. You can kill three birds with one stone. They want sexual balance and racial balance and representation, class representation. We have a freshman, black woman, how would you like her?" Albert agreed, and "Barbara Jordan was appointed to Steering and Policy, and that gave her [her] first real shot at being involved in the overall affairs of the House." Wright, interview by the authors, March 2001, Fort Worth, Texas.

8. Three women members served on the DSPC during the 99th and 103rd Congresses.

9. Two Republican women, Catherine May (WA) and Margaret Heckler (MA), did serve on the full RCC during this period. As Masters (1961) pointed out, however, the full committee merely ratified the decisions made by the smaller Executive Committee. The Republican Executive Committee, therefore, can be accurately described as a uniform (all male) committee using Rosabeth Moss Kanter's terms (1977).

10. This literature follows in the tradition of Kanter (1977), who first studied the effects of the proportions of women in groups.

11. Memorandum to Lagomarsino from Nancy [last name unknown] Re: Women's Representative on Committee on Committees, July 23, 1987, box 1, folder 24, Committee on Committees Files, 1986–1988, RG 5, Lagomarsino Collection.

12. Anonymous congressional member, interview by the authors, June 2002, Washington, D.C.; anonymous congressional member, telephone interview by the authors, October 2002.

13. Anonymous congressional member, telephone interview by the authors, August 2002. The member was successful in her quest to secure a female replacement on Ways and Means: "I traded my votes to get a woman on Ways and Means."

14. In this analysis, we accept Deering and Smith's (1997) categorization of Budget as an influence committee to maintain comparability of our findings with the many other works that use the Deering and Smith typology. As we illustrate in footnote 3 of this chapter, however, members evidence ambivalent attitudes toward service on the Budget Committee, and Budget is not an exclusive committee because members of Budget hold other committee assignments. Members of committees that are truly exclusive—Rules, Ways and Means, Appropriations, and in some years, Energy and Commerce—may not hold other committee assignments.

15. Anonymous congressional member, telephone interview by the authors, August 2002.

16. Anonymous congressional member, interview by the authors, June 2002, Washington, D.C.

17. Anonymous congressional member, telephone interview by the authors, August 2002.

18. Schneider to Michel, November 12, 1986, committee request letters, 100th Congress, Leadership Series, Michel Papers.

19. Schneider to Michel, November 1, 1988, committee request letters, 101st Congress, Leadership Series, Michel Papers.

20. Despite her electoral success, Schneider was significantly to the left of the Republican Conference during this period. Her average DW-NOMINATE score over the five Congresses was .05 compared with .30 for the conference as a whole ($t = 4.32, p = .000$).

21. Anonymous congressional member, interview by the authors, June 2002, Washington, D.C.

22. Anonymous congressional member, interview by the authors, June 2002, Washington, D.C.

23. See, however, Canon (1995); Friedman (1993, 1996); Mixon and Ressler (2001); and Swain (1993).

24. See chapter 8 and Frisch and Kelly (2004).

25. This discussion must remain speculative at this point. Extensive data analysis within each period would be nearly impossible given the small number of African Americans who have served during each epoch. Nonetheless, we believe that considering the history of African Americans in the House in three

periods is a compelling means for better understanding the highly contextual nature of the African American experience in the House.

26. Friedman (1996) found that in the 1960s, 75 percent of initial committee assignments for African American members were in the bottom third of Michael Munger's (1988) index of committee prestige compared with only 40 percent of the initial assignments of white male members.

27. "There are a lot more veterans in my district than there are trees," Chisholm commented after receiving the Veterans' Affairs assignment (Foerstel and Foerstel 1996, 97). Despite predictions that her act of defiance marked the end of her political career, Chisholm was rewarded with a transfer to the Education and Labor Committee at the start of her second term and ultimately was chosen by Speaker O'Neill to be a member of the powerful Rules Committee.

28. On the early history of the CBC, see Barnett (1975).

29. Stokes, telephone interview by the authors, May 2003.

30. Ibid.

31. The details of the Stokes-Vanik dispute can be found in a letter from Joseph W. Bartunek, chair of the Cuyahoga County Democratic Executive Committee, to majority meader Carl Albert (December 2, 1970, box 129, folder 49, Legislative Files, 91st Congress, Albert Papers).

32. Charles C. Diggs, Jr., et al., to Vanik, December 8, 1970, box 129, folder 49, Legislative Files, 91st Congress, Albert Papers.

33. Stokes, telephone interview by the authors, May 2003.

34. Chair Hebert was so displeased with the two new additions to "his" committee that he had Dellums literally share a chair with the other unwanted newcomer, Pat Schroeder.

35. Anonymous congressional member, telephone interview by the authors, March 2003.

36. Anonymous congressional member, telephone interview by the authors, May 2003.

37. Manley (1970) contends that the Ways and Means Committee of the time had a southern orientation, which could have played a role in African American members' limited committee advancement.

38. Wright, interview by the authors, March 2001, Fort Worth, Texas.

39. An internal listing of the DSPC membership for the 96th Congress, for example, includes the following appointed members' names along with parenthetical notations: "Rangel (Blacks), Gray (Freshmen) and Spellman (Women)." December 7, 1978, box 61, folder 9, Democratic Steering and Policy Committee, O'Neill Papers.

40. Of the eight, three serve ex officio—deputy whip Maxine Waters (CA), deputy whip John Lewis (GA), and Ways and Means Committee ranking member Charles Rangel (NY)—and five are appointees of Democratic Leader

Gephardt—James Clyburn (SC), Elijah Cummings (MD), William Jefferson (LA), Carolyn Kilpatrick (MI), and Bennie Thompson (MS). The appointment of five African Americans (listed above), of sixteen total appointees by Gephardt, brings the total African American representation proportional to the size of African Americans as a percentage of the Democratic Caucus.

41. Future Budget chair and Office of Management and Budget director Leon Panetta was the fifth ballot winner, with thirteen votes. Future senators Tim Wirth (CO) and Bill Nelson (FL) and representative Steven Solarz (NY) also won seats on Budget in the 1979 balloting. Ballot totals, January 1977, unprocessed file, Wright Papers.

42. Along similar lines, Barone and Ujifusa (1985) describe racial resentment surrounding Gray's election: "His election was an even more considerable achievement than first appears. . . . House Democrats were in no mood to elect a black as chairman at a time when most voters associated blacks with unpopular big-spending programs" (1148).

43. The CBC also lost representation on the Rules Committee (Alan Wheat failed in his bid for Missouri governor and was not replaced on the Democratic delegation on Rules, which now stands at four members) and on Ways and Means (William Jefferson of Florida lost his seat, and Mel Reynolds (IL) resigned from Congress and was not replaced on the committee by another CBC member).

44. Anonymous leadership aide, interview by the authors, June 2002, Washington, D.C.

45. The seventeenth new CBC member, Bennie Thompson (D-MS), was elected in a special election to replace secretary of agriculture appointee Mike Espy, and Thompson's request was therefore not included with the other first-term members. The briefing book did not list requests for two new members.

46. See, for example, Johnson and Secret (1996).

47. The nine "new style" members are Earl Hilliard (AL), Bobby L. Rusch (IL), Mel Reynolds (IL), Cleo Fields (LA), Albert Wynn (MD), Mel Watt (NC), James Clyburn (SC), Robert (Bobby) Scott (VA), and Sanford Bishop, Jr. (GA).

48. Anonymous congressional member, telephone interview by the authors, March 2003.

49. Ibid.

50. On average, African Americans received 10 percent more of the vote between the 80th and 105th Congresses than their white colleagues received ($t = 10.92, p < .001$).

CHAPTER 10

1. Exploration of the relationship between committee assignments and policy outcomes is beyond the scope of this book. For a look at the relationship

between committee composition and public spending, see Frisch and Kelly (2002). See also Frisch (1998).

APPENDIX 1

1. It is not the purpose of this appendix to provide a comprehensive review of these measures. For an introduction to measures of voting power, see Taylor (1995) and Felsenthal and Machover (1998).

REFERENCES

ARCHIVES

Albert, Carl. Papers. Carl Albert Center Congressional Archives. University of Oklahoma, Norman.

Arends, Leslie Cornelius. Papers. Leslie Arends Congressional Collection (1930–1975). The Ames Library, Illinois Wesleyan University, Bloomington.

Bevill, Thomas. Papers. W. S. Hoole Special Collections, University of Alabama, Tuscaloosa.

Boggs, Corinne "Lindy." Papers. Manuscripts Department. Tulane University, New Orleans, Louisiana.

Boggs, Hale. Papers. Manuscripts Department. Tulane University, New Orleans, Louisiana.

Bonior, David. Papers. Walter P. Reuther Library, Wayne State University, Detroit.

Burke, James A. Papers (1959–1978). John F. Kennedy Presidential Library, Boston.

Corman, James C. Congressman James C. Corman Collection. California State University Northridge.

Dixon, Julian. Collection. Public Officials Papers. Special Collections. California State University Los Angeles

Fenno, Richard F., Jr. Research Interview Notes of Richard F. Fenno, Jr., with Members of the U.S. House of Representatives, 1959–1965. Internet copy (http://www.archives.gov/records_of_congress/oral_histories/fenno/interview_notes.html), Special Collections, Records of Congress, National Archives, Washington, D.C.

Foley, Thomas S. Congressional Papers. Manuscripts, Archives, and Special Collections. Washington State University Libraries, Pullman.

Ford, Gerald R. Congressional Papers, 1949–1973. Gerald R. Ford Library, Ann Arbor.

Frenzel, William E. Papers (1962–1997). Public Affairs. Manuscripts Collection. Minnesota Historical Society, St. Paul.

Gejdenson, Samuel. Papers. Archives and Special Collections at the Thomas J. Dodd Research Center. University of Connecticut, Storrs.

Griffiths, Martha Wright. Papers (1956–1976). Political Collections. Bentley Historical Library. University of Michigan, Ann Arbor.

Halleck, Charles Abraham. Papers. Political Papers. Lilly Library. Indiana University, Bloomington.

Horton, Frank. Papers. Political History. Rare Books and Special Collections. Rush Rhees Library. University of Rochester.

Johnson, Lyndon Baines. Oral History Collection. Lyndon Baines Johnson Library and Museum, Austin.

Kennelly, Barbara B. Papers. Archives and Special Collections at the Thomas J. Dodd Research Center. University of Connecticut, Storrs.

Lagomarsino, Robert J. Collection. California State University, Channel Islands.

Livingston, Robert. Papers. Manuscripts Department. Tulane University, New Orleans, Louisiana.

McDade, Joseph M. Congressional Papers Collection. Special Collections and University Archives. Weinberg Memorial Library. University of Scranton.

Martin, Jr., Joseph W. Papers. Special Collections. Stonehill College, Easton, Massachusetts.

Michel, Robert H. Papers. Dirksen Congressional Center, Pekin, Illinois.

Mills, Wilbur. Papers. Hendrix College, Conway, Arkansas.

O'Neill, Jr., Thomas P. Papers. John J. Burns Library. Boston College.

Rayburn, Sam. Papers (1913–1961). Congressional History Collection. The Center for American History. University of Texas, Austin.

Rhodes, John J. Minority Leader Papers, 1968–1980. Arizona Collection. Arizona State University Libraries, Tempe.

Roybal, Edward R. Collection. Collection. Public Officials Papers. Special Collections. University of California, Los Angeles.

Smathers, George A. United States Senator, 1951–1969. Oral History Interviews. Senate Historical Office, Washington, D.C.

Wright, James. Speaker Jim Wright Collection. Special Collections. Texas Christian University Library.

BOOKS, PERIODICALS, AND OTHER SOURCES

Achen, Christopher H., and John S. Stolarek. 1974. "The Resolution of Congressional Committee Assignment Contests: Factors Influencing the Democratic

Committee on Committees." Paper prepared for the annual meeting of the American Political Science Association, Washington, D.C.

Adler, E. Scott. 2000. "Constituency Characteristics and the 'Guardian' Model of Appropriations Subcommittees, 1959–1998." *American Journal of Political Science* 44 (1):104–114.

———. 2002. *Why Congressional Reforms Fail: Reelection and the House Committee System*. Chicago: University of Chicago Press.

Adler, E. Scott, and John S. Lapinski. 1997. "Demand-Side Theory and Congressional Committee Composition: A Constituency Characteristics Approach." *American Journal of Political Science* 41(3):895–918.

Adler, E. Scott, and John D. Wilkerson. 2001. "The Second Face of Committee Power: The Potential for Committee Gatekeeping." Paper presented at the annual meeting of the American Political Science Association, San Francisco, California.

Arnold, Laura W., and Barbara M. King. 2000. "Women, Committees and Power in the Senate." Paper prepared for the Annual Meeting of the American Political Science Association, Washington, D.C.

———. 2002. "Women, Committees and Institutional Change in the Senate." In *Women Transforming Congress*, ed. Cindy Simon Rosenthal, 284–315. Norman: University of Oklahoma Press.

Arnold, R. Douglas. 1979. *Congress and the Bureaucracy: A Theory of Influence*. New Haven: Yale University Press.

Banzhaf, John F. 1965. "Weighted Voting Doesn't Work: A Mathematical Analysis." *Rutgers Law Review* 19:317–43.

Barnett, Marguerite Ross. 1975. "The Congressional Black Caucus." *Proceedings of the Academy of Political Science* 32(1):34–50.

Barone, Michael, and Grant Ujifusa. Various years, 1976–2004. *The Almanac of American Politics*. Washington, DC: National Journal.

Barrett, Edith J. 1997. "Gender and Race in the State House: The Legislative Experience." *Social Science Journal* 34:131–44.

Barry, John M. 1989. *The Ambition and the Power*. New York: Viking.

Berkman, Michael B., and Robert E. O'Connor. 1993. "Do Women Legislators Matter? Female Legislators and State Abortion Policy." *American Politics Quarterly* 21(1):102–124.

Bickers, Kenneth N., and Robert M. Stein. 1991. *Federal Domestic Outlays, 1983–1990*. Armonk, N.Y.: M.E. Sharpe.

Biggs, Jeffrey R., and Thomas S. Foley. 1999. *Honor in the House: Speaker Tom Foley*. Pullman: Washington State University Press.

Billings, Erin P. 2003. "Pelosi Revamps the Steering Committee." *Roll Call*, March 13.

———. 2004. "Pelosi Seeks Rules Change; Plan Discourages Dissension." *Roll Call*, March 22.

Bingham, Clara. 1997. *Women on the Hill: Challenging the Culture of Congress.* New York: Times Books.

Birnbaum, Jeffrey H., and Alan S. Murray. 1987. *Showdown at Gucci Gulch: Lawmakers, Lobbyists, and the Unlikely Triumph of Tax Reform.* New York: Vintage Books.

Blow, Richard. 1993. "Foley Flexes." *Mother Jones* 18(4):30 (also available at http://www.motherjones.com/news/feature/1993/07/blow.html).

Bolton, Alexander. 2003. "House Leaders Tighten Grip, Anger Centrists." *The Hill,* January 15.

Bratton, Kathleen A., and Kerry L. Haynie. 1999. "Agenda Setting and Legislative Success in State Legislatures: The Effects of Gender and Race." *Journal of Politics* 61(3):658–79.

Bresnahan, John. 2000. "Some GOP Freshmen Bristle at Ban on Top Panel Seats: Hastert's Stance on a Reversal from 1994, When Gingrich Put 19 New Members on Three A-Level Committees." *Roll Call,* December 4.

Brown, George Rothwell. 1922/1974. *The Leadership of Congress.* New York: Arno Press. (Orig. pub. 1922 by Bobbs-Merrill.)

Brown, Sherrod. 1999. *Congress from the Inside: Observations from the Majority and the Minority.* Kent, Ohio: Kent State University Press.

Bullock, Charles S. 1972. "Freshman Committee Assignments and Re-election in the United States House of Representatives." *The American Political Science Review* 66(3):996–1007.

———. 1973. "Committee Transfers in the United States House of Representatives." *The Journal of Politics* 35(1):85–120.

———. 1976. "Motivations for U.S. Congressional Committee Preferences: Freshmen of the 92nd Congress." *Legislative Studies Quarterly* 1(2):201–212.

Burger, Timothy J. 1993. "No Stomach for Purge: Democrats Let Eleven Targeted Chairmen Keep Posts." *Roll Call,* June 10.

Canon, David T. 1995. "Redistricting and the Congressional Black Caucus." *American Politics Quarterly* 23(2):159–89.

Canon, David T., Matthew M. Schousen, and Patrick J. Sellers. 1996. "The Supply of Congressional Redistricting: Race and Strategic Politicians, 1972–1992." *Journal of Politics* 58(3):846–62.

Carroll, Susan J. 2002. "Representing Women: Congresswomen's Perceptions of the Their Representational Roles." In *Women Transforming Congress,* ed. Cindy Simon Rosenthal, 50–68. Norman: University of Oklahoma Press.

Chisholm, Shirley. 1970. *Unbought and Unbossed.* Boston: Houghton Mifflin Company.

Chiu, Chang-Wei. 1928. *The Speaker of the House of Representatives Since 1896.* New York: Columbia University Press).

Clapp, Charles L. 1964. *The Congressman: His Work as He Sees It.* Garden City, N.Y.: Doubleday.

Cohodas, Nadine. 1985. "Black Members: The Drive for Recognition." *Congressional Quarterly Weekly Report,* April 13:676.

Churchman, Deborah. 1981. "Illinois Congresswoman Brings Her Frugal Style to Washington. *The Christian Science Monitor,* January 8, 17.

Clapp, Charles L. 1964. *The Congressman: His Work as He Sees It.* Garden City, N.Y.: Doubleday.

Cleveland Plain Dealer. 1992. "Ohio's Setback in Washington." December 14.

Cohen, Richard E. 1979. "The Mysterious Ways Congress Makes Committee Assignments. *The National Journal* 11(5):183.

Connelly, William F., Jr., and John J. Pitney, Jr. 1994. *Congress' Permanent Minority: Republicans in the House.* Lanham, Md.: Rowman and Littlefield.

Cooper, Kenneth J. 1992. "Old and New Sound Much the Same: Freshmen House Democrats Stress Traditional Concerns of Party." *Washington Post,* November 10.

Cox, Gary, and Mathew McCubbins. 1993a. "Data From Legislative Leviathan." http://mmccubbins.ucsd.edu/polisciexperlab/mccubbin/data/index.htm. Accessed September 1, 2001.

Cox, Gary, and Mathew McCubbins. 1993b. *Legislative Leviathan: Party Government in the House.* Berkeley: University of California Press.

Davis, Phillip A. 1991. "Norm Dicks." *CO Weekly,* December 17, 25.

Deering, Christopher J., and Steven S. Smith. 1997. *Committees in Congress.* 3rd ed. Washington, D.C.: Congressional Quarterly Press.

Dellums, Ronald V., and H. Lee Halterman. 2000. *Lying Down with the Lions: A Public Life from the Streets of Oakland to the Halls of Power.* Boston: Beacon Press.

Dodd, Lawrence C. 1977. "Congress and the Quest for Power." In *Congress Reconsidered,* ed. Lawrence C. Dodd and Bruce I. Oppenheimer, 269–307. New York: Praeger.

Dodd, Lawrence C. 2004. "Political Science and the Study of Congress: Trends and New Trajectories." Paper prepared for the annual meeting of the Association of Centers for the Study of Congress, Woodrow Wilson International Center, Washington, D.C.

Dodson, Debra L. 1998. "Representing Women's Interests in the U.S. House of Representatives." In *Women and Elective Office,* ed. Sue Thomas and Clyde Wilcox, 130–49. New York: Oxford University Press.

Duncan, Phillip D., and Christine C. Lawrence. Various years. *Congressional Quarterly's Politics in America.* Washington, D.C.: CQ Press.

Eulau, Heinz. 1984. "Legislative Committee Assignments." *Legislative Studies Quarterly* 9(4):587–93.

———. 1985. "Committee Selection." In *Handbook of Legislative Research,* ed. Gehard Lowenberg, Samuel C. Patterson, and Malcolm Jewell, 191–237. Cambridge, Mass.: Harvard University Press.

Eulau, Heinz, and Vera McGluggage. 1984. "Standing Committees in Legislatures: Three Decades of Research." *Legislative Studies Quarterly* 9(2):195–270.

Farrell, John A. 2001. *Tip O'Neill and the Democratic Century.* Boston: Little, Brown.

Felsenthal, Dan, and Moshe Machover. 1998. *The Measurement of Voting Power: Theory and Practice, Problems and Paradoxes.* Cheltenham, UK: Edward Elgar.

Fenno, Richard F., Jr. 1966. *The Power of the Purse.* Boston: Little, Brown.

———. 1973. *Congressmen in Committees.* Boston: Little, Brown.

———. 1977. *Home Style: House Members in Their Districts.* Boston: Little, Brown.

———. 2000. *Congress at the Grassroots: Representational Change in the South, 1970–1998.* Chapel Hill: University of North Carolina Press.

———. 2003. *Going Home: Black Representatives and Their Constituents.* Chicago: University of Chicago Press.

Ferejohn, John. 1974. *Pork Barrel Politics.* Stanford, Calif.: Stanford University Press.

Foerstel, Karen, and Herbert N. Foerstel. 1996. *Climbing the Hill: Gender and Conflict in Congress.* Westport, Conn.: Praeger.

Friedman, Sally. 1993. "Committee Advancement of Women and Blacks in Congress: A Test of the Responsible Legislator Thesis." *Women and Politics* 13(1):27–52.

———. 1996. "House Committee Assignments of Women and Minority Newcomers, 1965–1994." *Legislative Studies Quarterly* 21:73–81.

Frisch, Scott A. 1998. *The Politics of Pork: A Study of Congressional Appropriations Earmarks.* New York: Garland Publishing.

Frisch, Scott A., and Sean Q Kelly. 2001. "The Other Half of the Puzzle: Republican Committee Assignments in the House: 1965–1991." Paper prepared for the annual meeting of the American Political Science Association, San Francisco, California.

———. 2002. "Distributive Theory Reconsidered: Federal Spending and Committee Assignments Revisited." Paper prepared for the annual meeting of the Northeastern Political Science Association, Providence, Rhode Island.

———. 2003a. "Don't Have the Data? Make Them Up!: Congressional Archives as Untapped Data Sources." *PS: Political Science and Politics* 36(2):221–24.

———. 2003b. "A Place at the Table: Women's Committee Requests and Women's Committee Assignments in the U.S. House." *Women and Politics* 25(3):1–26.

———. 2004. "Self-Selection Reconsidered: House Committee Assignment Request and Constituency Characteristics." *Political Research Quarterly* 57(2):325–36.

Georges, Christopher. 1996. "Liars, Gays, Aliens, Hispanics, Women: It's All Their Fault." *Wall Street Journal*, November 20.

Gertzog, Irwin N. 1976. "The Routinization of Committee Assignments in the U.S. House of Representatives." *American Journal of Political Science* 20(4):693–712.

———. 1995. *Congressional Women: Their Recruitment, Integration, and Behavior.* 2nd ed. Westport, Conn.: Praeger.

Getlin, Josh. 1990. "What Makes Henry Tick?" *Los Angeles Times,* April 25.

Gist, John R., and R. Carter Hill. 1984. "Political and Economic Influences on Bureaucratic Allocation of Federal Funds: The Cast of Urban Development Action Grants." *Journal of Urban Economics* 16:158–72.

Goodwin, George, Jr. 1970. *The Little Legislatures: Committees in Congress.* Amherst: University of Massachusetts Press.

Granat, Diane. 1985. "1st Freshman Test: The Right Committee Seat." *CQ Weekly,* February 2, 172–75.

Groseclose, Timothy. 1994. "Testing Committee Composition Hypotheses for the U.S. Congress." *Journal of Politics* 56(2):440–58.

Groseclose, Timothy, and Charles Stewart III. 1998. "The Value of Committee Seats in the House, 1947–1991." *American Journal of Political Science* 42(2):453–74.

Grumm, John G. 1963. "A Factor Analysis of Legislative Behavior." *Midwest Journal of Political Science* 7:336–56.

Hall, Richard L. 1996. *Participation in Congress.* New Haven, Conn.: Yale University Press.

Hall, Richard L., and Bernard Grofman. 1990. "The Committee Assignment Process and the Conditional Nature of Committee Bias." *American Political Science Review* 84(4):1149–66.

Hasbrouck, Paul De Witt. 1927. *Party Government in the House of Representatives.* New York: The Macmillan Company.

Heberlig, Eric S. 2000. "I'm Giving at the Office: The Influence of Campaign Contributions by Members of Congress." Paper delivered at the annual meeting of the Southern Political Science Association, Atlanta, Georgia.

Heberlig, Eric S., and Bruce Larson. 2002. "Campaign Contributions by Members of Congress: The Spiraling Costs of the Permanent Campaign." Paper delivered at the annual meeting of the Midwest Political Science Association, Chicago, Illinois.

Hook, Janet. 1987. "Bitterness Lingers from GOP Assignments." *CQ Weekly,* May 16, 961.

ICPSR [Inter-university Consortium for Political and Social Research] and Carroll McKibbin. 1997. "Roster of United States Congressional Officeholders and Biographical Characteristics of Members of the United States Congress, 1789–1996: Merged Data." [Computer file] 10th ed. Ann Arbor, Mich.: ICPSR.

Jacobs, John. 1995. *A Rage for Justice: The Passion and Politics of Phillip Burton.* Berkeley: University of California Press.

Jewel, Malcom E., and Chu Chi-hung. 1974. "Membership Movement and Committee Attractiveness in the U.S. House of Representatives, 1963–1971." *Midwest Journal of Political Science* 18:433–41.

Johnson, James B., and Philip E. Secret. 1996. "Focus and Style: Representational Roles of Congressional Black and Hispanic Caucus Members." *Journal of Black Studies* 26(3):245–74.

Johnston, Robert J. 1978. "On the Measurement of Power: Some Restrictions to Laver." *Environment and Planning* 10:907–914.

Kanter, Rosabeth Moss. 1977. "Some Effects of Proportions on Group Life: Skewed Sex Ratios and Responses to Token Women." *American Journal of Sociology* 82(5):965–90.

Keller, Amy. 1997. "'I Want to Be Off and I Want to Be Off Immediately' Newly Released Papers of Former Minority Leader Bob Michel Reveal the Pleading, Cajoling, And Just Plain Begging That Members Stooped to in Order to Get On or Off House Committees." *Roll Call,* September 15.

Kennedy, David M. 1989. "Among Friends: Lynn Martin, Jerry Lewis, and the Race for the Chair of the House Republican Conference." Case Program 885, Kennedy School of Government. Cambridge, Mass.: The President and the Regents of Harvard College.

Kiewiet, D. Roderick, and Mathew D. McCubbins. 1991. *The Logic of Delegation: Congressional Parties and the Appropriations Process.* Chicago: University of Chicago Press.

Kim, Jae-On, and Charles Meuller. 1978. *Factor Analysis: Statistical Methods and Practical Issues.* Thousand Oaks, Calif.: Sage Publications.

Kingdon, John. 1973. *Congressmen's Voting Decisions.* Ann Arbor: University of Michigan Press.

Kluger, Richard. 1996. *Ashes to Ashes: America's Hundred-Year Cigarette War, the Public Health, and the Unabashed Triumph of Philip Morris.* New York: Alfred A. Knopf.

Kolodny, Robin. 1999. "Moderate Success: Majority Status and the Changing Nature of Factionalism in the House Republican Party." In *New Majority or Old Minority: The Impact of Republicans on Congress,* ed. Nicol C. Rae and Colton C. Campbell, 153–72. Lanham, Md.: Rowman and Littlefield.

Koopman, Douglas L. 1996. *Hostile Takeover: The House Republican Party, 1980–1995.* Lanham, Md.: Rowman and Littlefield.

Krehbiel, Keith. 1990. "Are Committees Composed of Preference Outliers?" *American Political Science Review* 84(1):149–63.

———. 1991. *Information and Legislative Organization.* Ann Arbor: University of Michigan Press.

Lawrence, Eric D., Forrest Maltzman, and Paul J Wahlbeck. 2001. "The Politics of Speaker Cannon's Committee Assignments." *American Journal of Political Science* 45(3):551.

Lehman, William. 2000. *Mr. Chairman: The Journal of a Congressional Appropriator.* Lanham, Md.: University Press of America.

Londregan, J., and J. M. Snyder, Jr. 1994. "Comparing Committee and Floor Preferences." *Legislative Studies Quarterly* 19(2):233–66.

Maass, Arthur. 1983. *Congress and the Common Good.* New York: Basic Books.

Machiavelli, Niccolò. 1950. *The Prince.* New York: Modern Library.

Maltzman, Forrest. 1999. *Competing Principals: Committees, Parties, and the Organization of Congress.* Ann Arbor: University of Michigan Press.

Manley, John F. 1970. *The Politics of Finance: The House Committee on Ways and Means.* Boston: Little, Brown.

Margulies, Herbert F. 1996. "James R. Mann's Apprenticeship in the House of Representatives, 1897–1908." *Congress and the Presidency* 26(1):21–40.

Martin, Joseph W., with Roberty J. Donovan. 1960. *My First Fifty Years in Politics.* New York: McGraw-Hill.

Masters, Nicholas A. 1961. "Committee Assignments in the U.S. House of Representatives." *American Political Science Review* 55(2):345–57.

Mayhew, David R. 1974. *Congress: The Electoral Connection.* New Haven: Yale University Press.

McGlen, Nancy E. and Karen O'Connor. 1998. *Women, Politics, and American Society.* 2nd ed. Upper Saddle River, N.J.: Prentice-Hall.

Mixon, Franklin G., Jr., and Rand W. Ressler. 2001. "Loyal Political Cartels and Committee Assignments in Congress: Evidence from the Congressional Black Caucus." *Public Choice* 108:313–30.

Mooney, Christopher Z. 1997. *Monte Carlo Simulation.* Thousand Oaks, Calif.: Sage Publications.

Mooney, Christopher Z., and Robert D. Duval. 1993. *Bootstrapping: A Non-Parametric Approach to Statistical Inference.* Newbury Park, Calif.: Sage Publications.

Munger, Michael. 1988. "Allocation of Desirable Committee Assignments: Extended Cues vs. Committee Expansion." *American Journal of Political Science* 32(2):317–44.

Nelson, Garrison and Clark H. Bensen. 1993–1994. *Committees in the U.S. Congress, 1947–1992.* Washington, D.C.: Congressional Quarterly Books, vol. 2.

Neustadt, Richard E. 1990. *Presidential Power and the Modern Presidents.* New York: Free Press.

Norton, Noelle. 1995. "Women, It's Not Enough to Be Elected: Committee Position Makes a Difference." In *Gender, Power, Leadership, and Governance,* ed. Georgia Duerst-Lahti and Rita Mae Kelly, 115–40. Ann Arbor: University of Michigan.

———. 1999. "Committee Influence over Controversial Policy: The Reproductive Policy Case." *Policy Studies Journal* 27:203–216.

———. 2002. "Transforming Policy from the Inside: Participation in Committee." In *Women Transforming Congress,* ed. Cindy Simon Rosenthal, 316–40. Norman: University of Oklahoma Press.

Olson, Mancur. 1965. *The Logic of Collective Action.* Cambridge, Mass.: Harvard University Press.

Owens, John R., and Larry L. Wade. 1984. "Federal Spending in Congressional Districts." *Western Political Quarterly* 37:404–423.

Parker, Glenn R., and Suzanne Parker. 1979. "Factions in Committees: The U.S. House of Representatives." *American Political Science Review* 73(1):85–102.

———. 1985. *Factions in House Committees*. Knoxville: University of Tennessee Press.

Peabody, Robert L. 1966. *The Ford-Halleck Minority Leader Contest, 1965*. Eagleton Institute, Cases in Practical Politics. New York: McGraw-Hill.

———. 1976. *Leadership in the House: Stability, Succession and Change*. Boston: Little, Brown.

Peters, Ronald M., Jr. 1997. *The American Speakership: The Office in Historical Perspective*. Baltimore, Md.: Johns Hopkins University Press.

Peterson, Geoffrey D., and Mark J. Wrighton. 1998. "The Continuing Puzzle of Committee Outliers: A Methodological Reassessment." *Congress and the Presidency* 25:67–79.

Petrocik, John R. 1996. "Issue Ownership in Presidential Elections with a 1980 Case Study." *American Journal of Political Science* 40(3):825–50.

Plott, Charles R. 1968. "Some Organizational Influences on Urban Renewal Decisions." *American Economic Review* 58:306–321.

Poole, Keith, and Howard Rosenthal. 1997. *Congress: A Political-Economic History of Roll Call Voting*. New York: Oxford University Press.

Price, David E. 1992. *The Congressional Experience: A View from the Hill*. Boulder, Colo.: Westview Press.

Rae, Nicol C. 1989. *The Decline and Fall of the Liberal Republicans: From 1952 to the Present*. New York: Oxford University Press.

Ray, Bruce A. 1980. "Federal Spending and the Selection of Committee Assignments in the U.S. House of Representatives." *American Journal of Political Science* 24(3):494–510.

———. 1981. "Military Committee Membership in the House of Representatives and the Allocation of Defense Department Outlays." *Western Political Quarterly* 34:222–34.

———. 1982a. "Causation in the Relationship Between Congressional Position and Federal Spending." *Polity* 14:676–90.

———. 1982b. "Committee Attractiveness in the U.S. House 1963–1981." *American Journal of Political Science* 26:609–613.

Reiter, Howard. 1981. "Intra-Party Cleavages in the United States Today." *Western Political Quarterly* 34:287–300.

Ripley, Randall B. 1969. *Majority Party Leadership in Congress*. Boston: Little, Brown.

Ritt, Leonard G. 1976. "Committee Position, Seniority and the Distribution of Government Expenditures." *Public Policy* 24(4):561–89.

Roberts, Steven V. 1983a. "Democrats Reward Loyalty in Giving Assignments." *New York Times,* January 6.

———. 1983b. "Four House Freshmen and the Jobs They Came to Do." *New York Times,* January 12.

Rohde, David W. 1991. *Parties and Leaders in the Postreform House.* Chicago: University of Chicago Press.

———. 1995. "Parties and Committees in the House: Member Motivations, Issues, and Institutional Arrangements." In *Positive Theories of Congressional Institutions,* ed. Kenneth A. Shepsle and Barry Weingast, 119–37. Ann Arbor: University of Michigan Press.

Rohde, David W., and Kenneth A. Shepsle. 1973. "Democratic Committee Assignments in the House of Representatives: Strategic Aspects of a Social Choice Process." *American Political Science Review* 67(3):889–905.

Rosenthal, Cindy Simon. 1998. "Getting Things Done: Women Committee Chairpersons in State Legislatures." In *Women and Elective Office,* ed. Sue Thomas and Clyde Wilcox, 175–87. New York: Oxford University Press.

Salant, Jonathan D. 1994. "Retrenching House Democrats Seek Solace in Seniority." *Congressional Quarterly Weekly Report 52, no. 49 (December 17): 3543–45.*

Schroedel, Jean Reith, and Tanya Buhler Corbin. 2002. "Gender Relations and Institutional Conflict Over Mifepristone." *Women and Politics* 24(3):35–59.

Schroeder, Pat. 1998. *24 Years of House Work and the Place Is Still a Mess: My Life in Politics.* Kansas City: Andrews McMeel Publishing.

Shapiro, Margaret. 1985. "Plums Hold House Democrats' Attention: Ways and Means Seats Are Among the Most Desired Prizes." *Washington Post,* January 20.

Sheppard, Burton D. 1985. *Rethinking Congressional Reform.* Cambridge, Mass.: Schenkman Books.

Shepsle, Kenneth A. 1978. *The Giant Jigsaw Puzzle: Democratic Committee Assignments in the Modern House.* Chicago: University of Chicago Press.

———. 1983a. "The Failure of Congressional Budgeting." *Society* 20:4–10.

———. 1983b. "Overgrazing the Budgetary Commons: Incentive-Compatible Solutions to the Problems of Deficits." In *The Economic Consequences of Government Deficits,* ed. Lawrence H. Meyer, 211–19. Boston: Kluwer-Nijhoff.

———. 1984. "The Congressional Budget Process: Diagnosis, Prescription, Prognosis." In W. Thomas Wander, F. Ted Hebert and Gary W. Copeland (eds.) *Congressional Budgeting: Politics, Process and Power.* Baltimore, Md.: Johns Hopkins University Press.

Shepsle, Kenneth A., and Barry R. Weingast. 1984. "Legislative Politics and Budget Outcomes." In *Federal Budget Policy in the 1980s,* ed. Gregory B. Mills and John L. Palmer, 343–67. Washington, D.C.: Urban Institute Press.

———. 1985. "Policy Consequences of Government by Congressional Subcommittees." In *Control of Federal Spending,* ed. C. Lowell Harris, 114–31. Proceedings of the Academy of Political Science, New York.

———. 1987. "The Institutional Foundations of Committee Power." *American Political Science Association* 81:929–45.

———. 1995. *Positive Theories of Congressional Institutions.* Ann Arbor: University of Michigan Press.

Sinclair, Barbara. 1988. "The Distribution of Committee Positions in the U.S. Senate: Explaining Institutional Change." *American Journal of Political Science* 43(2):963–73.

———. 1995. *Legislators, Leaders, and Lawmaking: The U.S. House of Representatives in the Postreform Era.* Baltimore, Md.: Johns Hopkins University Press.

Sisk, Bernie F., and Avrom I. Dickman. 1980. *The Memoir of Bernie Sisk: An Oral History Conducted by A. I. Dickman.* Fresno, Calif.: Panorama West.

Smith, Hedrick. 1996. "The Elected: The Presidency and Congress." The People and the Power Game, Program Two. VHS. Chevy Chase, Md.: Hedrick Smith Productions. (Original airdate on PBS: September 10, 1996.)

Smith, Robert C. 1981. "The Black Congressional Delegation." *Western Political Quarterly* 34:203–221.

Smith, Steven S., and Christopher J. Deering. 1984. *Committees in Congress.* Washington, D.C.: Congressional Quarterly Press.

Smith, Steven S., and Bruce A. Ray. 1983. "The Impact of Congressional Reform: House Democratic Committee Assignments." *Congress and the Presidency* 10:219–40.

Stein, Robert M., and Kenneth N. Bickers. 1995. *Perpetuating the Pork Barrel: Policy Subsystems and American Democracy.* Cambridge: University of Cambridge Press.

Stewart, Charles, III, and Jonathon Woon. 1998. "Congressional Committee Assignments, 103rd to 105th Congresses, 1993–1998: House." http://web.mit.edu/17.251/www/data_page.html. Accessed September 1, 2001.

Strahan, Randall. 1990. *New Ways and Means: Reform and Change in a Congressional Committee.* Chapel Hill: University of North Carolina Press.

Strand, Jonathan R. 1999. "State Power in a Multilateral Context: Voting Strength in the Asian Development Bank." *International Interactions* 25(3):265–86.

Swain, Carol M. 1993. *Black Faces, Black Interests: The Representation of African Americans in Congress.* Cambridge, Mass.: Harvard University Press.

Swers, Michele L. 2002a. *The Difference Women Make: The Policy Impact of Women in Congress.* Chicago: University of Chicago Press.

———. 2002b. "Transforming the Agenda: Analyzing Gender Differences in Women's Issue Bill Sponsorship." In *Women Transforming Congress,* ed. Cindy Simon Rosenthal, 260–84. Norman: University of Oklahoma Press.

Taylor, Alan D. 1995. *Mathematics and Politics: Strategy, Voting, Power and Proof.* New York: Springer-Verlag.

Thomas, Sue. 1994. *How Women Legislate.* Oxford: Oxford University Press.

Wagner, Anne. 2001. "Former House Speaker Newt Gingrich: Musical Chairs." *NationalJournal.com*, January 17.

Waldman, Sidney. 1980. "Majority Leadership in the House of Representatives." *Political Science Quarterly* 95(3):373–93.

Weber, Robert P. 1985. *Basic Content Analysis: Quantitative Applications in the Social Sciences.* No. 49. London: Sage Publications.

Weingast, Barry R., and William J. Marshall. 1988. "The Industrial Organization of Congress: Or, Why Legislatures, Like Firms, Are Not Organized as Markets." *Journal of Political Economy* 96(1):132–63.

White, Joseph. 1989. "The Functions and Power of the House Appropriations Committee." PhD dissertation, University of California, Berkeley.

Wilson, Woodrow. 1885/1981. *Congressional Government: A Study in American Politics.* Baltimore, Md.: Johns Hopkins University Press.

Wright, James C., Jr. 1996. *Balance of Power: Presidents and Congress from the Era of McCarthy to the Age of Gingrich.* Atlanta: Turner Publishing.

Zelizer, Julian E. 1998. *Taxing America: Wilbur Mills, Congress, and the State, 1945–1975.* Cambridge, UK: Cambridge University Press.

———. 2004. *On Capitol Hill: The Struggle to Reform Congress and Its Consequences, 1948–2000.* New York: Cambridge University Press.

Zuckman, Jill. 1992. "Committees: Most House Chairmen Hold On: Freshmen Win Choice Posts." *CQ Weekly*, December 12, 3785.

Name Index

Abdnor, James (R-SD), 88
Abourezk, Jim (D-SD), 271
Adler, E. Scott, 13
Akaka, Daniel (D-HI), 87
Albert, Carl (D-OK), 3, 155, 196–202, 283, 308, 355n21
Ambro, James Anthony, Jr. (D-NY), 206
Andrews, Mike (D-TX), 210–11
Archer, Bill (R-TX), 161
Arends, Leslie (R-IL), 185
Aspin, Les (D-WI), 92–93

Battin, James F. (R-MT), 185
Beilenson, Anthony (D-CA), 204, 369n50
Bennett, Marion T. (R-MO), 180
Bereuter, Doug (R-NE), 88
Berman, Howard (D-CA), 3, 251, 326
Bilbray, James (D-NV), 84
Boggs, Hale (D-LA), 196–97
Boland, Edward (D-MA), 366n31
Bolling, Richard (D-MO), 4, 155–56, 202, 204, 268, 355n21, 361n20

Bonior, David (D-MI), 206
Bono, Mary (R-CA), 302
Bono, Sonny (R-CA), 257
Boxer, Barbara (D-CA), 270
Brademas, John (D-IN), 200
Breaux, John (D-LA), 251
Brooks, Jack (D-TX), 204, 212
Broomfield (R-MI), 241
Brown, Hank (R-CO), 8, 140, 245
Bryant, John (D-TX), 214, 253
Buchanan, John H., Jr. (R-AL), 364n9
Buechner, Jack (R-MO), 86
Bunning, Jim (R-KY), 245
Burke, James (D-MA), 367n36
Burleson, Omar (D-TX), 206
Burton, Dan (R-IN), 261
Burton, Phil (D-CA), 204, 251–53, 326, 351n3, 369n50
Bush, George H. W. (R-TX), 141–42, 372n3
Bush, George W., 208
Byrne, Leslie (D-VA), 219, 371n71

Calkins, John T., 184

Cannon, Clarence (D-MO), 200

Cannon, Joseph (R-IL), 169, 179, 354n2

Carey, Hugh (D-NY), 140

Carroll, John (D-CO), 196–97

Carter, Jimmy, 240

Cederberg, Alfred (R-MI), 364n15

Chapman, Jim (D-TX), 212

Cheney, Richard (R-WY), 189, 249, 355n19

Chisholm, Shirley (D-NY), 304–306, 375n2, 378n27

Church, Frank (D-ID), 367n36

Clay, William (D-MO), 308

Clyburn, James (D-SC), 378n40

Coelho, Tony (D-CA), 251, 270, 310

Cohen William (R-ME), 83

Combs, Jesse Martin (D), 195, 197

Cooper, Jim (D-TN), 141

Coughlin, Lawrence (R-PA), 88

Coyne, William (D-PA), 210

Cummings, Elijah (D-MD), 378n40

Dannemeyer, William (R-CA), 372n10

Daschle, Tom (D-SD), 270–71

Davis, Jack (R-IL), 247, 363n56

Davis, Robert W. (R-MI), 186

Delaney, James Joseph (D-NY), 206

DeLay, Tom (R-TX), 160, 373n16

Dellums, Ronald (D-CA), 91–93, 305, 307–309, 331, 358n32, 378n34

Denney, Robert V. (R-NE), 183

Denton, Wilfred (D-OH), 198

Derrick, Butler (D-SC), 153–57, 205–206, 213

Dickinson, Bill (R-AL), 43, 184, 240

Dicks, Norman (D-WA), 271–72

Dingell, John (D-MI), 212–13, 251, 270

Ditka, Mike, 172

Donahue, Phil, 171

Donnelly, Brian (D-MA), 210

Dornan, Robert K. (R-CA), 163–70, 329–31

Doughton, Robert L. (D-NC), 365n27

Downey, Tom (D-NY), 164, 207

Drier, David (R-CA), 141

Duncan, John (R-TN), 140–41

Duncan, Richard (D-MO), 365n25

Dunn, Thomas (R-NY), 36

Durbin, Richard (D-IL), 81, 210

Edmondson, Ed (D-OK), 200

Edwards, Mickey (R-OK), 100

Engel, Eliot (D-NY), 84

Espy, Mike, 379n45

Fazio, Vic (D-CA), 64–65

Feighan, Mike (D-OH), 196–97

Fiedler, Bobbi (R-CA), 292, 301

Flippo, Ronnie (D-AL), 207

Foley, Thomas S. (D-WA), 132, 214–16, 270, 283

Forbes, Michael (R-NY), 365n24

Ford, Gerald R. (R-MI), 43, 82–83, 141–42, 181–82, 183–87, 364n9, 372n3

Fountain, L. C. (D-NC), 369n49

Fowler, Tillie (R-FL), 301

Fowler, Wyche (D-GA), 207

Franklin, Webb (R-MS), 81

Frenzel, Bill (R-MN), 33, 373n15

Fulbright, William (D-AR), 367n36

Fulton, James (R-PA), 185

Funderburk, Sapp, 155

Gemayel, Bachir, 109

Gephardt, Richard (D-MO), 65, 216–18, 378n40

Gillett, Frederick (R-MA), 35

Gingrich, Newt (R-GA), 51, 169, 189–93, 214, 355n19

Goldwater, Barry (R-AZ), 372n3

Goodell, Charles (R-NY), 185

Gore, Albert, Jr. (D-TN), 274–75

Gramm, Phil (D-TX), 211

Grandy, Fred (D-IA), 257
Gray, William H., III (D-PA), 310–11, 379n42
Gregg, Judd (R-NH), 224
Griffiths, Martha (D-MI), 291
Guarini, Frank (D-NJ), 207

Hall, Katie (D-IN), 87
Hall, Sam B., Jr. (D-TX), 206–208
Halleck, Charles (R-IN), 39, 43, 179, 181–83, 185
Hance, Kent (D-TX), 208–10
Hansen, Julia Butler (D-WA), 272
Hasbrouck, Paul DeWitt, 35
Hastert, Dennis (R-IL), 87, 172, 193, 249
Hebert, E. Edward (D-LA), 358n32
Hebert, F. Edward (D-LA), 92, 197, 308, 378n34
Heckler, Margaret M. (R-MA), 289, 376n9
Heftel, Cecil (D-HI), 207
Hollenbeck, Harold (R-NJ), 100
Horton, Frank (R-NY), 240, 373n15
Hunter, Duncan (R-CA), 91, 166

Jarman, John (D-OK), 200
Jefferson, Thomas, 13
Jefferson, William (D-LA), 378n40
Johnson, Harold T. ("Bizz") (D-CA), 203–204
Johnson, Lyndon Baines (D-TX), 134, 365n25
Jones, James (D-OK), 201, 310
Jordan, Barbara (D-TX), 376n7

Kasten, Bob (R-WI), 186
Kemp, Jack (R-NY), 112
Kennedy, John F., 199, 367n36
Kilpatrick, Carolyn (D-MI), 378n40
King, Cecil (D-CA), 195, 197
Kleczka, Gerald (D-WI), 142–43

Koch, Edward, 140
Kolbe, Jim (R-AZ), 160–62, 362n53

Lagomarsino, Robert J. (R-CA), 50, 292, 362n54
Landrum, Phil (D-GA), 198–99
Largent, Steve (R-OK), 257
Larsen, Billie, 203, 207
LeBoutillier, John, 368n43
Lehman, Rick (D-CA), 326
Lehman, William (D-FL), 311
Lewis, Jerry (R-CA), 166–67, 243–44, 362n55, 372n10
Lewis, John (D-GA), 378n40
Livingston, Robert (R-LA), 189–90, 192
Long, Gillis (D-LA), 326
Long, Russell (D-LA), 367n36
Lott, Trent (R-MS), 50, 189, 245, 247, 270

Macdonald, Torbert H. (D-MA), 96, 366n31
Madden, Ray J. (D-IN), 202, 356n21
Madigan, Edward (R-IL), 190
Madison, James, 12–13, 14, 352n14
Magnuson, Warren (D-WA), 271–72
Mahon, George (D-TX), 208–209
Mallary, Richard W. (R-VT), 44, 83
Mann, James R. (R-IL), 35–36, 354n2
Margulies, Herbert F., 36
Martin, Joseph W., Jr. (R-MA), 39, 179–81, 363n3, 364n4
Martin, Lynn (R-IL), 157–63, 247, 375n4
Masters, Nicholas, 28, 40–43
Mathias, Robert (R-CA), 82
Mattox. Jim (D-TX), 204–205
May, Catherine (R-WA), 376n9
Mayhew, David R., 18
McCloskey, Frank (D-IN), 359n13
McCormack, John W. (D-MA), 195, 197–202, 365n25

McCurdy, Dave (D-OK), 214–16
McDade, Joseph (R-PA), 240
McSpadden, Clem (D-OK), 201
Meek, Carrie (D-FL), 311–12
Michel, Robert H. (R-IL), 7, 50–51, 132, 158, 162, 179, 187–89, 232, 237–38, 270, 285, 362n54, 364n15
Mikva, Abner (D-IL), 207
Miller, George (D-CA), 214
Mills, Wilbur D. (D-AR), 57, 66, 144, 155, 194–98, 308, 365n25, 366n31, 375n24
Mitchell, Donald (D-NY), 142
Molinari, Guy (R-NY), 273
Molinari, Susan (R-NY), 273, 301
Moore, Henson (R-LA), 240
Moore, J. Hampton (R-PA), 36
Morse, Wayne (R-OR), 367n36
Moss, John E., Jr. (D-CA), 375n24
Mrazek, Robert (D-NY), 368n43
Murtha, John Patrick, Jr. (D-PA), 210, 251

Nelson, William (D-FL), 379n41
Neumann, Mark (R-WI), 190, 365n24

Oberstar, James (D-MN), 207, 210
O'Brien, Lawrence F., 199
O'Brien, Tom (D-IL), 195, 197
O'Neill, Thomas P. ("Tip"), Jr. (D-MA), 65, 92, 132, 156, 202–206, 268–70, 283, 355n21, 366n31, 366n33, 368n43, 369n50
Osborne, Tom (R-NE), 257

Panetta, Leon (D-CA), 86, 310, 379n41
Parker, Mike (R-MS), 371n71
Pashayan, Chip (R-CA), 87
Patterson, Jerry M. (D-CA), 167, 203–204, 369n47
Pease, Donald (D-OH), 171–72
Pelosi, Nancy (D-CA), 65, 88, 218–19, 357n24

Ploesser, Walter O. (R-MO), 180
Porter, John (R-IL), 158
Preyer, Richardson (D-NC), 4
Price, David (D-NC), 371n63

Rangel, Charles (D-NY), 305–306, 378n40
Rayburn, Samuel Taliaferro (D-TX), 181, 194–98, 364n6, 365n27, 366n33
Reagan, Ronald, 66, 209–10, 241
Rhodes, John J. (R-AZ), 7–8, 132, 183–87, 281
Richardson, Bill (D-NM), 270
Riley, John J. (D-SC), 199
Rockefeller, Nelson (R-NY), 372n3
Roemer, Buddy (D-LA), 326
Rogers, Harold (R-KY), 68
Rose, Charlie (D-NC), 214
Rostenkowski, Daniel (D-IL), 171–72, 207, 209–10, 212, 251, 373n14
Rumsfeld, Donald (R-IL), 182, 270
Russo, Martin (D-IL), 207

Sanchez, Loretta (D-CA), 169
Sanders, Bernie (I-VT), 218
Savage, Gus (D-IL), 83
Schneider, Claudine (R-RI), 293, 300–301
Schroeder, Patricia (D-CO), 92–93, 300, 331, 378n34
Schumer, Charles (D-NY), 113, 140
Sensenbrenner, James (R-WI), 351n8
Shannon, James (D-MA), 207
Siljander, Mark (R-MI), 109
Sisk, Bernie F. (D-CA), 203, 369n50
Slaughter, D. French (R-VA), 88
Smathers, George A. (D-FL), 367n36
Smith, Christopher (R-NJ), 85
Smith, H. Allen (R-CA), 82
Smith, Howard Worth (D-VA), 202
Solarz, Steven (D-NY), 379n41
Stangeland, Arlan (R-MN), 44, 66

Steed, Thomas (D-OK), 184, 200
Stockman, David (R-MI), 270
Stokes, Louis (D-OH), 170–71, 305–307
Swindall, Patrick (R-GA), 85

Taber, John (R-NY), 364n4
Taylor, Gene (R-MO), 8
Thomas, William (R-CA), 7–11
Thompson, Bennie (D-MS), 378n40, 379n45
Thompson, Frank (D-NJ), 251
Torres, Esteban (D-CA), 326
Tower, John (D-TX), 210
Traficant, James A., Jr. (D-OH), 170–73
Truman, Harry S., 365n27

Utt, James (R-CA), 185

Vanik, Charles A. (D-OH), 306–307
Vucanovich, Barbara (R-NV), 160

Wampler, William (R-VA), 7
Waters, Maxine (D-CA), 378n40

Waxman, Henry (D-CA), 3–6, 217, 251, 351n3, 361n20
Weber, Vin (R-MN), 160
Wheat, Alan (D-MO), 268, 379n43
Wilkinson, Jay (R-OK), 184
Wilson, Pete (R-CA), 8
Wilson, Woodrow, 11–13
Winslow, Samuel (R-MA), 36
Wirth, Tim (D-CO), 379n41
Wright, James (D-TX), 4, 65, 132, 150, 170, 175, 204, 206–14, 258, 283, 309, 376n7
Wyden, Ron (D-OR), 84
Wydler, Jack (R-NY), 182

Young, John (D-TX), 203, 205
Young, Stephen (D-OH), 197

Zablocki, Clement (D-WI), 84
Zeferetti, Leo (D-NY), 206
Zschau, Ed (R-CA), 109

General Index

Tables and Figures are identified by "t" and "f," respectively.

African Americans. *See* Congressional Black Caucus (CBC); Ethnic issues; Race; Women

African Growth and Opportunities Act, 10

Agriculture Committee: assignment politics and, 335; committee requests for, 101; constituent interests and, 71, 81–82, 97; distributive theory and, 25; federal spending and, 121–25; interest group scores and, 117–20; member justification for, 271; member motivation and, 7–8, 332; occupational background and, 148–50; party-cartel theory and, 23–24; race and, 313–14; self-selection hypothesis and, 107–108, 114–15; women and, 304

American Farm Bureau Federation (AFBF), 118–19t

American Federation of State, County, and Municipal Employees (AFSCME), 118–19t

American Federation of Teachers (AFT), 118–19t

American Security Council (ASC), 118–19t

Americans for Democratic Action (ADA), 204, 239t, 240

Andean Trade Preference Act, 10

Appropriations Committee: assignment politics and, 335; Carl Albert influence on, 200–201; committee assignments and, 105–106, 157–63, 166, 216, 231–32; deficit spending and, 134–36; DSPC and, 64; institutional power and, 72, 87–89; John McCormack influence on, 199; legislative process and, 27; member justification for, 141–42, 271–72; member motivation and, 74–75, 80–81; party-cartel theory and, 23–24; race and, 304–306, 310–12, 315; RCC and, 54, 362n50; seniority and, 101; women and, 294–95, 301

Armed Services Committee: committee assignments and, 159, 164–69, 232; committee requests for, 104, 329–32; constituent interests and, 82, 90–94; distributive theory and, 25; federal spending and, 121–25; interest group scores and, 117–20; occupational background and, 148–50; party-cartel theory and, 23–24; race and, 307–309; self-selection hypothesis and, 108–109, 114–15; women and, 294–95, 300

Banking and Finance Committee: committee assignments and, 232; committee requests for, 101, 105–106; federal spending and, 121–25; interest group scores, 118t; member justification for, 140–41; member motivation and, 85–86; occupational background and, 148–50; party-cartel theory and, 23–24; public policy role of, 78; race and, 303–304, 310, 315; self-selection hypothesis and, 113
Banzhaf Power Index (BPI), 35, 339–43
Blue Dog, Democrat, 151–52, 217
Breast and Cervical Cancer Mortality Prevention Act, 5
Bribery, 170, 172
Budget Committee: committee assignments and, 158–60; committee preferences and, 104; deficit spending and, 134–36; DSPC and, 64; institutional power and, 86; interest group scores, 118t; member motivation and, 80–81; occupational background and, 149t; party-cartel theory and, 23–24; public policy role of, 71–72; race and, 310, 315; RCC and, 54; seniority and, 101, 375n4; women and, 294–95

Campaigning: assignment process, 21, 138–39, 258, 268–70; fund raising, 152–53; PAC money and, 4, 9, 193, 361n20
CAP framework: assignment process and, 34, 139, 153, 173; committee composition and, 24–27; committee requests and, 19–20; constituent interests and, 96–97, 137; defined, 14–15, 31–32; diagram of, 16f; member motivation and, 68–69, 89, 94, 328–32; party differences and, 27–28; party leadership and, 175–76, 223; politics and the, 325, 332–35; process conflict, 255–57, 285; self-selection and, 22
Caribbean Basin Trade Partnership Act, 10
Caucuses, 140, 217–19, 222–23, 235. See also Democratic Caucus; Special interest groups
CBC. See Congressional Black Caucus (CBC)
Central Intelligence Agency (CIA), 171
Chamber of Commerce of the United States (COCUS), 118–19t, 239t
Cleavages: assignment process and, 333–35; defined, 226–28; identifying RCC, 237–40; large vs. small state, 229–31; RCC Executive Committee, 229–31, 238–40
Coalition building: committee assignments and, 177, 225–26, 373n15; committee composition and, 26–27; committee on committees, 372n12; conflict avoidance and, 170; defined, 226; DSPC, 238, 249–53; large vs. small state, 373n16; RCC, 160–61, 231, 238–40, 241f
COC score, 244t, 246t, 248t, 250t, 252t
Commerce Committee. See Energy and Commerce Committee

Committee assignment politics
framework. *See* CAP framework

Committee assignments: campaigning
for, 21, 138–39; caucuses and, 140,
217; committee system and, 16f,
24–26; competition for, 138–40; distributive theory and, 6, 30, 93–94, 126;
endorsements for, 139–40; exchange
theory, 259; family relationships
and, 19–20, 258, 260–66, 276t; fund
raising and, 152–53; gender and race,
21, 300–302; incumbents and, 133–34;
Informational theory and, 15; institutional power and, 175–78; majority
and minority status, 21–22, 66–67,
75; marginality thesis and, 260–66;
member justification for, 140–48, 350,
369n47; models for, 13; PAC money
and, 193; party-cartel theory and,
219–23; party leadership and, 131–33,
135t, 150–53, 175–78, 180, 211–12;
party loyalty, 19–20; personal background for, 19–20, 142, 148–50, 360n11;
political party, 27–31, 35–36, 55–57;
politics of, 14–17, 22, 31–34, 255–57;
327–28, 332–35, 362n53, 367n36; race
and, 302–309, 309, 311–12, 378–79n40;
RCC Executive Committee, 231–36,
362n50; reelection and, 17–18; self-
selection and, 20–24, 127–30; seniority
system and, 101–107; supply-and-
demand variables, 21, 279–81, 288,
364n9, 375n24; women and, 309

Committee on committees, 352n8;
CAP framework and, 34, 255;
changes in, 66–67; defined, 353n16;
member requests and, 96–97; party
leadership of, 135t; role of the, 13.
See also Democratic Steering and
Policy Committee (DSPC);
Republican committee on committees (RCC)

Committee on Political Education of
the AFL-CIO (COPE), 118–19t, 239t,
240, 242t, 244t, 246t, 248t, 250t, 252t

Committee requests: assignment
success and, 126–37, 260–66, 318t,
320t, 366n30; constituency characteristics, 110–11t; constituent
interests and, 96–97; data analysis
of, 29–31; distributive theory and,
89–91, 97; district interests and,
120–25; ethnic assimilation and,
312–21; first-term member, 277–81;
former staff member, 270–72; incumbents, 281–85; interest group scores
and, 115–20; member justification
for, 145t, 148–50, 350; member motivation and, 68–69, 74t, 76t, 77t, 79t,
153–73, 329–32, 345–50, 359n13;
models for success, 275–77, 279–81;
patterns in, 97–101; preferences in,
101–107, 316–17t; race and, 302–309,
311, 314–24; Ray thesis on, 121–25;
self-selection hypothesis, 107–15

Committee system: appointment vs.
balloting, 177; assignment politics
framework, 16f, 24–26; assignment
process, 20–24, 138–40, 157–63, 231–36,
255–57; family relationships and,
19–20, 258, 272–75, 276t; former
staff members and, 270–72; gender
differences in, 295t; legislative
process and, 352–53n15; marginality
thesis and, 260–66; member preferences and, 74t, 76t, 77t, 78–89, 153–57;
partisan politics and, 327–28; political party differences, 27–31, 33–34;
political style and, 163–70; power
indexes and, 34–35; predecessor
status and, 266–70; public policy
role of, 11–12; race and, 302–309;
reelection motivation and, 69–75;
selection process, 224–26

Community Development Block Grant (CDBG), 113

Conflict avoidance, 20–22, 153, 170–72, 226

Conflict of interest, committee membership and, 4–5

Congress at the Grassroots (Fenno), 353n17

Congressional Black Caucus (CBC), 379n45; committee assignments and, 305, 312–24, 335; committee system and, 306–309; declining influence of, 310–11, 321, 379n43; DSPC and, 217; endorsements, 140; formation of, 303; legislative role of, 305–306; party quota strategy and, 312, 317–19

Congressional Government (Wilson), 11–12

Congressional Quarterly, 205, 210, 346

Congressmen in Committees (Fenno), 72

Conservative Coalition, 212, 240, 242t, 244t, 246t, 248t, 250t, 252t

Conservative Opportunity Society, 160, 189

Constituent interests: CAP framework and, 96–97, 137; committee assignments and, 162–63, 312–13, 352n15; committee composition and, 24–27; committee preferences and, 81–83, 90t, 102t; committee requests and, 68–69, 74t, 76t, 77t, 96–97, 120–25, 353n17; federal spending and, 121–25; labor unions as, 112, 204; member motivation and, 17–19, 329–32; party-cartel theory and, 23–24; race and, 314–24; reelection motivation and, 70–73; self-selection hypothesis and, 114. *See also* Reelection; State representation

Criminal convictions, 172–73

Deficit spending, 134–36

Democrat Blue Dogs, 151–52

Democratic Caucus: committee assignments and, 304, 355–56n21; factions, 371n67; quota strategy, 152, 312, 317–19; race and, 310–11, 378–79n40; reforms, 57–63; rule changes, 219, 307; women and, 291

Democratic Committee on Committees. *See* Democratic Steering and Policy Committee (DSPC)

Democratic Party: assignment process, 21; committee assignments and, 14; committee preferences and, 77t, 79t, 89–94; committee request patterns, 101–107, 128–29t, 131–37; constituent interests and, 81–83; party loyalty and, 150; postwar leadership, 193–219; reforms, 133–37, 198, 201–202. *See also* Party leaders; Political parties

Democratic Policy Committee, 65

Democratic Select Committee, 305

Democratic Steering and Policy Committee (DSPC): assignment process, 231, 238; changes in, 216–19, 356n24; committee assignments and, 55–57, 150–53, 201–202, 214–15, 373n19; 86th Congress, 59t; 94th Congress, 57–58; 97th Congress, 59–60t, 62f; 107th Congress, 60–61t; party leadership, 193, 212–13; patterns in requests to, 97–101; regional representation, 58, 60, 63f; women and, 291, 376n7

Democratic Steering Committee (DSC), 31, 63–65

Democratic Study Group (DSG), 198

Department of Commerce, 122–25

Department of Housing and Urban Development (HUD), 113, 122–25

Department of Transportation, 122–25

Dirksen Congressional Center, 187, 232

Discrimination, 92, 299–300, 310–11, 378n34, 378n37. *See also* Party discipline; Prejudice; Race; Women

Distributive theory: assignment politics and, 335–37; assignment process and, 6, 22–23, 30, 93–94, 126, 226, 256; assignment success and, 278t; committee composition and, 25; committee requests and, 89–91, 97; interest group scores and, 116–20; member motivation and, 69–72; pork barrel spending and, 28; self interest and, 13, 18–19; self-selection hypothesis and, 107–15; women and, 376n5

District, electoral. *See* Constituent interests; Geography

District of Columbia Committee, 23–24, 307, 312

DSPC. *See* Democratic Steering and Policy Committee (DSPC)

DW-NOMINATE scores, 237, 240, 242t, 244t, 246t, 248t, 250t, 252t

80th Congress, 195–96

81st Congress, 197

83rd Congress, 36

86th Congress, 36–43

87th Congress, 43

88th Congress, 43, 182, 291

89th Congress, 43, 182

Education and Labor Committee: committee requests for, 101, 104, 105–106; constituent interests and, 78, 82; federal spending and, 121–25; interest group scores and, 117–20; occupational background and, 148–50; party-cartel theory and, 23–24; public policy role of, 72, 83;

race and, 303–304, 307, 315; self-selection hypothesis and, 114–15; women and, 294–96

Election to office: committee assignments and, 17–18; congressional staff, 270–72; endorsements, 184–86, 191–92; family relationships and, 19–20, 258, 272–75, 276t; gender discrimination and, 299–300; political parties and, 260; predecessor status and, 266–70. *See also* Reelection

Electoral district. *See* Constituent interests; Geography

Endorsements, 139–40, 144, 184–86, 191–92, 269–71

Energy and Commerce Committee: committee assignments and, 6, 212–13, 216, 231–32; committee requests for, 101, 104, 274–75; constituent interests and, 83, 85; federal spending and, 121–25; institutional power and, 72; interest group scores, 118t; member motivation and, 80; occupational background and, 148–50; party-cartel theory and, 23–24; public policy role of, 83–84; race and, 314–15; self-selection hypothesis and, 113–15; women and, 300–301

Entitlement policy, 8

Ethics Committee, 7, 351n8

Ethnic issues, 312–21, 376n7. *See also* Race

Exchange theory of committee assignments, 259, 281–85

Factions: defined, 226–28, 352n14; DSPC, 371n67; RCC, 235–36, 240–49; state, 354–55n10; systematic cleavages as, 237–40

Family relationships, 19–20, 258, 272–75, 276t

Federal Assistance Awards Data System (FAADS), 121

Federal Bureau of Investigation (FBI), 170–72

Federalist Papers (Madison), 14, 352n14

Foreign Affairs Committee: committee assignments and, 165–66; committee requests for, 104, 106–107; interest group scores, 118t; member motivation and, 84–85, 332; occupational background and, 149t; party-cartel theory and, 23–24; public policy role of, 72, 78; race and, 307; self-selection hypothesis and, 109, 114–15; women and, 294–95

Free trade agreements, 10

Gender: committee assignments and, 21, 334; committee preferences and, 91–93, 295t; political party differences, 291; women's issues and, 293–97. *See also* Women

Geography: committee assignments and, 20, 139–46, 150–53, 168, 352n15, 353n17; federal spending patterns and, 120–25; large vs. small state representation, 35–46; party cleavages and, 228; party leadership and, 210; party loyalty and, 206; race and, 314; special interest groups and, 115–20. *See also* State representation

Giant Jigsaw Puzzle, The (Shepsle), 12–13, 255

Goals: coalition building and, 226; committee preferences and, 69–75, 297–98; defined, 352n12; party leadership and, 176–77. *See also* Motivation

Going Home (Fenno), 353n17

Government Operations Committee: interest group scores, 119t; member motivation and, 78, 80, 85, 274–75; party-cartel theory and, 23–24; public policy role of, 73; self-selection hypothesis and, 113–14

Gulf War, 171

Health policy, 3–4, 5, 89, 169

Hispanic Caucus, 217, 312

Home Style (Fenno), 353n17

Homosexuality, 169

House Administration Committee, 23–24, 158

HUD. *See* Department of Housing and Urban Development (HUD)

Ideology: assignment success and, 281–85; DW-NOMINATE scores and, 237; member motivation and, 17–19; party cleavages and, 228–31; personal background and, 257–59

Incumbents: committee assignments and, 133–34, 138, 258–59; committee preferences and, 105t; committee requests, 98–101, 281–85; Congressional Black Caucus (CBC), 314; member justifications, 145t; supply-and-demand variables, 283–85. *See also* Seniority system

Influence. *See* Power, institutional

Informational theory: assignment politics and, 15, 335–37; assignment process and, 22–23; assignment success and, 278t, 281–85; committee composition and, 25–26; committee requests and, 120; member motivation and, 18–19, 70–72

Interest group: endorsements, 139–40; relationships to, 5–6; voting scores,

115–20, 237, 359n10. *See also* Special
interest groups
Interior Committee: committee
requests for, 274–75; constituent
interests and, 72, 82, 97; distributive
theory and, 25; federal spending
and, 121–25; interest group scores,
119t; member motivation and, 332;
occupational background and, 149t;
party-cartel theory and, 23–24; self-
selection hypothesis and, 114–15
Internal Revenue Service (IRS), 171
International Trade Organization
Charter, 196
Interstate and Foreign Commerce
Committee: committee requests for,
274–75; constituent interests and,
83; Waxman selection for, 3–5

Johnston Power Index (JPI), 35, 339–43
Judiciary Committee: committee
requests for, 106–107; interest group
scores, 119t; occupational background and, 148–50; party-cartel
theory and, 23–24; public policy
role of, 78; race and, 303–304; self-
selection hypothesis and, 113–14

Labor unions, 112, 118–19t, 204. *See
also* Committee on Political Education of the AFL-CIO (COPE)
League of Conservation Voters (LCV),
118–19t
League of Women Voters (LWV),
118–19t
Legislative process: coalition building
and, 26–27; committee role in,
11–14, 352n13; informational theory
and, 23–24; personal loyalty and,
194–98, 364n6, 365n26, 366n31; race
and, 305–306

Legislative Reorganization Act of
1946, 177
Lesbians for Motherhood, 169
Lobbyists, public policy and, 6

Majority/minority status: changes in,
216, 373n19; committee
assignments and, 21–22, 66–67, 75,
191, 216–18; committee requests
and, 98–101; informational theory
and, 23–24; interparty differences
and, 106; loss of committee positions, 312; marginality thesis and,
260–61; party loyalty and, 150–53;
Republican, 227, 372n2
Marginality thesis, 260–66, 283–85
Medical care. *See* Health policy
Medicare and Medicaid, 5
Merchant Marine and Fisheries
Committee: abolishment of, 312;
committee assignments and, 165;
constituent interests and, 83; party-
cartel theory and, 23–24; self-
selection hypothesis and, 113–15;
women and, 300–301
Minorities. *See* Ethnic issues; Race;
Women
Models, committee assignment, 13
Motivation: assignment politics and,
15, 335–37; committee request,
68–69, 74t, 76t, 77t, 79t, 345–50;
constituent interests and, 81–83;
defined, 352n12; institutional
power as, 7–9, 86–89; interest group
scores and, 115–20; member
interests and, 17–19, 31, 78–81,
297–98, 329–32; partisan politics
and, 327–28; party-cartel theory
and, 23–24; party leadership,
175–78, 225; personal background
as, 19–20, 142, 148–50, 360n11;

Motivation: (*continued*)
political party, 27–28, 89–94; public policy as, 6, 83–86; reelection concerns as, 9–10; self interest and, 3–4, 11–13; self-selection hypothesis and, 107. *See also* Goals

90th Congress, 141–42
91st Congress, 183
92nd Congress, 43–46
93rd Congress, 131–33, 307
94th Congress, 57–58, 87, 131–33, 177, 309
95th Congress, 165, 206–207, 368n46
96th Congress, 165, 203–204, 206–207
97th Congress, 8, 37–38t, 46–49, 62f, 158, 166, 208–209, 241
98th Congress, 93, 158–59, 209–10, 241–43, 244t
99th Congress, 159–60, 167, 170–71, 212, 227, 243, 246t, 261, 292
National Education Association (NEA), 118–19t
National Farmers' Organization (NFO), 118–19t
National Farmers' Union (NFU), 118–19t
National Federation of Independent Business (NFIB), 118–19t
National health care, 5
National interests, congressional policy and, 26–27
National Security Index (NSI), 239t, 242t, 244t, 246t, 248t, 250t, 252t
National Taxpayers Union (NTU), 118–19t, 160
Natural Resources Committee, 82
New Democrat Coalition, 217–18, 312
Nutrition Labeling and Education Act, 5

100th Congress, 49–50, 160, 167–68, 227, 245, 248t

101st Congress, 38t, 49–53, 87, 162, 187, 189, 249, 252t, 292–93, 310
102nd Congress, 162, 310–11, 314
103rd Congress, 93, 171–72, 310–11, 313
104th Congress, 53, 65, 171–72, 190, 219, 301, 312
105th Congress, 39t, 53–55
107th Congress, 65, 172
108th Congress, 218
Orphan Drug Act, 5

PAC. *See* Political action committees (PAC)
Partisan politics, 327–28
Party-cartel theory: assignment politics and, 336–37; assignment success and, 278t, 281–85; committee assignments and, 219–23; member motivation and, 23–24
Party discipline: committee assignments and, 172, 215; crossover votes, 209; party-unity scores and, 208. *See also* Discrimination
Party leaders: Albert, Carl (D-OK), 198–202; Cannon, Joseph W. (R-IL), 169, 179, 354n2; Foley, Tom (D-WA), 214–16; Ford, Gerald R. (R-MI), 181, 183–87; Gephardt, Richard (D-MO), 216–18; Gingrich, Newt (R-GA), 189–93; Halleck, Charles (R-IN), 179, 181–83; Hastert, Dennis (R-IL), 193; Martin, Joseph W, Jr. (R-MA), 179–81; McCormack, John W. (D-MA), 198–202; Michel, Robert H. (R-IL), 179, 187–89; O'Neill, Thomas P. "Tip" (D-MA), 202–206; Pelosi, Nancy (D-CA), 218–19; Rayburn, Samuel Taliaferro (D-TX), 181, 194–98; Rhodes, John J. (R-AZ), 183–87; Wright, James (D-TX), 206–14

Party leadership: assignment politics and, 336–37; assignment process and, 161–62, 211–12, 333–35, 364n4; assignment success and, 131–33, 135t, 366n30; DSPC and, 58, 61–62; ethics and, 214; geography vs. party loyalty, 203, 206, 210; legislative process and, 27, 364n6; party-cartel theory and, 24; political style and, 163–65; race and, 310, 317–24; RCC and, 53–55; women in, 293

Party loyalty: assignment success and, 281–85; committee assignments and, 19–20, 142–43, 150–51, 197, 219, 221t, 222t, 256–59; geography and, 206; incumbents and, 283–85; party-cartel theory and, 24, 220–23; party cleavages and, 228; party leadership and, 176, 225; political style and, 170–71; Tip O'Neill and, 207–208. *See also* Personal loyalty

Party-unity scores, 176, 203–204, 206, 208, 210, 220–23, 283

Patent Term Restoration and Drug Competition Act, 5

Permanent Select Committee on Intelligence, 215–16

Personal loyalty, 194–98, 364n6, 365n26, 366n31. *See also* Party loyalty

Personal popularity, 21, 199, 218

Pharmaceutical industry, conflict of interest and, 4–5

Policy, congressional: committee assignments and, 258, 352n13; committee composition and, 26–27, 92–93; DSPC and, 213, 218–19; interest group scores and, 115–20; partisan politics and, 327–28; party leadership and, 175–78, 261; party loyalty and, 150; reforms in, 133–37. *See also* Public policy

Political action committees (PAC), 4, 9, 193, 361n20

Political parties: assignment process and, 27–31, 176–77, 224–26; committee preferences and, 90t, 102t, 105t; committee requests and, 143–48; gender discrimination and, 291, 297–302; goals and motivations, 260; intraparty conflict and, 334; marginality thesis and, 261–66; partisan politics and, 327–28; party loyalty and, 150–53. *See also* Democratic Party; Majority/minority status; Republican Party

Political style: Derrick, Butler (D-SC), 153–57; Dornan, Robert K. (D-CA), 165–70; Martin, Lynn (R-IL), 157–63; party cleavages and, 228–31; party leadership and, 163–65, 176; personality and, 199; Traficant, James A., Jr. (D-OH), 170–73

Politics: assignment process, 14–17, 22, 31–34, 224–26, 257, 327–28, 332–35; committee assignment, 362n53, 369–70n50; committee composition and, 26–27, 92–93; committee preferences, 77t, 79t, 80t, 89–94; constituent interests and, 81–83; institutional power, 86–89, 367n36; marginality thesis and, 260–66; personality and, 163–70, 199; public policy and, 83–86; race and committee, 302–309

Popularity, personal, 21, 199, 218

Pork barrel politics, 3, 28, 70

Post Office and Civil Service Committee: abolishment of, 83, 312; committee preferences and, 105; constituent interests and, 72, 82–83; party-cartel theory and, 23–24; self-selection hypothesis and, 113–14

Power, institutional: appointment and
removal, 177; committee assignments
and, 163, 202; committee preferences
and, 86–89, 90t, 102t; committee
requests and, 68–69, 74t, 76t, 77t;
committee role in, 11–14, 352n13;
deficit spending and, 134–36;
member motivation and, 17–19,
357–58n24; party-cartel theory and,
23–24; party leadership and, 175–78;
race and, 311, 314–24; reelection
motivation and, 70–73; self interest
and, 7–9; seniority and, 375–76n4
Power indexes: defined, 34–35;
measuring, 339; 97th Congress, 48f,
62f; 101st Congress, 52f; 105th
Congress, 54f, 56f; RCC voting, 40f,
42t; regional representation, 49f, 52,
53f, 63f; state representation, 55. *See
also* Banzhaf Power Index (BPI);
Johnston Power Index (JPI)
Preference programs, free trade, 10
Prejudice, 92, 371n71, 379n42. *See also*
Discrimination
Public policy: assignment politics and,
15–17; committee composition and,
24–27; committee preferences and,
83–86, 90t, 102t; committee requests
and, 68–69, 74t, 76t, 77t; committee
role in, 11–14, 352n13; federal
spending and, 121–25; informational theory and, 23–24; interest
group scores and, 115–20; member
motivation and, 17–19, 329–32;
party-cartel theory and, 23–24; race
and, 314–24; reelection motivation
and, 70–73; self interest and, 6;
women and, 293–94, 297–99. *See also*
Policy, congressional
Public Works and Transportation
Committee: committee assignments
and, 159; committee requests for,

101, 105–106, 273–74; constituent
interests and, 82; federal spending
and, 121–25; interest group scores,
119t; occupational background and,
149t; party-cartel theory and, 23–24;
race and, 313–14

Quotas: negative, 318; party loyalty
and, 152; positive, 318–19; supply-
and-demand variables and, 310–12

Race: committee assignments and, 21,
334–35; committee politics and,
302–309; committee preferences
and, 91–92, 314–24; congressional
representation and, 375n1, 377n25,
378–79n40; discrimination toward,
92, 378n34, 378n37; increased representation by, 312–13, 371n67, 376n7;
quota strategy, 317–19; white backlash
toward, 311, 379n42. *See also* Discrimination; Ethnic issues; Prejudice
Racketeering, 172
Ray thesis, 120–25
RCC. *See* Republican committee on
committees (RCC)
RCC Executive Committee: creation
of, 43, 51; factions, 240–49; membership roster, 233–34t; party cleavages
and, 229–31; voting record, 236t;
women and, 291–93, 301–302
Reciprocal Trade Agreements Act, 196
Reelection: committee assignments
and, 17–18, 139, 150–53, 369n47;
committee requests and, 68–69, 74t,
76t, 77t, 146; committee role in,
352n13; distributive theory and, 6;
marginality thesis and, 260–66;
member motivation and, 3, 9–10,
70–76, 329–32; party leadership
and, 175. *See also* Constituent
interests; Election to office

Republican Committee on Committees (RCC): assignment process, 35–36, 226–29, 238–40; coalition building and, 160–61; committee assignments and, 150–53, 215, 362n50, 373n19; conservative reform, 164, 169; defined, 353–54n1; 83rd Congress, 36; 86th Congress, 36–43; 87th Congress, 43; 88th Congress, 43; 89th Congress, 43; 92nd Congress, 43–46; 97th Congress, 37–38t, 46–49; 100th Congress, 49–50; 101st Congress, 38t, 49–53; 104th Congress, 53; 105th Congress, 39t, 53–55, 56f; party leadership, 178–80; regional representation, 45f, 47, 49f, 55; requests to, 97–101; state representation, 55; women and, 376n9

Republican Party: assignment process, 21, 31, 33–34; committee assignments and, 14; committee preferences and, 77t, 79t, 89–94; committee request patterns, 101–107, 128–29t, 131–37; constituent interests and, 81–83; factions, 227–29; party loyalty and, 151; party unity, 372n2; postwar leadership, 178–93; reforms, 133–37, 181, 187. *See also* Party leaders; Political parties

Republican Policy Committee, 43

Rules Committee: Carl Albert influence on, 201–202, 355–56n21; committee assignments and, 158–59, 231–32, 268–70; DSPC and, 64; institutional power and, 86–87, 155–57; John McCormack influence on, 198–99; member motivation and, 8–9, 80–81, 369n47; party-cartel theory and, 23–24; party leadership and, 27, 104; public policy role of, 71–73; race and, 304–306; RCC and, 54; Sam Rayburn influence on,

197–98, 366–67n33; seniority and, 101; Tip O'Neill influence on, 203–206; women and, 294–95

Ryan White CARE Act, 5

79th Congress, 195

Safe Medical Devices Act, 5

Science, Space, and Technology Committee: committee assignments and, 165; committee requests for, 274–75; federal spending and, 121–25; occupational background and, 149t; party-cartel theory and, 23–24; public policy role of, 78; self-selection hypothesis and, 113–14; women and, 300–301

Self interest, 12–13, 17–19, 327–28

Self-selection: assignment process, 20–24, 225–26, 256, 285–88, 334; assignment process and, 352n15; assignment success and, 127–30, 277, 278t; distributive theory and, 97; Monte Carlo approach to, 107–15; supply-and-demand variables, 279–81, 288; women and, 376n5

Seniority system, 375–76n4; assignment preferences and, 101–107; career advancement and, 375n4; challenges to, 4–5, 190–91; committees and the, 12, 20; race and, 310–12; reform of, 133. *See also* Incumbents

Small Business Committee: federal spending and, 121–25; interest group scores, 119t; public policy role of, 78; self-selection hypothesis and, 113–14

Social Security, 196

Special interest groups: Americans for Democratic Action (ADA), 204, 239t, 240; Chamber of Commerce of the United States (COCUS),

Special interest groups: (*continued*) 118–19t, 239t; Committee on Political Education of the AFL-CIO (COPE), 239t, 240; committee requests and, 115–20; Congressional Black Caucus (CBC), 140, 217, 303, 312, 321, 379n43; Conservative Opportunity Society, 160, 189; Democrat Blue Dogs, 151–52, 217; distributive theory and, 6; endorsements, 139–40; Hispanic Caucus, 217, 312; Lesbians for Motherhood, 169; National Taxpayers Union (NTU), 160; New Democrat Coalition, 217–18, 312; organized labor, 112, 204; Women's Caucus, 217, 300, 312. *See also* Interest group

Standards of Official Conduct Committee. *See* Ethics Committee

State representation: assignment process and, 362n53; cleavages and, 229–31; committee assignments and, 375n24; committee term limits, 235; factions, 240–49, 354–55n10; intraparty conflict and, 334; large vs. small, 35–46, 55, 179–80, 229, 355n12, 372n5, 373n16; regional zones and, 58–63, 354n5. *See also* Constituent interests; Geography

Supply-and-demand variables: assignment process and, 21, 364n9; committee assignments and, 279–81, 288; quota strategy and, 310–12

Tax and entitlement policy, 8

Tax evasion, 172

Term limits, 175, 310

Tobacco industry, health policy and, 5

United Auto Workers (UAW), 118–19t

Urban Development Action Grant (UDAG), 113

Veteran's Affairs Committee: party-cartel theory and, 23–24; self-selection hypothesis and, 113–14; women and, 304

Vietnam War, 164–65, 308

Voting: committee assignments and, 177, 187, 188t, 223, 224–26; DW-NOMINATE scores, 237, 240, 242t, 244t, 246t, 248t, 250t, 252t; interest group scores, 115–20, 359n10; party-unity scores, 176, 203–204, 206, 208, 210, 283; RCC voting record, 231–36. *See also* Power indexes

Watergate, 3, 154, 186, 309

Ways and Means Committee: Carl Albert influence on, 200; committee assignments and, 104–106, 158–59, 216, 231–32, 366n30, 373n14; deficit spending and, 134–36; DSPC and, 57, 64; institutional power and, 71–72, 87–89; interest group scores, 119t; Jim Wright influence on, 206–12; John McCormack influence on, 198–99; member justification for, 140–42; member motivation and, 8–9, 80–81; occupational background and, 149t; party-cartel theory and, 23–24; race and, 304–306, 309, 378n37; RCC and, 54; Sam Rayburn influence on, 194–96; seniority and, 101; women and, 291, 293–94

Women: African American, 304–305, 376n7, 378n27; assignment success and, 296–97; committee assignments and, 290–93, 375n2, 376n5; committee preferences and, 295t, 297–302; committee requests and, 293–94; discrimination toward, 92, 371n71, 378n34; party differences toward, 334; party leadership and, 371n67; RCC and, 376n9. *See also* Prejudice

Women's Caucus, 217, 300, 312